Coin W

Guide to U.S. Coins, Prices & Value Trends

Written by
William T. Gibbs

Edited by William T. Gibbs
and
Suellen Ruttkay

Contributing Trends Editor
Stuart Segan

Twelfth Edition
2000

A SIGNET BOOK

Photograph reproduction of "Shoshone Mother," 26.5" high bronze sculpture by Glenna Goodacre, by kind permission of Daniel R. Anthony

Cover photograph reproduction of the Sacagawea dollar by kind permission of Daniel R. Anthony

SIGNET
Published by New American Library, a division of
Penguin Putnam Inc., 375 Hudson Street,
New York, New York 10014, U.S.A.
Penguin Books Ltd, 27 Wrights Lane,
London W8 5TZ, England
Penguin Books Australia Ltd, Ringwood,
Victoria, Australia
Penguin Books Canada Ltd, 10 Alcorn Avenue,
Toronto, Ontario, Canada M4V 3B2
Penguin Books (N.Z.) Ltd, 182–190 Wairau Road,
Auckland 10, New Zealand

Penguin Books Ltd, Registered Offices:
Harmondsworth, Middlesex, England

Published by Signet, an imprint of New American Library,
a division of Penguin Putnam Inc.

First Signet Printing, November 1999
10 9 8 7 6 5 4 3 2 1

Photographs from Coin World files and courtesy of Stack's And Bowers & Merena Inc.

Analysis and pricing information are based on historical information published in Coin World Trends. No information in this book should be confused as predictive. Past performance is not a guarantee of future performance.

Foreword

The information included in *The 2000 Coin World Guide to U.S. Coins, Prices & Value Trends* has been compiled by William T. Gibbs, *Coin World* news editor, and Beth Deisher, *Coin World* editor, with assistance from Paul Gilkes, senior staff writer. Price guide values have been researched by Stuart Segan, contributing Trends editor. The book was designed by Johanna L. Peters. The project director was Suellen Ruttkay, *Coin World* ancillary product manager.

For 40 years, since 1960, *Coin World* has reported on the people, laws, new issues, auctions, pricing trends — all the elements that affect the hobby and business of collecting coins and related items. Our mission is to enrich coin collecting through knowledge.

In the *Coin World Price Guide* the *Coin World* editors present in an easy-to-use format a wealth of information and insights. The Trends retail value guide included in the *Coin World Price Guide* is a regular feature in *Coin World*. The value of the information included in Trends has been proven over time.

To contact the editors of *Coin World* or request subscription information, write to Coin World, P.O. Box 150, Dept. 02, Sidney, Ohio 45365-0150. Visit *Coin World* Online at www.coinworld.com.

Contents

1 Introducing the Guide

Welcome to the world of coins. *Coin World's 2000 Guide to U.S. Coins, Prices and Value Trends* is designed for the collector, whether neophyte or advanced. However, it should also be useful to the noncollector who has inherited some old coins, or has just become interested in coins, and to the history buff interested in facets of American history virtually ignored in most history textbooks.

This year's annual feature focuses on the switch to a small-sized dollar that began in the 1970s and continues with the release of the 1999 Susan B. Anthony dollar and 2000 Sacagawea dollar. As with the ongoing State quarter dollars program, which began in 1999, these two coins will provide collectors with something new and exciting to collect directly from circulation.

Our comprehensive analysis of the rare coin market follows the annual feature, and then we get right in to what you buy this book for — the value trends of U.S. coins. Within the pricing section, we also present the technical specifications for each series, such as size, weight, composition and so on.

Following the pricing section are chapters devoted to mintages, Proof and Uncirculated Mint sets and commemorative coins. Then you'll find a chapter about the art and science of grading (determining a coin's level of preservation and ultimately its value), a background history of U.S. coins, and a look at the Mint facilities.

We then discuss the history and latest techniques of coin manufacturing, followed by an illustrated guide to error coins. You'll also find information about the great and mysterious rarities of the hobby, a glossary of often-encountered terms and a full index for quick and easy reference.

Why do people collect coins?

There are many different reasons for collecting coins. You may want to collect coins because of their historical significance. Coins reveal much about a nation. For example, the word Liberty, appearing on every United States coin, says volumes about Americans' love of freedom. The motto E Pluribus Unum, Latin for "out of many, one," defines the nation's character, forged from 50 states and the many peoples who make up such a diverse country.

You may collect coins for their artistic beauty. The country's greatest sculptor at the turn of the century, Augustus Saint-Gaudens, sculptured classical designs for gold $10 and $20 coins. Many other U.S. coins are amazing examples of the coiner's art.

You may, like some people, collect for financial reward. This book is not an investment advisory. Many authors are willing to give you their personal recommendations. However, we would be remiss if we did not point out that many individuals have profited from collecting U.S. coins. As is true for any investment, investing in rare coins is a calculated risk. It is essential that the investor knows exactly what he is buying and understands the risks. The risks may be great, but so may be the rewards.

You may collect simply for the love of collecting. A true collector can't explain to the uninitiated the inner joy that comes from owning a 160-year-old half cent that cost less than $25, or a unique misstruck coin pulled from circulation at face value, or an 1861 half dollar that may have been struck by the Confederate States of America after it took control of the three U.S. Mints located south of the Mason-Dixon Line.

Regardless of your vantage point, we hope you will find this book useful, educational and entertaining.

Tips for new collectors

Beginning collectors soon learn that there are right ways and wrong ways for just about everything. However, there are no "wrong" ways or "right" ways to collect coins and related numismatic items. No one way or method of collecting is objectively better than another.

However, there are right and wrong ways to do many things collectors routinely do. Some of the things to never do are:

• Never hold a coin by placing your fingers on the coin's surfaces. Instead, hold the coin by its edge. The human skin contains oil and contaminants that can damage a coin's surfaces.

• Never speak or sneeze while bending over a coin. While this advice may sound silly, it's practical. Saliva and mucus can also damage a coin's surfaces if contact is made.

• Avoid the natural impulse to clean your coins. There are chemicals that can be used safely to remove dirt and other substances from a coin; however, these are best left to the expert. Cleaning coins with abrasive cleaners like scouring powder or pencil erasers will also damage them. Coins that have been naturally toned should be left alone. The patina — the film that builds up on the surfaces of the coin — forms on copper and silver coins as a natural result of the chemical reaction of the coinage metal to the environment. It actually helps protect the metal from further reactions. Many collectors and dealers find natural toning attractive, and will even pay a premium for attractively toned coins.

There are also things all collectors should do:

• Store your coins properly. In recent years, hobbyists have found that certain types of plastic used in coin holders and flips (plastic holders creased in the middle, with the coin housed on one side) actually damage the coins placed in them. Avoid storage materials made of polyvinyl chloride (PVC); ask your dealer what is safe. Also, some forms of paper envelopes and albums contain high amounts of sulfur, a substance particularly damaging to copper coins. Do not leave your coins exposed to sunlight, high heat or high humidity for very long; all can damage a coin.

• Learn about grading. Chapter 8 discusses grading in more detail. Even a basic knowledge of what grading represents is important if you begin to buy coins from others. The higher the grade or condition a coin is in, the more it is worth.

Getting started

Collecting can be fun for the individual and for the entire family. It can be as easy as getting a couple of rolls of cents from the banks and placing the coins into folder-style albums, or a family trip to a local coin show (there are coin shows every weekend in some part of the United States; there's probably one in your area within the next few months).

A good place to start is with the Lincoln cent, particularly for the Lincoln Memorial design struck since 1959. It takes little effort to go to the bank, buy $5 worth (10 rolls) of cents and put individual dates and Mint marks into the holes of an inexpensive album or holder. Your local coin dealer or newsstand probably has them. After going through the rolls and saving the dates needed, take the unwanted coins back to the bank and get some more.

Sorting pocket change and searching new rolls from the bank brings enjoyment to many beginners. It's inexpensive and doesn't take a lot of time or effort. You may want to substitute Roosevelt dimes for the cents, or maybe the new State quarter dollars, but the goal is still the same — collecting an example of each date and Mint mark for any given series.

Coin collecting opens many doors: economics, history, art and technology, both old and new. Welcome to the world of numismatics and U.S. coins!

2 Two Women, Two Coins

One woman was a Shoshone slave in her teens, uneducated by the white man's standards yet wise in the ways of her people and land. The other woman was white and while free, like all women of her age was denied most rights guaranteed them today under the United States Constitution.

One helped a group of American explorers blaze a path to the Pacific Ocean, an act that helped set into motion the westward expansion of Americans and the destruction of the Indians' way of life. The other helped set into motion the movement that eventually enfranchised American women.

Sacagawea, the Shoshone guide of the Lewis and Clark Expedition, and Susan B. Anthony, pioneer in the women's rights movement, are being honored on circulating dollar coins struck the last two years of the 20th century. The revived Anthony dollar, last struck in 1981, went into production with the 1999 coin in mid-year. Production of the new Sacagawea dollar will begin in 2000, as the Western world celebrates the final year of the millennium and prepares for the new.

This chapter answers many questions. How were these two women selected to appear on circulating U.S. coins? Why did Anthony appear on a dollar coin that was substantially smaller than the Eisenhower dollar it replaced in 1979? Why did the Anthony dollar "fail," and why is it being struck again? Finally, why will the Sacagawea dollar look so different than the Anthony dollar?

To place the 1999 Anthony dollar and 2000 Sacagawea dollar in perspective, let's journey back in time to the end of the 18th century, when a young United States was striking its own coins for the first time. The Act of April 2, 1792, authorized a national coinage in three metals: copper, silver and gold. Five silver coins were authorized — the half dime, dime, quarter dollar, half dollar and silver dollar. Silver dollar production began in 1794. That coin was significantly larger than the 1999 and 2000 dollar coins. The 1794 Flowing Hair Liberty dollar was 39.5 millimeters in diameter and weighed 26.96 grams. In contrast, the Anthony dollar has a diameter of 26.5 mm and weight of 8.1 grams.

At the time, various silver coins of foreign origin circulated in the

United States as legal tender. Before the introduction of an American silver dollar, importers of foreign goods generally paid for their purchases with the Spanish dollar (an 8-real coin). Once an American silver dollar became available, however, it could be used in payment for imported goods. An unforeseen result was that few of the exported silver dollars were returned to the United States. The drain became so great that the U.S. government stopped minting silver dollars in 1804. It would be more than 20 years before new silver dollars were struck for circulation.

For a century, from 1836 to 1935, the U.S. government had a love-hate relationship with the silver dollar. After a few pieces were struck from 1836-39, silver dollar production resumed in earnest in 1840. It ended in 1873, the victim in part of a silver dollar surplus. A larger, heavier Trade silver dollar was produced for foreign use in 1873, even as production of a domestic silver dollar ceased. Domestic silver dollar production resumed in 1878 after passage of a law requiring the government to purchase $2 million to $4 million of silver every month and turn the metal into silver dollars (vaults were already choked with lower denomination silver coins). Production ended again in 1904, once silver bullion supplies became exhausted (an 1890 law required the government to buy 4.5 million ounces of silver every month for conversion into silver dollars); millions of silver dollars sat unused in government vaults. A 1918 law required the melting of hundreds of millions of silver dollars. Shortly thereafter, the price of silver dropped and the government resumed buying more silver. Silver dollar production resumed in 1921 and continued until 1935. Except for a small number of 1964 silver dollars that were all melted before entering circulation, silver dollar production for circulation had ended.

The death of Dwight D. Eisenhower and the landing of man on the moon, both in 1969, prompted production of a new dollar coin beginning in 1971, although there was no clear public need for a circulating dollar coin. It may have been politically easier to authorize a new denomination rather than replace one of the five dead presidents depicted on the cent through half dollar.

The Eisenhower coin was given the same diameter as the silver dollars since 1840, 38.1 mm, but composed of a copper-nickel clad composition (authority to strike 90 percent silver coins ceased in 1965). The Eisenhower dollar never circulated well. An entire generation of Americans had grown up without a circulating dollar coin. Most preferred the $1 Federal Reserve note to the large and heavy Eisenhower dollar. Production ended in 1978.

RTI report

Meanwhile, the Treasury Department commissioned a private research organization in North Carolina, the Research Triangle Institute, to study U.S. coinage system requirements expected through 1990. The RTI report was released in September 1976 with various recommendations: that the cent and half dollar be eliminated (the elimination of the cent has always proven unpopular and thus never acted upon) and that a smaller dollar be introduced to replace the Eisenhower dollar.

The RTI blamed the dollar's lack of circulation largely on its size. "A conveniently sized dollar coin would significantly broaden the capabilities of consumers for cash transactions, especially with machines," the report said. "Members of the automated merchandising industry have expressed a strong interest in a smaller dollar, indicating their willingness to adapt their machinery to its use." To make room in cash register drawers for the dollar, the RTI report recommended eliminating the half dollar, for which there was a "handy substitute — two quarters," according to the report. The report noted that dollar coins are a financially sound idea. For every dollar note replaced with the dollar coin, the government saves on production costs; dollar bills last an average of 18 months before they have to be replaced, while dollar coins last decades.

The report recommended the new dollar be 26.54 mm in diameter, be composed of the same composition as the dime, quarter dollar and half dollar, and possess a distinctive edge to help users distinguish it from other reeded edge coins.

While the report was strongly in favor of a smaller dollar, it noted that about half of those in the business and banking industries surveyed by RTI showed little interest in a smaller dollar coin. "That response is interpreted as revealing their preference for not handling the present dollar and, therefore, a reluctance to change," the report said. The report strongly urged the government to promote the use of a new dollar coin through public-relations campaign.

Treasury Secretary Michael Blumenthal voiced support for a downsized dollar coin in March 1977. Mint officials studied a new dollar coin through 1977 and even briefly considered striking an 11-sided coin to make it distinctive. However, technical problems forced the Mint to drop that intriguing idea. Chief Engraver Frank Gasparro began work on two designs — a Flowing Hair Liberty obverse and Flying Eagle reverse — that updated classic designs of the previous centuries.

Meanwhile, technical issues were being resolved. The final diameter, 26.5 mm, was about that recommended in the RTI report, and the Mint officials followed the recommendations on composition. However, they gave the new dollar coin the same reeded edge as the similarly sized quarter dollar, a decision that they would later regret. The Mint did, however, experiment with unusual rims, finally settling on a distinctive 11-sided rim rather than the traditional round rim.

Meanwhile, disagreement was brewing in Congress over what designs the coin should show. Blumenthal preferred the allegorical Liberty concept, which was also a favorite with many coin collectors tired of seeing uninteresting designs depicting dead presidents. However, many in Congress, the Carter administration and the women's rights movement believed it was time that a circulating U.S. coin depict a real American woman rather than an allegorical figure. The only appearances of real women had been on a handful of commemorative coins not intended to circulate.

Anthony dollar
obverse

Anthony dollar
reverse

Anthony dollar

Susan B. Anthony, a heroine of the women's rights movement, was the clear choice of those favoring this approach. Anthony, born in 1820, fought tirelessly for temperance, abolitionism, woman suffrage and equal rights for women. Anthony died in 1906, living long enough to see the slaves freed but before passage of the amendment to the

Constitution that gave women the right to vote in 1920.

Many collectors, however, clearly favored anyone other than Anthony. Some criticized Anthony's physical appearance (although few who called her "ugly" ever said the same thing about Abraham Lincoln), her supposed religious beliefs (some writers claimed she was an atheist) and the women's rights movement that encouraged her selection. Collector anger grew once Gasparro's design, depicting a stern-faced Anthony, was made public. Gasparro was ordered not to soften Anthony's portrait and to base his design on a particular portrait.

Interestingly, the Apollo 11 design used on the Eisenhower dollar was retained on the Anthony dollar. Artistically and historically, this made no sense. It had nothing to do with Anthony or her causes. The use of the moon landing design was somewhat appropriate on the Eisenhower dollar (although Eisenhower supported an early space program, the design would have been more appropriate on the Kennedy half dollar, since it was President Kennedy who ordered the moon landing missions).

Congress passed the Anthony dollar legislation and it became law Oct. 10, 1978. The Mint began striking test pieces on Dec. 13, 1978. However, Mint officials decided to wait until 500 million Anthony dollars were struck before they were released into circulation. The Mint claimed it did so to prevent hoarding if the coins were introduced into circulation in smaller quantities. The coins were finally released in July 1979 (although some got out ahead of time, prompting a legal investigation).

The coin proved to be as big a flop as the Eisenhower dollar. Mint officials need not have worried about the coins being hoarded; they couldn't get the coins to circulate. Production of circulation strikes continued into 1980, despite a lack of interest in the coin by the American public. Facing up to reality, the Mint struck Anthony dollars in 1981 for inclusion in Proof and Uncirculated Mint sets, but not for circulation. As 1981 ended, the Treasury Department had in its vaults 800 million Anthony dollars that no one wanted.

Why did the Anthony dollar fail? The reasons were many.

First and foremost, the government continued to issue the dollar bill. Americans stuck with what they were comfortable with, not with the new dollar coin. Had the government stopped issuing the dollar bill, the public would have been forced to use the dollar coin and it would have been a success. Other nations, including Canada and Great

Britain, learned from the Americans' mistake. Both nations stopped production of the paper money equivalent of their new dollar and £1 coins, respectively, and forced their citizens into using the new coins.

Second, many had difficulty distinguishing between the new dollar and the quarter dollar. The quarter, with a diameter of 24.26 mm, is only slightly smaller than the dollar. Some Americans found themselves spending the dollars as quarters, prompting some wags to call the dollar the Carter quarter. Few Americans had the patience to use a coin that they faced losing three-quarters of its value if spent by mistake.

Third, the decision to use the same composition as the quarter dollar and a reeded edge only made things worse. Many believed that the dollar coin might have had a better chance of circulating had it been of a different color than the quarter and if it had a distinctive edge. Again, Canada and Great Britain gave their dollar and pound coins a distinctive color and edge to help citizens distinguish the coins from other denominations.

The twin failures of the Eisenhower and Anthony dollars soured many in government on the idea of a dollar coin. It would take nearly two decades, in fact, before the government seriously considered a resumption of dollar coinage.

Meanwhile, what could the government do with all of the Anthony dollars? The government couldn't melt them; it would lose money on every coin it destroyed. So the Mint just let the bags of coins sit in its vault. In an effort to get rid of some of the coins, the Mint began offering 1979 and 1980 Anthony dollars to its collector clientele in 1985, in sets and in Mint-sewn bags. Almost a decade after collector sales began, other sources began using the Anthony dollar. Treasury stocks began to fall.

The United States Postal Service in March 1993 began installing 9,000 stamp-dispensing machines that use the Anthony dollar. Beginning in 1994, demand grew from several metropolitan transit agencies. All of this increased demand forced Treasury officials to begin considering a resumption of dollar coin production. Mint Director Philip N. Diehl told a House subcommittee on June 26, 1997, that the Mint could strike new Anthony dollars overnight once dies were produced (the Treasury Department has authority to strike the Anthony dollar at any time). By October 1997, Treasury officials were predicting that at current drawdown rates, the existing stocks would be depleted in 30 months. However, officials wanted to avoid striking additional

Anthony dollars and proposed an alternative; the result was authorization to begin striking a new, golden-colored dollar, to be released beginning in 2000.

Despite a reluctance to strike additional Anthony dollars, Mint officials were prepared to do so if required before a new dollar coin could be introduced. Faced with that possibility, the Mint's engraving department created a model for a 1999-dated Anthony dollar. Finally, on May 20, 1999, Mint officials announced a decision to strike 1999-dated Anthony dollars sometime before the end of the year. The decision was timely. Less than a month later, the Treasury Department's vaults were emptied of Anthony dollars many believed would never circulate. Production of the 1999 Anthony dollars began during the summer.

Sacagawea dollar

When Mint officials found themselves faced with striking more dollar coins, they wanted to avoid, if at all possible, resuming production of the Anthony dollar. Some in Congress, too, favored a small dollar coin to replace the Anthony dollar. Other members of Congress said they would support a new dollar coin only if no effort was made to stop production of the $1 Federal Reserve note. (As noted, other nations that have produced successful dollar-equivalent coins have withdrawn the corresponding note, forcing use of the coin to ensure the coin's success.)

During a hearing before a House subcommittee on June 26, 1997, officials from the Mint, Bureau of Engraving and Printing, Treasury and the General Accounting Office discussed the impact that introduction of a new dollar coin could have. GAO officials recommended the "biggest hurdle" to introducing a new dollar coin would be eliminating the dollar note, and recommended educating the public on using the dollar coin. Rep. Joseph P. Kennedy II, D-Mass., voiced he did not like the idea of forcing the public to accept a new dollar coin. Subcommittee Chairman Michael Castle, R-Del., promised to pursue legislation for a dollar coin, and introduced H.R. 2637, which sought a dollar coin. Castle decided to avoid the controversy over eliminating the dollar note, so the legislation did not address that point. He acknowledged, however, that withdrawing the note would enhance the chances of success for the dollar coin.

Castle held another hearing Oct. 21, 1997, during which Treasury officials reversed 17 years of policy on a dollar coin. Nancy Killefer, assistant secretary for management and chief financial officer for the Treasury Department, proposed a new dollar coin to replace the Anthony dollar. Killefer told members of the House Banking Subcommittee on Domestic and International Monetary Policy that Treasury officials wanted a coin with features they hoped would encourage its use and make it distinguishable from the quarter dollar. Killefer called for a dollar coin that would be golden in color and feature a distinctive edge.

Mint Director Diehl, speaking during the same hearing, said the Mint needed 30 months of development time before a new dollar coin could be introduced into circulation, although the time could be shortened if necessary.

Congress approved a Senate amended version of Castle's bill on Nov. 13, 1997, and President Clinton signed it into law.

While Congress was debating the dollar coin legislation, discussion began over who or what should be depicted on the coin. Some wanted the coin to depict Anthony or some other woman or women of historical significance. Others wanted an allegorical image of Liberty. A strong candidate was an image of the Statue of Liberty (the choice of Rep. Castle).

Private minters, artists and collectors began working on suggested designs. Ron Landis of the Gallery Mint Museum, Eureka Springs, Ark., created several "One Concept" pieces depicting different renditions of the Statue of Liberty or a more generic Liberty figure. Another artist, D. Carr, published images of an Astronaut dollar design concept; he wanted the coin to reflect 21st century ideals rather than depicting images similar to those used in the 18th and 19th centuries. Many collectors favored older concepts. Some collectors even wanted to resurrect Gasparro's abandoned Flowing Hair, Flying Eagle designs that had been superseded by the Anthony dollar designs. Still others recommended Sacagawea, the teenage Shoshone guide of the Lewis and Clark expedition.

To address the issue, Treasury Secretary Robert Rubin appointed the Dollar Coin Advisory Committee to examine the options and make recommendations as to what should appear on the coin. The committee met in private and then held public hearings June 8, 1998, in Philadelphia at the Philadelphia Federal Reserve. The committee announced its recommendations during that hearing: The committee recommended the coin "depict Liberty as represented by a Native-American inspired by Sacagawea." Castle was the sole dissenter serving on the committee; he still preferred the Statue of Liberty. Castle introduced legislation, H.R. 4329, on July 24, 1998, that if it had passed, would have required the Treasury Department to depict the Statue of on the coin. The bill failed to gain support before the 105th Congress ended its session at the end of 1998. Castle's earlier legislation required a General Accounting Office study of the public's preferences for design concepts.

Sacajawea dollar obverse

Sacajawea dollar reverse

Rubin supported the recommendation of the panel, assuring that Sacagawea would be primary design element concept. Mint officials invited artists to submit designs for the dollar coin. The invitation, mailed the second week of September 1998, included a requirement that the designs depict a woman of clearly Native-American heritage rather than a woman of European heritage wearing Indian garb or headdress (a common practice on 19th century coins).

Mint officials conducted a semi-public viewing of the designs in Washington, D.C., the week of Nov. 16. The Mint placed on display 80 obverse designs and 41 reverse designs, at Casa Italiana, a small church adjacent to the Mint headquarters. About 400 area numismatists, artists and historians were invited to view the designs and make comments. The Commission of Fine Arts met Nov. 20 to consider the 121 designs. Following that meeting, a Mint design selection panel narrowed the designs to six obverses and seven reverses, and placed all 13 designs on its Internet site for additional public comment. The panel considered those comments and others from focus groups before narrowing the designs further. The Commission of Fine Arts made its recommendations Dec. 17.

Winning its approval was an obverse design by Glenna Goodacre, an artist living in Santa Fe, N.M. (whose most famous work is the bronze Vietnam Women's Memorial in Washington, D.C.). The recommended obverse, in its original form, depicted a woman portraying Sacagawea with her baby on her back. Goodacre located a 22-year-old Shoshone college student who modeled for her. The recommended reverse depicted an eagle standing on a rock that was inscribed with petrographs, and was submitted by Thomas G. Rogers Sr. of the Mint.

The selected obverse met with criticism from members of the Lemhi-Shoshone tribe, of which Sacagawea was a member. They noted that the model was of the Shoshone-Bannock tribe, whose members, the critics said, have different facial features than the Lemhi-Shoshone. Those same critics pointed out historical inaccuracies in the hair and the lack of a cradleboard, which they said Sacagawea would have used to carry her baby.

To go with Goodacre's obverse design, Treasury officials selected a Flying Eagle design by Rogers. The design depicts 17 stars, one each for the 17 states in the Union during the Lewis and Clark expedition.

Whether the Sacagawea dollar will be more successful than Eisenhower and Anthony dollars is a question the future will answer.

Collecting the small dollars

Collectors seeking to collect the nation's downsized dollars will find it an easy, inexpensive hobby.

The smallest collection would contain just those Anthony dollars originally struck for circulation. That set comprises the 1979-P, 1979-D, 1979-S, 1980-P, 1980-D and 1980-S Anthony dollars. (Incidentally, the 1979 Anthony dollar struck at the Philadelphia Mint became the first such coin to bear a P Mint mark since the 1942-45 Jefferson, Wartime Alloy 5-cent coins. The San Francisco dollars were the first S Mint mark coins struck for circulation since the 1974-S cents.)

This six-coin set will cost collectors about $10.50 for coins grading Mint State 63. Mint State 65 specimens will cost about $9 each, except for the 1980-S dollar, valued at about $6.

An expanded set would contain two more coins, the 1981-P and

1981-D Anthony dollars. These coins were not struck for circulation. Instead, they were produced only for inclusion in the 1981 Uncirculated Mint sets. Values for these two coins in MS-63 are $4 for the 1981-P coin and $2.75 for the 1981-D dollar. Values are considerably higher for MS-65 specimens ñ $75 for the Philadelphia coin and $30 for the Denver coin. (Those values are due to the overall poor quality of surviving Mint State specimens.)

A third goal to complete a set of Anthony dollars would be to include the normal Proof coins. A Proof 65 1979-S Anthony dollar is valued at about $3.75, the 1980-S at $5 and the 1981-S at $5.

Collectors interested in die varieties and who don't mind paying a bit more for recent coins will want to include three additional pieces, each with subtle though discernable differences.

The first of these is the 1979-P Anthony, Near Date dollar. A Near Date specimen grading MS-63 is valued at about $7, with an MS-65 specimen costing about $25.

The second die variety to added to the collection is the "abnormal" Proof 1979-S Anthony, Clear S dollar. Well into the year, the Mint mark punch being used to punch Mint marks into the dollar and other denomination dies had worn so much that the S was barely identifiable. A second Mint mark punch was substituted, creating two varieties for the year. The Clear S variety is the scarcer of the two coins, bringing about $48 for a Proof 63 coin and $60 for a Proof 65 coin.

The new S Mint mark punch was replaced again in 1981, with the new Clear S variety of the Proof 1981-S Anthony dollar being the scarcer. It brings about $55 in Proof 63 and $75 in Proof 65.

A "complete" set of pre-1999 Anthony dollars, including the die varieties, totals 14 coins.

Collectors also will want to add the 1999 Anthony dollars to their collection as they become available. The Mint began striking 1999-P Anthony dollars in mid-summer; production had not begun at the Denver Mint at press time. Mint officials have already revealed a copper-nickel Proof version would also be offered, presumably with the S Mint mark. It was not known whether a 90 percent silver Proof version would be offered. The Mint now offers two versions of the Proof dime, quarter dollar and half dollar ñ a copper-nickel clad version of each and a 90 percent silver version. Collectors would likely welcome the first and only silver version of the Anthony dollar.

Collectors will have various collecting options beginning in 2000 when the Sacagawea dollar is released. The Philadelphia and Denver Mints will likely strike circulating specimens. A Proof version is planned. Collectors should be able to find the circulating specimens at their banks once the coins are released. The Proof versions will be available from the U.S. Mint.

The move from a big, heavy dollar coin has been an interesting one. Who knows what their future will bring.

3 Coin Market Analysis

1999 was a banner year for rare coins. One pattern piece, a 1907 Saint-Gaudens, Ultra High Relief $20 double eagle, sold for $1.21 million, a world's record for a United States gold coin sold at public auction. Numerous U.S. coins, too many to list individually, sold for well into hundreds of thousands of dollars. The "collage" of auctions that took place in June with nearly every major rare coin auction house in America participating prior, during and right after the Long Beach (Calif.) Coin and Stamp Expo was possibly the most concentrated offering of rare coins in the history of the U.S. market.

Collectors were very busy throughout the year because of programs introduced by the United States Mint in 1999. It was most definitely the year of the Washington quarter dollar. From the moment the Washington, Delaware quarter dollar hit circulation, *Coin World* readers were contacting the publication daily with reports of "sightings" of the new coins and to discuss variety and error coins pertaining to the new quarters. How the Mint would package the new quarters in the 1999 Proof sets was also uppermost in many collectors' minds.

If 1999 was the year of the quarter, it also was the year of the Internet as collectors and sellers found novel ways to buy and sell coins. At least one transaction for more than six figures took place on one of the more popular Internet "auction" sites. This site does not offer an auction of rare coins in the traditional sense since in this day of the Internet, anyone can be an auctioneer. Perhaps not coincidentally, the seller of this $100,000-plus item was a longtime dealer who had just started "dabbling on the net."

That rare coins did so spectacularly well in light of weak precious metals prices and Year 2000 promotions that did nothing really to energize the core community of rare coin collectors bodes well for 2000. To be a coin collector in America today means to enjoy the hobby whether purchasing Lincoln cents for a few dollars or major rarities for $10,000 and more.

Auctions

The biggest "name" auction of the year took place in May 1999 when the Harry Bass Jr. collection of U.S. paper money and pattern coinage was sold by Auctions by Bowers and Merena. While Bass' paper money and pattern collections were world class in their own right, Bass was maybe better known for his love and collection of early U.S. gold coinage. The gold portion of the Bass collection was set for auction in October 1999 by the same company.

The general strength of the market brought out many coins that had been in hiding since the weaker days of the early 1990s. Those collectors who joined the market in the early 1990s found much to choose from and at price levels significantly below those of 1988 to 1991. Therefore, some of the material that had been salted away for just a few years was auctioned during a very busy 1999 auction calendar.

January 1999 saw Heritage Numismatic Auctions Inc. hold one of its Signature sales in conjunction with the Florida United Numismatists show, held annually in January and one of the premier shows of the entire U.S. show calendar.

Featured in the Heritage auction were consignments from numerous specialized collections ranging from Charlotte and Dahlonega gold coins to two silver dollar collections and a portion of the Ed Trompeter Proof gold coin collection. This blockbuster sale got the year off to a rousing start with total prices realized of $10,115,861.15.

In February, Superior Stamp & Coin of Beverly Hills, Calif., auctioned the Dr. Juan Suros Collection. A very specialized collection, it featured overdate and other die variety coins. An overdate coin features a date that has been stamped or hubbed over the residue of another date, as on the 1799/8 Draped Bust cent and 1942/1 Winged Liberty Head dime. The majority of overdate coins were produced during a much more primitive era of the United States Mint when the date was applied to the die by hand. Many of these overdate coins were probably not "errors" (a term that suggests the overdate happened by accident) but were deliberately created when Mint officials salvaged a usable die by "changing" its date. At the time, Mint officials did not care that they were creating die varieties that would be eagerly collected by collectors of a later age, unlike officials at today's Mint who do everything they can to prevent such varieties.

One coin of particular note in the Suros auction is the Proof 1823/2 Capped Bust quarter dollar. The coin is unique in Proof format and the provenance of this one and only piece is quite interesting. The coin first appeared at auction in Germany around 1900. At that time noted dealer Burdette Johnson of St. Louis brought the coin home. At one time this piece resided in the Newcomer collection, an important collection assembled in Baltimore. Later, the composer Jerome Kern, a connoisseur of United States coins, purchased this piece. After the sale of the Kern collection, a member of the illustrious Gugghenhiemer family of New York acquired the coin. The coin was recently graded Proof 64 by Numismatic Guaranty Corporation of America; this unique and desirable piece realized $138,000.

The June Long Beach Coin and Stamp Exposition was "surrounded" by auctions with no less than five major auctions conducted by five different auction houses during a span of 10 days. Collectors and dealers were most happy to have such a spread of auctions and coins to choose from and the entire batch of auctions indicated just how healthy the rare coin market is currently. The combined prices realized for these five auctions totaled $24.73 million!

Discoveries

The release of the State quarter dollars into circulation gave error and variety collectors a whole new area in which to expend their energies. Among the many reports received by *Coin World* were State quarter dollars with parts of various mottoes missing caused by filled dies to more exotic blunders such as a State quarter dollar being struck on a planchet intended for a 5-cent coin or one struck multiple times.

Among the more esoteric rare coins, many new varieties were reported to specialized collector clubs, but no varieties were reported that captured the imagination of the entire coin collecting community. The Mint appears to have eliminated the production of doubled dies through changes in the die-production process, although there was one unconfirmed report of an extremely minor doubled die being found on the reverse of a 1998 cent.

It has sometimes been said that when it comes to rare coins there is an ever-dwindling supply since no more of these "rare coins" will be made. However, there is the instance when coins struck 100 or more years ago are lost to the coin collecting community and only discovered much later.

In May, Auctions by Bowers and Merena Inc. brought to the coin collecting community a hoard of gold coins that sunk with the *SS Brother Jonathan* steamship on July 30, 1865. Having departed San Francisco just two days prior, the sidewheel steamship carried with it an unknown amount of coins that had been struck in San Francisco. The auction contained no less than 400 1865-S Coronet Head $20 double eagles, many in very high grade. This one find literally multiplied 10-fold or more the number of available high-grade specimens of this formerly extremely rare date in Uncirculated condition.

Precious Metals

All the commotion surrounding how to prepare for year 2000 computer glitches bodes well for the precious metals market. By March premiums on $1,000 face value bags of 90 percent U.S. silver coins had skyrocketed as had the premiums on pre-1933 U.S. gold coins. However, other fundamental issues, most notably announced sales of gold by European central banks, seemed to put a damper on the precious metals market and with it the premiums above and beyond the price of the metal evaporated just as quickly as the price of gold by the ounce eroded. By mid-summer, gold hovered at 20-year lows or less than $255 an ounce. Silver, which had reached $7 in 1998, never saw such lofty levels during 1999 and went below $5 an ounce on numerous occasions. If there is anything to say about precious metals as it concerns coin collecting, it is that except for some of the "old school" dealers and collectors, the two markets have very much gone their separate ways.

Grading Services

No rare coin market analysis is complete without reference to improvements in the grading of United States coins. At this point, third-party grading services have been in existence for more than a decade and professional grading and encapsulation of coins is reaching its maturity. Three independent grading services, Professional Coin Grading Service of Newport Beach, Calif., ANACS of Columbus, Ohio, and Numismatic Guaranty Corporation of America of Parsippany, N.J., actively continue to grade and encapsulate coins. A fourth service, Independent Coin Grading of Boulder, Colo., is a relative newcomer but in just its first year it has gained enough market share that in a short time collectors may think of "the big four" when it comes to grading services. While third-party grading has gone a long way toward eliminating much of the arbitrary whim of collectors and dealers with respect to the grading (and therefore the valuations) of coins, the last word on precision grading has not been written. Therefore, when viewing the valuations in Trends and noting that a coin might "jump" dramatically in price from one grade to the next, realize that these grade definitions are not scientifically determined. What it comes down to is, "Am I willing to purchase a coin I like for my collection at the asking price?" using the *Coin World Price Guide* as a guide, not the deciding factor.

More importantly, just because a coin is encapsulated with a grade on it, doesn't mean that the coin is worth exactly what is listed in this price guide. Market acceptance of a given coin at a given grade level has mostly to do with the individual coin's merits, though in some cases the market acceptance of a particular grading service can come into play. As third-party grading continues to expand, a large portion of coins offered to the collecting public are in these third-party professional grading holders.

Year 2000 Outlook

As we head into the new millennium there is every indication that coin collecting and the more detailed study of coins known as numismatics is quite healthy. Specialty publications abound, and new ventures being formed on the Internet such as *Coin World* and Numismatists Online have brought the hobby of kings into the new technology era. A robust economy continues to fuel collector spending. As the State quarter program heads into its second year, more novices will develop into true collectors. All of this is good for supporting the valuations of United States coins at their current levels.

4 Values of U.S. Coins

Rare coin prices rise and fall based upon the interest of collectors, investors and dealers, the overall economy, changes in precious metals prices and a host of other factors.

In 1979-80, rare coins enjoyed immense popularity and prices soared. Rare coins became a very popular investment medium as investors who had never considered coins turned to the numismatic hobby. That market peak coincided with higher precious metals prices, high inflation rates, interest rates that were many points higher than they are today, oil prices that were much higher than they are currently and an otherwise weak national economy.

The rare coin boom was good for dealers, many of whom found themselves making more money than ever before. The average collector, on the other hand, found himself locked out of the booming market by high prices. Coins that a few years earlier were well within the budget of the average collector suddenly were being offered at prices that in many cases exceeded the collector's total annual budget for coins. Numismatic publications of the boom period were filled with letters from disgruntled collectors angry over the high cost of collecting. Many said they were leaving the hobby, possibly forever.

However, interest in rare coins as investments waned as inflation seemed to be tamed and the national economy improved. Other, more traditional investments like the stock market began bringing higher returns than rare coins, and precious metals prices dropped. Common-date gold double eagles — $20 coins struck from 1850 to 1933 — that were worth $774 in precious metals value alone when gold was worth $800 an ounce dropped in value intrinsically as the price of gold lost half of its value in the early to mid-1980s. Most market observers consider the bottom of the rare coin market to have coincided with the recession in the summer of 1982.

Problems in the numismatic market also helped decrease investor interest in rare coins. As prices dropped, dealers and others sought to maintain the values of their holdings. Grading standards tightened; in order to keep a value of a Mint State 65 coin, for example, a specimen would have to grade at a level that a few months earlier would have been called Mint State 66 or even higher. Collectors, dealers and investors found their holdings would have to pass stricter scrutiny. What would have been accepted as one grade level in 1979 — Mint State 65, for example — may have been accepted as only a Mint State 63 several years later, with a corresponding drop in price. Investors who were already losing money because of falling prices lost even more money as new grading standards made their coins worth even less.

From 1982 to 1987, grading standards changed and the market wavered. Some years were better than others, but the market didn't approach the levels achieved in 1979-80. That's not to say the market was dead. Indeed, many major collections entered the market through public auctions. Collections built over the span of decades by such collector greats as Virgil Brand, Emery May Norweb, Amon G. Carter Jr. and Robinson Brown were sold, often in auctions spaced over 18 months to three years. Prices for the classic rarities — coins such as the 1804 silver dollars and 1913 Liberty Head 5-cent coins — generally did not reach the lofty levels generated in 1979-80. In fact, some of the same pieces selling for record highs in those two years realized much lower prices when they reappeared at auction from 1981-87.

However, a new force began to emerge beginning in late 1987. The collector, who had all but abandoned the rare coin field since the boom period, began to return. Collector rarities became the most sought-after pieces, as well as common-date coins in top-notch conditions preferred by investors.

Meanwhile, investors were also re-examining the rare coin market. Coins that many collectors have always considered common suddenly became rare in the eyes of some dealers and investors. Franklin half dollars, struck from 1948 to 1963, became a hot item. Sharply struck specimens in the higher levels of Mint State began realizing prices that only a few years earlier would have been unthinkable. The market reached another peak in 1989.

Collector strength continued during the 1990s. Specialty clubs, often focusing on a single denomination, series or design, flourished. Interest in die varieties increased.

The growth of interest in the late 1980s and throughout the 1990s in die varieties — the differences between coins struck from a particular pair of dies from those struck by another set of dies — has prompted one of the most important and exciting areas of growth in the coin collecting community: publication of a number of books on individual series. These highly specialized books represent years of work by dedicated collectors, dealers and researchers (many times, all three labels can be applied to one person), showing the love and respect the authors have for their area of specialty. Publishers have produced, since the late 1980s and throughout the current decade, books that represent new areas of research or major upgrades to works published in the 1940s and 1950s, which of course were decades out of date. Subjects include Middle Date large cents (1816-39) and Late Date large cents (1840-57) in individual books, Lincoln cents (at least two major works on die varieties), 2-cent coins, Barber dimes, quarter dollars and half dollars (in three separate books), Winged Liberty Head dimes, Shield and Liberty Head 5-cent coins, Flowing Hair, Draped Bust and Capped Bust half dollars (in a major revision to the classic reference about the subject), and much more. Many other books are in progress and will be published over the next few years.

As the 1990s close, the collector market remains strong in many areas. Three collector coins have brought more than $1 million each at public auction.

Chapter 3 in this book reviews the collector coin market over the past 12 months.

Trends values

We make no predictions in these pages about what the future may bring for rare coins. We provide the reader with information. The Trends listings provide a guide for retail value.

We will note that historically, the rare coin market appears to move in cycles. Q. David Bowers, a longtime and well-respected dealer, was one of the first in the hobby to write about price cycles. The overall market moves in cycles, with peaks in 1973-74 and 1979-80, and slumps in 1975-76 and 1981 to late 1987. In 1979-80, the cycle peaked, with prices and interest higher than ever before, until another peak was reached in 1989.

Individual series also experience cyclical movements, with gold coins popular in some years, Proof sets and rolls in other years, and silver dollars at other times.

How coins become rare

The first factor that makes a coin rare is its mintage. The term mintage is the number of specimens struck for any given date at a specific Mint. However, mintage figures are often deceptive. For example, the United States Mint struck 312,500 1933 Indian Head eagles, a $10 gold coin. However, price records indicate that the coin is much rarer than the mintage would indicate; perhaps as few as 30-40 pieces exist.

What happened? The coins were struck shortly before President Franklin D. Roosevelt signed an executive order forbidding Americans to own gold coins. The only gold coins not banned from private ownership were those with numismatic value held by collectors and dealers. Only a few of the 1933 Indian Head eagles struck were released into circulation; the rest were melted before they ever left the Mint. (The 1933 Saint-Gaudens double eagle, a $20 gold coin, was *never* released into circulation. However, a few pieces turned up in dealers' hands, including one within the last couple of years, only to be confiscated or withdrawn from circulation. Treasury officials deem it illegal to own the coin since it was never officially released.)

Another case of how mintage figures can be misleading is raised by the 1883 Liberty Head 5-cent varieties. Two distinct varieties were struck that year. The first bears the denomination on the reverse in the form of the Roman numeral V; the word CENTS does not appear. After larcenous individuals began gold-plating the Liberty Head, No CENTS 5-cent coin and passing it off as the similarly sized $5 gold half eagle, a new variety was struck. The second variety bears the word CENTS in addition to the Roman numeral V. Approximately three times as many of the second, With CENTS variety were struck (mintage: 16 million) as the first, No CENTS variety (mintage: 5.5 million). However, prices for the more "common" variety are much higher than for the lower mintage piece.

The sudden replacement of the 1883 Liberty, No CENTS 5-cent variety led to the quick withdrawal of the coin by the public, certain they had a rarity. The much more common variety entered circulation and stayed there, with many more pieces eventually consigned to the melting pot as they became too worn and were withdrawn by banks. Thus, collectors saved many more specimens of the first variety than the second version.

As noted, most coins end up in the melting pot. As coins circulate, they become worn, scratched and damaged. Eventually, they are returned to the Mint for melting. Gold and silver coins have been melted in large quantities by the government and by private individuals. When gold surpassed $800 an ounce and silver reached $50 an ounce in January 1980, millions of common-date gold and silver coins were melted for their precious metal content. A worn 1964 quarter dollar, for example, worth a dollar or less to a collector in 1978 had a bullion value of $9.04 when silver hit $50 an ounce!

Researchers study survival rates by degree of preservation. One author traced the appearances of all U.S. gold coins sold at auction by grade. Several grading services now publish population reports of the coins they grade, another indicator of the survival rate for a particular coin in a particular condition. These population reports can be misleading, however, in that a single coin may be submitted to a grading service many times by an owner hoping to get a higher grade for the piece at some point. A coin submitted a half dozen times may be listed in the firm's population report a half dozen times, thus artificially inflating the number of coins with that grade.

Unexpected supplies of coins turning up on the market can also have an impact on the rare coin market. A 1903-O Morgan silver dollar in Uncirculated was listed in a popular price guide published in 1962 as being valued at $1,500, and a 1904-O Morgan dollar, also in Uncirculated condition, was priced at $350. A year later, in the next edition of the same price guide, the 1903-O dollar was priced at $30 in the same grade, a loss of more than $1,400, and the 1904-O dollar was worth just $3.50, 1 percent of its value a year earlier!

What had happened was that the Treasury Department emptied some of its vaults as citizens turned in ever-increasing numbers of silver certificates in exchange for silver dollars. Numerous bags of the 1903-O and 1904-O dollars, in storage for nearly 60 years, were suddenly dumped onto the market at face value. Prices plummeted.

It is unlikely that such extreme examples will occur again. The Treasury Department sold the last of its silver dollar holdings beginning in 1972 in a series of seven sales, through the General Services Administration. However, some private hoards of certain coins still exist.

Demand and dealer promotion can also affect the price of a coin. For example, certain types of error coins are promoted as part of the regular series although in actuality, they are not. For example, the 1955 Lincoln, Doubled Die cent is heavily promoted, as is the 1972 Lincoln, Doubled Die cent. Activity is high for both coins, collector albums often have a space reserved for them, and dealers heavily promote them. However, other doubled die cents, much rarer than the 1955 and 1972 coins, are promoted only by a few dealers specializing in error coins. Their prices are often much lower than the heavily promoted pieces because their existence is known only to a few specialists and the supply is greater than the demand.

About the Trends values

The values in this price guide were compiled by *Coin World* Trends Editor Stuart Segan through July 1999. *Coin World's* Trends is a comprehensive retail value guide of U.S. coins, published consecutively in a three-week cycle in *Coin World.* Many different sources are used in determining the Trends, including dealer price lists (both buy and sell), prices quoted on several dealer trading networks, Internet transactions, public auction prices, realistic private transactions and any additional information acquired by the staff. In addition, demand and rarity are key considerations in compiling Trends. Values are for properly graded, problem-free, original and uncleaned coins with attractive color. Values given here are generally for sight-seen coins (coins that dealers demand to see before bidding on them), as opposed to sight-unseen coins (which dealers offer to buy without looking at them first, although at considerably lower bids than sight-seen coins). A sight-seen coin is generally acknowledged to be of higher quality than a sight-unseen coin, even if the two coins bear the same grade.

Coin World neither buys nor sells coins. Trends values are published as a reader service and may or may not be the same as an individual's or a firm's buy or sell prices.

Unless otherwise noted, condition (grade) designations are for the lowest possible level of each grade range. See **Chapter 8** for additional information concerning grading.

Reading a Trends listing

It is not possible to configure each line of Trends to the market peculiarities of each date and variety of every series of U.S. coin. Therefore, gaps may appear in the listing.

A dash listed among the values usually indicates a coin for which accurate market information is not available due to rarity or lack of activity in the marketplace. An asterisk indicates no coins issued. FV means the coin is commonly available at face value.

Liberty Cap, Left half cent

Date of authorization: April 2, 1792
Dates of issue: 1793
Designer/Engraver: Adam Eckfeldt
Diameter: 23.50 mm/0.93 inch
Weight: 6.74 grams/0.22 ounce
Metallic content: 100% copper
Edge: Lettered (TWO HUNDRED FOR A DOLLAR)
Mint mark: None

	AG-3	G-4	VG-8	F-12	VF-20	VF-30	EF-40	EF-45
1793	800.	1425.	2200.	3600.	5200.	6900.	10750.	14500.

Liberty Cap, Right half cent

Date of authorization: April 2, 1792
Dates of issue: 1794-1797
Designers: (Large Head): Robert Scot
(Small Head): Scot-John Gardner
Engraver: Robert Scot
Diameter: 23.50 mm/0.93 inch
Weight: 1794-1795: 6.74 grams/0.22 ounce
1795-1797: 5.44 grams/0.18 ounce
Metallic content: 100% copper
Edge: 1794-1797: None
17978: Lettered (TWO HUNDRED FOR A DOLLAR)
1797: Gripped
Mint mark: None

	AG-3	G-4	VG-8	F-12	VF-20	VF-30	EF-40	EF-45
1794	145.	305.	625.	900.	1350.	2500.	3600.	5000.
1795 Lettered Edge, Pole	140.	300.	550.	875.	1300.	2250.	3500.	4250.
1795 Plain Edge, Pole, Punctuated Date	95.00	275.	550.	750.	1150.	2200.	3250.	4500.
1795 Plain Edge, No Pole	85.00	225.	375.	625.	1100.	2050.	3050.	3750.
1795 Lettered Edge, Pole, Punctuated Date	175.	350.	675.	1000.	1600.	2900.	4500.	5500.
1796 With Pole	5500.	9000.	13500.	16500.	20500.	24500.	30000.	37500.
1796 No Pole	8500.	19000.	27500.	38500.	65000.	——	——	——
1797 Plain Edge	150.	275.	400.	800.	1250.	2200.	4500.	5500.
1797 Plain Edge, 1 above 1	115.	225.	350.	675.	1100.	1750.	2900.	4000.
1797 Lettered Edge	390.	685.	1225.	2500.	5350.	——	——	——
1797 Gripped Edge	5250.	9500.	19000.	——	——	——	——	——

—— = Insufficient pricing data

Draped Bust half cent

Date of authorization: April 2, 1792
Dates of issue: 1800-1808
Designers: Obverse: GIlbert Stuart-Robert Scot
Reverse: Scot-John Gardner
Engraver: Robert Scot
Diameter: 23.50 mm/0.93 inch
Weight: 5.44 grams/0.18 ounce
Metallic content: 100% copper
Edge: Plain
Mint mark: None

	G-4	VG-8	F-12	VF-20	VF-30	EF-40	AU-50	MS-60
1800	35.00	60.00	120.	200.	325.	415.	650.	1400.
1802/0 Reverse of 1802	475.	1200.	2400.	8000.	——	——	——	——
1802/0 Reverse of 1800	13500.	25000.	35000.	——	——	——	——	——
1803	35.00	55.00	130.	240.	375.	675.	1500.	3000.
1804 Plain 4, Stemless	35.00	42.50	55.00	105.	170.	265.	500.	1175.
1804 Plain 4, Stems	50.00	95.00	175.	300.	800.	——	——	——
1804 Crosslet 4, Stemless	40.00	50.00	70.00	115.	300.	450.	625.	1300.
1804 Crosslet 4, Stems	35.00	42.50	65.00	110.	200.	300.	575.	1500.
1804 Spiked Chin	40.00	55.00	80.00	150.	235.	375.	550.	1450.
1805 Medium 5, Stemless	35.00	55.00	65.00	125.	175.	340.	585.	1250.
1805 Large 5, Stems	35.00	55.00	80.00	135.	275.	390.	675.	——
1805 Small 5, Stems	585.	2000.	3500.	——	——	——	——	——
1806 Small 6, Stemless	35.00	45.00	55.00	80.00	105.	180.	385.	975.
1806 Large 6, Stems	35.00	42.50	60.00	100.	150.	230.	450.	1000.
1806 Small 6, Stems	200.	375.	675.	1250.	1450.	2650.	——	——
1807	35.00	45.00	80.00	130.	225.	350.	650.	2100.
1808	35.00	55.00	80.00	160.	375.	475.	1200.	2400.
1808/7	175.	350.	675.	1100.	2700.	3750.	9500.	——

—— = Insufficient pricing data

Classic Head half cent

Date of authorization: April 2, 1792
Dates of issue: 1809-1835
Designer/Engraver: John Reich
Diameter: 23.50 mm/0.93 inch
Weight: 5.44 grams/0.18 ounce
Metallic content: 100% copper
Edge: Plain
Mint mark: None

	G-4	VG-8	F-12	VF-20	VF-30	EF-40	AU-50	MS-60
1809	30.00	37.00	47.50	65.00	90.00	150.	325.	850.
1809 Circle in O	35.00	48.00	72.50	100.	200.	375.	700.	——
1809/6	30.00	37.00	45.00	85.00	110.	175.	500.	1050.
1810	35.00	40.00	80.00	190.	285.	550.	1100.	2050.
1811	115.	325.	600.	1050.	2100.	4350.	7500.	——
1825	35.00	40.00	55.00	77.50	100.	140.	350.	750.
1826	30.00	37.00	45.00	62.50	75.00	115.	215.	400.
1828 13 Stars	30.00	37.00	45.00	60.00	67.50	80.00	125.	225.
1828 12 Stars	30.00	38.00	45.00	85.00	105.	205.	390.	1275.
1829	30.00	35.00	45.00	60.00	67.50	100.	160.	235.
1831 Originals and Restrikes: Orig. VF-25 $8600; VF-30 $10250; Prf-65 Br $22500; Restrike Prf-64 R&B $12500; Prf-66 red $24500.								
1832	30.00	35.00	44.00	55.00	60.00	70.00	135.	205.
1833	30.00	35.00	44.00	55.00	60.00	70.00	130.	200.
1834	30.00	35.00	44.00	55.00	60.00	70.00	130.	200.
1835	30.00	35.00	44.00	55.00	60.00	70.00	130.	200.
1836 Originals and Restrikes: Original Prf-15 $2100; Prf-60 $3500; Prf-63 $5500; Prf-64 $12000; 2nd Restrike Prf-64 $12500; Prf-65 red $45000.								

—— = Insufficient pricing data

Coronet half cent

Date of authorization:	April 2, 1792
Dates of issue:	1849-1857
Designers:	Obverse: Robert Scot-Christian Gobrecht Reverse: John Reich-Gobrecht
Engraver:	Christian Gobrecht
Diameter:	23.50 mm/0.93 inch
Weight:	5.44 grams/0.18 ounce
Metallic content:	100% copper
Edge:	Plain
Mint mark:	None

	G-4	VG-8	F-12	VF-20	VF-30	EF-40	AU-50	MS-60	MS-63
1840-49 Originals and Restrikes VF-20 $1500; AU-50 $2750; Prf-60 $3800; Prf-63 red and brown $5500; Prf-64 red and brown $8050; Prf-65 red $15000.									
1849 Large Date	35.00	40.00	47.00	62.00	70.00	105.	185.	325.	875.
1850	34.00	42.00	50.00	67.00	75.00	125.	225.	500.	1600.
1851	29.00	35.00	40.00	50.00	55.00	75.00	135.	210.	400.
1852 Restrikes: 1st Restrike Small Berries Prf-60 $2600; Prf-62 $4000; Prf-63 $4500; Prf-64 Br $4750; Prf-65 R&B $11500; Large Berries Prf-63 Br $90000.									
1853	29.00	35.00	45.00	55.00	60.00	75.00	125.	180.	370.
1854	30.00	36.00	42.00	50.00	55.00	75.00	125.	180.	385.
1855	30.00	35.00	42.00	50.00	55.00	75.00	130.	180.	365.
1856	32.00	37.00	43.00	60.00	65.00	85.00	145.	225.	435.
1857	40.00	45.00	60.00	80.00	90.00	125.	200.	300.	500.

Flowing Hair, Chain cent

Date of authorization:	April 2, 1792
Dates of issue:	1793
Designer/Engraver:	Henry Voigt
Diameter:	28.50 mm/1.13 inches
Weight:	13.48 grams/0.43 ounce
Metallic content:	100% Copper
Edge:	Vine and bars, or lettered (ONE HUNDRED FOR A DOLLAR)
Mint mark:	None

	AG-3	G-4	VG-8	F-12	VF-20	VF-30	EF-40	AU-50
1793 AMERICA	1025.	2450.	3850.	6000.	8500.	12750.	19000.	35000.
1793 AMERICA, Periods	1200.	2550.	4000.	6100.	9750.	13500.	20000.	40000.
1793 AMERI.	1300.	2750.	4150.	6500.	11500.	14500.	20500.	41500.

Flowing Hair, Wreath cent

Date of authorization: April 2, 1792
Dates of issue: 1793
Designers: Obverse: Henry Voigt-Adam Eckfeldt
Reverse: Eckfeldt
Engraver: Adam Eckfeldt
Diameter: 28.50 mm/1.13 inches
Weight: 13.48 grams/0.43 ounce
Metallic content: 100% copper
Edge: Vine and bars, lettered (ONE HUNDRED FOR A DOLLAR)
Mint mark: None

	AG-3	G-4	VG-8	F-12	VF-20	VF-30	EF-40	AU-50
1793 Vine and Bars	450.	850.	1250.	2500.	3550.	5750.	7250.	12250.
1793 Lettered Edge	575.	1050.	1400.	2800.	4150.	6250.	9250.	18500.
1793 Strawberry Leaf	75000.	125000.	250000.	——	——	——	——	——

—— = Insufficient pricing data

Liberty Cap cent

Date of authorization: April 2, 1792
Dates of issue: 1793-1796
Designers: (1793-1794): Joseph Wright
(1794-1796): Wright-John Gardner
Engravers: (1793-1794): Joseph Wright
(1794-1796): Robert Scot
Diameter: 28.50 mm/1.13 inches
Weight: 1793-1795: 13.48 grams/0.43 ounce
1795-1796: 10.89 grams/0.35 ounce
Metallic content: 100% copper
Edge: Plain, or lettered (ONE HUNDRED FOR A DOLLAR)
Mint mark: None

	AG-3	G-4	VG-8	F-12	VF-20	VF-30	EF-40	AU-50
1793	1100.	2100.	3750.	6750.	15000.	21000.	30000.	——
1794 Head of 1793	475.	1050.	2150.	3250.	7750.	9750.	16500.	——
1794 Head of 1794	85.00	165.	325.	475.	935.	1375.	2250.	4350.
1794 Head of 1795 S-72	100.	180.	400.	550.	1100.	1800.	3000.	4950.
1794 Starred Reverse	4500.	8750.	17000.	35000.	57500.	70000.	95000.	——
1795 Plain Edge	85.00	150.	235.	450.	700.	1200.	1850.	3150.
1795 Lettered Edge	110.	225.	465.	900.	1750.	2250.	4500.	6500.
1795 Jefferson Head, Plain Edge	3750.	7250.	12500.	20500.	40000.	75000.	——	——
1796	105.	175.	335.	675.	1400.	2050.	3450.	6350.

—— = Insufficient pricing data

Draped Bust cent

Date of authorization: April 2, 1792
Dates of issue: 1796-1807
Designers: Obverse: Gilbert Stuart-Robert Scot
Reverse: Joseph Wright-Scot
Engraver: Robert Scot
Diameter: 28.50 mm/1.13 inches
Weight: 10.89 grams/0.35 ounce
Metallic content: 100% copper
Edge: Plain, lettered (ONE HUNDRED FOR A DOLLAR), gripped
Mint mark: None

	AG-3	G-4	VG-8	F-12	VF-20	VF-30	EF-40	AU-50
1796 Reverse of 1794	95.00	195.	575.	1150.	2000.	2350.	3400.	7250.
1796 Reverse of 1796	70.00	130.	230.	475.	925.	1175.	2150.	4750.
1796 Reverse of 1797	65.00	120.	225.	460.	850.	1125.	2000.	3750.
1796 LIHERTY	135.	250.	550.	1150.	2250.	3750.	7000.	—
1797 Reverse of 1797, Stems	30.00	60.00	140.	275.	525.	825.	1400.	2600.
1797 Reverse of 1796, Gripped Edge	42.50	80.00	180.	350.	800.	1150.	2250.	4000.
1797 Reverse of 1796, Plain Edge	50.00	85.00	235.	425.	850.	1350.	2500.	—
1797 Reverse of 1797, Stemless	80.00	150.	310.	575.	1300.	2250.	3750.	8500.
1798 1st Hair Style	21.00	50.00	150.	335.	775.	1075.	2050.	3750.
1798 2nd Hair Style	20.00	40.00	90.00	225.	475.	1150.	1550.	3300.
1798 Reverse of 1796	52.50	100.	290.	550.	1450.	3300.	6600.	9000.
1798/7 1st Hair Style	77.50	145.	315.	525.	1050.	2500.	3500.	9250.
1799	875.	1750.	3500.	7000.	13750.	22500.	57500.	—
1799/8	950.	2050.	4250.	8000.	17000.	—	—	—
1800 Normal Date	18.00	40.00	92.50	240.	550.	725.	1250.	4750.
1800/798 1st Hair Style	22.50	57.50	175.	550.	1250.	2650.	4000.	8000.
1800 80/79 2nd Hair Style	20.50	45.00	120.	310.	600.	1500.	2000.	5750.

— = Insufficient pricing data

	AG-3	G-4	VG-8	F-12	VF-20	VF-30	EF-40	AU-50
1801	12.50	39.00	75.00	160.	400.	525.	750.	1900.
1801 3 Errors	47.50	140.	385.	750.	1550.	4250.	6000.	11500.
1801 1/000	20.00	42.50	90.00	200.	450.	900.	2000.	5000.
1801 100/000	25.00	85.00	165.	235.	560.	1000.	1900.	4000.
1802	13.00	38.00	72.50	185.	275.	425.	700.	1550.
1802 Stemless	13.50	38.00	90.00	165.	325.	475.	725.	1350.
1802 1/000	14.00	45.00	115.	250.	415.	725.	975.	2500.
1803 Small Date	11.50	38.00	57.50	115.	255.	375.	675.	1300.
1803 Large Date, Small Fraction S-264	2450.	5500.	10250.	17500.	37500.	75000.	——	——
1803 Large Date, Large Fraction S-265	32.50	92.50	225.	400.	875.	1950.	2850.	5500.
1803 Stemless S-243	16.00	38.00	80.00	225.	540.	635.	1200.	2300.
1803 100/000 S-249	18.50	40.00	105.	215.	635.	850.	1500.	3000.
1804	300.	600.	1350.	2350.	3100.	5500.	7950.	19000.
1804 restrike (c. 1860)	——	——	——	350.	375.	400.	455.	500.
1805 Pointed 1	12.00	38.00	70.00	175.	375.	500.	925.	2300.
1805 Blunt 1 S-267	12.00	38.00	70.00	165.	295.	400.	800.	1550.
1806	22.50	42.00	110.	245.	425.	625.	1300.	4000.
1807 Large Fraction	15.00	38.00	57.50	160.	345.	450.	865.	1600.
1807 Small Fraction	15.50	40.00	90.00	250.	525.	1200.	2750.	——
1807 Small Fraction, Comet	22.50	40.00	80.00	225.	500.	1200.	2850.	——
1807/6 Large 7	19.00	38.00	75.00	195.	400.	500.	925.	2250.
1807/6 Small 7	1600.	2750.	4400.	9000.	17500.	——	——	——

—— = Insufficient pricing data

Classic Head cent

Date of authorization: April 2, 1792
Dates of issue: 1808-1814
Designer/Engraver: John Reich
Diameter: 28.50 mm/1.13 inches
Weight: 10.89 grams/0.36 ounce
Metallic content: 100% copper
Edge: Plain
Mint mark: None

	AG-3	G-4	VG-8	F-12	VF-20	VF-30	EF-40	AU-50
1808	18.00	40.00	120.	325.	525.	1100.	1750.	3500.
1809	25.00	110.	225.	440.	825.	1750.	2400.	4500.
1810	16.00	36.00	80.00	200.	425.	540.	825.	1800.
1810 10/09	17.00	45.00	110.	250.	540.	850.	1300.	3250.
1811	25.00	110.	160.	400.	775.	1350.	2250.	3400.
1811/0	26.00	115.	210.	465.	1075.	2100.	3850.	9750.
1812	15.00	34.00	72.50	200.	435.	540.	875.	2000.
1813	23.00	60.00	115.	240.	525.	675.	1350.	2400.
1814 Plain 4	17.00	40.00	80.00	225.	500.	575.	925.	2275.
1814 Crosslet 4	17.00	40.00	80.00	225.	500.	575.	1000.	1950.

Coronet cent

Date of authorization: April 2, 1792
Dates of issue: 1816-1857
Designers: (1816-1835)
Obverse: Robert Scot
Reverse: John Reich
(1835-1839)
Obverse: Scot-Christian Gobrecht
Reverse: Reich
(1839-1857)
Obverse: Scot-Gobrecht
Reverse: Reich-Gobrecht
Engravers: (1816-1835)
Obverse: Scot
Reverse: Reich
(1835-1839)
Obverse: Gobrecht
Reverse: Reich
(1839-1857)
Obverse: Gobrecht
Reverse: Gobrecht
Diameter: 28.50 mm/1.13 inches
Weight: 10.89 grams/0.35 ounce
Metallic content: 100% copper
Edge: Plain
Mint mark: None

	G-4	VG-8	F-12	VF-20	EF-40	AU-50	AU-55	MS-60	MS-63
1816	11.75	23.00	37.50	90.00	185.	295.	350.	500.	1200.
1817 13 Stars	12.00	22.00	30.00	67.50	175.	240.	290.	425.	700.
1817 15 Stars	15.00	27.00	45.00	145.	425.	825.	1450.	3150.	——
1818	11.00	21.50	29.00	55.00	145.	185.	210.	275.	475.
1819	11.50	22.00	30.00	55.00	150.	215.	250.	375.	800.
1819/8	19.00	29.00	45.00	100.	220.	350.	500.	950.	2250.
1820	11.75	22.50	30.00	55.00	175.	230.	275.	375.	725.

—— = Insufficient pricing data

	G-4	VG-8	F-12	VF-20	EF-40	AU-50	AU-55	MS-60	MS-63
1820/19	12.00	24.50	45.00	120.	400.	800.	1250.	1750.	2500.
1820 Small Date, Curled 2	11.75	23.00	30.00	55.00	425.	700.	1100.	1500.	——
1820 Large Date, Curled 2	15.00	27.00	60.00	110.	750.	1950.	——	——	——
1820 Large Date, Plain 2	11.75	23.00	30.00	55.00	190.	225.	275.	375.	475.
1821	30.00	55.00	150.	525.	1325.	2750.	3750.	8000.	17500.
1822	11.50	23.00	45.00	105.	300.	600.	800.	1275.	3500.
1823	65.00	175.	350.	875.	2400.	5500.	7500.	12500.	——
1823/2	57.00	115.	290.	775.	2100.	5000.	6900.	12250.	——
1823 restrike	——	——	——	——	450.	600.	750.	875.	1100.
1824	11.75	27.00	57.50	150.	475.	1250.	1750.	2250.	3750.
1824/2	15.00	32.00	80.00	280.	1100.	2500.	3000.	6250.	22500.
1825	11.50	22.00	50.00	140.	375.	850.	1400.	2100.	4250.
1826	11.00	19.00	45.00	105.	285.	400.	575.	900.	2750.
1826/5	30.00	75.00	190.	400.	850.	1600.	2100.	3500.	8850.
1827	11.00	17.00	40.00	100.	265.	425.	550.	850.	1350.
1828 Large Date	10.75	14.50	29.00	75.00	225.	325.	400.	650.	1275.
1828 Small Date	14.50	25.00	65.00	135.	300.	575.	700.	1050.	2050.
1829 Large Letters	10.75	15.00	37.00	80.00	230.	575.	675.	975.	1650.
1829 Small Letters	27.50	65.00	145.	475.	1250.	3000.	——	——	——
1830 Large Letters	10.75	13.50	28.00	60.00	185.	250.	375.	550.	1250.
1830 Small Letters	18.00	32.50	125.	385.	950.	2400.	3850.	——	——
1831	10.00	13.50	28.00	55.00	165.	250.	385.	600.	1150.
1832	11.00	13.50	27.00	55.00	155.	245.	360.	565.	925.
1833	10.00	13.00	26.00	54.00	140.	235.	300.	425.	800.
1834 Small 8, Large Stars, Medium Letters	10.75	13.50	27.00	55.00	205.	325.	450.	700.	1400.
1834 Large 8, Small Stars, Medium Letters	10.75	13.50	27.00	55.00	205.	300.	400.	700.	1400.
1834 Large 8, Large Stars, Medium Letters N-5	95.00	195.	315.	575.	2050.	4350.	——	——	——
1835	10.00	13.00	27.50	55.00	135.	225.	250.	375.	575.
1835 Small 8, Small Stars	10.00	13.00	27.50	55.00	250.	400.	500.	850.	——
1835 Large 8, Large Stars	10.00	14.00	34.00	70.00	365.	675.	800.	1500.	——
1835 Type of 1836	10.00	12.00	24.50	57.50	150.	220.	325.	500.	750.
1836	10.00	12.00	24.00	52.00	95.00	200.	250.	425.	625.
1837 Plain Cord, Large Letters	10.00	11.00	20.00	51.00	90.00	160.	230.	450.	800.
1837 Plain Cord, Small Letters	10.00	11.00	25.00	57.00	130.	225.	350.	700.	——
1837 Beaded Cord	10.00	11.00	20.00	50.00	87.00	160.	225.	460.	——
1838	10.00	11.25	20.00	50.00	85.00	150.	210.	315.	635.
1839 Head of 1838	11.25	15.50	23.00	58.00	130.	275.	325.	650.	1450.
1839/6	215.	415.	1250.	2500.	6000.	13000.	——	——	——
1839 Silly Head	11.50	15.25	26.00	67.50	210.	400.	480.	1200.	2750.
1839 Booby Head	10.50	15.00	28.00	70.00	185.	460.	675.	950.	2250.
CORONET, MODIFIED PORTRAIT; NO HAIR CURL ON LIBERTY'S CHEEK									
1839 Type of 1840, Newcomb 8	9.50	12.25	19.00	40.00	90.00	185.	240.	425.	800.
1840 Large Date	9.15	11.50	17.00	32.00	70.00	175.	235.	350.	625.

—— = Insufficient pricing data

	G-4	VG-8	F-12	VF-20	EF-40	AU-50	AU-55	MS-60	MS-63
1840 Small Date	9.15	11.50	17.00	32.00	70.00	170.	225.	245.	600.
1840 Small Date, Large 18, N-2	11.00	13.50	25.00	52.50	150.	275.	325.	450.	750.
1841	9.20	12.50	24.00	50.00	100.	265.	315.	385.	550.
1842	9.15	12.00	15.00	25.00	75.00	170.	225.	250.	400.
1843 Petite Head, Small Letters	9.15	11.50	19.00	35.00	75.00	180.	240.	280.	650.
1843 Mature Head , Large Letters	9.15	14.00	15.00	35.00	105.	200.	255.	335.	455.
1843 Petite Head, Large Letters, N-4	14.50	21.00	42.50	120.	295.	525.	775.	1050.	1850.
1844	9.00	11.00	13.50	30.00	85.00	150.	230.	300.	400.
1844/81 N-2	16.00	25.00	45.00	130.	400.	725.	900.	1450.	——
1845	9.00	11.00	12.50	21.00	62.50	115.	175.	210.	335.
1846 Medium Date, N-11	9.00	11.00	12.50	19.00	60.00	130.	190.	255.	775.
1846 Small Date	9.00	11.00	14.00	27.50	92.00	215.	275.	375.	825.
1846 Tall Date	9.00	11.00	16.00	30.00	100.	210.	285.	425.	——
1847	9.15	11.25	13.25	21.00	67.50	125.	190.	225.	575.
1847 7/Small 7	13.00	22.00	35.00	55.00	175.	300.	——	600.	——
1848	9.00	10.50	12.50	20.00	42.00	100.	155.	215.	350.
1849	9.00	10.50	12.75	21.00	55.00	110.	165.	220.	340.
1850	9.00	10.50	12.50	18.00	42.00	90.00	145.	175.	285.
1851	9.00	10.50	12.50	18.00	42.00	90.00	145.	175.	285.
1851/81 N-3	13.75	18.00	26.00	55.00	125.	250.	325.	450.	1100.
1852	9.00	10.50	12.50	18.00	42.00	90.00	145.	175.	285.
1853	9.00	10.50	12.50	18.00	42.00	90.00	145.	175.	285.
1854	9.15	10.50	12.50	18.00	42.00	90.00	145.	175.	285.
1855	9.25	11.15	13.25	20.00	43.00	100.	155.	225.	400.
1855 Knob Ear N-9	10.40	12.25	17.00	32.50	75.00	210.	290.	425.	1150.
1856	9.20	10.75	12.75	19.00	42.00	90.00	145.	210.	350.
1857	32.00	41.00	50.00	55.00	95.00	175.	200.	250.	525.
1857 Large Date N-1	26.50	32.00	40.00	55.00	95.00	180.	225.	310.	575.

—— = Insufficient pricing data

Flying Eagle cent

Date of authorization: Feb. 21, 1857
Dates of issue: 1856-1858
Designers: Obverse: Christian Gobrecht-James B. Longacre
Reverse: Longacre
Engraver: James B. Longacre
Diameter: 19.30 mm/0.76 inches
Weight: 4.67 grams/0.15 ounce
Metallic content: 88% copper, 12% nickel
Edge: Plain
Mint mark: None

Note: Mint State 65 and Proof 65 copper values are for coins with full red original color; lower Mint State and Proof grades reflect specimens that are red and brown.

	G-4	VG-8	F-12	VF-20	EF-40	AU-50	MS-60	MS-63	MS-64	MS-65R
1856	3850.	4400.	4850.	5250.	5750.	6150.	7050.	10750.	16500.	27500.
1857	17.00	19.00	24.00	33.00	85.00	150.	220.	525.	950.	2550.
1858 Large Letters	17.00	19.00	24.00	34.00	97.50	180.	245.	525.	950.	2450.
1858 Small Letters	17.00	19.00	24.00	32.50	92.50	170.	220.	525.	1100.	2750.
1858/7 early die state	63.00	90.00	175.	350.	500.	950.	1750.	4850.	9500.	——

—— = Insufficient pricing data

Indian Head cent

Date of authorization:	Feb. 21, 1857
Dates of issue:	1859-1909
Designer/Engraver:	James B. Longacre
Diameter:	1859-1864: 19.30 mm/0.76 inch 1864-1909: 19.05 grams/0.75 inch
Weight:	1859-1864: 4.67 grams/0.15 ounce 1864-1909: 3.11 grams/0.10 ounce
Metallic content:	1859-1864: 88% copper, 12% nickel 1864-1909: 95% copper, 5% tin and zinc
Edge:	Plain
Mint mark:	1908-1909, reverse under wreath

Note: Mint State 65 and Proof 65 copper values are for coins with full red original color; lower Mint State and Proof grades reflect specimens that are red and brown.

	G-4	VG-8	F-12	VF-20	EF-40	AU-50	MS-60	MS-63	MS-64	MS-65R
1859	8.00	10.00	15.00	35.00	80.00	130.	220.	410.	900.	2450.
SHIELD ADDED										
1860 Broad Bust T 2	6.00	8.00	9.00	13.50	42.00	75.00	130.	225.	375.	725.
1860 Narrow Bust	8.50	11.50	15.00	40.00	75.00	130.	235.	350.	900.	5250.
1861	16.00	19.00	26.00	36.00	72.00	145.	180.	235.	325.	800.
1862	5.50	6.00	7.50	11.00	23.00	54.00	95.00	150.	275.	685.
1863	5.50	6.00	7.00	10.00	21.00	40.00	65.00	150.	270.	750.
1864	15.00	19.00	21.00	26.00	44.00	72.00	135.	210.	315.	1025.
BRONZE										
1864 Initial L	36.00	55.00	85.00	110.	175.	225.	300.	425.	700.	2500.
1864	6.00	8.00	11.00	22.00	36.00	48.00	80.00	135.	175.	850.
1865	6.00	7.00	12.00	17.00	30.00	45.00	77.50	125.	170.	750.
1866	30.00	36.00	48.00	82.50	165.	200.	245.	385.	600.	3500.
1867	31.00	38.00	50.00	90.00	150.	180.	225.	400.	625.	4950.
1867/7	45.00	55.00	75.00	150.	250.	350.	450.	750.	1350.	——
1868	27.00	29.00	45.00	67.00	115.	160.	255.	340.	575.	2600.
1869	43.00	65.00	170.	215.	260.	350.	450.	515.	650.	3750.
1870	36.00	55.00	150.	210.	260.	340.	435.	525.	675.	3450.
1871	43.00	60.00	195.	250.	310.	390.	450.	625.	825.	7950.

—— = Insufficient pricing data

INDIAN HEAD CENT (CONTINUED)

	G-4	VG-8	F-12	VF-20	EF-40	AU-50	MS-60	MS-63	MS-64	MS-65R
1872	58.00	90.00	210.	275.	350.	425.	550.	800.	1425.	12500.
1873 Closed 3	16.00	25.00	37.50	60.00	90.00	260.	325.	600.	875.	9750.
1873 Doubled LIBERTY Die 1 bold	100.	250.	600.	1100.	2250.	3400.	5850.	13500.	26000.	——
1873 Open 3	14.00	20.00	26.00	42.00	85.00	120.	175.	275.	450.	3750.
1874	14.00	17.00	25.00	35.00	80.00	110.	135.	210.	275.	2100.
1875	14.00	20.00	33.00	40.00	75.00	110.	140.	225.	315.	2100.
1876	24.00	29.00	40.00	48.00	95.00	130.	205.	280.	365.	3600.
1877	475.	575.	750.	900.	1375.	1700.	2150.	3375.	5250.	14000.
1878	24.00	30.00	44.00	63.00	105.	160.	190.	300.	490.	1650.
1879	5.00	7.00	9.00	23.00	45.00	55.00	62.50	125.	200.	660.
1880	3.00	3.75	4.50	7.50	22.00	35.00	57.50	105.	175.	650.
1881	3.00	3.75	4.00	6.50	15.00	23.50	37.50	75.00	130.	550.
1882	3.00	3.75	4.00	6.00	14.25	22.00	35.00	75.00	125.	480.
1883	2.75	3.15	3.75	6.00	14.00	21.50	35.00	75.00	140.	465.
1884	3.00	3.50	5.00	9.00	16.00	28.00	52.50	125.	175.	700.
1885	5.00	5.00	9.75	19.00	45.00	60.00	90.00	190.	300.	1800.
1886 feather between I and C	3.50	4.25	12.00	35.00	80.00	95.00	135.	225.	375.	3100.
1886 feather between C and A	4.50	5.75	15.00	50.00	90.00	140.	250.	525.	1150.	10000.
1887	1.75	1.80	3.00	5.50	11.50	18.50	32.00	67.50	150.	750.
1888/7	450.	825.	1100.	1400.	1750.	2500.	——	35000.	——	——
1888	1.75	1.80	2.90	5.50	12.00	20.00	36.00	150.	325.	3250.
1889	1.50	1.80	2.90	4.75	9.75	18.00	30.50	65.00	165.	2150.
1890	1.50	1.65	2.45	3.75	9.50	16.50	29.50	62.00	150.	1650.
1891	1.50	1.65	2.40	3.75	9.50	17.00	30.00	65.00	150.	950.
1892	1.50	1.65	2.40	3.75	9.50	16.50	29.50	60.00	120.	1325.
1893	1.50	1.65	2.40	3.75	9.50	17.00	28.75	62.00	115.	600.
1894	2.00	2.50	6.25	8.75	15.00	25.00	45.00	95.00	150.	650.
1895	1.50	1.65	2.40	3.50	9.00	16.00	28.00	50.00	110.	385.
1896	1.50	1.65	2.40	3.50	8.75	15.00	27.50	50.00	120.	900.
1897	1.50	1.65	2.15	3.25	8.50	15.00	27.50	50.00	100.	390.
1898	1.50	1.65	2.15	3.25	8.00	14.00	26.00	45.00	85.00	315.
1899	1.50	1.65	2.15	3.25	8.00	14.00	26.00	45.00	70.00	285.
1900	1.30	1.45	1.90	2.25	6.50	12.75	21.00	37.00	65.00	285.
1901	1.30	1.45	1.90	2.25	6.00	12.50	20.00	37.00	65.00	270.
1902	1.30	1.45	1.90	2.25	6.00	12.50	20.00	37.00	65.00	285.
1903	1.30	1.45	1.90	2.25	6.00	12.50	20.00	37.00	65.00	285.
1904	1.30	1.45	1.90	2.25	6.00	12.50	20.00	37.00	55.00	270.
1905	1.30	1.45	1.90	2.25	6.00	12.50	20.00	37.00	55.00	285.
1906	1.30	1.45	1.90	2.25	6.50	12.75	20.50	37.00	60.00	285.
1907	1.30	1.45	1.90	2.25	6.00	12.50	20.00	37.00	55.00	285.
1908	1.30	1.45	1.90	2.25	6.50	13.00	21.00	37.00	55.00	285.
1908-S	40.00	45.00	50.00	57.50	75.00	125.	180.	335.	450.	1525.
1909	2.50	2.75	3.00	3.50	8.50	13.50	26.00	40.00	60.00	300.
1909-S	225.	265.	325.	375.	410.	435.	500.	650.	750.	2750.

—— = Insufficient pricing data

Lincoln, Wheat Ears cent

Date of authorization: Feb. 21, 1857
Dates of issue: 1909-1958
Designer: Victor D. Brenner
Engraver: Charles Barber
Diameter: 19.05 mm/0.75 inch
Weight: 1909-1942, 1944-1958:
3.11 grams/0.10 ounce
1943: 2.69 grams/0.09 ounce;
2.75 grams/0.09 ounce
Metallic content: 1909-1942: 95% copper, 5% zinc and tin
1942: 95% copper, 5% zinc
1943: zinc-plated steel
1944-1946: 95% copper, 5% zinc
1947-1958: 95% copper, 5% zinc and tin
Edge: Plain
Mint mark: Obverse under date

Note: Mint State 65 and Proof 65 copper values are for coins with full red original color; lower Mint State and Proof grades reflect specimens that are red and brown.

	G-4	VG-8	F-12	VF-20	EF-40	AU-50	MS-60	MS-63	MS-64	MS-65R
1909 VDB	2.25	2.50	2.65	2.85	3.50	4.50	9.50	13.50	23.00	40.00
1909-S VDB	375.	400.	445.	525.	575.	650.	715.	825.	1050.	2325.
1909	0.75	0.85	1.30	1.75	2.75	6.50	12.50	17.50	22.50	65.00
1909-S	35.00	42.00	50.00	65.00	90.00	110.	125.	150.	190.	435.
1909-S over Horizontal S	42.00	50.00	60.00	75.00	95.00	135.	190.	265.	325.	600.
1910	0.15	0.20	0.30	0.75	2.00	4.50	14.00	22.00	30.00	80.00
1910-S	5.75	7.00	8.00	9.50	19.00	50.00	55.00	60.00	70.00	265.
1911	0.20	0.30	0.75	1.50	4.00	8.00	19.00	32.50	55.00	175.
1911-D	4.00	4.75	7.00	11.50	30.00	55.00	70.00	95.00	160.	750.
1911-S	12.75	14.50	16.00	20.00	33.00	65.00	125.	175.	255.	1025.
1912	0.95	1.15	1.50	3.50	7.50	13.00	25.00	35.00	60.00	175.
1912-D	4.00	4.75	7.00	14.00	35.00	58.00	115.	175.	250.	825.
1912-S	9.00	10.00	11.50	17.00	35.00	55.00	95.00	125.	300.	1350.
1913	0.40	0.55	1.00	3.00	9.00	15.00	22.00	40.00	65.00	225.
1913-D	1.75	2.50	4.00	6.50	20.00	45.00	65.00	95.00	300.	1000.
1913-S	4.25	5.00	7.00	10.50	24.00	50.00	110.	160.	250.	1775.
1914	0.35	0.50	1.50	3.00	8.50	20.00	35.00	50.00	65.00	200.
1914-D	80.00	100.	130.	195.	425.	625.	1075.	1750.	2625.	7950.

	G-4	VG-8	F-12	VF-20	EF-40	AU-50	MS-60	MS-63	MS-64	MS-65R
1914-S	7.00	9.00	11.00	17.00	40.00	90.00	190.	385.	600.	6750.
1915	1.00	1.50	4.50	9.00	31.00	55.00	80.00	105.	130.	425.
1915-D	0.70	0.95	1.75	3.75	10.00	22.00	50.00	77.50	145.	400.
1915-S	5.25	6.00	7.50	11.75	27.00	50.00	100.	185.	400.	2100.
1916	0.15	0.20	0.40	1.10	2.50	6.00	12.00	22.50	45.00	100.
1916-D	0.25	0.35	1.25	3.00	7.75	19.50	48.00	85.00	140.	1350.
1916-S	0.75	0.95	1.60	2.75	8.00	20.00	62.50	95.00	350.	3600.
1917	0.15	0.20	0.30	1.00	2.25	5.50	12.00	24.00	30.00	125.
1917 Doubled Die	70.00	100.	240.	400.	900.	1100.	1500.	2250.	3500.	12000.
1917-D	0.25	0.35	1.75	4.00	9.00	19.00	60.00	130.	200.	800.
1917-S	0.40	0.50	0.75	1.75	6.75	16.00	62.50	140.	260.	2150.
1918	0.15	0.20	0.30	0.90	2.00	4.75	10.00	27.50	65.00	135.
1918-D	0.25	0.35	1.50	3.00	8.00	19.50	47.50	115.	160.	1025.
1918-S	0.35	0.45	1.00	2.00	6.00	21.00	57.50	145.	425.	3800.
1919	0.15	0.20	0.30	0.75	2.00	4.50	9.00	22.50	27.00	65.00
1919-D	0.20	0.35	0.60	1.50	4.50	18.00	45.00	87.50	175.	750.
1919-S	0.20	0.25	0.40	1.15	2.00	12.50	35.00	80.00	300.	2300.
1920	0.15	0.20	0.35	0.70	2.00	4.50	10.50	20.00	26.00	70.00
1920-D	0.20	0.30	0.65	2.00	5.75	16.00	55.00	85.00	140.	750.
1920-S	0.20	0.30	0.60	1.15	3.75	20.00	90.00	190.	350.	4900.
1921	0.20	0.25	0.50	1.55	4.50	14.00	35.00	50.00	65.00	140.
1921-S	0.65	0.80	1.50	3.50	11.50	50.00	85.00	150.	375.	3100.
1922 Missing D, Die Pair 2	190.	265.	385.	550.	1350.	2600.	5500.	15000.	27500.	45000.
1922-D	5.50	6.50	7.50	10.00	17.50	42.50	60.00	77.50	150.	700.
1923	0.15	0.20	0.30	0.85	2.75	6.00	14.50	25.00	70.00	185.
1923-S	1.50	1.85	2.75	5.25	17.00	60.00	175.	400.	675.	3350.
1924	0.15	0.20	0.30	0.80	3.00	8.50	21.00	42.50	60.00	135.
1924-D	8.00	8.75	11.50	20.00	50.00	110.	230.	325.	515.	3500.
1924-S	0.75	1.00	1.30	2.25	9.50	40.00	95.00	210.	500.	5250.
1925	0.10	0.15	0.20	0.60	1.75	5.00	9.25	19.50	28.50	60.00
1925-D	0.25	0.40	0.60	2.00	7.00	16.50	45.00	77.50	175.	975.
1925-S	0.15	0.30	0.50	1.00	4.50	18.00	55.00	140.	650.	4200.
1926	0.10	0.15	0.20	0.60	1.75	3.75	8.00	12.50	19.00	40.00
1926-D	0.25	0.30	0.60	1.50	5.50	16.00	35.00	85.00	300.	1100.
1926-S	2.00	2.25	2.75	4.00	10.00	45.00	110.	275.	925.	9250.
1927	0.10	0.15	0.20	0.75	1.75	3.85	9.00	14.00	27.00	75.00
1927-D	0.20	0.30	0.50	1.00	3.50	11.00	35.00	67.50	140.	900.
1927-S	0.50	0.75	1.10	1.75	7.00	21.50	60.00	125.	250.	3300.
1928	0.10	0.15	0.20	0.45	1.45	3.00	8.50	14.00	26.50	60.00
1928-D	0.20	0.30	0.40	1.00	2.50	9.50	24.00	55.00	75.00	475.
1928-S	0.45	0.50	0.60	1.50	3.50	14.50	44.00	80.00	165.	1050.
1929	0.10	0.15	0.20	0.45	1.25	3.50	6.50	12.50	25.00	60.00
1929-D	0.20	0.25	0.35	0.60	1.75	6.00	17.00	28.50	45.00	160.
1929-S	0.15	0.25	0.35	0.50	1.40	3.00	9.00	19.00	28.00	110.
1930	0.10	0.15	0.20	0.35	1.00	2.25	4.75	6.50	10.00	35.00

	G-4	VG-8	F-12	VF-20	EF-40	AU-50	MS-60	MS-63	MS-64	MS-65R
1930-D	0.15	0.25	0.35	0.80	1.75	4.50	13.00	23.50	28.00	70.00
1930-S	0.20	0.25	0.35	0.65	1.15	3.00	6.50	12.50	25.00	45.00
1931	0.45	0.55	0.65	1.15	1.85	6.75	15.00	28.00	37.50	80.00
1931-D	2.25	2.75	3.25	3.85	8.00	30.00	45.00	78.00	110.	550.
1931-S	29.00	31.00	35.00	40.00	45.00	55.00	57.50	65.00	80.00	225.
1932	1.20	1.50	1.75	2.00	3.50	9.00	16.50	19.50	25.00	60.00
1932-D	0.90	1.05	1.25	1.50	2.00	7.00	14.00	26.50	33.50	55.00
1933	1.00	1.15	1.35	1.75	2.50	8.50	15.00	22.00	26.50	55.00
1933-D	1.75	2.00	2.50	2.75	3.75	10.50	16.00	21.50	24.00	50.00

	F-12	VF-20	EF-40	AU-50	AU-55	MS-60	MS-63	MS-64	MS-65R	PF-65
1934	0.25	0.40	0.75	1.50	1.75	3.00	4.75	6.75	15.00	*
1934-D	0.35	0.55	5.00	8.75	9.25	11.50	13.50	15.00	35.00	*
1935	0.22	0.40	0.65	0.90	1.00	1.25	4.50	5.00	12.00	*
1935-D	0.40	0.45	0.85	1.65	1.90	3.25	5.00	7.25	15.00	*
1935-S	0.65	1.50	2.50	4.25	5.00	6.50	9.00	17.00	45.00	*
1936	0.22	0.40	0.70	0.90	1.00	1.25	2.25	3.00	6.00	850.
1936-D	0.30	0.40	0.85	1.00	1.20	1.85	3.75	4.50	10.00	*
1936-S	0.32	0.50	1.00	1.60	1.80	2.65	4.00	4.75	10.75	*
1937	0.20	0.30	0.50	0.60	0.65	0.80	1.50	2.00	6.00	110.
1937-D	0.25	0.40	0.65	1.00	1.20	2.25	2.85	4.00	6.50	*
1937-S	0.25	0.40	0.65	1.00	1.10	2.00	2.75	3.50	8.00	*
1938	0.20	0.30	0.60	1.00	1.10	1.25	1.75	2.50	6.00	100.
1938-D	0.40	0.75	0.85	1.00	1.25	1.85	3.75	4.25	6.50	*
1938-S	0.35	0.55	0.80	1.00	1.10	2.50	3.00	4.00	9.50	*
1939	0.15	0.25	0.30	0.40	0.45	0.50	1.00	2.00	6.00	95.00
1939-D	0.40	0.75	1.00	1.30	1.50	1.75	4.00	5.50	10.00	*
1939-S	0.25	0.40	0.75	1.00	1.10	1.30	2.00	4.50	12.50	*
1940	0.20	0.30	0.40	0.45	0.50	0.60	1.00	2.00	3.00	90.00
1940-D	0.30	0.50	0.60	0.70	0.80	0.90	1.00	2.25	3.75	*
1940-S	0.30	0.50	0.60	0.90	0.95	1.25	1.85	2.75	5.75	*
1941	0.23	0.40	0.50	0.55	0.60	0.80	1.00	2.50	4.00	75.00
1941-D	0.40	0.60	0.90	1.45	1.50	1.65	2.50	3.75	6.00	*
1941-S	0.50	0.70	0.80	1.00	1.10	1.75	2.50	4.75	9.50	*
1942	0.20	0.30	0.40	0.45	0.50	0.65	0.75	1.75	2.75	87.00
1942-D	0.25	0.35	0.40	0.45	0.50	0.60	0.70	2.00	3.75	*
1942-S	0.55	0.75	1.00	1.50	1.65	2.50	5.00	8.50	20.00	*
ZINC-COATED STEEL										
1943	0.20	0.30	0.40	0.65	0.70	0.80	1.40	1.75	4.00	*
1943-D	0.25	0.45	0.60	0.75	0.80	0.90	1.65	2.75	6.50	*
1943-S	0.35	0.55	0.75	1.00	1.10	1.40	2.65	4.50	10.00	*
SHELL-CASE BRASS										
1944	0.10	0.15	0.20	0.35	0.39	0.42	0.65	1.25	1.75	*
1944-D	0.20	0.25	0.30	0.35	0.38	0.40	0.50	1.50	2.50	*
1944-D/S Variety 1	75.00	115.	175.	245.	260.	325.	425.	675.	1700.	*

* = None issued

	F-12	VF-20	EF-40	AU-50	AU-55	MS-60	MS-63	MS-64	MS-65R	PF-65
1944-D/S Variety 2	32.50	47.50	90.00	100.	110.	145.	275.	350.	750.	*
1944-S	0.15	0.20	0.25	0.35	0.38	0.40	0.55	——	2.50	*
1945	0.10	0.15	0.24	0.40	0.45	0.55	0.65	——	1.70	*
1945-D	0.15	0.20	0.25	0.40	0.42	0.45	0.50	——	1.60	*
1945-S	0.15	0.20	0.25	0.30	0.35	0.40	0.45	——	2.00	*
1946	0.10	0.15	0.20	0.25	——	0.30	0.50	——	1.25	*
1946-D	0.15	0.18	0.20	0.25	——	0.30	0.50	——	1.50	*
1946-S	0.20	0.25	0.30	0.35	——	0.40	0.50	——	2.00	*
1946-S/D	——	——	——	——	——	175.	300.	400.	600.	*
BRONZE ALLOY RESUMED										
1947	0.20	0.30	0.40	0.75	——	1.15	1.50	——	3.00	*
1947-D	0.15	0.18	0.20	0.25	——	0.30	0.40	——	1.75	*
1947-S	0.16	0.22	0.26	0.35	——	0.50	0.75	——	2.00	*
1948	0.20	0.25	0.30	0.35	——	0.40	0.50	——	2.25	*
1948-D	0.25	0.30	0.35	0.40	——	0.45	0.50	——	2.50	*
1948-S	0.30	0.40	0.50	0.85	——	0.90	1.35	——	3.00	*
1949	0.20	0.30	0.40	0.50	——	0.55	0.65	——	3.00	*
1949-D	0.30	0.40	0.45	0.50	——	0.55	0.65	——	3.50	*
1949-S	0.30	0.45	0.60	0.75	——	1.00	1.25	——	7.00	*
1950	0.07	0.15	0.25	0.40	——	0.55	0.75	——	2.00	40.00
1950-D	0.05	0.14	0.20	0.25	——	0.45	0.65	——	1.50	*
1950-S	0.07	0.15	0.25	0.55	——	0.65	0.85	——	2.65	*
1951	0.07	0.15	0.25	0.40	——	0.55	0.65	——	2.00	30.00
1951-D	0.05	0.10	0.20	0.25	——	0.30	0.35	——	1.65	*
1951-S	0.20	0.25	0.35	0.40	——	0.45	0.55	——	3.00	*
1952	0.07	0.12	0.25	0.35	——	0.50	0.55	——	2.75	25.00
1952-D	0.04	0.08	0.15	0.20	——	0.23	0.25	——	1.60	*
1952-S	0.07	0.12	0.25	0.50	——	0.75	1.40	——	3.30	*
1953	0.05	0.09	0.15	0.16	——	0.18	0.20	——	1.20	22.00
1953-D	0.04	0.08	0.15	0.16	——	0.18	0.20	——	1.25	*
1953-S	0.07	0.12	0.16	0.26	——	0.35	0.50	——	1.75	*
1954	0.12	0.16	0.20	0.30	——	0.35	0.40	——	1.50	12.00
1954-D	0.04	0.07	0.10	0.20	——	0.25	0.35	——	0.50	*
1954-S	0.05	0.06	0.08	0.10	——	0.12	0.15	——	0.60	*
1955	0.04	0.07	0.09	0.10	——	0.12	0.15	——	0.75	11.50
1955 Doubled Die	325.	425.	480.	675.	725.	900.	1575.	3050.	22750.	*
1955-D	0.04	0.07	0.09	0.10	——	0.12	0.15	——	0.80	*
1955-S	0.15	0.18	0.20	0.22	——	0.25	0.40	——	1.25	*
1956	0.03	0.04	0.05	0.10	——	0.12	0.15	——	0.60	3.50
1956-D	0.03	0.04	0.05	0.10	——	0.12	0.15	——	0.60	*
1957	0.03	0.04	0.05	0.10	——	0.12	0.15	——	0.60	2.50
1957-D	0.03	0.04	0.05	0.10	——	0.12	0.15	——	0.60	*
1958	0.03	0.04	0.05	0.10	——	0.12	0.15	——	0.50	2.00
1958-D	0.03	0.04	0.05	0.10	——	0.12	0.15	——	0.50	*

—— = Insufficient pricing data * = None issued

Lincoln, Memorial cent

Date of authorization: Feb. 21, 1857
Dates of issue: 1959-present
Designers: Obverse: Victor D. Brenner
Reverse: Frank Gasparro
Engravers: Obverse: Charles Barber
Reverse: Gilroy Roberts
Diameter: 19.05 mm/0.75 inch
Weight: 1959-1982: 3.11 grams/0.10 ounce
1982-present: 2.50 grams/0.08 ounce
Metallic content: 1959-1962: 95% copper, 5% zinc and tin
1962-1982: 95% copper, 5% zinc
1982-present: 97.5% zinc, 2.5% copper (99.2% zinc, 0.8% copper planchet plated with pure copper)
Edge: Plain
Mint mark: Obverse under date

Note: Mint State 65 and Proof 65 copper values are for coins with full red original color; lower Mint State and Proof grades reflect specimens that are red and brown.

	F-12	VF-20	EF-40	AU-50	MS-60	MS-63	MS-65R	PF-65
1959	FV	FV	FV	FV	FV	0.15	0.50	1.50
1959-D	FV	FV	FV	FV	FV	0.15	0.50	*
1960 Large Date	FV	FV	FV	FV	FV	0.15	0.50	1.25
1960 Small Date	0.40	0.50	0.85	1.00	1.25	1.50	6.00	19.00
1960-D Large Date	FV	FV	FV	FV	FV	0.15	0.50	*
1960-D Small Date	0.03	0.05	0.10	0.12	0.15	0.20	1.65	*
1961	FV	FV	FV	FV	FV	0.15	0.50	0.75
1961-D	FV	FV	FV	FV	FV	0.15	0.50	*
BRASS ALLOY								
1962	FV	FV	FV	FV	FV	0.15	0.50	0.75
1962-D	FV	FV	FV	FV	FV	0.15	0.50	*
1963	FV	FV	FV	FV	FV	0.15	0.50	1.00
1963-D	FV	FV	FV	FV	FV	0.15	0.50	*
1964	FV	FV	FV	FV	FV	0.15	0.50	0.75
1964-D	FV	FV	FV	FV	FV	0.15	0.50	*

* = None issued FV = Face Value

	F-12	VF-20	EF-40	AU-50	MS-60	MS-63	MS-65R	PF-65
1965	FV	FV	FV	FV	FV	0.15	0.55	*
1966	FV	FV	FV	FV	FV	0.25	0.60	*
1967	FV	FV	FV	FV	FV	0.15	0.55	*
1968	FV	FV	FV	FV	FV	0.15	0.50	*
1968-D	FV	FV	FV	FV	FV	0.15	0.50	*
1968-S	FV	FV	FV	FV	FV	0.15	0.85	0.90
1969	FV	FV	FV	FV	FV	0.25	1.35	*
1969-D	FV	FV	FV	FV	FV	0.15	0.50	*
1969-S	FV	FV	FV	FV	FV	0.15	0.50	0.90
1969-S Doubled Die	——	5750.	6500.	7750.	——	——	20000.	
1970	FV	FV	FV	FV	FV	0.25	1.00	*
1970-D	FV	FV	FV	FV	FV	0.15	0.50	*
1970-S Low 7	FV	FV	FV	FV	FV	0.15	0.50	0.90
1970-S Level 7	5.00	7.50	9.50	11.00	19.00	24.00	62.50	55.00
1971	FV	FV	FV	FV	FV	0.25	1.35	*
1971-D	FV	FV	FV	FV	FV	0.25	1.10	*
1971-S	FV	FV	FV	FV	FV	0.15	1.00	0.90
1972	FV	FV	FV	FV	FV	0.15	0.50	*
1972-D	FV	FV	FV	FV	FV	0.15	0.50	*
1972-S	FV	FV	FV	FV	FV	0.20	0.50	0.90
1972 Doubled Die	——	——	——	145.	170.	205.	405.	*
1973	FV	FV	FV	FV	FV	0.15	0.50	*
1973-D	FV	FV	FV	FV	FV	0.15	0.50	*
1973-S	FV	FV	FV	FV	FV	0.25	0.50	0.75
1974	FV	FV	FV	FV	FV	0.15	0.50	*
1974-D	FV	FV	FV	FV	FV	0.15	0.50	*
1974-S	FV	FV	FV	FV	FV	0.25	0.85	0.75
1975	FV	FV	FV	FV	FV	0.15	0.50	*
1975-D	FV	FV	FV	FV	FV	0.15	0.50	*
1975-S	*	*	*	*	*	*	*	3.50
1976	FV	FV	FV	FV	FV	0.15	0.50	*
1976-D	FV	FV	FV	FV	FV	0.15	0.50	*
1976-S	*	*	*	*	*	*	*	2.50
1977	FV	FV	FV	FV	FV	0.15	0.50	*
1977-D	FV	FV	FV	FV	FV	0.15	0.50	*
1977-S	*	*	*	*	*	*	*	2.00
1978	FV	FV	FV	FV	FV	0.15	0.50	*
1978-D	FV	FV	FV	FV	FV	0.15	0.50	*
1978-S	*	*	*	*	*	*	*	1.60
1979	FV	FV	FV	FV	FV	0.15	0.50	*
1979-D	FV	FV	FV	FV	FV	0.15	0.50	*
1979-S Filled S	*	*	*	*	*	*	*	2.50
1979-S Clear S	*	*	*	*	*	*	*	3.00
1980	FV	FV	FV	FV	FV	0.15	0.50	*
1980-D	FV	FV	FV	FV	FV	0.15	0.50	*
1980-S	*	*	*	*	*	*	*	1.00

—— = Insufficient pricing data * = None issued FV = Face Value

	F-12	VF-20	EF-40	AU-50	MS-60	MS-63	MS-65R	PF-65
1981	FV	FV	FV	FV	FV	0.15	0.50	*
1981-D	FV	FV	FV	FV	FV	0.15	0.50	*
1981-S	*	*	*	*	*	*	*	1.50
1982 Large Date	FV	FV	FV	FV	0.12	0.20	0.50	*
1982 Small Date	FV	FV	FV	FV	0.17	0.30	1.00	*
1982-D Large Date	FV	FV	FV	FV	0.12	0.20	0.70	*
COPPER-PLATED ZINC								
1982 Large Date	FV	FV	FV	FV	0.22	0.25	0.95	*
1982 Small Date	FV	FV	FV	FV	0.67	0.75	1.75	*
1982-D Large Date	FV	FV	FV	FV	0.17	0.30	1.20	*
1982-D Small Date	FV	FV	FV	FV	0.14	0.24	0.85	*
1982-S	*	*	*	*	*	*	*	2.00
1983	FV	FV	FV	FV	FV	0.15	0.50	*
1983-D	FV	FV	FV	FV	FV	0.15	0.50	*
1983-S	*	*	*	*	*	*	*	2.75
1983 Doubled Die	——	——	——	130.	145.	170.	300.	*
1984	FV	FV	FV	FV	FV	0.15	0.50	*
1984-D	FV	FV	FV	FV	0.17	0.30	0.75	*
1984-S	*	*	*	*	*	*	*	2.00
1984 Doubled Die	——	——	——	90.00	135.	155.	190.	*
1985	FV	FV	FV	FV	FV	0.50	0.50	*
1985-D	FV	FV	FV	FV	FV	0.15	0.50	*
1985-S	*	*	*	*	*	*	*	3.00
1986	FV	FV	FV	FV	0.15	0.75	0.90	*
1986-D	FV	FV	FV	FV	FV	0.20	0.50	*
1986-S	*	*	*	*	*	*	*	5.50
1987	FV	FV	FV	FV	FV	0.50	0.50	*
1987-D	FV	FV	FV	FV	FV	0.15	0.50	*
1987-S	*	*	*	*	*	*	*	2.50
1988	FV	FV	FV	FV	FV	0.15	0.50	*
1988-D	FV	FV	FV	FV	FV	0.15	0.50	*
1988-S	*	*	*	*	*	*	*	2.00
1989	FV	FV	FV	FV	FV	0.15	0.50	*
1989-D	FV	FV	FV	FV	FV	0.15	0.50	*
1989-S	*	*	*	*	*	*	*	2.50
1990	FV	FV	FV	FV	FV	0.15	0.50	*
1990-D	FV	FV	FV	FV	FV	0.15	0.50	*
1990-S	*	*	*	*	*	*	*	3.75
1990-S No S	*	*	*	*	*	*	*	1200.
1991	FV	FV	FV	FV	FV	0.15	0.50	*
1991-D	FV	FV	FV	FV	FV	0.15	0.50	*
1991-S	*	*	*	*	*	*	*	5.00
1992	FV	FV	FV	FV	FV	0.15	0.50	*
1992-D	FV	FV	FV	FV	FV	0.15	0.50	*
1992-S	*	*	*	*	*	*	*	5.00
1993	FV	FV	FV	FV	FV	0.15	0.50	*

—— = Insufficient pricing data   * = None issued   FV = Face Value

	F-12	VF-20	EF-40	AU-50	MS-60	MS-63	MS-65R	PF-65
1993-D	FV	FV	FV	FV	FV	0.15	0.50	*
1993-S	*	*	*	*	*	*	*	6.00
1994	FV	FV	FV	FV	FV	0.15	0.50	*
1994-D	FV	FV	FV	FV	FV	0.15	0.50	*
1994-S	*	*	*	*	*	*	*	6.00
1995	FV	FV	FV	FV	FV	0.15	0.50	*
1995 Doubled Die, early die state	6.00	9.00	12.00	14.00	19.00	22.00	25.00	*
1995-D	FV	FV	FV	FV	FV	0.15	0.50	*
1995-S	*	*	*	*	*	*	*	5.50
1996	FV	FV	FV	FV	FV	0.15	0.50	*
1996-D	FV	FV	FV	FV	FV	0.15	0.50	*
1996-S	*	*	*	*	*	*	*	4.50
1997	FV	FV	FV	FV	FV	0.15	0.50	*
1997-D	FV	FV	FV	FV	FV	0.15	0.50	*
1997-S	*	*	*	*	*	*	*	5.00
1998	FV	FV	FV	FV	FV	0.15	0.50	*
1998-D	FV	FV	FV	FV	FV	0.15	0.50	*
1998-S	*	*	*	*	*	*	*	5.00
1999	—	—	—	—	—	—	—	*
1999-D	—	—	—	—	—	—	—	*
1999-S	*	*	*	*	*	*	*	—

—— = Insufficient pricing data   * = None issued   FV = Face Value

2 cents

Date of authorization: April 22, 1864
Dates of issue: 1864-1872
Designer/Engraver: James B. Longacre
Diameter: 23.00 mm/0.91 inch
Weight: 6.22 grams/0.20 ounce
Metallic content: 95% copper, 5% zinc and tin
Edge: Plain
Mint mark: None

	F-12	VF-20	EF-40	AU-50	MS-60	MS-63	MS-64	MS-65	PF-63	PF-65
1864 Small Motto	110.	200.	330.	415.	515.	725.	1150.	3000.	13500.	65000.
1864 Large Motto	22.00	24.00	30.00	50.00	90.00	145.	215.	935.	635.	3900.
1865	22.00	24.00	30.00	52.50	100.	165.	250.	1025.	475.	3050.
1866	22.00	25.00	30.00	56.00	110.	165.	250.	1575.	450.	1775.
1867	22.00	24.00	30.00	65.00	115.	170.	285.	1500.	450.	1950.
1868	22.00	24.00	31.50	75.00	120.	180.	290.	1600.	450.	1825.
1869	22.00	26.00	40.00	85.00	120.	190.	390.	1425.	450.	1775.
1869/9	—	—	—	—	—	—	—	—	—	—
1870	22.50	35.00	60.00	95.00	160.	300.	600.	1700.	475.	1775.
1871	25.00	40.00	77.50	125.	215.	425.	800.	2200.	480.	1775.
1872	165.	285.	400.	585.	750.	1100.	1650.	2850.	505.	1900.
1873 Closed 3 Proofs Only				1000.	1150.	—	—	—	1390.	2900.
1873 Open 3 Restrike Proofs Only				—	1450.	—	—	—	1975.	6000.

— = Insufficient pricing data

Copper-nickel 3 cents

Date of authorization: April 22, 1864
Dates of issue: 1865-1889
Designer/Engraver: James B. Longacre
Diameter: 17.90 mm/0.71 inch
Weight: 1.94 grams/0.06 ounce
Metallic content: 75% copper, 25% nickel
Edge: Plain
Mint mark: None

	F-12	VF-20	EF-40	AU-50	MS-60	MS-63	MS-64	MS-65	PF-65
1865	14.00	15.00	18.00	35.00	80.00	120.	230.	675.	5500.
1866	14.00	15.00	18.00	35.00	80.00	125.	235.	685.	1950.
1867	14.00	15.00	18.00	36.00	82.00	130.	240.	750.	1100.
1868	14.00	15.00	18.00	37.00	83.00	130.	235.	685.	1225.
1869	14.00	15.00	18.00	38.00	90.00	135.	250.	775.	975.
1870	14.00	15.00	18.00	40.00	95.00	145.	275.	750.	1100.
1871	14.00	15.00	20.00	50.00	105.	160.	280.	750.	1000.
1872	14.00	15.00	19.00	48.00	100.	175.	350.	1200.	950.
1873 Closed 3	14.00	22.00	35.00	65.00	140.	265.	425.	2100.	925.
1873 Open 3	14.00	18.00	22.00	40.00	95.00	180.	450.	2250.	——
1874	14.00	15.00	22.00	48.00	105.	170.	315.	1500.	950.
1875	15.00	21.00	30.00	70.00	125.	175.	280.	690.	1050.
1876	16.00	23.00	38.00	80.00	165.	275.	400.	1750.	800.
1877 (Proofs only)	1025.	1050.	1075.	1100.	1125.	1175.	1500.	*	2250.
1878 (Proofs only)	385.	400.	425.	450.	475.	500.	550.	*	615.
1879	60.00	65.00	85.00	135.	220.	300.	425.	825.	525.
1880	80.00	90.00	135.	180.	230.	325.	350.	690.	520.
1881	14.00	15.00	18.00	36.00	80.00	130.	230.	750.	515.
1882	68.00	90.00	120.	165.	245.	350.	575.	950.	515.
1883	175.	200.	245.	280.	375.	925.	1350.	2800.	490.
1884	335.	365.	390.	430.	485.	1200.	1450.	3750.	525.
1885	440.	475.	500.	600.	700.	1050.	1175.	2000.	535.
1886 (Proofs only)	250.	275.	300.	325.	375.	425.	450.	*	550.
1887/6 (Proofs only)	300.	325.	350.	375.	400.	450.	500.	*	625.
1887	250.	285.	305.	325.	365.	550.	675.	1000.	1000.
1888	41.00	47.00	60.00	95.00	180.	300.	385.	675.	500.
1889	77.00	89.00	100.	115.	220.	350.	425.	665.	500.

—— = Insufficient pricing data * = None issued

Silver 3 cents

Date of authorization: March 3, 1851
Dates of issue: 1851-1873
Designer/Engraver: James B. Longacre
Diameter: 14.00 mm/0.55 inch
Weight: (1851-1853): 0.80 grams/0.03 ounce
(1854-1873): 0.75 grams/0.02 ounce
Metallic content: (1851-1853): 75% silver, 25% copper
(1854-1873): 90% silver, 10% copper
Weight of pure silver: (1851-1853): 0.60 grams/0.02 ounce
(1854-1873): 0.67 grams/0.02 ounce
Edge: Plain
Mint mark: 1851-O only, reverse right field

	VG-8	F-12	VF-20	EF-40	AU-50	MS-60	MS-63	MS-64	MS-65	PF-65
1 OUTLINE OF STAR										
1851	20.00	23.00	29.00	58.00	125.	145.	250.	380.	925.	6600.
1851-O	25.00	33.00	60.00	110.	210.	300.	450.	825.	1975.	——
1852	20.00	23.00	29.00	58.00	125.	145.	250.	380.	925.	*
1853	20.00	23.00	29.00	58.00	125.	145.	260.	425.	1000.	*
3 OUTLINES OF STAR										
1854	20.00	24.00	40.00	90.00	215.	325.	700.	1500.	3500.	34000.
1855	35.00	45.00	85.00	150.	250.	550.	1100.	2750.	10500.	15000.
1856	19.00	23.00	43.00	85.00	165.	310.	550.	1750.	3700.	12500.
1857	19.00	25.00	42.00	85.00	220.	290.	600.	1525.	3425.	10250.
1858	19.00	23.00	40.00	85.00	165.	260.	550.	1275.	3375.	7500.
2 OUTLINES OF STAR										
1859	18.00	23.00	36.00	60.00	125.	160.	250.	425.	925.	2350.
1860	18.00	24.00	36.00	65.00	125.	160.	370.	425.	1000.	3500.
1861	18.00	24.00	35.00	60.00	125.	160.	250.	420.	925.	2100.
1862	18.00	24.00	40.00	62.00	125.	160.	305.	415.	925.	1600.
1862/1	20.00	30.00	40.00	75.00	140.	210.	350.	550.	1000.	——

	AU-50	MS-60	MS-62	MS-63	MS-64	MS-65	PF-60	PF-63	PF-64	PF-65
1863	400.	525.	625.	775.	1125.	1600.	325.	450.	700.	1425.
1863/2 (Proofs only)	475.	*	*	*	*	*	440.	500.	2000.	4500.
1864	425.	525.	660.	965.	1150.	1500.	325.	460.	700.	1350.
1865	425.	535.	635.	825.	1100.	1700.	330.	475.	710.	1375.
1866	400.	535.	635.	825.	1075.	1550.	325.	470.	700.	1350.
1867	425.	550.	685.	1150.	1600.	2900.	340.	465.	690.	1325.

—— = Insufficient pricing data * = None issued

	AU-50	MS-60	MS-62	MS-63	MS-64	MS-65	PF-60	PF-63	PF-64	PF-65
1868	425.	560.	700.	1200.	2350.	5750.	330.	465.	700.	1400.
1869	425.	575.	675.	890.	1400.	2750.	330.	465.	700.	1375.
1869/8 (Proofs only)	625.	*	*	*	*	*	850.	1750.	2500.	4900.
1870	425.	585.	685.	935.	1250.	3250.	345.	480.	700.	1400.
1871	425.	565.	650.	835.	1100.	1500.	350.	550.	725.	1300.
1872	575.	700.	825.	1350.	2450.	6000.	425.	650.	800.	1325.
1873 Closed 3 (Proofs only)	575.	*	*	*	*	*	650.	800.	1050.	1600.

Enlarged to show detail

One outline of star

Three outlines

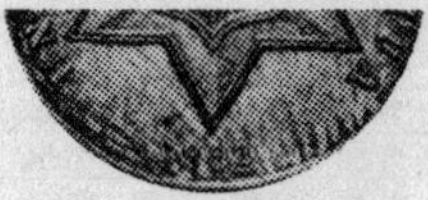

Two outlines

* = None issued

Shield 5 cents

Rays Removed

Date of authorization: May 16, 1886
Dates of issue: 1866-1883
Designer/Engraver: James B. Longacre
Diameter: 20.50 mm/0.81 inch
Weight: 5.00 grams/0.16 ounce
Metallic content: 75% copper, 25% nickel
Edge: Plain
Mint mark: None

	G-4	VG-8	F-12	VF-20	EF-40	AU-50	MS-60	MS-63	MS-64	MS-65
1866	17.50	19.00	22.00	38.00	100.	145.	200.	390.	600.	2300.
1867	19.00	22.50	27.00	44.00	130.	190.	265.	500.	1075.	3400.
RAYS REMOVED FROM REVERSE										
1867	12.50	14.00	15.00	16.00	32.00	57.00	90.00	150.	295.	650.
1868	12.50	14.00	15.00	16.00	32.00	59.00	90.00	150.	275.	650.
1869	12.50	14.00	15.00	16.00	35.00	62.00	95.00	185.	275.	650.
1870	12.50	14.00	17.00	21.00	37.00	70.00	115.	265.	375.	900.
1871	30.00	42.00	55.00	75.00	125.	175.	275.	500.	800.	1250.
1872	12.50	14.00	15.00	19.00	37.00	70.00	125.	295.	675.	1000.
1873 Closed 3	22.50	30.00	37.50	72.50	115.	155.	225.	400.	750.	1100.
1873 Open 3	12.50	14.00	16.00	30.00	40.00	72.50	115.	260.	400.	800.
1874	12.50	14.00	24.00	30.00	55.00	80.00	130.	275.	475.	1150.
1875	14.00	18.00	30.00	42.00	60.00	95.00	145.	345.	525.	1750.
1876	12.50	17.00	26.00	35.00	60.00	82.50	130.	275.	400.	975.
1877 (Proofs only)	950.	1000.	1050.	1100.	1150.	1200.	1250.	1350.	1650.	2200.
1878 (Proofs only)	425.	450.	475.	500.	525.	550.	600.	650.	700.	800.
1879	235.	290.	350.	400.	450.	500.	585.	825.	1125.	1500.
1880	290.	350.	390.	450.	525.	640.	1050.	1650.	2300.	3950.
1881	140.	185.	225.	275.	360.	400.	560.	725.	900.	1150.
1882	12.50	14.00	15.00	16.00	35.00	57.00	92.50	165.	265.	650.
1883	12.50	14.00	15.00	17.50	38.00	57.00	92.50	150.	260.	650.
1883/2	65.00	90.00	120.	165.	210.	260.	350.	650.	925.	2425.

Liberty Head 5 cents

No CENTS

With CENTS

Date of authorization: May 16, 1886
Dates of issue: 1883-1912
Designer/Engraver: Charles Barber
Diameter: 21.21 mm/0.84 inch
Weight: 5.00 grams/0.16 ounce
Metallic content: 75% copper, 25% nickel
Edge: Plain
Mint mark: 1912 only, reverse left of CENTS

	VG-8	F-12	VF-20	EF-40	AU-50	AU-55	MS-60	MS-63	MS-64	MS-65
1883	4.50	5.00	6.00	7.50	11.00	15.00	22.50	45.00	70.00	235.
CENTS ADDED BELOW WREATH ON REVERSE										
1883	10.00	13.50	20.00	38.00	60.00	65.00	85.00	100.	235.	500.
1884	15.00	15.00	20.00	42.50	77.50	90.00	125.	225.	375.	775.
1885	290.	360.	425.	590.	685.	750.	800.	1150.	1425.	2175.
1886	110.	160.	210.	285.	365.	425.	500.	700.	1075.	2350.
1887	9.50	17.00	21.00	42.50	62.50	70.00	85.00	150.	300.	600.
1888	13.50	19.50	40.00	55.00	100.	115.	150.	190.	325.	750.
1889	7.50	15.00	17.50	36.00	60.00	65.00	85.00	145.	300.	600.
1890	10.00	15.00	19.00	38.00	65.00	70.00	90.00	155.	300.	850.
1891	6.00	11.00	15.50	37.00	60.00	65.00	85.00	140.	275.	775.
1892	6.00	11.50	17.00	36.00	65.00	70.00	100.	155.	275.	725.
1893	5.50	11.00	15.50	35.00	60.00	65.00	85.00	145.	275.	715.
1894	12.00	45.00	72.50	140.	160.	170.	190.	240.	405.	775.
1895	4.50	14.00	18.00	38.00	60.00	65.00	105.	160.	325.	900.
1896	7.25	16.00	22.00	41.00	70.00	80.00	105.	175.	375.	1025.
1897	3.50	7.00	10.00	24.00	45.00	57.50	75.00	145.	375.	800.
1898	3.00	7.00	10.00	27.50	55.00	62.50	85.00	150.	225.	725.
1899	1.75	4.50	9.00	24.00	45.00	55.00	75.00	95.00	170.	475.
1900	1.75	4.35	8.00	27.50	48.00	52.50	65.00	95.00	170.	475.
1901	1.75	4.50	8.00	24.00	42.50	47.50	55.00	85.00	170.	475.
1902	1.75	4.25	7.00	24.00	42.50	47.50	55.00	85.00	170.	475.
1903	1.75	4.50	8.00	24.00	42.50	47.50	55.00	85.00	170.	475.
1904	1.75	4.75	8.00	26.00	42.50	47.50	55.00	85.00	170.	475.
1905	1.75	3.75	7.00	24.00	42.50	47.50	55.00	85.00	170.	475.
1906	1.75	3.75	7.00	24.00	42.50	47.50	55.00	85.00	170.	475.
1907	1.75	3.75	7.00	24.00	42.50	47.50	55.00	85.00	175.	550.
1908	1.75	3.75	7.50	24.00	42.50	47.50	55.00	85.00	180.	575.

LIBERTY HEAD 5 CENTS (CONTINUED)

	VG-8	F-12	VF-20	EF-40	AU-50	AU-55	MS-60	MS-63	MS-64	MS-65
1909	2.00	3.75	8.00	26.00	42.50	47.50	65.00	95.00	185.	575
1910	1.75	3.75	7.00	20.00	42.50	47.50	55.00	85.00	170.	525.
1911	1.75	3.75	7.00	20.00	42.50	47.50	55.00	85.00	170.	475.
1912	1.75	3.75	7.00	20.00	42.50	47.50	55.00	85.00	175.	475.
1912-D	2.00	5.00	20.00	47.50	105.	120.	200.	265.	375.	975.
1912-S	55.00	95.00	250.	475.	650.	685.	750.	1000.	1500.	2350.

1913 Five struck. Eliasberg now Proof 66 (NGC) sold for $1.485 million.

Indian Head 5 cents

Bison on Mound Bison on Plain

"Buffalo nickel"

Date of authorization: May 16, 1886
Dates of issue: 1913-1938
Designer: James Earle Fraser
Engraver: Charles Barber
Diameter: 21.21 mm/0.84 inch
Weight: 5.00 grams/0.16 ounce
Metallic content: 75% copper, 25% nickel
Edge: Plain
Mint mark: Reverse below FIVE CENTS

	G-4	VG-8	F-12	VF-20	EF-40	AU-50	MS-60	MS-63	MS-64	MS-65
BISON STANDING ON MOUND										
1913	4.75	5.50	6.00	8.00	12.00	20.00	30.00	40.00	55.00	100.
1913-D	7.00	9.00	10.00	12.50	19.00	36.00	48.00	60.00	80.00	180.
1913-S	12.00	15.00	20.00	27.00	42.00	50.00	65.00	100.	175.	650.
BISON STANDING ON PLAIN										
1913	6.00	7.00	7.00	8.00	12.00	22.00	32.00	52.00	115.	310.
1913-D	42.00	45.00	58.00	65.00	75.00	120.	175.	260.	400.	800.
1913-S	90.00	130.	155.	175.	200.	265.	335.	550.	1000.	2825.
1914	9.00	10.00	10.00	12.00	16.00	26.00	41.00	70.00	140.	305.
1914/3	175.	450.	700.	1000.	1500.	3000.	3950.	6000.	——	——
1914-D	35.00	45.00	58.00	70.00	105.	135.	205.	315.	600.	1300.
1914-S	8.50	9.00	16.00	22.50	35.00	55.00	180.	350.	575.	1625.
1915	4.50	5.00	5.50	6.50	12.00	21.00	42.00	63.00	115.	250.
1915-D	9.00	12.00	21.00	34.00	55.00	75.00	145.	290.	595.	1800.

—— = Insufficient pricing data

	G-4	VG-8	F-12	VF-20	EF-40	AU-50	MS-60	MS-63	MS-64	MS-65
1915-S	14.00	20.00	40.00	70.00	135.	210.	460.	625.	1025.	2100.
1916	2.25	2.50	3.00	3.75	7.50	14.00	40.00	65.00	85.00	265.
1916 Doubled Die	1900.	3000.	4900.	7250.	11000.	17000.	24500.	60000.	——	——
1916-D	6.50	9.00	13.00	21.00	50.00	70.00	135.	275.	385.	1800.
1916-S	4.50	5.00	11.00	20.00	45.00	75.00	145.	315.	525.	2325.
1917	2.00	2.50	2.75	5.25	10.00	26.00	43.00	115.	185.	450.
1917-D	7.00	10.00	18.00	40.00	82.50	140.	315.	650.	950.	2650.
1917-S	7.00	12.00	25.00	47.50	135.	215.	390.	1100.	1600.	2800.
1918	1.75	3.00	4.00	8.25	18.00	33.00	45.00	220.	440.	1350.
1918/7-D	350.	650.	1075.	2050.	4400.	7500.	16000.	42500.	75000.	——
1918-D	6.50	10.00	21.50	75.00	165.	225.	385.	1125.	1750.	3750.
1918-S	6.00	12.00	20.00	65.00	135.	240.	650.	2600.	6250.	22500.
1919	1.50	1.75	2.00	3.50	9.00	21.00	40.00	82.50	165.	435.
1919-D	7.00	11.00	27.00	75.00	175.	240.	445.	1250.	2300.	4400.
1919-S	5.00	10.00	22.00	65.00	180.	265.	535.	1350.	3575.	10500.
1920	1.25	1.75	2.00	4.00	9.00	23.00	40.00	120.	175.	575.
1920-D	5.00	9.00	21.00	75.00	205.	295.	490.	1500.	2250.	4750.
1920-S	3.50	5.50	14.00	65.00	150.	215.	365.	1450.	3750.	17500.
1921	2.50	2.75	3.00	9.00	25.00	40.00	80.00	150.	325.	600.
1921-S	22.00	36.00	75.00	360.	675.	875.	1350.	1950.	2675.	4950.
1923	1.50	1.75	2.00	3.75	9.00	18.00	35.00	75.00	180.	450.
1923-S	3.50	4.00	10.00	80.00	200.	260.	435.	700.	1250.	8500.
1924	1.50	1.75	2.00	4.00	9.50	27.00	45.00	82.00	225.	550.
1924-D	3.50	4.50	10.00	55.00	150.	185.	375.	750.	1175.	3250.
1924-S	6.00	10.00	52.50	350.	1100.	1375.	1750.	3250.	4750.	8900.
1925	1.75	1.75	2.00	3.50	9.00	20.00	31.00	75.00	125.	500.
1925-D	5.50	10.00	24.00	62.50	145.	215.	425.	675.	1200.	3450.
1925-S	3.50	7.00	12.50	52.50	155.	220.	435.	1725.	4175.	32500.
1926	1.00	1.25	1.50	2.50	6.00	16.00	28.00	55.00	75.00	140.
1926-D	4.00	7.00	17.00	60.00	120.	175.	200.	475.	1250.	3450.
1926-S	7.00	10.00	30.00	325.	725.	1250.	2400.	6250.	10500.	35000.
1927	0.75	1.00	1.25	2.25	6.00	16.00	28.00	52.00	80.00	205.
1927-D	1.75	3.25	5.00	17.50	48.00	70.00	115.	275.	550.	3350.
1927-S	1.00	1.50	2.25	20.00	60.00	115.	400.	2000.	3450.	14500.
1928	0.90	1.00	1.25	2.00	6.00	16.00	25.00	45.00	95.00	225.
1928-D	1.05	2.00	3.00	9.50	22.00	30.00	38.00	80.00	130.	625.
1928-S	1.00	1.75	2.50	6.00	16.00	40.00	130.	490.	1075.	3750.
1929	0.60	0.65	0.80	1.75	5.00	14.00	21.00	35.00	75.00	275.
1929-D	1.05	1.40	2.00	5.00	25.00	35.00	43.00	105.	275.	1400.
1929-S	0.70	0.80	1.05	1.50	10.00	20.00	40.00	70.00	125.	325.
1930	0.65	0.70	0.85	2.00	4.50	14.00	23.00	45.00	67.50	115.
1930-S	0.65	0.70	1.05	1.50	7.25	20.00	32.00	65.00	165.	425.
1931-S	3.50	4.00	4.00	5.00	14.00	28.00	43.00	67.00	95.00	200.
1934	0.60	0.65	0.75	2.25	4.50	12.00	23.00	40.00	75.00	300.
1934-D	0.65	0.75	1.30	3.75	10.00	25.00	40.00	75.00	210.	1050.
1935	0.60	0.65	0.75	1.00	2.10	7.75	16.00	23.50	35.00	85.00

—— = Insufficient pricing data

	G-4	VG-8	F-12	VF-20	EF-40	AU-50	MS-60	MS-63	MS-64	MS-65
1935 Doubled Die	30.00	40.00	75.00	150.	400.	1200.	2500.	5000.	——	——
1935-D	0.65	0.80	1.55	4.00	10.00	25.00	32.00	55.00	120.	360.
1935-S	0.65	0.70	0.80	1.15	3.00	11.00	23.00	49.00	75.00	145.
1936	0.60	0.65	0.70	1.00	2.35	6.75	13.00	25.00	32.00	75.00
1936-D	0.60	0.65	0.75	1.25	4.00	11.00	17.00	23.00	30.00	95.00
1936-S	0.60	0.65	0.75	1.15	3.00	11.00	15.00	25.00	40.00	85.00
1937	0.60	0.65	0.70	1.00	2.25	6.50	11.00	17.00	21.00	40.00
1937-D	0.60	0.65	0.75	1.15	2.75	7.75	14.50	20.00	27.00	50.00
1937-D 3 Legs	150.	220.	250.	335.	410.	525.	1350.	3075.	4750.	14000.
1937-S	0.60	0.65	0.75	1.15	3.00	8.50	13.00	20.00	27.00	50.00
1938-D	0.90	1.25	1.40	1.75	2.50	7.50	11.50	16.00	22.00	40.00
1938-D/D	1.75	2.75	4.00	5.25	7.00	11.00	19.00	25.00	30.00	50.00
1938-D/S	5.00	6.75	7.50	9.00	15.00	26.00	35.00	53.00	90.00	150.

Jefferson 5 cents

Date of authorization:	May 16, 1866; March 27, 1942
Dates of issue:	1938-present
Designer:	Felix Schlag
Engraver:	John R. Sinnock
Diameter:	21.21 mm/0.84 inch
Weight:	5.00 grams/0.16 ounce
Metallic content:	(1938-1942): 75% copper, 25% nickel (1942-1945): 56% copper, 35% silver, 9% manganese (1946-present): 75% copper, 25% nickel
Weight of pure silver:	(1942-1945): 1/75 grams/0.06 ounce
Edge:	Plain
Mint mark:	(1938-1964): Reverse right of building (1942-1945, silver): Reverse above dome (1968-present): Obverse below Jefferson's ponytail

	VG-8	F-12	VF-20	EF-40	AU-50	MS-60	MS-63	MS-64	MS-65	PF-65
1938	0.15	0.35	0.45	0.65	0.90	2.25	2.75	3.00	4.50	80.00

—— = Insufficient pricing data

JEFFERSON 5 CENTS (CONTINUED)

	VG-8	F-12	VF-20	EF-40	AU-50	MS-60	MS-63	MS-64	MS-65	PF-65
1938-D	0.65	0.70	1.00	1.75	2.25	3.50	5.00	7.00	12.00	*
1938-S	1.35	1.75	2.05	2.25	2.75	3.75	4.50	8.00	16.00	*
1939	0.08	0.18	0.25	0.45	0.75	1.35	2.50	2.90	4.00	60.00
1939 Doubled MONTICELLO	24.00	40.00	60.00	70.00	125.	165.	300.	400.	575.	*
1939-D	3.00	3.25	4.00	7.50	20.00	30.00	42.00	50.00	70.00	*
1939-S	0.75	1.00	1.75	3.25	7.75	14.00	22.00	25.00	35.00	*
1940	FV	0.10	0.20	0.25	0.60	0.75	1.35	1.50	2.85	60.00
1940-D	0.13	0.20	0.30	0.50	1.45	2.25	2.75	3.00	5.50	*
1940-S	0.14	0.20	0.35	0.55	1.00	1.90	3.35	3.75	5.00	*
1941	FV	0.10	0.20	0.30	0.40	0.65	1.25	1.50	2.10	55.00
1941-D	0.10	0.15	0.30	0.55	1.40	2.15	3.00	3.25	4.85	*
1941-S	0.10	0.15	0.30	0.60	1.75	2.75	4.00	4.50	6.00	*
1942	0.10	0.15	0.20	0.45	0.70	1.25	4.25	4.75	6.25	50.00
1942-P	0.35	0.65	0.75	1.10	3.00	5.25	8.00	9.00	11.50	80.00
1942-D	0.35	0.45	1.25	2.75	7.00	14.00	17.00	19.00	35.00	*
1942-D/Horizontal D	——	30.00	45.00	——	——	475.	750.	1550.	2850.	*
1942-S	0.45	1.00	1.45	2.00	2.75	5.00	8.00	10.00	25.00	*
1943/2-P	35.00	42.50	65.00	90.00	150.	200.	235.	300.	625.	*
1943-P	0.35	0.60	0.75	1.10	1.75	2.75	4.00	4.75	15.00	*
1943-P Doubled Eye	17.00	24.00	30.00	49.00	87.50	115.	150.	250.	400.	*
1943-D	0.55	0.75	1.00	1.50	2.10	2.50	4.00	5.50	13.00	*
1943-S	0.35	0.60	0.75	1.10	1.75	2.90	5.00	6.50	13.25	*
1944-P	0.40	0.65	0.80	1.15	2.00	2.75	4.00	5.00	17.00	*
1944-D	0.50	0.85	1.00	1.80	3.00	6.50	9.00	10.00	13.50	*
1944-S	0.60	0.90	1.25	1.90	3.00	3.75	4.75	7.00	13.00	*
1945-P	0.40	0.65	0.80	1.50	2.00	2.65	4.75	7.00	12.00	*
1945-P Doubled Die	——	15.00	20.00	30.00	47.50	75.00	120.	190.	440.	*
1945-D	0.60	1.00	1.35	1.75	2.35	2.65	4.00	4.75	7.50	*
1945-S	0.35	0.55	0.70	1.25	1.50	2.15	3.75	4.50	7.25	*
1946	FV	0.07	0.15	0.20	0.30	0.50	0.70	0.90	1.85	*
1946-D	0.07	0.10	0.15	0.30	0.45	0.55	0.80	2.00	5.50	*
1946-D/Horizontal D	42.50	65.00	80.00	140.	225.	275.	400.	650.	1350.	*
1946-S	0.10	0.20	0.25	0.35	0.40	0.50	0.55	2.00	5.00	*
1947	FV	0.07	0.15	0.20	0.30	0.55	0.95	1.15	2.00	*
1947-D	0.06	0.08	0.15	0.40	0.60	0.70	1.20	1.35	2.25	*
1947-S	0.06	0.08	0.15	0.25	0.30	0.35	0.45	0.75	2.00	*
1948	FV	0.07	0.10	0.20	0.32	0.40	0.55	0.85	1.80	*
1948-D	0.07	0.10	0.30	0.45	0.60	0.85	1.35	1.50	2.65	*
1948-S	0.10	0.20	0.35	0.40	0.45	0.50	0.60	1.00	2.25	*
1949	0.08	0.15	0.20	0.30	0.45	0.65	0.75	1.40	3.25	*
1949-D	0.07	0.10	0.25	0.45	0.55	0.75	1.50	2.00	4.00	*
1949-D/S	——	——	35.00	70.00	105.	145.	185.	225.	390.	*

—— = Insufficient pricing data * = None issued FV = Face Value

	VG-8	F-12	VF-20	EF-40	AU-50	MS-60	MS-63	MS-64	MS-65	PF-65
1949-S	0.35	0.45	0.60	0.75	0.90	1.15	1.45	2.75	5.00	*
1950	0.15	0.20	0.30	0.45	0.70	0.80	0.90	1.75	3.65	42.50
1950-D	4.75	5.00	5.15	5.25	5.35	6.00	7.00	9.00	14.00	*
1951	FV	0.07	0.15	0.30	0.35	0.75	1.40	1.75	2.75	37.50
1951-D	FV	0.07	0.25	0.45	0.55	0.65	1.00	1.45	2.65	*
1951-S	0.25	0.30	0.45	0.70	1.00	1.50	2.25	2.75	5.00	*
1952	FV	0.07	0.08	0.10	0.50	0.70	0.95	1.15	2.25	27.00
1952-D	FV	0.07	0.15	0.25	0.75	1.00	1.25	1.50	3.35	*
1952-S	0.07	0.10	0.15	0.25	0.35	0.60	1.00	1.45	2.50	*
1953	FV	0.07	0.08	0.10	0.20	0.22	0.35	0.50	1.10	26.50
1953-D	FV	0.07	0.10	0.15	0.18	0.21	0.35	0.50	1.25	*
1953-S	0.08	0.15	0.20	0.25	0.30	0.38	0.75	1.65	3.50	*
1954	FV	0.07	0.08	0.10	0.15	0.19	0.35	0.50	1.25	20.00
1954-D	FV	0.07	0.08	0.10	0.15	0.19	0.35	0.50	1.35	*
1954-S	FV	0.07	0.08	0.10	0.20	0.23	0.40	0.60	1.75	*
1954 S/D	——	——	9.00	16.00	22.00	30.00	45.00	60.00	110.	*
1955	0.15	0.22	0.25	0.30	0.35	0.40	0.75	2.00	6.00	10.00
1955-D	FV	0.07	0.08	0.10	0.15	0.19	0.30	0.50	2.00	*
1955 D/S Variety 1	——	——	10.00	17.00	26.00	30.00	50.00	75.00	130.	*
1956	FV	FV	FV	FV	FV	0.16	0.25	0.35	0.75	4.00
1956-D	FV	FV	FV	FV	FV	0.16	0.25	0.35	0.75	*
1957	FV	FV	FV	FV	FV	0.17	0.25	0.40	0.85	1.75
1957-D	FV	FV	FV	FV	FV	0.16	0.25	0.35	0.75	*
1958	0.06	0.08	0.12	0.17	0.20	0.25	0.35	0.65	1.65	2.50
1958-D	FV	FV	FV	FV	FV	0.16	0.25	0.35	0.75	*
1959	FV	FV	FV	FV	FV	0.16	0.25	0.35	0.75	1.75
1959-D	FV	FV	FV	FV	FV	0.16	0.25	0.35	0.75	*
1960	FV	FV	FV	FV	FV	0.16	0.25	0.35	0.75	0.65
1960-D	FV	FV	FV	FV	FV	0.16	0.25	0.35	0.75	*
1961	FV	FV	FV	FV	FV	0.16	0.25	0.35	0.75	0.50
1961-D	FV	FV	FV	FV	FV	0.16	0.25	0.35	0.75	*
1962	FV	FV	FV	FV	FV	0.16	0.25	0.35	0.75	0.50
1962-D	FV	FV	FV	FV	FV	0.16	0.25	0.35	0.75	*
1963	FV	FV	FV	FV	FV	0.16	0.25	0.35	0.75	0.50
1963-D	FV	FV	FV	FV	FV	0.16	0.25	0.35	0.75	*
1964	FV	FV	FV	FV	FV	0.16	0.25	0.35	0.75	0.50
1964-D	FV	FV	FV	FV	FV	0.16	0.25	0.35	0.75	*
1965	FV	FV	FV	FV	FV	0.13	0.25	0.35	0.85	*
1966	FV	FV	FV	FV	FV	0.13	0.25	0.35	0.85	*
1967	FV	FV	FV	FV	FV	0.13	0.25	0.35	0.85	*
1968-D	FV	FV	FV	FV	FV	0.13	0.25	0.30	0.35	*
1968-S	FV	FV	FV	FV	FV	0.13	0.25	0.30	0.35	0.75
1969-D	FV	FV	FV	FV	FV	0.13	0.25	0.30	0.35	*
1969-S	FV	FV	FV	FV	FV	0.13	0.25	0.30	0.35	0.75
1970-D	FV	FV	FV	FV	FV	0.13	0.25	0.30	0.35	*
1970-S	FV	FV	FV	FV	FV	0.13	0.25	0.30	0.35	0.75

—— = Insufficient pricing data   * = None issued   FV = Face Value

	VG-8	F-12	VF-20	EF-40	AU-50	MS-60	MS-63	MS-64	MS-65	PF-65
1971	FV	FV	FV	FV	FV	0.45	0.75	1.00	2.00	*
1971-D	FV	FV	FV	FV	FV	0.20	0.50	0.60	1.50	*
1971-S	*	*	*	*	*	*	*	*	*	1.50
1971-S No S	*	*	*	*	*	*	*	*	*	500.
1972	FV	FV	FV	FV	FV	0.13	0.25	0.30	0.35	*
1972-D	FV	FV	FV	FV	FV	0.13	0.25	0.30	0.35	*
1972-S	*	*	*	*	*	*	*	*	*	1.50
1973	FV	FV	FV	FV	FV	0.13	0.25	0.30	0.35	*
1973-D	FV	FV	FV	FV	FV	0.13	0.25	0.30	0.35	*
1973-S	*	*	*	*	*	*	*	*	*	1.25
1974	FV	FV	FV	FV	FV	0.13	0.25	0.30	0.35	*
1974-D	FV	FV	FV	FV	FV	0.15	0.27	0.35	0.45	*
1974-S	*	*	*	*	*	*	*	*	*	1.00
1975	FV	FV	FV	FV	FV	0.25	0.40	0.55	0.75	*
1975-D	FV	FV	FV	FV	FV	0.20	0.35	0.40	0.60	*
1975-S	*	*	*	*	*	*	*	*	*	1.00
1976	0.09	0.10	0.11	0.12	0.14	0.25	0.45	0.55	0.85	*
1976-D	FV	FV	FV	FV	FV	0.30	0.45	0.85	1.50	*
1976-S	*	*	*	*	*	*	*	*	*	1.25
1977	FV	FV	FV	FV	FV	0.13	0.25	0.30	0.35	*
1977-D	FV	FV	FV	FV	FV	0.28	0.40	0.65	1.25	*
1977-S	*	*	*	*	*	*	*	*	*	1.25
1978	FV	FV	FV	FV	FV	0.13	0.25	0.30	0.35	*
1978-D	FV	FV	FV	FV	FV	0.15	0.35	0.45	1.00	*
1978-S	*	*	*	*	*	*	*	*	*	1.25
1979	FV	FV	FV	FV	FV	0.13	0.25	0.30	0.35	*
1979-D	FV	FV	FV	FV	FV	0.13	0.27	0.30	0.35	*
1979-S Filled S	*	*	*	*	*	*	*	*	*	1.25
1979-S Clear S	*	*	*	*	*	*	*	*	*	1.75
1980-P	FV	FV	FV	FV	FV	0.13	0.25	0.30	0.35	*
1980-D	FV	FV	FV	FV	FV	0.13	0.25	0.30	0.35	*
1980-S	*	*	*	*	*	*	*	*	*	0.75
1981-P	FV	FV	FV	FV	FV	0.13	0.25	0.30	0.35	*
1981-D	FV	FV	FV	FV	FV	0.13	0.25	0.30	0.35	*
1981-S Filled S	*	*	*	*	*	*	*	*	*	0.75
1981-S Clear S	*	*	*	*	*	*	*	*	*	1.75
1982-P	FV	FV	FV	FV	FV	0.14	0.75	1.00	2.00	*
1982-D	FV	FV	FV	FV	FV	0.25	1.25	1.50	3.00	*
1982-S	*	*	*	*	*	*	*	*	*	1.50
1983-P	FV	FV	FV	FV	FV	0.87	0.90	1.10	1.50	*
1983-D	FV	FV	FV	FV	FV	0.80	0.90	1.25	1.75	*
1983-S	*	*	*	*	*	*	*	*	*	1.50
1984-P	FV	FV	FV	FV	FV	0.10	0.45	0.55	0.85	*
1984-D	FV	FV	FV	FV	FV	0.15	0.45	0.65	1.25	*
1984-S	*	*	*	*	*	*	*	*	*	2.75
1985-P	FV	FV	FV	FV	FV	0.13	0.45	0.55	0.85	*
1985-D	FV	FV	FV	FV	FV	0.15	0.45	0.65	1.25	*

* = None issued FV = Face Value

	VG-8	F-12	VF-20	EF-40	AU-50	MS-60	MS-63	MS-64	MS-65	PF-65
1985-S	*	*	*	*	*	*	*	*	*	2.25
1986-P	FV	FV	FV	FV	FV	0.10	0.45	0.55	0.85	*
1986-D	FV	FV	FV	FV	FV	0.15	0.85	1.25	1.65	*
1986-S	*	*	*	*	*	*	*	*	*	4.50

	MS-63	MS-64	MS-65	PF-65
1987-P	0.25	0.30	0.35	*
1987-D	0.25	0.30	0.35	*
1987-S	*	*	*	2.25
1988-P	0.25	0.30	0.35	*
1988-D	0.25	0.30	0.35	*
1988-S	*	*	*	2.50
1989-P	0.25	0.30	0.35	*
1989-D	0.25	0.30	0.35	*
1989-S	*	*	*	2.00
1990-P	0.25	0.30	0.35	*
1990-D	0.25	0.30	0.35	*
1990-S	*	*	*	3.00
1991-P	0.25	0.30	0.35	*
1991-D	0.25	0.30	0.35	*
1991-S	*	*	*	4.00
1992-P	0.25	0.30	0.35	*
1992-D	0.25	0.30	0.35	*
1992-S	*	*	*	3.00
1993-P	0.25	0.30	0.35	*
1993-D	0.25	0.30	0.35	*
1993-S				3.00
1994-P	0.25	0.30	0.35	*
1994-P Matte Finish from Jefferson Coin & Currency set: -64 $60; -65 $75; -66 $95; -67 $110; -68 $130; and -69 $200.				
1994-D	0.25	0.30	0.35	*
1994-S	*	*	*	3.00
1995-P	0.25	0.30	0.35	*
1995-D	0.25	0.30	0.35	*
1995-S	*	*	*	4.50
1996-P	0.25	0.30	0.35	*
1996-D	0.25	0.30	0.35	*
1996-S	*	*	*	3.00
1997-P	0.25	0.30	0.35	*
1997-D	0.25	0.30	0.35	*
1997-S	*	*	*	3.00
1998-P	0.25	0.30	0.35	*
1998-D	0.25	0.30	0.35	*
1998-S	*	*	*	3.00
1999-P	——	——	——	*
1999-D	——	——	——	*
1999-S	*	*	*	——

—— = Insufficient pricing data   * = None issued   FV = Face Value

Flowing Hair half dime

Half disme pattern — Flowing Hair

Date of authorization:	April 2, 1792
Dates of issue:	1792 (half disme); 1794-1795
Designer/Engraver:	Robert Scot
Diameter:	16.50 mm/0.65 inch
Weight:	1.348 grams/0.04 ounce
Metallic content:	89.25% silver, 10.75% copper
Weight of pure silver:	1.20 grams/0.04 ounce
Edge:	Reeded
Mint mark:	None

	AG-3	G-4	VG-8	F-12	VF-20	EF-40	AU-50
HALF DISME PATTERN							
1792	3500.	4250.	6000.	8500.	14500.	21000.	26000.
FLOWING HAIR							
1794	350.	675.	800.	1250.	1800.	3000.	4750.
1795	315.	515.	675.	900.	1325.	2100.	2925.

Draped Bust half dime

Small Eagle

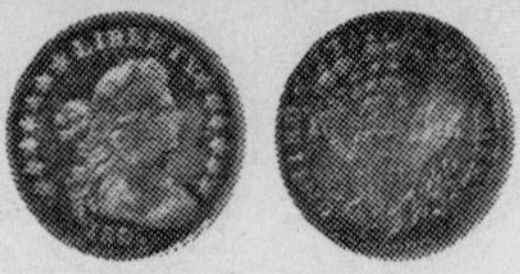

Heraldic Eagle

Date of authorization: April 2, 1792
Dates of issue: 1796-1805
Designer: Obverse: Gilbert Stuart-Robert Scot
Reverse:
(1796-1797): Robert Scot-John Eckstein
(1800-1805): Robert Scot
Engraver: Robert Scot
Diameter: 16.50 mm/0.65 inch
Weight: 1.35 grams/0.04 ounce
Metallic content: 89.25% silver, 10.75% copper
Weight of pure silver: 1.20 grams/0.04 ounce
Edge: Reeded
Mint mark: None

	AG-3	G-4	VG-8	F-12	VF-20	EF-40	AU-50
SMALL EAGLE							
1796/5	405.	700.	850.	1400.	2450.	4350.	10500.
1796 LIBERTY	375.	675.	800.	1200.	1950.	3400.	5000.
1796 LIKERTY	375.	675.	800.	1300.	1975.	3600.	6750.
1797 15 Stars	350.	625.	800.	1200.	1825.	3150.	3900.
1797 16 Stars	365.	625.	800.	1250.	1850.	3250.	4750.
1797 13 Stars	425.	725.	950.	1400.	2550.	4500.	7250.
HERALDIC EAGLE							
1800	200.	425.	575.	750.	1175.	2300.	3300.
1800 LIBEKTY	205.	435.	580.	750.	1225.	2350.	3500.
1801	245.	475.	600.	825.	1250.	2400.	3800.
1802	4750.	7750.	11500.	18500.	32500.	60000.	——
1803	210.	450.	600.	800.	1200.	2325.	3450.
1805	300.	625.	725.	900.	1600.	3000.	5500.

—— = Insufficient pricing data

Capped Bust half dime

Date of authorization:	April 2, 1792
Dates of issue:	1829-1837
Designers:	John Reich-William Kneass
Engraver:	William Kneass
Diameter:	15.50 mm/0.61 inch
Weight:	1.35 grams/0.04 ounce
Metallic content:	89.25% silver, 10.75% copper
Weight of pure silver:	1.20 grams/0.04 ounce
Edge:	Reeded
Mint mark:	None

	G-4	VG-8	F-12	VF-20	EF-40	AU-50	AU-55	MS-60	MS-62	MS-63
1829	20.00	27.50	30.00	60.00	125.	185.	250.	290.	400.	600.
1830	19.00	27.50	29.00	55.00	115.	180.	235.	285.	400.	575.
1831	17.00	25.00	29.00	55.00	115.	180.	235.	280.	395.	575.
1832	17.00	25.00	29.00	55.00	115.	185.	240.	285.	400.	600.
1833	17.00	25.00	29.00	55.00	115.	180.	235.	280.	395.	575.
1834	17.00	25.00	29.00	55.00	115.	185.	240.	280.	395.	575.
1835 all varieties	17.00	25.00	29.00	55.00	115.	180.	235.	280.	395.	575.
1836 all varieties	17.00	25.00	32.50	55.00	115.	190.	245.	285.	400.	580.
1837 Small 5c	22.00	30.00	40.00	95.00	175.	350.	500.	750.	975.	1650.
1837 Large 5c	19.00	25.00	29.00	55.00	115.	185.	240.	280.	450.	675.

Seated Liberty, half dime

Date of authorization:	April 2, 1792
Dates of issue:	1837-1873
Designers:	(1837-1840): Christian Gobrecht (1840-1859): Obverse: Gobrecht-Robert B. Hughes Reverse: Christian Gobrecht (1860-1873): Obverse: Christian Gobrecht-Robert B. Hughes-James B. Longacre Reverse: James B. Longacre
Engraver:	(1837-1840): Christian Gobrecht (1840-1859): Christian Gobrecht (1860-1873): James B. Longacre
Diameter:	15.50 mm/0.61 inch
Weight:	(1837-1853): 1.34 grams/0.04 ounce (1853-1873): 1.24 grams/0.04 ounce
Metallic content:	90% silver, 10% copper
Weight of pure silver:	(1837-1853): 1.20 grams/0.04 ounce (1853-1873): 1.12 grams/0.04 ounce
Edge:	Reeded
Mint mark:	Reverse within or below wreath

	G-4	VG-8	F-12	VF-20	EF-40	AU-50	AU-55	MS-60	MS-63
NO STARS									
1837 Large or Small Date	24.00	33.00	48.00	90.00	180.	340.	400.	575.	825.
1838-O	67.50	100.	200.	390.	650.	1375.	1800.	4000.	8800.
NO DRAPERY									
1838	9.00	10.00	12.50	22.00	60.00	125.	160.	240.	375.
1838 Small Stars	13.00	27.50	45.00	85.00	145.	265.	350.	575.	950.
1839	9.00	10.50	12.50	22.00	60.00	125.	160.	240.	375.
1839-O	10.00	14.00	19.00	32.00	75.00	180.	275.	475.	1275.
1839-O Large O	325.	625.	1100.	——	——	3750.	——	——	——
1840	9.50	10.50	12.50	22.00	65.00	125.	165.	275.	425.
1840-O	10.00	11.50	20.00	35.00	80.00	210.	300.	525.	1600.
DRAPERY									
1840	18.00	30.00	45.00	85.00	160.	275.	350.	525.	900.
1840-O	28.00	45.00	80.00	165.	265.	800.	——	——	——

—— = Insufficient pricing data

	G-4	VG-8	F-12	VF-20	EF-40	AU-50	AU-55	MS-60	MS-63
1841	9.00	10.00	12.00	20.00	45.00	100.	120.	155.	325.
1841-O	11.00	16.00	22.50	37.50	120.	300.	360.	600.	1300.
1842	9.00	10.00	12.00	20.00	45.00	100.	130.	165.	300.
1842-O	24.00	35.00	62.00	175.	375.	1500.	1750.	2600.	4750.
1843	9.00	12.00	14.00	20.00	44.00	100.	120.	145.	300.
1844	9.00	11.00	12.50	22.00	50.00	110.	135.	170.	375.
1844-O Small O	60.00	130.	250.	515.	850.	1700.	2150.	4900.	——
1844-O Large O	65.00	110.	175.	350.	700.	——	——	4000.	——
1845	9.00	10.00	12.00	21.00	45.00	92.00	110.	145.	300.
1846	190.	280.	475.	650.	1500.	3100.	——	——	——
1847	9.00	10.00	12.00	20.00	43.00	92.00	110.	145.	300.
1848 Medium Date	9.50	10.00	12.00	20.00	43.00	92.00	110.	145.	425.
1848 Large Date	12.50	17.50	28.00	40.00	75.00	190.	265.	475.	1350.
1848-O	11.00	15.00	27.50	42.50	100.	225.	315.	425.	725.
1849/6	10.00	13.00	26.00	45.00	77.00	145.	185.	375.	750.
1849/8	13.50	16.50	30.00	48.00	100.	185.	235.	400.	800.
1849	9.00	10.00	12.00	19.50	45.00	95.00	110.	145.	390.
1849-O	19.00	35.00	80.00	185.	450.	950.	1350.	2200.	5500.
1850	9.00	10.00	12.00	19.50	42.00	95.00	110.	150.	385.
1850-O	12.00	16.00	25.00	50.00	110.	245.	335.	650.	1550.
1851	9.00	10.00	12.00	19.50	42.00	95.00	115.	155.	390.
1851-O	9.00	13.00	24.00	35.00	72.00	175.	215.	335.	725.
1852	9.00	10.00	12.00	19.50	42.00	95.00	115.	155.	300.
1852-O	22.00	33.00	65.00	100.	235.	450.	650.	1150.	2500.
1853	25.00	34.00	55.00	90.00	195.	350.	390.	500.	985.
1853-O	145.	215.	300.	585.	1275.	2950.	3650.	6800.	——
ARROWS									
1853	9.00	10.00	12.00	15.00	45.00	80.00	120.	160.	290.
1853-O	12.00	14.00	13.00	20.00	52.00	135.	165.	275.	1050.
1854	9.00	10.00	12.00	15.00	45.00	82.00	125.	175.	285.
1854-O	10.00	12.00	13.00	20.00	55.00	145.	185.	325.	950.
1855	9.00	10.00	12.00	17.00	45.00	85.00	125.	175.	350.
1855-O	16.00	21.00	27.50	55.00	120.	235.	275.	425.	1400.
NO ARROWS									
1856	9.00	10.00	12.00	18.00	40.00	80.00	110.	130.	225.
1856-O	10.00	12.00	19.00	35.00	70.00	185.	250.	385.	1075.
1857	9.00	10.00	12.00	18.00	40.00	77.00	105.	120.	225.
1857-O	10.00	12.50	16.00	29.00	55.00	130.	160.	250.	425.
1858	9.00	10.00	12.50	18.00	40.00	77.00	105.	120.	225.
1858/Inverted Date	28.00	45.00	55.00	115.	200.	300.	350.	475.	750.
1858/1858	35.00	50.00	75.00	155.	245.	325.	350.	675.	1300.
1858-O	9.00	10.00	16.00	32.00	57.50	150.	180.	240.	390.
1859	9.00	12.00	18.00	31.00	53.00	105.	130.	155.	290.
1859-O	15.00	18.00	23.00	45.00	95.00	175.	195.	255.	425.
1860 Transitional	——	——	——	——	——	——	——	1800.	3250.

—— = Insufficient pricing data

	G-4	VG-8	F-12	VF-20	EF-40	AU-50	AU-55	MS-60	MS-63
LEGEND OBVERSE									
1860	9.00	10.00	12.00	17.50	31.00	67.00	77.00	115.	185.
1860-O	10.00	12.00	18.00	23.00	45.00	87.00	97.00	135.	275.
1861	9.00	10.00	12.00	18.00	31.00	67.00	77.00	115.	180.
1861/0	20.50	30.00	45.00	75.00	150.	275.	315.	450.	675.
1862	9.00	10.00	12.00	18.00	31.00	67.00	77.00	110.	175.
1863	115.	160.	225.	290.	340.	450.	475.	500.	800.
1863-S	20.00	25.00	35.00	60.00	105.	285.	340.	450.	975.
1864	250.	325.	405.	525.	700.	800.	850.	925.	1175.
1864-S	35.00	45.00	70.00	100.	200.	375.	425.	660.	1300.
1865	245.	285.	345.	390.	475.	550.	600.	750.	950.
1865-S	18.00	24.00	30.00	50.00	105.	370.	435.	700.	1650.
1866	235.	270.	335.	425.	540.	600.	625.	725.	925.
1866-S	18.00	25.00	30.00	55.00	105.	290.	350.	550.	925.
1867	325.	365.	435.	525.	600.	725.	750.	790.	1050.
1867-S	16.00	20.00	34.00	57.00	90.00	225.	265.	350.	750.
1868	37.50	55.00	90.00	160.	235.	310.	335.	425.	675.
1868-S	10.00	12.50	19.00	27.00	50.00	145.	190.	275.	515.
1869	10.00	10.00	18.50	26.50	48.00	95.00	135.	225.	375.
1869-S	9.00	11.00	17.50	25.00	50.00	130.	175.	255.	725.
1870	9.00	10.00	12.25	13.50	32.50	65.00	75.00	115.	175.
1870-S Unique - Graded (PCGS) MS-63	——	——	——	——	——	——	——	——	——
1871	9.00	10.00	12.00	14.50	29.00	62.50	72.00	110.	175.
1871-S	10.00	18.00	32.00	45.00	65.00	135.	185.	245.	425.
1872	9.00	10.00	12.00	13.50	29.00	60.00	70.00	105.	170.
1872-S S in Wreath	9.00	10.00	12.25	14.50	30.00	60.00	70.00	105.	170.
1872-S S Below Wreath	9.00	10.00	12.25	14.50	30.00	60.00	70.00	105.	170.
1873	9.00	8.25	12.50	13.50	29.00	60.00	70.00	105.	170.
1873-S	9.75	11.50	15.00	20.00	42.00	80.00	90.00	115.	180.

—— = Insufficient pricing data

Draped Bust dime

Small Eagle Heraldic Eagle

Date of authorization: April 2, 1792
Dates of issue: 1796-1805
Designer: Obverse: Gilbert Stuart-Robert Scot
Reverse:
(1796-1797): Robert Scot-John Eckstein
(1800-1805): Robert Scot
Engraver: Robert Scot
Diameter: 16.50 mm/0.65 inch
Weight: 1.35 grams/0.04 ounce
Metallic content: 89.25% silver, 10.75% copper
Weight of pure silver: 1.20 grams/0.04 ounce
Edge: Reeded
Mint mark: None

	G-4	VG-8	F-12	VF-20	EF-40	AU-50	AU-55	MS-60
1796	950.	1400.	1700.	2850.	4400.	5650.	6750.	7750.
1797 16 Stars	1000.	1500.	1800.	3000.	4750.	6900.	8000.	12500.
1797 13 Stars	1000.	1500.	1800.	3000.	5250.	7500.	9000.	15000.
1798/97 16 Stars	525.	625.	850.	1250.	2500.	3500.	4750.	6250.
1798/97 13 Stars	1650.	2750.	4300.	6500.	—	—	—	—
1798	425.	475.	650.	1000.	1750.	2200.	3350.	4000.
1798 Small 8	525.	700.	1000.	1750.	2750.	4750.	5750.	9500.
1800	425.	475.	625.	950.	1825.	2500.	3500.	4800.
1801	425.	475.	750.	1200.	2650.	5250.	6500.	9000.
1802	650.	900.	1475.	2700.	4950.	8750.	17500.	27500.
1803	450.	525.	725.	1000.	2200.	3100.	5250.	8250.
1804 13 Star	975.	1500.	2400.	4500.	10000.	20000.	—	—
1804 14 Star	1100.	1650.	2750.	5000.	12500.	27500.	—	—
1805 4 Berries	375.	450.	600.	775.	1450.	2000.	3150.	3800.
1805 5 Berries	450.	500.	750.	1250.	2150.	4250.	—	—
1807	375.	450.	600.	800.	1450.	1925.	3000.	3750.

— = Insufficient pricing data

Capped Bust dime

Date of authorization: April 2, 1792
Dates of issue: 1809-1837
Designer/Engraver: John Reich
Diameter: (1809-1828): 18.80 mm/0.74 inch
(1828-1837): 17.90 mm/0.71 inch
Weight: 2.70 grams/0.09 ounce
Metallic content: 89.25% silver, 10.75% copper
Weight of pure silver: 2.41 grams/0.08 ounce
Edge: Reeded
Mint mark: None

	G-4	VG-8	F-12	VF-20	EF-40	AU-50	AU-55	MS-60
Open Collar Strikes								
1809	95.00	175.	325.	500.	1000.	1650.	2250.	4250.
1811/09	120.	190.	285.	450.	950.	1500.	1850.	2400.
1814 Small Date	35.00	60.00	105.	225.	400.	675.	1025.	1850.
1814 Large Date	25.00	34.00	55.00	140.	345.	535.	625.	975.
1814 STATESOFAMERICA	25.00	40.00	72.00	175.	375.	640.	725.	1150.
1820 Large O	20.00	32.00	45.00	110.	325.	575.	685.	925.
1820 Small O	20.00	33.00	45.00	130.	345.	550.	675.	950.
1820 STATESOFAMERICA	22.50	35.00	60.00	165.	425.	825.	900.	1650.
1821 Small Date	22.50	35.00	55.00	115.	335.	650.	725.	1200.
1821 Large Date	20.00	25.00	40.00	90.00	270.	500.	600.	900.
1822	325.	485.	775.	1375.	2250.	4250.	5250.	9750.
1823/2 Large E reverse	20.00	30.00	40.00	85.00	275.	505.	605.	900.
1823/2 Small E reverse	20.00	30.00	40.00	85.00	275.	505.	605.	925.
1824/2	26.00	45.00	88.00	260.	475.	1050.	1250.	1800.
1825	18.00	25.00	35.00	85.00	260.	490.	590.	850.
1827	18.00	25.00	35.00	85.00	260.	490.	590.	850.

	G-4	VG-8	F-12	VF-20	EF-40	AU-50	AU-55	MS-60	MS-63	MS-64
Closed Collar Strikes										
1828 Large Date	65.00	90.00	165.	275.	575.	925.	1150.	2400.	3750.	——
1828 Small Date	25.00	40.00	65.00	150.	335.	600.	650.	1000.	2450.	3850.
1829 Curl Base 2	3850.	5750.	8000.	16000.	——	——	——	——	——	——
1829 Small 10c	18.00	25.00	40.00	75.00	180.	300.	475.	775.	1250.	2550.
1829 Med. 10c	18.00	25.00	40.00	75.00	200.	350.	550.	900.	1400.	2750.
1829 Large 10c	32.50	48.00	95.00	175.	400.	585.	750.	1000.	1750.	3500.
1830	16.00	18.00	25.00	55.00	175.	275.	380.	615.	1150.	2200.

—— = Insufficient pricing data

	G-4	VG-8	F-12	VF-20	EF-40	AU-50	AU-55	MS-60	MS-63	MS-64
1830/29	35.00	57.50	85.00	145.	350.	575.	625.	1200.	3500.	5250.
1831	16.00	18.00	25.00	52.50	175.	275.	360.	600.	1150.	2075.
1832	16.00	18.00	25.00	52.50	175.	275.	370.	615.	1150.	2100.
1833	16.00	18.00	25.00	52.50	175.	275.	360.	610.	1150.	2100.
1834	16.00	18.00	25.00	52.50	175.	275.	360.	610.	1150.	2100.
1835	16.00	18.00	25.00	52.50	175.	275.	360.	600.	1150.	2100.
1836	16.00	18.00	25.00	52.50	175.	275.	360.	625.	1150.	2300.
1837	16.00	18.00	25.00	52.50	175.	275.	360.	625.	1150.	2350.

Seated Liberty dime

Date of authorization: April 2, 1792
Dates of issue: 1837-1891
Designer: (1837-1840)
Obverse: Thomas Sully-Christian Gobrecht
Reverse: Christian Gobrecht
(1840-1860)
Obverse: John Hughes-Gobrecht-Sully
Reverse: Christian Gobrecht
(1860-1891)
Obverse: James B. Longacre-Hughes-Gobrecht-Sully
Reverse: James B. Longacre
Engraver: (1837-1840): Christian Gobrecht
(1840-1860): Christian Gobrecht
(1860-1891): James B. Longacre
Diameter: 17.90 mm/0.71 inch
Weight: (1837-1853): 2.67 grams/0.09 ounce
(1853-1873): 2.49 grams/0.08 ounce
Metallic content:: 90% silver, 10% copper
Weight of pure silver: (1837-1853): 2.41 grams/0.08 ounce
(1853-1873): 2.24 grams/0.07 ounce
Edge: Reeded
Mint mark: Reverse within or below wreath

	G-4	VG-8	F-12	VF-20	EF-40	AU-50	AU-55	MS-60	MS-63
1837	25.00	35.00	70.00	250.	475.	650.	775.	950.	1850.
1838-O	30.00	45.00	95.00	290.	625.	1175.	1375.	2475.	7500.

	G-4	VG-8	F-12	VF-20	EF-40	AU-50	AU-55	MS-60	MS-63
NO DRAPERY									
1838 Sm Stars	18.00	27.50	47.50	72.50	155.	310.	350.	600.	1125.
1838 Lg Stars	9.75	11.00	15.00	25.00	60.00	150.	185.	285.	675.
1838 Partial Drapery	20.00	30.00	50.00	90.00	175.	275.	340.	425.	1325.
1839	9.75	11.00	15.50	26.00	55.00	145.	180.	270.	675.
1839-O Reverse of 1838	115.	200.	350.	475.	750.	—	—	—	—
1839-O	10.75	13.00	23.00	44.00	90.00	225.	375.	600.	1350.
1840	9.25	10.75	14.00	26.00	52.50	135.	180.	270.	675.
1840-O	11.00	14.00	24.00	50.00	100.	260.	400.	950.	2500.
DRAPERY									
1840	24.00	40.00	75.00	135.	265.	575.	800.	1750.	—
1841	8.75	10.50	14.00	25.00	55.00	130.	175.	270.	635.
1841-O Open Bud Reverse	9.25	11.00	17.00	37.50	85.00	215.	375.	900.	1950.
1842	8.75	10.50	13.00	18.00	37.00	120.	155.	265.	625.
1842-O	10.25	13.50	22.50	45.00	200.	1200.	1450.	2750.	5500.
1843	8.75	10.00	13.00	18.00	37.00	125.	170.	275.	750.
1843/1843	11.25	17.50	27.00	60.00	115.	185.	250.	375.	—
1843-O	32.50	50.00	130.	215.	500.	1200.	1800.	2700.	—
1844	125.	250.	375.	600.	975.	1900.	—	—	16000.
1845	8.75	10.00	12.50	19.00	37.00	110.	145.	225.	675.
1845/1845	11.50	20.00	37.00	50.00	150.	415.	—	—	—
1845-O	17.00	25.00	62.50	190.	600.	1300.	—	—	3850.
1846	60.00	95.00	165.	285.	775.	1750.	—	—	—
1847	11.50	17.00	35.00	60.00	120.	325.	385.	575.	1675.
1848	9.50	11.50	16.00	37.00	75.00	175.	285.	600.	1275.
1849	9.25	11.00	15.00	25.00	52.00	140.	190.	300.	1050.
1849-O	10.75	16.00	45.00	90.00	300.	775.	1500.	3000.	5500.
1850	8.75	10.00	12.00	18.00	37.00	115.	150.	225.	675.
1850-O	10.50	14.50	37.00	75.00	175.	325.	475.	1350.	2750.
1851	9.50	10.00	12.00	17.00	37.00	110.	180.	290.	900.
1851-O	11.25	15.00	27.00	75.00	200.	500.	800.	1750.	3150.
1852	8.75	10.00	12.00	18.00	37.00	105.	140.	230.	625.
1852-O	12.50	19.00	40.00	77.00	210.	475.	850.	1550.	2900.
1853	55.00	80.00	110.	160.	290.	450.	550.	775.	1425.
ARROWS AT DATE									
1853	8.50	9.00	10.50	16.00	38.00	120.	185.	275.	650.
1853-O	9.00	13.00	24.00	35.00	90.00	345.	500.	850.	2900.
1854	8.50	9.75	10.75	16.00	38.00	120.	195.	300.	750.
1854-O	8.75	9.00	10.50	21.00	65.00	175.	260.	525.	1100.
1855	8.50	9.25	11.25	16.50	50.00	135.	215.	400.	850.
ARROWS REMOVED									
1856 Small Date	8.50	9.50	11.50	16.00	35.00	115.	150.	225.	620.
1856 Large Date	9.00	11.00	14.00	19.00	50.00	160.	195.	275.	700.
1856-O	9.00	10.00	14.00	25.00	75.00	210.	285.	600.	1950.
1856-S	85.00	145.	225.	425.	750.	1750.	2350.	3500.	9250.

—— = Insufficient pricing data

	G-4	VG-8	F-12	VF-20	EF-40	AU-50	AU-55	MS-60	MS-63
1857	8.50	10.00	11.50	13.00	35.00	100.	130.	230.	600.
1857-O	8.75	10.50	12.00	24.00	65.00	175.	225.	315.	975.
1858	8.50	9.50	11.50	13.00	35.00	100.	130.	225.	630.
1858-O	12.75	21.00	35.00	70.00	125.	350.	425.	675.	1500.
1858-S	75.00	140.	225.	375.	675.	1300.	1750.	2750.	7500.
1859	9.00	10.00	11.50	21.00	55.00	145.	180.	300.	600.
1859-O	9.25	13.50	23.50	37.00	80.00	185.	245.	315.	650.
1859-S	85.00	145.	230.	425.	900.	1750.	2400.	——	——
1860-S	25.00	31.00	47.00	115.	275.	700.	1000.	2250.	6250.
LEGEND OBVERSE									
1860	8.15	10.00	14.00	20.00	37.00	70.00	85.00	150.	340.
1860-O	300.	475.	625.	1000.	2650.	5250.	6500.	10250.	26500.
1861	8.00	9.50	13.00	18.00	36.00	65.00	75.00	140.	325.
1861-S	47.50	77.50	120.	225.	390.	700.	900.	1800.	——
1862	7.75	9.50	13.00	18.00	36.00	65.00	75.00	165.	335.
1862-S	31.00	47.50	77.50	165.	365.	685.	785.	1600.	2850.
1863	250.	360.	415.	565.	700.	775.	875.	1175.	1550.
1863-S	25.00	30.00	45.00	85.00	165.	550.	725.	1550.	2600.
1864	185.	300.	375.	475.	675.	750.	825.	925.	1250.
1864-S	23.00	28.00	40.00	80.00	160.	375.	590.	875.	1775.
1865	250.	370.	460.	560.	685.	800.	875.	925.	1150.
1865-S	23.00	30.00	50.00	95.00	260.	675.	1125.	2300.	6250.
1866	260.	385.	535.	685.	800.	950.	1050.	1175.	1450.
1866-S	23.00	28.50	47.50	100.	250.	475.	775.	1900.	——
1867	300.	475.	575.	675.	750.	1050.	1150.	1350.	1850.
1867-S	32.50	40.00	60.00	125.	225.	490.	900.	2200.	4500.
1868	10.25	13.00	20.00	32.50	60.00	135.	185.	350.	725.
1868-S	14.00	21.00	32.00	65.00	115.	210.	270.	665.	——
1869	13.00	20.00	28.00	50.00	105.	205.	265.	585.	1200.
1869-S	11.50	20.00	30.00	45.00	75.00	145.	210.	450.	1075.
1870	8.25	9.00	11.50	23.00	50.00	125.	150.	225.	525.
1870-S	190.	275.	340.	435.	585.	950.	1150.	1900.	2750.
1871	8.00	9.00	11.00	20.00	37.00	130.	180.	310.	675.
1871-CC	850.	1150.	1550.	2900.	5000.	7250.	9000.	14500.	——
1871-S	14.00	20.00	32.00	67.50	155.	350.	425.	685.	1500.
1872	7.75	9.00	11.00	18.00	34.00	90.00	115.	150.	305.
1872-CC	350.	575.	900.	1950.	3400.	7000.	13500.	26000.	——
1872-S	21.00	35.00	72.50	125.	225.	425.	600.	1050.	2300.
1873 Closed 3	10.25	14.00	20.00	30.00	40.00	85.00	110.	170.	340.
1873 Open 3	14.50	19.00	40.00	60.00	105.	210.	270.	550.	——
1873-CC (unique) Eliasberg specimen MS-65 $550000.									
ARROWS AT DATE									
1873	9.75	13.00	20.00	40.00	135.	235.	315.	425.	925.
1873 Doubled Die (Shield)	——	350.	500.	775.	1000.	——	——	——	——
1873-CC	675.	925.	1950.	3500.	4850.	8250.	10500.	22500.	50000.
1873-S	13.00	19.00	30.00	60.00	175.	300.	450.	700.	2100.

—— = Insufficient pricing data

Legend obverse

	G-4	VG-8	F-12	VF-20	EF-40	AU-50	AU-55	MS-60	MS-63
1874	9.50	12.50	20.00	40.00	135.	260.	325.	440.	950.
1874-CC	2150.	4850.	6500.	10750.	18500.	24500.	27500.	37500.	——
1874-S	16.50	32.50	50.00	115.	275.	500.	600.	925.	2400.

	G-4	VG-8	F-12	VF-20	EF-40	AU-50	AU-55	MS-60	MS-63
ARROWS REMOVED									
1875	8.50	9.00	11.00	12.00	25.00	65.00	75.00	120.	210.
1875-CC	9.25	12.00	24.00	35.00	60.00	125.	170.	265.	575.
1875-CC in Wreath	9.00	10.00	14.00	24.00	39.00	70.00	105.	200.	360.
1875-S	8.50	9.00	11.00	12.50	20.00	65.00	75.00	130.	225.
1875-S S in Wreath	8.50	9.00	11.00	12.00	20.25	65.00	75.00	130.	225.
1876	8.50	9.00	11.00	12.00	20.00	65.00	75.00	130.	205.
1876-CC	8.75	9.75	12.00	16.00	32.50	67.50	97.50	200.	390.
1876-CC Doubled Die	15.00	30.00	50.00	85.00	225.	315.	390.	475.	1250.
1876-S	9.00	9.00	11.00	16.00	34.00	65.00	75.00	130.	235.
1877	8.50	9.00	11.00	12.00	20.00	65.00	75.00	120.	230.
1877-CC	8.75	9.50	11.50	15.00	30.00	65.00	75.00	155.	275.
1877-S	9.75	11.00	14.00	19.00	28.00	65.00	75.00	120.	300.
1878	8.75	9.50	12.25	16.00	24.50	65.00	75.00	185.	350.
1878-CC	45.00	62.50	100.	160.	240.	480.	515.	725.	1575.
1879	160.	200.	235.	280.	330.	435.	440.	500.	675.
1880	135.	175.	210.	240.	275.	350.	400.	455.	610.
1881	135.	175.	215.	275.	340.	375.	415.	460.	665.
1882	8.50	9.00	11.00	12.00	20.00	65.00	75.00	120.	210.
1883	8.50	9.00	11.00	12.00	20.00	65.00	75.00	120.	210.
1884	8.50	9.00	11.00	12.00	20.00	65.00	75.00	120.	210.
1884-S	14.00	18.00	24.00	35.00	85.00	225.	325.	635.	1350.
1885	8.50	9.00	11.00	12.00	20.00	65.00	75.00	120.	220.
1885-S	375.	475.	750.	1400.	2250.	3400.	4000.	5750.	9000.
1886	8.50	9.00	11.00	12.00	20.00	65.00	75.00	120.	210.
1886-S	35.00	42.50	55.00	85.00	115.	225.	270.	525.	1100.
1887	8.50	9.00	11.00	12.00	20.00	65.00	75.00	120.	210.
1887-S	8.50	9.00	11.00	13.50	24.00	65.00	75.00	135.	280.
1888	8.50	9.00	11.00	12.00	20.00	65.00	75.00	120.	215.
1888-S	8.60	9.00	11.00	13.00	32.00	85.00	115.	235.	460.
1889	8.50	9.00	11.00	12.00	20.00	65.00	75.00	120.	210.
1889-S	9.50	12.00	22.00	35.00	70.00	210.	265.	465.	1075.
1890	8.50	9.00	11.00	12.00	20.00	65.00	75.00	120.	210.
1890-S	12.00	17.00	25.00	39.00	60.00	150.	185.	325.	700.

—— = Insufficient pricing data

	G-4	VG-8	F-12	VF-20	EF-40	AU-50	AU-55	MS-60	MS-63
1891	8.50	9.00	11.00	12.00	20.00	65.00	75.00	120.	210.
1891-O	8.75	9.25	11.50	13.00	25.00	65.00	80.00	135.	290.
1891-O/Horizontal O	50.00	80.00	115.	165.	225.	425.	——	——	——
1891-S	8.50	9.00	11.25	14.00	30.00	70.00	85.00	155.	350.

Barber dime

Date of authorization: April 2, 1792
Dates of issue: 1892-1916
Designer: Obverse: Charles Barber
Reverse: James B. Longacre
Engraver: Charles Barber
Diameter: 17.91 mm/0.71 inch
Weight: 2.50 grams/0.08 ounce
Metallic content: 90% silver, 10% copper
Weight of pure silver: 2.25 grams/0.07 ounce
Edge: Reeded
Mint mark: Reverse within or below wreath

	G-4	VG-8	F-12	VF-20	EF-40	AU-50	AU-55	MS-60	MS-63	MS-64
1892	3.50	5.10	14.00	19.00	25.00	60.00	65.00	95.00	155.	240.
1892-O	6.75	12.00	27.00	38.00	50.00	75.00	90.00	140.	290.	515.
1892-S	38.00	70.00	150.	180.	220.	250.	285.	375.	750.	1550.
1893	6.00	11.00	18.00	25.00	37.00	60.00	75.00	105.	170.	250.
1893/2	——	——	——	130.	275.	400.	475.	550.	1350.	2200.
1893-O	17.00	33.00	100.	110.	140.	170.	200.	265.	485.	1000.
1893-S	8.00	19.00	25.00	39.00	55.00	125.	150.	250.	525.	1500.
1894	10.00	22.50	90.00	105.	125.	175.	225.	275.	440.	750.
1894-O	38.00	77.50	165.	225.	325.	625.	900.	1500.	2600.	4575.
1894-S (Proof only) Prf-4 $40000, Prf-60 $ 65000, Prf-63 $125000, Prf-65 $450000										
1895	65.00	115.	290.	400.	475.	525.	565.	650.	1150.	1650.
1895-O	225.	315.	700.	975.	1850.	2600.	2750.	3250.	4750.	8250.
1895-S	26.00	42.50	95.00	140.	200.	285.	340.	475.	1000.	3050.
1896	8.50	20.00	40.00	62.50	75.00	110.	135.	175.	375.	600.

—— = Insufficient pricing data

	G-4	VG-8	F-12	VF-20	EF-40	AU-50	AU-55	MS-60	MS-63	MS-64
1896-O	50.00	100.	235.	300.	390.	575.	675.	1050.	2125.	4000.
1896-S	58.00	90.00	200.	275.	350.	450.	525.	675.	1650.	3250.
1897	2.50	3.00	6.50	10.00	25.00	55.00	65.00	100.	155.	240.
1897-O	42.00	70.00	245.	315.	390.	505.	585.	775.	1400.	2650.
1897-S	9.50	22.00	65.00	87.00	125.	225.	290.	400.	1000.	2500.
1898	1.50	2.25	6.50	10.00	23.00	55.00	65.00	90.00	140.	240.
1898-O	6.00	15.00	75.00	95.00	145.	230.	295.	450.	1150.	2550.
1898-S	4.75	12.00	25.00	35.00	58.00	115.	165.	285.	950.	2625.
1899	1.50	2.00	6.50	9.00	22.50	55.00	65.00	85.00	140.	240.
1899-O	5.00	11.00	63.00	80.00	140.	235.	300.	465.	1150.	2900.
1899-S	5.00	10.75	17.00	25.00	39.00	105.	150.	290.	600.	1700.
1900	1.60	2.00	6.50	9.00	21.00	55.00	65.00	85.00	140.	245.
1900-O	7.00	18.00	80.00	100.	225.	425.	575.	750.	1400.	3250.
1900-S	2.75	4.00	9.75	13.00	24.00	75.00	90.00	190.	475.	760.
1901	1.50	1.90	5.00	8.50	20.50	50.00	60.00	85.00	140.	235.
1901-O	3.00	5.25	12.00	19.00	45.00	125.	175.	370.	1050.	1850.
1901-S	40.00	65.00	275.	345.	435.	650.	750.	1025.	2050.	2850.
1902	1.50	1.90	5.00	7.50	20.50	50.00	60.00	85.00	140.	240.
1902-O	2.90	7.00	14.00	25.00	46.00	140.	215.	425.	825.	1800.
1902-S	7.00	12.00	45.00	70.00	110.	160.	200.	350.	690.	1950.
1903	1.50	1.90	5.00	7.50	20.50	50.00	60.00	85.00	150.	300.
1903-O	2.25	5.50	9.50	17.00	30.00	100.	140.	250.	575.	1250.
1903-S	38.00	70.00	290.	450.	750.	850.	1100.	1250.	1750.	2175.
1904	1.50	2.50	5.50	10.00	20.50	55.00	65.00	85.00	200.	365.
1904-S	25.00	42.50	150.	185.	275.	440.	585.	785.	1350.	2650.
1905	1.50	1.90	5.00	7.50	20.00	50.00	60.00	85.00	140.	240.
1905-O	3.00	6.00	32.00	45.00	65.00	120.	140.	225.	500.	900.
1905-O Micro O	18.00	35.00	65.00	92.00	150.	300.	400.	850.	1650.	2850.
1905-S	2.25	5.00	8.00	13.00	32.00	80.00	95.00	165.	315.	465.
1906	1.50	1.90	4.50	7.50	20.00	50.00	60.00	85.00	140.	240.
1906-D	3.00	4.75	10.00	15.50	31.00	75.00	85.00	160.	285.	925.
1906-O	5.00	10.50	45.00	60.00	90.00	125.	150.	210.	325.	500.
1906-S	2.75	6.00	11.00	19.00	40.00	90.00	130.	240.	365.	800.
1907	1.50	1.90	4.25	7.50	20.00	50.00	60.00	85.00	155.	240.
1907-D	3.00	5.00	9.00	16.00	40.00	95.00	125.	235.	775.	1700.
1907-O	2.00	3.50	32.00	45.00	55.00	80.00	100.	190.	330.	675.
1907-S	2.75	6.00	9.50	19.00	43.00	100.	155.	300.	800.	1575.
1908	1.50	1.90	4.00	7.50	20.00	50.00	60.00	85.00	140.	240.
1908-D	1.85	3.00	7.50	12.00	32.00	60.00	65.00	120.	200.	425.
1908-O	4.00	12.50	45.00	60.00	80.00	160.	195.	290.	475.	700.
1908-S	2.75	5.00	9.00	16.00	35.00	140.	175.	265.	535.	1425.
1909	1.70	2.25	4.00	7.50	20.00	50.00	60.00	85.00	150.	240.
1909-D	5.00	15.00	60.00	90.00	120.	235.	260.	475.	1075.	1450.
1909-O	2.75	5.00	9.00	18.00	30.00	85.00	115.	170.	460.	700.
1909-S	4.00	14.00	80.00	110.	155.	285.	350.	575.	1350.	1900.
1910	1.50	2.50	7.00	10.00	20.00	55.00	65.00	85.00	140.	240.
1910-D	2.50	5.00	8.00	17.00	42.00	95.00	110.	185.	490.	675.

	G-4	VG-8	F-12	VF-20	EF-40	AU-50	AU-55	MS-60	MS-63	MS-64
1910-S	3.25	10.00	52.00	70.00	105.	175.	200.	275.	700.	1250.
1911	1.50	2.05	4.00	7.50	20.00	50.00	60.00	85.00	140.	240.
1911-D	1.50	2.05	4.50	8.00	21.00	55.00	70.00	95.00	170.	240.
1911-S	1.75	3.25	9.00	16.00	35.00	83.00	92.00	135.	240.	600.
1912	1.50	2.05	4.00	7.75	21.00	50.00	60.00	85.00	140.	240.
1912-D	1.50	2.00	4.25	8.00	20.50	50.00	65.00	90.00	150.	250.
1912-S	1.75	3.00	8.00	13.00	33.00	85.00	95.00	175.	315.	525.
1913	1.50	2.00	4.00	7.50	20.00	50.00	60.00	85.00	140.	240.
1913-S	8.00	17.50	80.00	115.	190.	275.	325.	400.	650.	850.
1914	1.50	2.05	4.00	7.50	20.00	50.00	60.00	85.00	140.	240.
1914-D	1.50	2.05	4.00	7.75	21.00	55.00	65.00	90.00	155.	280.
1914-S	1.75	3.00	9.00	15.00	34.00	70.00	87.50	125.	350.	600.
1915	1.50	2.05	4.00	8.25	20.00	50.00	60.00	85.00	140.	240.
1915-S	2.30	6.00	28.00	40.00	60.00	130.	155.	250.	475.	640.
1916	1.50	2.25	4.00	7.75	20.00	50.00	60.00	85.00	140.	240.
1916-S	1.75	2.75	5.75	8.00	21.00	55.00	65.00	90.00	165.	260.

Winged Liberty Head dime

"Mercury dime"

Date of authorization: April 2, 1792
Dates of issue: 1916-1945
Designer: Adolph Weinman
Engraver: Charles Barber
Diameter: 17.91 mm/0.71 inch
Weight: 2.50 grams/0..08 ounce
Metallic content: 90% silver, 10% copper
Weight of pure silver: 2.25 grams/0.07 ounce
Edge: Reeded
Mint mark: Reverse left of base of fasces (bundle of rods)

NOTE: B refers to Full Split Bands on the fasces on the reverse.

	VG-8	F-12	VF-20	EF-40	AU-50	MS-60	MS-63	MS-64	MS-65	MS-65B
1916	2.40	4.50	6.00	9.00	20.00	26.00	40.00	46.00	85.00	115.
1916-D	725.	1250.	1500.	2450.	3750.	4500.	5500.	6250.	14500.	30000.
1916-S	4.00	6.00	8.00	15.00	20.00	35.00	60.00	80.00	225.	550.
1917	1.70	2.60	4.50	6.00	13.00	23.00	55.00	77.50	140.	375.

WINGED LIBERTY HEAD DIME (CONTINUED)

	VG-8	F-12	VF-20	EF-40	AU-50	MS-60	MS-63	MS-64	MS-65	MS-65B
1917-D	5.00	9.00	16.00	37.00	70.00	135.	350.	475.	1350.	6000.
1917-S	2.25	3.25	5.00	9.00	26.00	55.00	150.	210.	465.	1000.
1918	2.00	5.25	9.50	26.00	38.00	67.50	95.00	130.	350.	1050.
1918-D	2.25	4.25	9.00	18.00	39.00	95.00	215.	365.	725.	——
1918-S	2.35	4.00	7.00	13.00	30.00	80.00	250.	375.	600.	5750.
1919	1.95	3.00	5.00	9.00	21.00	29.00	95.00	125.	300.	650.
1919-D	5.00	9.00	15.00	30.00	68.00	190.	400.	625.	1600.	——
1919-S	3.75	6.00	12.00	28.00	65.00	170.	395.	700.	850.	9750.
1920	1.80	2.50	4.00	7.00	14.00	24.00	70.00	95.00	225.	450.
1920-D	2.40	3.50	6.75	15.00	40.00	100.	350.	390.	750.	4025.
1920-S	2.25	4.00	7.00	14.75	34.00	95.00	315.	515.	1350.	7000.
1921	35.00	73.00	210.	440.	685.	900.	1300.	1525.	2900.	3500.
1921-D	58.00	110.	230.	460.	750.	1000.	1475.	1850.	2900.	4600.
1923	1.75	2.50	3.75	6.00	13.00	27.00	38.00	45.00	100.	275.
1923-S	2.35	5.00	10.00	47.00	85.00	160.	375.	775.	1500.	5850.
1924	1.60	2.50	5.00	9.00	23.00	33.00	80.00	105.	185.	545.
1924-D	3.00	4.50	11.00	42.00	90.00	140.	325.	565.	1250.	1575.
1924-S	2.00	3.00	9.00	37.00	88.00	140.	450.	625.	1025.	10750.
1925	1.60	2.50	5.00	7.00	18.00	31.00	75.00	110.	200.	750.
1925-D	3.75	9.00	30.00	95.00	180.	375.	650.	900.	1600.	2950.
1925-S	2.25	3.50	9.00	43.00	85.00	165.	525.	800.	1700.	4250.
1926	1.50	2.00	3.50	4.75	12.50	24.00	58.00	105.	265.	575.
1926-D	2.00	3.75	7.00	18.00	39.00	95.00	225.	300.	550.	2400.
1926-S	6.00	14.00	37.00	170.	400.	775.	1300.	1500.	2950.	6000.
1927	1.55	2.25	3.50	5.00	11.00	20.00	45.00	77.00	165.	450.
1927-D	4.00	5.00	18.00	43.00	95.00	200.	335.	475.	1375.	6500.
1927-S	1.85	2.75	6.00	21.00	48.00	235.	485.	725.	1750.	5500.
1928	1.45	2.10	3.50	5.00	15.00	24.00	45.00	55.00	140.	295.
1928-D	3.65	5.50	18.00	40.00	80.00	125.	295.	400.	800.	2650.
1928-S	2.00	2.75	4.25	13.00	35.00	85.00	225.	290.	475.	1750.
1929	1.45	2.25	3.30	4.25	10.00	19.00	30.00	36.00	60.00	215.
1929-D	2.50	3.75	7.00	11.50	21.00	28.00	37.50	42.50	80.00	240.
1929-S	1.75	2.50	3.50	6.50	20.00	37.50	50.00	65.00	130.	480.
1930	1.70	2.25	3.50	5.50	13.00	25.00	45.00	50.00	145.	550.
1930-S	3.00	4.00	5.75	12.00	38.00	67.00	90.00	95.00	155.	450.
1931	2.25	3.00	4.00	9.00	20.00	35.00	55.00	75.00	140.	750.
1931-D	5.50	8.75	16.00	30.00	45.00	80.00	95.00	110.	210.	275.
1931-S	2.35	3.50	6.00	12.00	33.00	65.00	100.	130.	210.	1775.
1934	0.55	1.25	2.25	4.00	7.00	14.00	19.00	21.00	38.00	145.
1934-D	1.30	2.75	6.00	11.00	21.00	33.00	40.00	50.00	75.00	325.
1935	0.55	1.00	1.35	2.50	5.00	8.00	15.00	24.00	37.00	70.00
1935-D	1.25	2.25	5.00	10.00	19.50	29.00	35.00	42.50	65.00	500.
1935-S	1.00	1.25	1.85	3.25	9.00	19.00	24.00	27.50	36.00	450.
1936	0.55	1.00	1.35	2.00	3.25	8.00	15.00	20.00	25.00	85.00
1936-D	1.05	1.45	3.00	6.00	12.00	20.00	25.00	32.00	42.00	325.
1936-S	0.95	1.10	1.80	3.50	9.00	15.00	18.00	23.00	27.50	60.00
1937	0.55	1.00	1.35	1.95	4.00	8.00	12.00	15.00	23.00	35.00

—— = Insufficient pricing data

	VG-8	F-12	VF-20	EF-40	AU-50	MS-60	MS-63	MS-64	MS-65	MS-65B
1937-D	0.95	1.25	2.00	4.00	8.00	18.00	22.50	27.00	45.00	110.
1937-S	0.95	1.25	2.25	3.00	7.00	16.00	23.00	29.00	35.00	180.
1938	0.55	0.95	1.30	2.50	6.00	10.00	12.50	16.50	21.00	60.00
1938-D	1.50	1.75	2.25	4.50	9.00	12.50	16.00	18.00	30.00	55.00
1938-S	1.00	1.20	1.75	3.00	6.00	13.50	18.00	27.00	33.00	135.
1939	0.55	1.00	1.30	1.95	3.00	8.00	12.00	17.00	25.00	170.
1939-D	0.95	1.10	1.50	2.00	4.00	7.00	10.00	17.00	22.50	35.00
1939-S	1.25	1.50	2.00	4.00	9.00	19.00	27.00	35.00	40.00	500.
1940	0.50	0.85	1.00	1.95	2.75	5.00	10.00	17.00	25.00	40.00
1940-D	0.50	0.95	1.25	2.50	5.00	6.75	11.00	20.00	25.00	45.00
1940-S	0.50	0.95	1.25	1.75	3.00	7.00	12.00	16.00	24.00	100.
1941	0.50	0.85	1.00	1.50	2.00	5.50	9.00	13.50	18.00	30.00
1941-D	0.50	0.95	1.25	1.85	4.00	7.00	11.00	15.00	22.50	43.00
1941-S	0.50	0.95	1.25	1.85	2.50	9.00	12.50	16.00	23.00	35.00
1942/1	275.	320.	350.	385.	500.	1450.	3300.	4850.	6850.	12500.
1942/1-D	275.	350.	385.	475.	1050.	1750.	2850.	4000.	5750.	12000.
1942	0.50	0.85	1.00	1.50	2.00	5.00	9.00	12.50	17.00	40.00
1942-D	0.50	0.95	1.25	1.85	2.75	7.00	12.00	16.00	23.00	25.00
1942-S	0.50	0.95	1.35	2.00	2.50	9.00	13.00	20.00	25.00	100.
1943	0.50	0.85	1.00	1.50	2.25	5.50	9.00	12.50	17.00	40.00
1943-D	0.50	0.95	1.25	1.85	2.50	7.00	10.50	13.00	22.50	29.50
1943-S	0.50	0.95	1.25	1.85	2.75	9.00	12.00	17.00	22.00	60.00
1944	0.50	0.85	1.00	1.25	2.00	5.00	11.00	13.00	17.00	75.00
1944-D	0.50	0.95	1.25	1.85	2.50	7.00	12.00	13.50	22.00	29.00
1944-S	0.50	0.95	1.25	1.75	2.25	7.50	11.50	20.00	23.00	40.00
1945	0.50	0.85	1.00	1.25	2.25	5.50	10.00	15.00	22.00	5500.
1945-D	0.50	0.95	1.25	2.00	3.50	7.00	10.00	17.00	22.00	29.50
1945-S	0.50	0.95	1.25	1.90	2.50	7.00	13.00	18.00	25.00	100.
1945-S Micro S	1.25	1.50	2.50	5.00	15.00	19.50	26.50	30.00	57.00	550.

* = None issued

Roosevelt dime

Date of authorization: April 2, 1792; July 23, 1965
Dates of issue: 1946-present
Designer/Engraver: John R. Sinnock
Diameter: 17.91 mm/0.71 inch
Weight: (1946-1964, 1992-present silver Proofs only): 2.50 grams/0.08 ounce
(1965-present): 2.27 grams/0.07 ounce

Metallic content: (1946-1964, 1992-present silver Proofs only): 90% silver, 10% copper
(1965-present): 75% copper, 25% nickel clad to pure copper core
Weight of pure silver: (1946-1964, 1992-present silver Proofs only) 2.25 grams/0.07 ounce
Edge: Reeded
Mint mark: (1946-1964): Reverse left of base of torch
(1968-present): Obverse above date

	VG-8	F-12	VF-20	EF-40	AU-50	MS-60	MS-63	MS-65	PF-65
1946	0.50	0.55	0.60	0.68	0.70	0.75	0.85	4.75	*
1946-D	0.40	0.50	0.55	0.65	0.70	0.85	1.00	7.00	*
1946-S	0.40	0.50	0.55	1.15	1.25	1.50	2.25	10.50	*
1947	0.40	0.50	0.55	0.70	0.90	1.40	1.75	4.50	*
1947-D	0.45	0.60	0.75	1.35	1.75	2.20	2.75	11.00	*
1947-S	0.50	0.65	0.80	0.90	1.25	1.75	2.50	13.00	*
1948	0.40	0.50	0.65	0.90	1.55	4.00	5.50	14.00	*
1948-D	0.45	0.60	0.75	1.35	2.00	2.50	3.50	10.00	*
1948-S	0.40	0.50	0.50	0.95	1.25	1.90	2.25	12.00	*
1949	0.95	1.25	1.75	2.25	4.00	9.00	11.00	18.00	*
1949-D	0.40	0.60	0.90	1.65	3.25	3.75	5.00	13.00	*
1949-S	0.75	1.50	2.25	3.50	6.25	15.00	17.50	37.50	*
1950	0.40	0.50	0.80	1.25	1.40	1.90	2.50	8.00	37.50
1950-D	0.40	0.50	0.70	0.85	1.00	3.00	3.75	8.00	*
1950-S	0.95	1.35	1.75	2.85	6.00	9.50	10.00	22.50	*
1951	0.40	0.50	0.55	0.70	0.75	1.30	1.70	3.75	29.00
1951-D	0.40	0.50	0.55	0.75	0.85	1.40	1.80	4.00	*
1951-S	0.55	1.05	1.15	1.75	3.50	5.25	6.50	10.00	*
1952	0.40	0.50	0.55	0.80	0.85	1.75	1.85	4.00	20.00
1952-D	0.40	0.45	0.55	0.75	0.80	1.00	1.25	4.25	*
1952-S	0.50	1.00	1.15	1.25	1.50	3.75	5.00	9.50	*
1953	0.40	0.45	0.50	0.85	0.95	1.10	1.40	4.25	18.50
1953-D	0.40	0.45	0.55	0.65	0.70	0.90	1.10	3.75	*
1953-S	0.40	0.45	0.50	0.55	0.60	0.75	0.85	3.30	*
1954	0.40	0.45	0.50	0.57	0.58	0.60	0.80	3.35	9.00
1954-D	0.40	0.45	0.50	0.57	0.58	0.60	0.80	3.20	*
1954-S	0.40	0.45	0.50	0.60	0.65	0.70	0.75	3.20	*
1955	0.55	0.57	0.60	0.70	0.75	0.80	0.95	5.00	8.50
1955-D	0.45	0.50	0.55	0.67	0.68	0.70	0.75	3.40	*
1955-S	0.45	0.50	0.55	0.67	0.68	0.70	0.75	4.75	*
1956	0.40	0.45	0.50	0.58	0.60	0.63	0.75	2.90	3.50
1956-D	0.40	0.45	0.50	0.60	0.62	0.65	0.90	2.80	*

* = None issued

	VG-8	F-12	VF-20	EF-40	AU-50	MS-60	MS-63	MS-65	PF-65
1957	0.40	0.45	0.50	0.58	0.60	0.63	0.75	2.90	3.00
1957-D	0.40	0.45	0.50	0.60	0.65	0.70	0.90	3.85	*
1958	0.40	0.45	0.50	0.60	0.62	0.65	0.75	4.00	3.50
1958-D	0.40	0.45	0.50	0.57	0.58	0.60	0.75	3.75	*
1959	0.40	0.45	0.50	0.57	0.58	0.60	0.75	2.60	2.00
1959-D	0.40	0.45	0.50	0.60	0.62	0.65	0.75	3.00	*
1960	0.40	0.45	0.50	0.55	0.58	0.60	0.70	2.55	1.00
1960-D	0.40	0.45	0.50	0.55	0.58	0.60	0.70	2.55	*
1961	0.40	0.45	0.50	0.55	0.58	0.60	0.70	2.30	0.95
1961-D	0.40	0.45	0.50	0.55	0.58	0.60	0.70	2.30	*
1962	0.40	0.45	0.50	0.55	0.58	0.60	0.70	2.30	0.95
1962-D	0.40	0.45	0.50	0.55	0.58	0.60	0.70	2.75	*
1963	0.40	0.45	0.50	0.55	0.58	0.60	0.70	2.25	0.95
1963-D	0.40	0.45	0.50	0.55	0.58	0.60	0.70	2.25	*
1964	0.40	0.45	0.50	0.55	0.58	0.60	0.70	2.25	0.95
1964-D	0.40	0.45	0.50	0.55	0.58	0.60	0.70	2.25	*

	MS-60	MS-63	MS-65	PF-65
COPPER-NICKEL CLAD				
1965	0.23	0.40	0.70	*
1966	0.25	0.40	0.70	*
1967	0.23	0.40	0.70	*
1968	0.23	0.40	0.70	*
1968-D	0.23	0.40	0.70	*
1968-S	*	*	*	0.60
1968-S No S	*	*	*	4850.
1969	0.35	0.75	1.00	*
1969-D	0.25	0.40	0.65	*
1969-S	*	*	*	0.60
1970	0.23	0.40	0.65	*
1970-D	0.23	0.40	0.65	*
1970-S	*	*	*	0.60
1970-S No S	*	*	*	350.
1971	0.27	0.45	0.75	*
1971-D	0.23	0.40	0.65	*
1971-S	*	*	*	0.75
1972	0.27	0.40	0.70	*
1972-D	0.25	0.40	0.65	*
1972-S	*	*	*	0.95
1973	0.23	0.40	0.65	*
1973-D	0.23	0.40	0.65	*
1973-S	*	*	*	0.70
1974	0.23	0.40	0.65	*
1974-D	0.23	0.40	0.65	*
1974-S	*	*	*	0.80
1975	0.25	0.45	0.70	*
1975-D	0.25	0.40	0.65	*

* = None issued

	MS-60	MS-63	MS-65	PF-65
1975-S	*	*	*	1.00
1975-S No S	*	*	*	28000.
1976	0.25	0.55	0.80	*
1976-D	0.25	0.55	0.80	*
1976-S	*	*	*	0.75
1977	0.20	0.35	0.65	*
1977-D	0.21	0.35	0.70	*
1977-S	*	*	*	1.50
1978	0.20	0.35	0.65	*
1978-D	0.21	0.35	0.70	*
1978-S	*	*	*	0.60
1979	0.20	0.35	0.65	*
1979-D	0.20	0.35	0.65	*
1979-S Filled S	*	*	*	0.75
1979-S Clear S	*	*	*	1.50
1980-P	0.20	0.35	0.50	*
1980-D	0.20	0.35	0.50	*
1980-S	*	*	*	0.80
1981-P	0.20	0.35	0.50	*
1981-D	0.20	0.35	0.50	*
1981-S	*	*	*	0.80
1982 No Mint mark, Strong Strike	85.00	90.00	125.	*
1982-P	0.85	1.45	——	*
1982-D	0.30	0.55	——	*
1982-S	*	*	*	1.00
1983-P	0.30	0.95	——	*
1983-D	0.28	0.95	——	*
1983-S	*	*	*	1.00
1983-S No S	*	*	*	250.
1984-P	0.20	0.50	——	*
1984-D	0.20	0.55	——	*
1984-S	*	*	*	1.50
1985-P	0.21	0.60	——	*
1985-D	0.20	0.50	——	*
1985-S	*	*	*	1.25
1986-P	0.20	0.75	——	*
1986-D	0.20	0.75	——	*
1986-S	*	*	*	1.50
1987-P	0.20	0.35	——	*
1987-D	0.20	0.35	——	*
1987-S	*	*	*	1.50
1988-P	0.20	0.40	——	*
1988-D	0.20	0.35	——	*
1988-S	*	*	*	1.50
1989-P	0.20	0.35	——	*
1989-D	0.20	0.35	——	*
1989-S	*	*	*	1.50

—— = Insufficient pricing data   * = None issued

	MS-60	MS-63	MS-65	PF-65
1990-P	0.20	0.35	——	*
1990-D	0.20	0.35	——	*
1990-S	*	*	*	1.60
1991-P	0.20	0.35	——	*
1991-D	0.20	0.35	——	*
1991-S	*	*	*	3.00
1992-P	0.20	0.35	——	*
1992-D	0.20	0.35	——	*
1992-S Clad	*	*	*	3.50
1992-S Silver	*	*	*	7.00
1993-P	0.20	0.35	——	*
1993-D	0.20	0.35	——	*
1993-S Clad	*	*	*	5.00
1993-S Silver	*	*	*	6.00
1994-P	0.20	0.35	——	*
1994-D	0.20	0.35	——	*
1994-S Clad	*	*	*	3.50
1994-S Silver	*	*	*	5.50
1995-P	0.20	0.35	——	*
1995-D	0.20	0.35	——	*
1995-S Clad	*	*	*	4.00
1995-S Silver	*	*	*	4.75
1996-P	0.20	0.35	——	*
1996-W	7.00	7.25	12.00	*
1996-D	0.20	0.35	——	*
1996-S Clad	*	*	*	2.50
1996-S Silver	*	*	*	4.75
1997-P	0.20	0.35	——	*
1997-D	0.20	0.35	——	*
1997-S Clad	*	*	*	3.00
1997-S Silver	*	*	*	4.25
1998-P	0.20	0.35	——	*
1998-D	0.20	0.35	——	*
1998-S Clad	*	*	*	2.50
1998-S Silver	*	*	*	5.00
1999-P	——	——	——	*
1999-D	——	——	——	*
1999-S Clad	*	*	*	——
1999-S Silver	*	*	*	——

—— = Insufficient pricing data   * = None issued

Seated Liberty 20 cents

Date of authorization: March 3, 1875
Dates of issue: 1875-1876
Designers: Obverse: Thomas Sully-Christian Gobrecht-John Hughes-Willaim Barber
Reverse: William Barber
Engraver: William Barber
Diameter: 22.50 mm/0.89 inch
Weight: 5.00 grams/0.16 ounce
Metallic content: 90% silver, 10% copper
Weight of pure silver: 4.50 grams/0.14 ounce
Edge: Plain
Mint mark: Reverse below eagle

	F-12	VF-20	EF-40	AU-50	MS-60	MS-62	MS-63	MS-64	MS-65	PF-65
1875	75.00	100.	185.	325.	540.	725.	1175.	2000.	5500.	8500.
1875-CC	87.00	155.	210.	450.	725.	900.	1250.	2750.	8500.	——
1875-S	70.00	100.	160.	275.	460.	675.	1050.	1675.	5000.	45000.
1876	140.	200.	330.	450.	640.	925.	1400.	2175.	5500.	8500.
1876-CC Eliasberg sale - April 1997, Cataloged as MS-65 $148,500										
1877 Proofs only	1450.	1600.	1750.	1900.	1950.	2200.	2600.	3450.	8000.	8000.
1878 Proofs only	1200.	1300.	1400.	1550.	1625.	1750.	2100.	3450.	8000.	8000.

—— = Insufficient pricing data

Draped Bust quarter dollar

Small Eagle

Heraldic Eagle

Date of authorization:	April 2, 1792
Dates of issue:	1796, 1804-1807
Designers:	Obverse: Gilbert Stuart-Robert Scot Reverse: (1796): Robert Scot-John Eckstein (1804-1807): Robert Scot
Engraver:	Robert Scot
Diameter:	27 mm/1.07 inches
Weight:	6.74 grams/0.22 ounce
Metallic content:	89.25% silver, 10.75% copper
Weight of pure silver:	6.02 grams/0.19 ounce
Edge:	Reeded
Mint Mark:	None

	G-4	VG-8	F-12	VF-20	EF-40	AU-50	AU-55	MS-60	MS-62	MS-63
SMALL EAGLE										
1796	4250.	6250.	8250.	9750.	14000.	16750.	19500.	24500.	28750.	35000.
HERALDIC EAGLE										
1804	1025.	1225.	2250.	3250.	7750.	16000.	20000.	35000.	47500.	75000.
1805	180.	265.	400.	700.	1550.	2350.	3150.	6250.	8500.	12000.
1806/5	180.	255.	410.	825.	1850.	3100.	4750.	7750.	12000.	22500.
1806	175.	245.	365.	675.	1500.	2150.	2600.	3900.	4500.	7500.
1807	175.	245.	360.	690.	1475.	2100.	2550.	3850.	4750.	7500.

Capped Bust quarter dollar

Date of authorization: April 2, 1792
Dates of issue: 1815-1838
Designer/Engraver: John Reich
Diameter: 1815-1828: 27.00mm/1.07 inches
1831-1838: 24.26mm/0.96 inch
Weight: 6.74 grams/0.22 ounce
Metallic content: 89.25% silver, 10.75% copper
Weight of pure silver: 6.02 grams/0.19 ounce
Edge: Reeded
Mint mark: None

	G-4	VG-8	F-12	VF-20	EF-40	AU-50	AU-55	MS-60	MS-62	MS-63
MOTTO, Open Collar Strike										
1815	57.50	75.00	110.	280.	685.	1050.	1450.	2100.	2350.	3650.
1818/5	50.00	93.00	125.	315.	700.	1125.	1600.	2250.	2500.	4250.
1818	48.00	65.00	100.	280.	660.	1000.	1350.	1950.	2250.	3500.
1819	48.00	60.00	90.00	265.	660.	1000.	1400.	1950.	2450.	4700.
1820 Small 0	48.00	65.00	100.	280.	675.	1050.	1500.	2200.	2750.	5000.
1820 Large 0	48.00	60.00	90.00	275.	650.	975.	1400.	1950.	2550.	4650.
1821	48.00	60.00	90.00	265.	650.	975.	1325.	1950.	2300.	3650.
1822	60.00	100.	140.	325.	815.	1600.	2300.	2550.	2900.	4900.
1822 25/50c	1650.	3250.	4100.	5250.	8500.	15000.	—	25000.	—	—
1823/2	9250.	13500.	18000.	22500.	32500.	50000.	—	—	—	—
1824/2	75.00	115.	190.	525.	1325.	2150.	2800.	6000.	—	—
1825/2	145.	185.	300.	550.	1100.	1900.	2500.	3750.	—	6500.
1825/3	48.00	60.00	90.00	250.	640.	950.	1325.	1950.	2300.	3500.
1825/4	48.00	60.00	90.00	250.	640.	950.	1350.	2100.	2400.	3500.
1827/3 Originals and Restrikes: Original VF-20/30 $40000; Prf-60 $58500; Prf-64 $120000; Restrike Prf-62 $46000; Prf-63 $55000; Prf-65 $100000										
1828	48.00	60.00	90.00	250.	640.	1100.	1375.	2150.	2450.	4000.
1828 25/50c	140.	280.	400.	850.	1550.	3600.	—	8500.	13000.	—
CAPPED BUST, NO MOTTO, Closed Collar Strike										
1831 Small Letters	39.00	45.00	55.00	85.00	200.	525.	590.	800.	1100.	1975.
1832	39.00	45.00	55.00	85.00	200.	525.	600.	925.	1450.	2350.
1833	42.50	45.00	60.00	115.	280.	725.	800.	1350.	1800.	3350.
1834	39.00	45.00	55.00	85.00	200.	525.	590.	800.	1150.	1975.

— = Insufficient pricing data

	G-4	VG-8	F-12	VF-20	EF-40	AU-50	AU-55	MS-60	MS-62	MS-63
1835	39.00	45.00	55.00	85.00	200.	525.	590.	775.	1150.	1975.
1836	39.00	45.00	55.00	85.00	200.	550.	625.	1200.	1800.	3250.
1837	39.00	45.00	55.00	85.00	200.	550.	615.	825.	1175.	1975.
1838	39.00	45.00	55.00	85.00	200.	525.	590.	850.	1250.	2050.

Seated Liberty quarter dollar

Date of authorization: April 2, 1792
Dates of issue: 1838-1891
Designers: (1838-1840):
Obverse: Thomas Sully-Christian Gobrecht
Reverse: John Reich-William Kneass-Gobrecht-Sully
(1840-1891):
Obverse: Robert B. Hughes-Gobrecht-Sully
Reverse: Hughes-Gobrecht-Sully
Engravers: Obverse: Christian Gobrecht
Reverse:
(1838-1853): Christian Gobrecht
(1853-1891): James B. Longacre
Diameter:24.26 mm/0.96 inch
Weight: (1838-1873): 6.22 grams/0.20 ounce
(1873-1891): 6.25 grams/0.20 ounce
Metallic content: 90% silver, 10% copper
Weight of pure silver: (1838-1873): 5.60 grams/0.18 ounce
(1873-1891): 5.63 grams/0.18 ounce
Edge: Reeded
Mint mark: Reverse below eagle

	G-4	VG-8	F-12	VF-20	EF-40	AU-50	AU-55	MS-60	MS-63
NO DRAPERY AT ELBOW									
1838	14.00	18.00	30.00	70.00	265.	525.	600.	975.	3400.
1839	14.00	18.00	30.00	65.00	250.	500.	575.	1000.	3650.
1840-O	16.00	20.00	35.00	95.00	300.	575.	685.	1200.	4100.
DRAPERY AT ELBOW									

	G-4	VG-8	F-12	VF-20	EF-40	AU-50	AU-55	MS-60	MS-63
1840	19.00	29.00	45.00	80.00	180.	340.	500.	900.	3050.
1840-O Small O	23.00	37.00	57.50	125.	250.	525.	625.	1050.	3450.
1840-O Large O	300.	360.	600.	1100.	——	——	——	——	——
1841	44.50	57.50	87.50	140.	255.	435.	525.	1050.	2200.
1841-O	18.00	23.00	40.00	70.00	150.	310.	400.	700.	1800.
1842 Small Date Proofs only	——	——	——	——	——	——		25000.	50000.
1842 Large Date	70.00	97.50	175.	250.	375.	875.	1250.	2800.	4750.
1842-O Small Date	400.	600.	1150.	2000.	4750.	7500.	——	16500.	——
1842-O Large Date	16.25	19.25	36.00	70.00	175.	585.	775.	1950.	4500.
1843	14.00	16.00	25.00	35.00	62.50	190.	230.	475.	1075.
1843-O Small O	18.50	26.50	50.00	100.	235.	800.	1550.	——	——
1843-O Large O	75.00	110.	200.	400.	800.	——	——	——	——
1844	13.00	16.00	23.00	35.00	65.00	185.	220.	475.	1200.
1844-O	15.75	17.50	35.00	60.00	145.	350.	600.	1950.	4250.
1845	13.00	16.00	22.50	35.00	75.00	200.	240.	490.	1150.
1845/5	15.75	19.00	32.50	55.00	115.	265.	325.	725.	——
1846	14.50	16.50	27.00	35.00	67.50	190.	235.	480.	1275.
1846/1846	15.75	19.50	35.00	57.50	155.	325.	500.	——	——
1847	13.00	16.00	25.00	32.50	65.00	185.	220.	450.	1200.
1847/7	16.00	25.00	50.00	62.50	125.	285.	475.	——	——
1847-O	19.50	35.00	57.50	97.50	315.	685.	1450.	3200.	6250.
1848 (triple date)	25.00	37.50	82.50	140.	210.	400.	550.	1050.	2850.
1848/1848	40.00	55.00	87.50	170.	235.	590.	1150.	——	——
1849	18.00	25.00	37.50	67.50	135.	300.	485.	775.	——
1849-O	385.	610.	1025.	1600.	3100.	5750.	6250.	7500.	——
1850	22.50	35.00	60.00	82.50	165.	330.	550.	875.	2400.
1850-O	17.75	27.00	55.00	85.00	200.	490.	900.	1400.	3750.
1851	32.50	45.00	80.00	125.	190.	315.	415.	800.	1825.
1851-O	150.	250.	390.	625.	1400.	2650.	3800.	5050.	——
1852	31.50	42.50	80.00	135.	200.	360.	435.	875.	1200.
1852-O	175.	245.	400.	725.	1400.	3500.	4500.	7000.	19000.
1853/53 Recut Date	195.	285.	425.	600.	875.	1700.	2000.	2450.	4900.
ARROWS AND RAYS									
1853	12.50	16.00	23.50	37.00	130.	300.	400.	775.	2025.
1853/4	35.00	52.50	145.	200.	450.	800.	1250.	2350.	5500.
1853-O	14.75	18.00	28.50	57.50	200.	1275.	1950.	2650.	7500.
1853-O/Horizontal O	27.50	40.00	75.00	150.	400.	1800.	——	——	——

Arrows at date, Rays on Reverse

—— = Insufficient pricing data

	G-4	VG-8	F-12	VF-20	EF-40	AU-50	AU-55	MS-60	MS-63
ARROWS, NO RAYS									
1854	12.75	16.00	22.00	29.00	75.00	235.	285.	475.	1175.
1854-O Large O	13.50	16.50	30.00	50.00	115.	305.	550.	975.	1800.
1854-O Huge O	90.00	145.	190.	350.	750.	—	6000.	—	—
1855	12.50	16.00	21.50	28.00	70.00	235.	295.	550.	1275.
1855-O	32.50	50.00	100.	250.	550.	1200.	1975.	2950.	8000.
1855-S	30.00	34.00	65.00	140.	425.	1000.	1450.	1950.	4750.
NO ARROWS									
1856	13.00	16.00	21.50	27.00	50.00	130.	185.	290.	625.
1856-O	14.00	18.00	24.00	45.00	100.	425.	600.	1200.	2250.
1856-S	35.00	52.50	85.00	185.	435.	1025.	2500.	3250.	7500.
1856-S/ Small S	42.50	65.00	135.	275.	775.	1600.	—	—	—
1857	13.00	16.00	21.50	27.00	50.00	120.	165.	280.	550.
1857-O	13.25	16.00	27.00	45.00	75.00	285.	525.	1100.	3100.
1857-S	60.00	115.	205.	325.	505.	1150.	1900.	2900.	6500.
1858	13.00	16.00	21.50	27.00	50.00	120.	165.	285.	550.
1858-O	16.75	19.50	32.00	52.50	115.	445.	675.	1500.	4200.
1858-S	50.00	100.	165.	250.	625.	1900.	2650.	—	—
1859	13.25	16.00	22.00	29.00	65.00	145.	200.	395.	1200.
1859-O	17.50	24.50	33.50	52.50	110.	375.	650.	1450.	—
1859-S	85.00	125.	210.	320.	1250.	3100.	7000.	—	—
1860	13.00	16.00	21.50	29.00	62.50	135.	190.	385.	825.
1860-O	16.25	21.00	36.00	47.50	90.00	325.	500.	1050.	2200.
1860-S	170.	315.	425.	900.	4250.	10000.	—	—	—
1861	13.00	16.00	21.50	28.50	55.00	120.	165.	290.	550.
1861-S	55.00	80.00	190.	285.	800.	3250.	—	—	—
1862	13.75	17.00	24.00	31.00	57.50	140.	200.	375.	575.
1862-S	50.00	77.50	175.	250.	490.	975.	1650.	2750.	5000.
1863	28.50	40.00	52.50	72.50	170.	285.	375.	750.	1250.
1864	47.50	60.00	105.	160.	235.	430.	525.	850.	1700.
1864-S	290.	475.	650.	1050.	1850.	3500.	4500.	—	23000.
1865	55.00	70.00	145.	200.	290.	365.	485.	775.	1350.
1865-S	70.00	115.	200.	300.	475.	1200.	1500.	2000.	3500.
1866	—	—	—	—	—	—	—	—	—
WITH MOTTO									
1866	275.	405.	480.	575.	685.	1050.	1250.	1600.	2450.
1866-S	195.	300.	500.	800.	1350.	1900.	2600.	3850.	—
1867	155.	200.	275.	315.	440.	600.	710.	975.	1800.
1867-S	155.	240.	350.	490.	725.	1750.	2500.	4500.	—
1868	87.50	105.	200.	260.	330.	415.	575.	675.	1600.
1868-S	55.00	70.00	130.	215.	590.	1300.	1700.	2800.	6000.
1869	240.	325.	430.	485.	675.	950.	1200.	1750.	3000.
1869-S	70.00	100.	175.	265.	525.	1350.	1750.	2550.	4150.
1870	47.50	65.00	95.00	145.	235.	350.	435.	800.	1750.
1870-CC	1850.	2750.	5500.	10500.	19500.	37500.	—	—	—
1871	32.50	40.00	52.50	87.50	155.	300.	400.	750.	1100.

— = Insufficient pricing data

	G-4	VG-8	F-12	VF-20	EF-40	AU-50	AU-55	MS-60	MS-63
1871-CC	1150.	2400.	3500.	8000.	13500.	27500.	——	——	——
1871-S	285.	365.	465.	575.	900.	1500.	1975.	3000.	3750.
1872	30.00	37.50	52.50	82.50	145.	260.	315.	875.	1975.
1872-CC	400.	640.	1300.	2250.	4150.	9500.	15000.	25000.	——
1872-S	450.	750.	1200.	1900.	3850.	5650.	——	7500.	14000.
1873 Closed 3	160.	225.	350.	460.	610.	1125.	1450.	2900.	——
1873 Open 3	30.00	35.00	52.50	95.00	175.	275.	325.	550.	1200.
1873-CC R. Henry Norweb Specimen MS-64 (PCGS) sold for $209000 on 2/9/98.									
ARROWS ADDED									
1873	14.50	18.50	29.00	55.00	185.	375.	425.	675.	1475.
1873-CC	1300.	2550.	4750.	8500.	14000.	——	32500.	——	100000.
1873-S	25.00	40.00	80.00	160.	300.	575.	750.	1200.	3000.
1874	16.75	21.00	32.50	60.00	185.	360.	425.	750.	1550.
1874-S	20.00	32.50	60.00	130.	275.	500.	600.	825.	1450.
ARROWS REMOVED									
1875	13.00	16.00	21.25	27.00	50.00	110.	145.	230.	405.
1875-CC	50.00	85.00	140.	250.	410.	660.	825.	1400.	2250.
1875-S	39.00	52.50	72.50	110.	150.	285.	325.	550.	1400.
1876	13.00	16.00	21.25	27.00	50.00	110.	145.	225.	405.
1876-CC	13.35	16.00	22.00	31.00	55.00	145.	200.	315.	700.
1876-S	13.25	16.00	21.25	27.00	52.50	130.	165.	230.	415.
1877	13.00	16.00	21.25	27.00	50.00	110.	145.	225.	405.
1877-CC	13.25	16.50	22.50	32.00	60.00	140.	175.	275.	600.
1877-S	13.00	16.00	22.00	28.00	51.00	110.	140.	235.	410.
1877-S/Horizontal S	25.00	37.50	75.00	175.	225.	275.	375.	750.	2250.
1878	13.00	16.00	21.25	27.00	50.00	110.	145.	240.	450.
1878-CC	18.00	27.50	40.00	60.00	105.	210.	255.	340.	850.
1878-S	75.00	140.	190.	265.	435.	750.	800.	1275.	2900.
1879	140.	180.	205.	250.	320.	350.	395.	420.	725.
1880	140.	185.	210.	250.	330.	355.	405.	415.	700.
1881	145.	190.	215.	265.	315.	350.	400.	445.	750.
1882	150.	195.	215.	265.	330.	365.	420.	500.	765.
1883	145.	190.	215.	265.	325.	360.	415.	495.	775.
1884	175.	225.	260.	320.	350.	370.	455.	575.	800.
1885	145.	190.	215.	260.	330.	355.	395.	415.	725.
1886	190.	235.	275.	325.	450.	700.	750.	850.	1000.
1887	160.	205.	245.	285.	345.	375.	465.	500.	765.
1888	160.	205.	245.	285.	345.	375.	465.	500.	675.
1888-S	13.35	16.00	22.00	28.00	51.00	140.	210.	390.	725.
1889	145.	205.	245.	280.	350.	385.	450.	525.	700.
1890	50.00	57.50	85.00	110.	155.	200.	330.	425.	650.
1891	13.00	16.00	21.50	27.00	50.00	110.	145.	235.	405.
1891-O	135.	165.	300.	475.	775.	1550.	1950.	2950.	7500.
1891-S	13.50	16.00	23.00	32.50	52.00	145.	185.	275.	475.

—— = Insufficient pricing data

Barber quarter dollar

Date of authorization: April 2, 1792
Dates of issue: 1892-1916
Designer/Engraver: Charles Barber
Diameter: 24.26 mm/0.96 inch
Weight: 6.25 grams/0.20 ounce
Metallic content: 90% silver, 10% copper
Weight of pure silver: 5.63 grams/0.18 ounce
Edge: Reeded
Mint mark: Reverse below

	G-4	VG-8	F-12	VF-20	EF-40	AU-50	MS-60	MS-62	MS-63
1892	4.00	5.00	20.00	30.00	72.50	125.	160.	195.	250.
1892-O	6.00	9.50	24.00	37.00	80.00	150.	260.	310.	400.
1892-S	14.00	27.00	55.00	75.00	125.	275.	400.	550.	750.
1892-S/S	21.00	40.00	65.00	87.50	195.	375.	500.	725.	1100.
1893	4.00	6.50	23.00	30.00	72.50	125.	220.	260.	310.
1893-O	5.00	7.75	25.00	44.50	77.50	155.	265.	380.	550.
1893-S	7.50	14.00	37.50	65.00	130.	275.	420.	650.	950.
1894	5.00	6.00	24.00	37.00	75.00	135.	220.	270.	365.
1894-O	5.50	7.75	30.00	45.00	85.00	195.	345.	525.	700.
1894-S	6.00	8.00	28.00	47.50	80.00	175.	325.	500.	750.
1895	5.00	6.00	24.00	30.00	72.50	135.	225.	360.	475.
1895-O	6.50	9.00	35.00	50.00	95.00	220.	420.	650.	950.
1895-S	7.50	11.50	38.00	65.00	100.	220.	375.	575.	1000.
1895-S/S	10.50	19.00	50.00	85.00	150.	300.	450.	750.	1250.
1896	5.00	6.00	24.00	30.00	72.50	135.	230.	300.	400.
1896-O	7.00	13.00	65.00	190.	335.	625.	875.	1275.	1850.
1896-S	300.	465.	625.	925.	1600.	3000.	4400.	6000.	7850.
1897	4.00	4.50	20.00	30.00	72.50	125.	175.	210.	275.
1897-O	7.50	14.50	75.00	170.	350.	625.	850.	1250.	1700.
1897-S	12.00	28.00	110.	175.	325.	650.	950.	1325.	1750.
1898	4.00	4.50	20.00	30.00	70.00	125.	175.	200.	275.
1898-O	6.00	14.00	55.00	105.	205.	415.	650.	950.	1500.
1898-S	5.00	12.00	32.00	50.00	75.00	180.	425.	800.	1200.
1899	4.00	4.50	20.00	32.00	65.00	125.	175.	200.	275.
1899-O	5.00	12.00	28.00	45.00	92.50	260.	400.	600.	800.
1899-S	8.50	18.00	40.00	65.00	105.	230.	440.	650.	1200.
1900	4.00	4.50	18.50	30.00	65.00	125.	175.	200.	275.
1900-O	6.50	14.00	48.00	75.00	125.	325.	600.	750.	950.
1900-S	6.00	9.50	35.00	48.00	65.00	125.	400.	650.	975.

	G-4	VG-8	F-12	VF-20	EF-40	AU-50	MS-60	MS-62	MS-63
1901	6.00	7.00	20.00	30.00	65.00	125.	170.	200.	275.
1901-O	23.00	38.00	85.00	175.	350.	615.	825.	1350.	2000.
1901-S	1750.	2800.	4500.	6000.	8000.	10000.	14500.	17500.	21500.
1902	3.50	4.50	19.00	30.00	65.00	125.	175.	200.	275.
1902-O	5.00	9.50	35.00	55.00	100.	200.	425.	675.	1250.
1902-S	8.00	14.00	35.00	55.00	85.00	200.	425.	575.	825.
1903	3.50	4.50	19.00	30.00	65.00	125.	175.	300.	475.
1903-O	5.50	7.50	33.00	48.00	85.00	225.	400.	775.	1200.
1903-S	8.00	19.00	38.00	60.00	110.	250.	430.	575.	850.
1904	3.50	4.50	19.00	30.00	65.00	125.	175.	210.	300.
1904-O	7.00	10.00	45.00	70.00	175.	375.	765.	1025.	1350.
1905	3.50	4.50	23.00	35.00	65.00	125.	175.	225.	375.
1905-O	9.00	14.00	60.00	100.	200.	345.	475.	750.	1100.
1905-S	7.00	11.00	35.00	48.00	90.00	210.	350.	650.	1000.
1906	3.50	4.50	19.50	30.00	65.00	125.	165.	195.	250.
1906-D	4.00	5.00	23.00	38.00	65.00	145.	240.	315.	475.
1906-O	3.50	5.00	29.00	43.00	85.00	200.	300.	375.	500.
1907	3.50	4.50	19.00	30.00	65.00	125.	165.	195.	250.
1907-D	3.50	4.50	25.00	40.00	80.00	175.	250.	375.	775.
1907-O	3.50	4.50	19.00	30.00	65.00	135.	185.	265.	400.
1907-S	5.50	7.50	38.00	55.00	110.	250.	475.	700.	975.
1908	3.50	4.50	19.00	30.00	65.00	125.	200.	235.	300.
1908-D	3.50	4.50	19.00	30.00	65.00	125.	225.	285.	390.
1908-O	3.50	4.50	19.00	30.00	65.00	125.	200.	250.	310.
1908-S	9.00	21.00	63.00	105.	250.	425.	700.	950.	1400.
1909	3.50	4.50	19.00	30.00	65.00	110.	165.	195.	250.
1909-D	3.50	4.50	19.00	30.00	65.00	150.	195.	250.	335.
1909-O	13.00	25.00	72.00	150.	285.	465.	750.	1025.	1475.
1909-S	3.50	5.50	28.00	40.00	65.00	180.	325.	475.	800.
1910	3.50	4.50	22.00	32.00	65.00	140.	190.	225.	300.
1910-D	4.50	6.50	36.00	55.00	100.	225.	335.	550.	1025.
1911	3.50	4.50	19.00	30.00	72.00	130.	165.	195.	275.
1911-D	5.00	8.00	65.00	175.	285.	450.	650.	850.	1250.
1911-S	5.00	8.00	45.00	55.00	135.	285.	400.	525.	725.
1912	3.50	4.50	19.00	30.00	60.00	125.	165.	195.	275.
1912-S	5.00	6.50	38.00	55.00	100.	220.	400.	675.	1050.
1913	10.00	17.00	58.00	140.	375.	525.	950.	1025.	1200.
1913-D	6.00	7.00	30.00	43.00	80.00	160.	275.	325.	425.
1913-S	450.	700.	1750.	2750.	3500.	4250.	5150.	6100.	7300.
1914	3.50	5.00	16.00	29.00	60.00	110.	165.	195.	275.
1914-D	3.50	5.00	16.00	29.00	65.00	110.	165.	200.	275.
1914-S	55.00	75.00	145.	185.	385.	575.	925.	1150.	1375.
1915	3.50	4.00	16.00	29.00	65.00	110.	165.	200.	285.
1915-D	3.50	4.00	16.00	29.00	65.00	110.	165.	195.	285.
1915-S	4.00	6.00	27.00	38.00	75.00	185.	240.	325.	450.
1916	3.50	4.00	17.00	29.00	60.00	110.	165.	195.	275.
1916-D	3.50	4.00	16.00	29.00	60.00	110.	165.	195.	275.
1916-D Large D/Small D	——	21.00	40.00	60.00	110.	185.	300.	450.	700.

—— = Insufficient pricing data

Standing Liberty quarter dollar

Bare breast, No stars below eagle

Date of authorization:	April 2, 1792
Dates of issue:	1916-1930
Designer:	Hermon MacNeil
Engravers:	Obverse: Hermon McNeil
	Reverse: MacNeil, Charles Barber
Diameter:	24.26 mm/0.96 inch
Weight:	6.25 grams/0.20 ounce
Metallic content:	90% silver, 10% copper
Weight of pure silver:	5.63 grams/0.18 ounce
Edge:	Reeded
Mint mark:	Obverse left of date

NOTE: H refers to full head.

	G-4	F-12	VF-20	EF-40	AU-50	MS-60	MS-63	MS-63H	MS-65	MS-65H
BARE BREAST										
1916	1400.	2000.	2450.	3050.	4100.	5250.	7150.	8300.	14000.	23500.
1917	15.00	27.00	43.00	60.00	115.	150.	240.	315.	700.	1350.
1917-D	17.00	28.00	53.00	85.00	135.	225.	365.	450.	950.	1800.
1917-S	17.00	28.00	63.00	130.	180.	280.	375.	550.	1650.	2400.
MAILED BREAST, STARS BELOW EAGLE										
1917	14.00	20.00	25.00	47.50	72.00	120.	175.	275.	625.	850.
1917-D	24.00	50.00	63.00	90.00	125.	150.	300.	750.	1400.	3350.
1917-S	21.00	37.00	55.00	75.00	105.	160.	310.	775.	925.	3250.
1918	15.00	22.00	32.50	45.00	80.00	135.	185.	350.	625.	1650.
1918-D	27.00	43.00	61.00	82.50	140.	215.	325.	1150.	1350.	5500.
1918-S	17.00	27.00	33.00	45.00	80.00	170.	300.	1550.	1275.	17500.
1918/7-S	1200.	1925.	2250.	4500.	7800.	14500.	30500.	——	85000.	——
1919	30.00	42.00	48.00	67.50	92.50	140.	190.	350.	600.	1275.
1919-D	65.00	115.	175.	280.	485.	625.	1100.	3750.	2250.	24000.
1919-S	60.00	115.	225.	375.	525.	875.	1650.	3850.	3000.	30000.
1920	15.00	21.00	25.00	35.00	65.00	125.	165.	325.	500.	1875.
1920-D	33.00	60.00	82.00	105.	165.	210.	610.	1650.	1750.	5900.
1920-S	20.00	27.00	35.00	55.00	94.00	225.	775.	8500.	2250.	34000.
1921	75.00	145.	190.	275.	335.	440.	700.	1250.	1550.	3975.
1923	14.50	25.00	30.00	37.00	65.00	120.	170.	700.	500.	3900.
1923-S	150.	260.	330.	435.	500.	600.	900.	1500.	1750.	3450.

—— = Insufficient pricing data

Mailed breast, Stars below eagle

	G-4	F-12	VF-20	EF-40	AU-50	MS-60	MS-63	MS-63H	MS-65	MS-65H
1924	14.00	20.00	24.00	32.00	63.00	115.	160.	315.	480.	1400.
1924-D	38.00	46.00	65.00	90.00	120.	145.	195.	1275.	550.	4500.
1924-S	22.00	27.50	35.00	85.00	175.	350.	850.	1600.	1950.	5650.
1925	3.00	5.00	14.50	26.50	57.00	105.	155.	315.	525.	900.
1926	3.00	5.00	12.50	25.00	55.00	105.	155.	315.	480.	1975.
1926-D	6.50	14.00	27.00	45.00	80.00	110.	160.	6500.	525.	25000.
1926-S	3.50	10.00	24.00	95.00	215.	345.	850.	6250.	2050.	26500.
1927	3.00	5.00	12.50	26.00	50.00	100.	155.	300.	480.	950.
1927-D	7.00	14.00	39.00	80.00	132.	155.	200.	675.	480.	2900.
1927-S	9.00	52.50	155.	1000.	3200.	3800.	5500.	——	9750.	——
1928	3.00	5.00	12.50	26.00	52.00	100.	155.	375.	480.	1400.
1928-D	4.50	7.00	19.50	37.50	77.50	135.	175.	1975.	500.	——
1928-S	3.00	6.00	12.50	30.00	67.00	130.	170.	350.	475.	825.
1929	3.00	5.00	12.50	25.00	52.00	100.	155.	300.	480.	700.
1929-D	4.50	8.00	14.00	31.50	65.00	135.	165.	1050.	525.	6250.
1929-S	3.00	5.50	15.00	29.00	60.00	115.	150.	295.	450.	700.
1930	3.00	4.50	12.50	25.00	52.00	95.00	150.	290.	450.	700.
1930-S	3.00	4.50	12.50	25.00	58.00	115.	165.	400.	500.	800.

—— = Insufficient pricing data

Washington quarter dollar

Date of authorization: April 2, 1792; July 23, 1965; Oct. 18, 1973
Dates of issue: 1932-present
Designers: John Flanagan
(Bicentennial Reverse): Jack L. Ahr
Engravers: John R. Sinnock
(Bicentennial Reverse): Frank Gasparro
Diameter: 24.26mm/0.96 inch
Weight: (1932-1964, 1992-presnet silver Proofs only): 6.25 grams/0.20 ounce
(1965-present): 5.67 grams/0.18 ounce
1976 Bientennial Proof and Uncirculated: 5.75 grams/0.18 ounce
Metallic content: (1932-1964, 1992-present silver Proofs only): 90% silver, 10% copper
(1976 Bicentennial Proof and Uncirculated sets only): 80% silver, 20% copper bonded to a core of 21.5% silver, 78.5% copper
Weight of pure silver: (1932-1964, 1992-present silver Proofs only): 5.63 grams/0.18 ounce
(1976 Bicentennail Proof and Uncirculated sets only): 2.30 grams/0.07 ounce
Edge: Reeded
Mint mark: (1932-1964): Reverse below eagle
(1968-present): Obverse right of Washington's ponytail

	G-4	VG-8	F-12	VF-20	EF-40	AU-50	MS-60	MS-63	MS-65	PF-65
1932	4.00	3.60	5.00	7.00	9.00	15.00	20.00	35.00	225.	*
1932-D	38.00	42.00	47.00	60.00	155.	240.	465.	850.	5600.	*
1932-S	40.00	44.00	48.00	50.00	64.00	130.	260.	400.	2650.	*

* = None issued

	G-4	VG-8	F-12	VF-20	EF-40	AU-50	MS-60	MS-63	MS-65	PF-65
1934	1.40	2.00	2.25	3.00	4.75	7.50	20.00	27.50	65.00	*
1934 Light Motto	1.75	3.50	4.50	7.00	8.50	11.00	26.00	50.00	175.	*
1934 Doubled Die	30.00	32.50	37.50	75.00	125.	230.	565.	750.	2850.	*
1934-D	3.25	3.75	5.75	7.50	16.50	70.00	175.	225.	975.	*
1935	1.40	2.00	2.25	3.00	4.00	8.00	20.00	26.00	65.00	*
1935-D	2.15	3.50	5.00	7.25	14.50	100.	200.	260.	575.	*
1935-S	2.00	2.50	3.75	5.00	10.00	25.00	55.00	75.00	190.	*
1936	1.40	1.75	2.00	3.00	4.00	7.75	18.00	24.00	55.00	1000.
1936-D	2.50	3.00	4.75	14.00	34.00	175.	300.	350.	625.	*
1936-S	2.00	2.85	3.50	6.25	12.00	40.00	55.00	68.00	125.	*
1937	1.30	1.85	2.75	3.25	4.00	15.00	20.00	27.50	80.00	335.
1937-D	1.90	2.50	3.50	6.00	9.00	24.00	40.00	42.50	90.00	*
1937-S	3.00	3.75	6.00	10.00	20.00	65.00	90.00	110.	200.	*
1938	2.00	2.75	4.00	8.00	14.00	30.00	55.00	65.00	125.	220.
1938-S	2.75	3.00	4.00	8.25	14.50	30.00	55.00	60.00	140.	*
1939	1.50	1.75	1.90	2.50	3.50	7.00	12.50	22.00	55.00	167.
1939-D	1.75	2.25	3.75	6.00	8.50	13.00	30.00	33.00	80.00	*
1939-S	2.50	3.00	4.00	6.00	13.00	40.00	60.00	65.00	125.	*
1940	1.20	1.60	1.90	2.15	3.00	6.00	10.00	15.00	55.00	145.
1940-D	2.60	3.50	5.25	8.50	15.00	40.00	60.00	70.00	120.	*
1940-S	1.75	2.00	2.75	3.00	3.25	10.00	14.00	22.50	50.00	*
1941	1.20	1.30	2.00	2.15	2.75	3.50	5.00	7.00	42.50	138.
1941-D	1.20	1.30	2.00	2.85	3.50	6.00	14.00	25.00	52.50	*
1941-S	1.20	1.30	2.00	2.60	3.25	6.00	15.00	22.00	75.00	*
1942	1.20	1.30	2.00	2.50	3.00	3.50	4.00	6.50	35.00	125.
1942-D	1.20	1.60	2.35	2.85	3.40	5.25	8.00	12.50	40.00	*
1942-S	1.25	1.65	2.45	3.00	5.00	15.00	45.00	50.00	90.00	*
1943	1.20	1.30	2.00	2.60	2.75	3.00	3.75	6.25	40.00	*
1943-D	1.20	1.30	2.00	2.50	3.10	6.00	15.00	20.00	40.00	*
1943-S	1.20	1.30	2.00	2.60	4.00	11.00	17.00	25.00	45.00	*
1943-S Doubled Die	40.00	50.00	75.00	125.	185.	225.	375.	600.	1550.	*
1944	1.20	1.30	2.00	2.15	2.65	3.00	3.50	4.75	40.00	*
1944-D	1.20	1.30	2.00	2.15	2.75	4.75	7.00	10.00	40.00	*
1944-S	1.20	1.30	2.00	2.15	2.75	4.50	6.00	12.00	40.00	*
1945	1.20	1.30	2.00	2.15	2.35	2.40	2.50	4.25	40.00	*
1945-D	1.20	1.60	2.45	2.75	3.20	4.25	5.75	8.50	40.00	*
1945-S	1.20	1.30	2.00	2.35	2.80	3.75	4.25	6.00	40.00	*
1946	1.20	1.30	2.00	2.15	2.55	2.75	3.75	5.50	40.00	*
1946-D	1.20	1.30	2.00	2.35	2.60	2.90	3.25	4.50	40.00	*
1946-S	1.20	1.35	2.45	2.50	2.75	2.85	3.00	4.50	40.00	*
1947	1.20	1.30	2.00	2.15	2.55	3.75	5.25	6.50	40.00	*
1947-D	1.20	1.30	2.00	2.35	2.80	3.00	3.75	5.00	40.00	*
1947-S	1.20	1.30	2.00	2.35	2.80	3.00	3.25	4.50	40.00	*

* = None issued

	G-4	VG-8	F-12	VF-20	EF-40	AU-50	MS-60	MS-63	MS-65	PF-65
1948	1.20	1.30	2.00	2.15	2.55	3.00	3.25	4.00	40.00	*
1948-D	1.20	1.30	2.00	2.35	2.80	3.15	3.50	4.75	40.00	*
1948-S	1.20	1.30	2.00	2.35	2.80	3.15	4.00	5.00	40.00	*
1949	1.20	1.30	2.00	2.85	3.45	7.00	15.00	18.00	40.00	*
1949-D	1.20	1.30	2.00	2.35	2.80	4.00	6.00	8.00	45.00	*
1950	1.20	1.30	2.00	2.15	2.55	2.85	3.00	3.75	20.00	60.00
1950-D	1.20	1.30	2.00	2.15	2.55	2.90	3.25	4.00	22.00	*
1950-D/S	——	29.00	37.50	70.00	125.	175.	225.	300.	825.	*
1950-S	1.20	1.30	2.00	2.15	2.55	4.00	5.50	6.50	23.00	*
1950-S/D	——	35.00	45.00	77.50	145.	200.	275.	350.	600.	*
1951	1.20	1.30	2.00	2.15	2.55	2.75	3.00	4.00	20.00	45.00
1951-D	1.20	1.30	2.00	2.15	2.55	2.75	2.90	3.75	20.00	*
1951-S	1.20	1.30	2.00	2.15	2.55	6.50	8.50	14.00	35.00	*
1952	1.20	1.30	2.00	2.15	2.35	2.55	2.65	3.50	20.00	37.50
1952-D	1.20	1.30	2.00	2.15	2.50	2.65	2.75	3.50	20.00	*
1952-S	1.20	1.30	2.00	2.15	2.45	4.50	6.75	9.00	25.00	*
1953	1.20	1.30	2.35	2.45	2.50	2.55	2.65	3.50	20.00	24.00
1953-D	1.20	1.30	1.85	1.90	1.95	2.00	2.05	3.25	20.00	*
1953-S	1.20	1.30	2.20	2.35	2.40	2.50	2.75	4.25	20.00	*
1954	1.20	1.30	1.35	1.45	1.55	1.65	1.75	3.25	20.00	12.50
1954-D	1.20	1.30	1.35	1.40	1.45	1.50	1.55	2.75	20.00	*
1954-S	1.20	1.30	1.80	1.85	1.90	1.95	2.00	3.25	20.00	*
1955	1.20	1.30	1.65	1.75	1.80	1.85	1.90	3.25	20.00	10.50
1955-D	1.20	1.30	1.65	1.90	2.00	2.05	2.15	2.75	20.00	*
1956	1.20	1.30	1.36	1.50	1.60	1.65	1.70	2.50	18.00	8.50
1956-D	1.20	1.30	1.65	1.75	1.85	1.95	2.15	3.00	20.00	*
1957	1.20	1.30	1.35	1.50	1.60	1.65	1.70	2.50	18.00	4.00
1957-D	1.20	1.30	1.35	1.50	1.60	1.65	1.70	2.50	18.00	*
1958	1.20	1.30	1.50	1.60	1.65	1.70	1.75	2.50	18.00	7.00
1958-D	1.20	1.30	1.35	1.40	1.45	1.50	1.65	2.25	18.00	*
1959	1.20	1.30	1.35	1.50	1.55	1.60	1.55	2.25	18.00	5.00
1959-D	1.20	1.30	1.35	1.40	1.45	1.50	1.55	2.50	18.00	*
1960	1.20	1.30	1.35	1.40	1.45	1.50	1.60	2.25	18.00	2.25
1960-D	1.20	1.30	1.35	1.40	1.45	1.50	1.60	2.25	16.00	*
1961	1.20	1.30	1.35	1.40	1.45	1.50	1.60	3.00	17.00	1.75
1961-D	1.20	1.30	1.35	1.40	1.45	1.50	1.55	2.25	16.00	*
1962	1.20	1.30	1.35	1.40	1.45	1.50	1.55	2.25	16.00	1.75
1962-D	1.20	1.30	1.35	1.40	1.45	1.50	1.60	2.25	16.00	*
1963	1.20	1.30	1.35	1.40	1.45	1.50	1.55	2.00	15.00	1.75
1963-D	1.20	1.30	1.35	1.40	1.45	1.50	1.55	3.00	15.00	*
1964	1.20	1.30	1.35	1.40	1.45	1.50	1.55	2.00	15.00	1.75
1964-D	1.20	1.30	1.35	1.40	1.45	1.50	1.55	2.00	15.00	*
COPPER-NICKEL CLAD										
1965	FV	FV	FV	FV	FV	FV	0.50	0.70	3.00	*
1966	FV	FV	FV	FV	FV	FV	0.50	0.70	3.00	*
1967	FV	FV	FV	FV	FV	FV	0.50	0.95	3.50	*

—— = Insufficient pricing data * = None issued

Bicentennial date reverse

	G-4	VG-8	F-12	VF-20	EF-40	AU-50	MS-60	MS-63	MS-65	PF-65
1968	FV	FV	FV	FV	FV	FV	0.40	0.95	3.00	*
1968-D	FV	FV	FV	FV	FV	FV	0.42	0.95	3.25	*
1968-S	*	*	*	*	*	*	*	*	*	0.85
1969	FV	FV	FV	FV	FV	FV	0.40	0.95	3.00	*
1969-D	FV	FV	FV	FV	FV	FV	0.50	0.95	3.25	*
1969-S	*	*	*	*	*	*	*	*	*	0.85
1970	FV	FV	FV	FV	FV	FV	0.35	0.55	2.00	*
1970-D	FV	FV	FV	FV	FV	FV	0.35	0.55	2.00	*
1970-S	*	*	*	*	*	*	*	*	*	0.85
1971	FV	FV	FV	FV	FV	0.35	0.50	0.95	2.50	*
1971-D	FV	FV	FV	FV	FV	0.35	0.40	0.95	2.25	*
1971-S	*	*	*	*	*	*	*	*	*	1.00
1972	FV	FV	FV	FV	FV	FV	0.35	0.65	2.00	*
1972-D	FV	FV	FV	FV	FV	FV	0.35	0.65	2.00	*
1972-S	*	*	*	*	*	*	*	*	*	1.00
1973	FV	FV	FV	FV	FV	FV	0.30	0.65	2.00	*
1973-D	FV	FV	FV	FV	FV	FV	0.30	0.65	2.00	*
1973-S	*	*	*	*	*	*	*	*	*	0.75
1974	FV	FV	FV	FV	FV	FV	0.30	0.75	2.00	*
1974-D	FV	FV	FV	FV	FV	FV	0.30	0.75	2.00	*
1974-S	*	*	*	*	*	*	*	*	*	0.65
DUAL DATE, BICENTENNIAL REVERSE										
1776-1976	0.27	0.28	0.29	0.30	0.31	0.32	0.41	0.75	1.00	*
1776-1976-D	0.27	0.28	0.29	0.30	0.31	0.32	0.41	0.75	1.00	*
1776-1976-S	*	*	*	*	*	*	*	*	*	0.75
1776-1976-S 40% silver	——	——	——	——	——	——	1.50	2.50	3.75	2.00
EAGLE REVERSE RESUMED										
1977	FV	FV	FV	FV	FV	FV	0.30	0.55	1.00	*
1977-D	FV	FV	FV	FV	FV	FV	0.30	0.55	1.00	*
1977-S	*	*	*	*	*	*	*	*	*	0.85
1978	FV	FV	FV	FV	FV	FV	——	0.55	——	*
1978-D	FV	FV	FV	FV	FV	FV	——	0.55	——	*
1978-S	*	*	*	*	*	*	*	*	*	0.85

—— = Insufficient pricing data * = None issued

	G-4	VG-8	F-12	VF-20	EF-40	AU-50	MS-60	MS-63	MS-65	PF-65
1979	FV	FV	FV	FV	FV	FV	0.40	0.65	——	*
1979-D	FV	FV	FV	FV	FV	FV	0.40	0.65	——	*
1979-S Filled S	*	*	*	*	*	*	*	*	*	0.85
1979-S Clear S	*	*	*	*	*	*	*	*	*	1.25
1980-P	FV	FV	FV	FV	FV	FV	——	0.55	——	*
1980-D	FV	FV	FV	FV	FV	FV	——	0.55	——	*
1980-S	*	*	*	*	*	*	*	*	*	0.85
1981-P	FV	FV	FV	FV	FV	FV	——	0.55	——	*
1981-D	FV	FV	FV	FV	FV	FV	——	0.55	——	*
1981-S	*	*	*	*	*	*	*	*	*	0.85
1982-P	FV	FV	FV	FV	FV	1.50	2.25	4.00	——	*
1982-D	FV	FV	FV	FV	FV	FV	——	1.50	——	*
1982-S	*	*	*	*	*	*	*	*	*	1.00
1983-P	FV	FV	FV	FV	1.50	2.50	3.35	7.50	——	*
1983-D	FV	FV	FV	FV	FV	1.10	2.00	5.00	——	*
1983-S	*	*	*	*	*	*	*	*	*	1.65
1984-P	FV	FV	FV	FV	FV	FV	——	1.25	——	*
1984-D	FV	FV	FV	FV	FV	1.10	1.25	2.50	——	*
1984-S	*	*	*	*	*	*	*	*	*	1.00
1985-P	FV	FV	FV	FV	FV	1.10	1.25	2.50	——	*
1985-D	FV	FV	FV	FV	1.25	1.75	2.25	4.00	——	*
1985-S	*	*	*	*	*	*	*	*	*	0.65
1986-P	FV	FV	FV	FV	1.25	1.75	2.50	5.00	——	*
1986-D	FV	FV	FV	FV	1.00	1.50	2.00	4.00	——	*
1986-S	*	*	*	*	*	*	*	*	*	1.50

	MS-63	MS-65	PF-64	PF-65
1987-P	0.55	——	*	*
1987-D	0.55	——	*	*
1987-S	*	*	0.65	0.85
1988-P	1.65	——	*	*
1988-D	0.60	——	*	*
1988-S	*	*	0.65	0.85
1989-P	0.85	——	*	*
1989-D	0.85	——	*	*
1989-S	*	*	0.65	0.85
1990-P	0.55	——	*	*
1990-D	0.55	——	*	*
1990-S	*	*	1.50	2.00
1991-P	0.55	——	*	*
1991-D	0.55	——	*	*
1991-S	*	*	2.00	2.75
1992-P	0.55	——	*	*
1992-D	0.55	——	*	*
1992-S Clad	*	*	2.70	3.75
1992-S Silver	*	*	3.50	4.50
1993-P	0.55	——	*	*

—— = Insufficient pricing data * = None issued

	MS-63	MS-65	PF-64	PF-65
1993-D	0.55	——	*	*
1993-S Clad	*	*	4.00	5.00
1993-S Silver	*	*	6.00	7.00
1994-P	0.55	——	*	*
1994-D	0.55	——	*	*
1994-S Clad	*	*	3.00	4.00
1994-S Silver	*	*	5.50	6.25
1995-P	0.55	——	*	*
1995-D	0.55	——	*	*
1995-S Clad	*	*	2.75	3.50
1995-S Silver	*	*	4.00	5.00
1996-P	0.55	——	*	*
1996-D	0.55	——	*	*
1996-S Clad	*	*	1.50	3.00
1996-S Silver	*	*	3.75	4.75
1997-P	0.55	——	*	*
1997-D	0.55	——	*	*
1997-S Clad	*	*	1.50	2.00
1997-S Silver	*	*	3.75	4.25
1998-P	0.55	——	*	*
1998-D	0.55	——	*	*
1998-S Clad	*	*	2.85	3.50
1998-S Silver	*	*	5.00	6.00
1999-P Delaware	——	——	*	*
1999-D Delaware	——	——	*	*
1999-S Delaware Clad	*	*	——	——
1999-S Delaware Silver	*	*	——	——
1999-P Pennsylvania	——	——	*	*
1999-D Pennsylvania	——	——	*	*
1999-S Pennsylvania Clad	*	*	——	——
1999-S Pennsylvania Silver	*	*	——	——
1999-P New Jersey	——	——	*	*
1999-D New Jersey	——	——	*	*
1999-S New Jersey Clad	*	*	——	——
1999-S New Jersey Silver	*	*	——	——
1999-P Georgia	——	——	*	*
1999-D Georgia	——	——	*	*
1999-S Georgia Clad	*	*	——	——
1999-S Georgia Silver	*	*	——	——
1999-P Connecticut	——	——	*	*
1999-D Connecticut	——	——	*	*
1999-S Connecticut Clad	*	*	——	——
1999-S Connecticut Silver	*	*	——	——

—— = Insufficient pricing data * = None issued

Flowing Hair half dollar

Date of authorization: April 2, 1792
Dates of issue: 1794-1795
Designer: Robert Scot
Engravers: Robert Scot, John S. Gardner
Diameter: 32.50 mm/1.28 inches
Weight: 13.48 grams/0.43 ounce
Metallic content: 90% silver, 10% copper
Weight of pure silver: 12.13 grams/0.39 ounce
Edge: Lettered (FIFTY CENTS OR HALF A DOLLAR)
Mint mark: None

	AG-3	G-4	VG-8	F-12	VF-20	EF-40	EF-45	AU-50	MS-60
1794	725.	1200.	2100.	3000.	7250.	13000.	18500.	28500.	40000.
1795 2 Leaves	290.	385.	600.	850.	1400.	4350.	5800.	8750.	23000.
1795 3 Leaves	550.	975.	1750.	3250.	6500.	12000.	16500.	25000.	——

—— = Insufficient pricing data

Draped Bust half dollar

Small Eagle reverse

Heraldic Eagle reverse

Date of authorization: April 2, 1792
Dates of issue: 1796-1797, 1801-1807
Designers: Obverse: Gilbert Stuart-Robert Scot
Reverse:
(1796-1797): Scot-John Eckstein
(1801-1807): Robert Scot
Engraver: Robert Scot
Diameter: 32.50 mm/1.28 inches
Weight: 13.48 grams/0.43 ounce
Metallic content: 89.25% silver, 10.75% copper
Weight of pure silver: 12.03 grams/0.39 ounce
Edge: Lettered (FIFTY CENTS OR HALF A DOLLAR)
Mint mark: None

	AG-3	G-4	VG-8	F-12	VF-20	EF-40	EF-45	AU-50	MS-60
SMALL EAGLE									
1796 15 Stars	7750.	10000.	14000.	18750.	22500.	43000.	46000.	65000.	——
1796 16 Stars	8000.	12000.	15000.	20000.	27500.	47500.	52500.	70000.	105000.
1797 15 Stars	7500.	10500.	14500.	19250.	24000.	43000.	50000.	63500.	97500.
HERALDIC EAGLE									
1801	92.00	190.	300.	500.	775.	3500.	4750.	9000.	27500.
1802	85.00	180.	250.	450.	750.	3200.	4750.	9250.	——
1803 Small 3	72.00	150.	210.	315.	500.	1175.	1700.	3250.	7150.
1803 Large 3	60.00	135.	170.	230.	345.	825.	1200.	2350.	5400.
1805/4	105.	205.	300.	480.	635.	1900.	3750.	6500.	25000.
1805	57.00	135.	170.	235.	345.	850.	1250.	2450.	5650.
1806/5	37.00	135.	170.	225.	340.	700.	1050.	2050.	5150.
1806/Inverted 6	90.00	190.	285.	450.	825.	1800.	2400.	3850.	8750.
1806 Knobbed 6, No Stem, VF-35 $57,500.									
1806 Knobbed 6, Stems	60.00	135.	165.	215.	345.	685.	850.	1700.	4400.
1806 Pointed 6, Stems	57.00	125.	160.	210.	330.	650.	775.	1650.	4300.
1806 Pointed 6, No Stem	57.00	125.	160.	210.	330.	650.	775.	1650.	4300.
1807	57.00	125.	160.	210.	330.	650.	775.	1650.	4300.

—— = Insufficient pricing data

Capped Bust half dollar

Date of authorization: April 2, 1792
Dates of issue: 1807-1839
Designers: Obverse: John Reich
Reverse:
(1807-1836): John Reich
(1836-1839): Reich-Christian Gobrecht
Engraver: John Reich
Diameter: (1807-1836): 32.50 mm/1.28 inches
(1836-1839): 30.61 mm/1.21 inches
Weight: (1807-1836): 13.48 grams/0.43 ounce
(1836-1839): 13.37 grams/0.43 ounce
Metallic Content: (1807-1836): 89.25% silver, 10.75% copper
(1836-1839): 90% silver, 10% silver
Weight of pure silver: (1807-1836): 12.03 grams/0.39 ounce
(1836-1839): 12.03 grams/0.39 ounce
Edge: (1807-1836): Lettered (FIFTY CENTS OR HALF ADOLLAR)
(1836-1839): Reeded
Mint mark: 1838-1839 only, obverse above date

	G-4	VG-8	F-12	VF-20	EF-40	AU-50	MS-60	MS-63
1807 Small Stars	62.00	95.00	190.	345.	800.	2200.	3800.	10000.
1807 Large Stars	45.00	67.00	180.	290.	825.	2350.	4500.	12500.
1807 50/20C	41.00	85.00	155.	250.	475.	1750.	3500.	8500.
1807 Bearded Goddess	300.	465.	775.	1250.	2500.	7250.	—	—
1808/7	40.00	53.00	80.00	160.	435.	825.	2250.	6250.
1808	38.00	45.00	60.00	100.	210.	545.	1450.	3900.
1809 Plain Edge	37.00	45.00	60.00	95.00	200.	525.	1500.	3850.
1809 XXXX Edge	40.00	45.00	60.00	110.	230.	650.	1800.	—
1809 IIII Edge	42.00	50.00	65.00	115.	245.	650.	2000.	6000.
1810	35.00	40.00	50.00	75.00	165.	400.	1300.	3500.

— = Insufficient pricing data

	G-4	VG-8	F-12	VF-20	EF-40	AU-50	MS-60	MS-63
1811 Small 8	35.00	40.00	57.00	80.00	160.	385.	900.	1850.
1811 Large 8	35.00	40.00	57.00	80.00	170.	500.	1000.	2450.
1811/0	36.00	45.00	80.00	145.	300.	585.	1250.	7000.
1812/1 Small 8	37.00	60.00	80.00	165.	365.	675.	1700.	5850.
1812/1 Large 8	1550.	2500.	3750.	6750.	11000.	——	——	——
1812	35.00	40.00	50.00	65.00	135.	375.	685.	2150.
1813	35.00	40.00	52.00	73.00	160.	380.	925.	2850.
1813 50C/UNI	36.00	45.00	70.00	135.	270.	550.	1900.	6750.
1814	35.00	40.00	52.00	75.00	185.	410.	1050.	3250.
1814 Single Leaf	38.00	55.00	80.00	120.	325.	750.	2000.	——
1814/3	50.00	57.00	92.00	150.	375.	675.	2050.	5300.
1815/2	610.	800.	1275.	1550.	2650.	4000.	9500.	24500.
1817/3	80.00	105.	175.	350.	675.	1600.	4750.	18500.
1817/4	——	——	52500.	110000.	——	——	——	——
1817	35.00	40.00	45.00	63.00	170.	340.	950.	2900.
1817 Single Leaf	35.00	55.00	80.00	120.	240.	750.	2150.	——
1818/7	35.00	42.00	50.00	75.00	180.	625.	1250.	7000.
1818	35.00	38.00	45.00	55.00	130.	280.	675.	2100.
1819/8 Small 9	35.00	42.00	50.00	72.00	150.	425.	900.	2050.
1819/8 Large 9	35.00	42.00	50.00	72.00	150.	425.	900.	2500.
1819	35.00	38.00	45.00	55.00	135.	275.	775.	2750.
1820/19 Curl 2	35.00	41.00	65.00	140.	275.	625.	1400.	4000.
1820/19 Square 2	37.00	43.00	70.00	150.	350.	800.	1600.	4350.
1820 Large Date	35.00	42.00	60.00	115.	250.	525.	1100.	3250.
1820 Small Date	38.00	45.00	65.00	125.	275.	585.	1250.	4100.
1821	35.00	38.00	45.00	62.00	145.	450.	800.	2250.
1822	35.00	38.00	45.00	60.00	135.	265.	675.	2000.
1822/1	45.00	55.00	70.00	135.	275.	635.	1200.	2900.
1823	35.00	38.00	45.00	58.00	125.	275.	600.	1850.
1823 Broken 3	40.00	52.00	72.00	125.	415.	725.	1650.	3500.
1823 Patched 3	35.00	40.00	60.00	80.00	150.	500.	1400.	3000.
1823 Ugly 3	35.00	45.00	65.00	90.00	165.	575.	1450.	3100.
1824/1	35.00	40.00	45.00	95.00	210.	350.	885.	2850.
1824/2/0	35.00	40.00	45.00	55.00	150.	550.	1100.	5000.
1824/4	35.00	40.00	45.00	55.00	145.	325.	825.	1950.
1824	35.00	38.00	45.00	50.00	105.	265.	575.	1500.
1825	35.00	38.00	45.00	50.00	100.	225.	525.	1325.
1826	35.00	38.00	45.00	50.00	90.00	190.	505.	1250.
1827/6	35.00	38.00	45.00	85.00	200.	375.	950.	2325.
1827 Square 2	35.00	38.00	45.00	55.00	87.00	190.	600.	1400.
1827 Curl 2	35.00	40.00	50.00	70.00	110.	225.	525.	1275.
1828	35.00	38.00	45.00	50.00	75.00	175.	500.	1250.
1828 Small Letters	40.00	50.00	75.00	100.	195.	625.	1300.	2600.
1828 Large 8s	35.00	38.00	45.00	55.00	85.00	235.	500.	1250.
1828 Small 8s	35.00	38.00	45.00	50.00	77.00	230.	500.	1250.
1829/7	35.00	40.00	48.00	60.00	125.	350.	950.	2750.
1829	35.00	38.00	45.00	50.00	75.00	180.	500.	1250.

—— = Insufficient pricing data

CAPPED BUST HALF DOLLAR (CONTINUED)

	G-4	VG-8	F-12	VF-20	EF-40	AU-50	MS-60	MS-63
1830 Large 0	35.00	38.00	45.00	50.00	75.00	180.	475.	1250.
1830 Small 0	35.00	38.00	45.00	50.00	75.00	185.	450.	1250.
1830 Large Letters	1500.	2100.	3000.	3850.	4500.	7750.	15000.	——
1831	35.00	38.00	45.00	50.00	75.00	180.	425.	1250.
1832 Normal	35.00	38.00	45.00	50.00	75.00	180.	425.	1250.
1832 Large Letters	35.00	38.00	45.00	85.00	135.	225.	525.	1750.
1833	35.00	38.00	45.00	50.00	75.00	180.	450.	1275.
1834 All varieties	35.00	38.00	45.00	50.00	75.00	180.	450.	1250.
1835	35.00	38.00	45.00	50.00	75.00	180.	425.	1325.
1836	35.00	38.00	45.00	50.00	75.00	180.	425.	1250.
1836/1336	35.00	38.00	45.00	50.00	75.00	210.	500.	1300.
1836 50/00	37.00	55.00	75.00	165.	250.	685.	1600.	3950.

CAPPED BUST, REEDED EDGE HALF DOLLAR

50 CENTS reverse

HALF DOL. reverse

	G-4	VG-8	F-12	VF-20	EF-40	AU-50	AU-55	MS-60	MS-62	MS-63
50 CENTS REVERSE										
1836	625.	775.	900.	1250.	1800.	3400.	4750.	9000.	11500.	17500.
1837	32.00	36.00	45.00	75.00	120.	250.	325.	600.	975.	1650.
HALF DOL. REVERSE										
1838	32.00	36.00	45.00	75.00	120.	290.	340.	625.	1075.	1750.
1838-O Proofs only	——	——	——	——	42500.	80000.	——	115000.	165000.	300000.
1839	32.00	36.00	45.00	85.00	150.	350.	450.	950.	1550.	2500.
1839-O	135.	175.	250.	310.	585.	1125.	1550.	2800.	4000.	5600.

—— = Insufficient pricing data

Seated Liberty half dollar

Date of authorization: April 2, 1792
Dates of issue: 1839-1891
Designers: Obverse: Christian Gobrecht
Reverse: John Reich-Gobrecht
Engraver: Christian Gobrecht
Diameter: 30.61 mm/1.21 inches
Weight: (1839-1853): 13.37 grams/0.43 ounce
(1853-1873): 12.4 grams/0.40 ounce
(1873-1891): 12.50 grams/0.40 ounce
Metallic Content: 90% silver, 10% copper
Weight of pure silver: (1839-1853): 12.03 grams/0.39 ounce
(1853-1873): 11.20 grams/0.36 ounce
(1873-1891): 11.25 grams/0.36 ounce
Edge: Reeded
Mint mark: Reverse below eagle

	G-4	VG-8	F-12	VF-20	EF-40	AU-50	MS-60	MS-63
NO DRAPERY								
1839	40.00	55.00	115.	265.	615.	1400.	4000.	9500.
DRAPERY AT ELBOW								
1839	21.00	30.00	48.00	85.00	135.	275.	550.	2250.
1840 Small Letters	24.00	35.00	53.00	75.00	110.	250.	585.	1475.
1840 Medium Letters	105.	165.	225.	295.	525.	1100.	2750.	6000.
1840-O	21.00	30.00	50.00	70.00	105.	230.	600.	2250.
1841	32.00	43.00	85.00	150.	250.	425.	1200.	2750.
1841-O	17.00	27.00	48.00	88.00	125.	235.	800.	2400.
1842 Small Date	25.00	39.00	55.00	70.00	175.	400.	875.	2350.
1842 Medium Date	20.00	31.00	49.00	62.00	90.00	185.	400.	1450.
1842-O Medium Date	17.00	28.00	40.00	57.00	120.	300.	725.	4500.
1842-O Small Date	575.	800.	1350.	2000.	4150.	8500.	——	——
1843	17.00	26.00	43.00	53.00	73.00	180.	395.	1150.
1843-O	17.25	28.00	47.00	60.00	90.00	195.	700.	1900.
1844	17.00	26.00	40.00	48.00	70.00	175.	390.	1200.
1844-O	17.00	26.00	40.00	48.00	82.00	225.	735.	1950.
1844-O Doubled Date	300.	650.	1100.	1550.	2100.	5750.	12000.	——

—— = Insufficient pricing data

	G-4	VG-8	F-12	VF-20	EF-40	AU-50	MS-60	MS-63
1845	23.00	31.00	55.00	87.50	180.	340.	900.	3750.
1845-O	17.00	26.00	40.00	58.00	125.	255.	725.	2050.
1845-O No Drapery	24.00	35.00	75.00	100.	185.	325.	975.	4000.
1846 Medium Date	17.00	27.00	40.00	52.00	88.00	200.	400.	1450.
1846 Tall Date	19.00	30.00	43.00	60.00	120.	250.	535.	1700.
1846/Horizontal 6	125.	225.	275.	340.	500.	1200.	3500.	——
1846-O Medium Date	18.50	25.00	40.00	53.00	95.00	250.	750.	2200.
1846-O Tall Date	130.	290.	360.	475.	1100.	2000.	3950.	10000.
1847	17.00	24.00	40.00	48.00	80.00	160.	400.	1150.
1847-O	19.00	26.00	40.00	55.00	125.	290.	800.	2250.
1847/6	——	2000.	2850.	3600.	6750.	——	——	24000.
1848	34.00	55.00	75.00	125.	215.	475.	775.	1600.
1848-O	17.00	29.00	40.00	48.00	130.	325.	810.	1850.
1849	28.00	35.00	48.00	68.00	140.	350.	805.	1400.
1849 Doubled Date, bold	1400.	1800.	2750.	3750.	5150.	8500.	——	——
1849-O	19.00	29.00	43.00	59.00	115.	245.	650.	1950.
1850	180.	255.	335.	415.	550.	825.	1650.	4650.
1850-O	18.50	28.00	42.00	57.00	110.	235.	550.	1600.
1851	250.	350.	415.	500.	600.	775.	1200.	2350.
1851-O	20.00	30.00	53.00	85.00	185.	385.	675.	1400.
1852	300.	450.	525.	700.	900.	1100.	1325.	1900.
1852-O	45.00	90.00	175.	350.	515.	1150.	3750.	7500.
1853-O (Beware Alterations)	125000.	190000.		——				

Arrows at date, Rays on reverse

ARROWS AND RAYS

	G-4	VG-8	F-12	VF-20	EF-40	AU-50	MS-60	MS-63
1853	18.00	29.00	44.00	80.00	225.	450.	1275.	3550.
1853-O	20.00	33.00	55.00	150.	250.	850.	2750.	5750.

RAYS REMOVED

	G-4	VG-8	F-12	VF-20	EF-40	AU-50	MS-60	MS-63
1854	16.00	26.00	40.00	45.00	100.	255.	585.	1450.
1854-O	16.00	25.00	40.00	45.00	90.00	250.	475.	1450.
1855/1854	55.00	75.00	140.	225.	375.	700.	1800.	——
1855	18.00	29.00	41.00	60.00	110.	280.	750.	1900.
1855-O	16.00	26.00	40.00	45.00	100.	270.	675.	1475.
1855-S	325.	485.	850.	1350.	3100.	6700.	14500.	——

—— = Insufficient pricing data

	G-4	VG-8	F-12	VF-20	EF-40	AU-50	MS-60	MS-63
ARROWS REMOVED								
1856	16.00	24.00	40.00	48.00	75.00	160.	375.	800.
1856-O	16.00	26.00	40.00	48.00	75.00	165.	405.	775.
1856-S	42.50	55.00	100.	205.	375.	1300.	3500.	——
1857	16.00	24.00	40.00	48.00	75.00	160.	380.	800.
1857-O	17.00	28.00	43.00	58.00	125.	225.	725.	2600.
1857-S	60.00	80.00	140.	250.	525.	900.	3350.	6250.
1858	16.00	24.00	40.00	48.00	75.00	160.	375.	750.
1858-O	16.00	25.00	40.00	48.00	75.00	180.	400.	900.
1858-S	18.00	29.00	55.00	90.00	140.	340.	1050.	3250.
1859	23.00	31.00	49.00	68.00	100.	210.	395.	925.
1859-O	16.00	25.00	40.00	48.00	75.00	200.	390.	750.
1859-S	18.00	29.00	50.00	85.00	165.	290.	925.	2900.
1860	18.00	28.00	45.00	60.00	110.	235.	600.	1200.
1860-O	15.50	28.00	43.00	56.00	75.00	180.	380.	740.
1860-S	18.00	27.00	44.00	58.00	110.	240.	650.	2600.
1861	16.00	24.00	40.00	48.00	75.00	160.	375.	750.
1861-O	16.00	27.00	42.00	55.00	80.00	215.	400.	800.
1861-O struck by CSA, obverse die crack	50.00	75.00	125.	175.	250.	385.	925.	3000.
1861-S	17.00	26.00	40.00	58.00	130.	265.	900.	3550.
1862	26.00	40.00	58.00	90.00	185.	310.	525.	1050.
1862-S	16.00	24.00	40.00	49.00	85.00	250.	475.	2550.
1863	18.00	30.00	47.00	63.00	135.	265.	460.	950.
1863-S	16.00	28.00	43.00	50.00	85.00	245.	510.	2150.
1864	21.00	32.00	51.00	75.00	150.	275.	500.	1025.
1864-S	16.50	28.00	42.00	53.00	85.00	255.	550.	2350.
1865	22.00	33.00	48.00	70.00	140.	285.	515.	1300.
1865 Doubled Date	40.00	60.00	90.00	165.	235.	375.	——	——
1865-S	16.00	27.00	42.00	58.00	105.	275.	835.	2750.
1866-S	70.00	115.	215.	335.	825.	1850.	4650.	10000.
1866 Unique Trial Piece								
MOTTO ABOVE EAGLE								
1866	17.00	29.00	43.00	65.00	95.00	175.	385.	1000.
1866-S	16.00	25.00	40.00	63.00	100.	265.	475.	2350.
1867	24.00	40.00	57.00	95.00	145.	255.	435.	1050.
1867-S	16.00	25.00	40.00	48.00	80.00	170.	500.	2400.
1868	40.00	55.00	80.00	145.	265.	375.	525.	950.
1868-S	17.00	28.00	40.00	52.00	110.	235.	700.	2750.
1869	20.00	31.00	40.00	51.00	90.00	175.	365.	950.
1869-S	17.00	26.00	42.00	54.00	115.	400.	975.	3450.
1870	21.00	29.00	40.00	58.00	105.	190.	345.	1000.
1870-CC	450.	725.	1500.	2800.	10000.	15000.	——	47500.
1870-S	17.00	30.00	43.00	63.00	120.	265.	650.	2750.
1871	17.00	26.00	40.00	58.00	73.00	165.	340.	900.
1871-CC	115.	185.	325.	550.	1000.	1900.	5000.	42500.
1871-S	16.00	24.00	40.00	45.00	80.00	225.	575.	1750.

—— = Insufficient pricing data

	G-4	VG-8	F-12	VF-20	EF-40	AU-50	MS-60	MS-63
1872	16.00	26.00	40.00	48.00	70.00	180.	335.	900.
1872-CC	55.00	100.	225.	300.	675.	1500.	3250.	——
1872-S	24.00	35.00	60.00	90.00	190.	350.	1275.	3150.
1873 Closed 3	26.00	43.00	66.00	88.00	140.	300.	410.	1100.
1873 Open 3	2400.	3000.	4200.	5900.	7750.	11500.	25000.	57500.
1873-CC	150.	225.	325.	650.	1400.	4250.	9500.	35000.
ARROWS AT DATE								
1873	18.00	27.00	40.00	73.00	190.	350.	875.	2250.
1873-CC	110.	160.	285.	525.	1500.	2800.	5850.	13000.
1873-S	40.00	65.00	115.	190.	390.	850.	2000.	6250.
1874	18.00	27.00	40.00	70.00	190.	350.	875.	2000.
1874-CC	240.	365.	565.	1000.	1700.	3500.	7000.	24500.
1874-S	32.00	40.00	73.00	145.	290.	650.	1600.	3400.
ARROWS REMOVED								
1875	16.00	24.00	40.00	45.00	68.00	160.	335.	540.
1875-CC	19.00	38.00	60.00	80.00	170.	300.	600.	1200.
1875-S	16.00	26.00	47.00	60.00	90.00	165.	345.	650.
1876	16.00	24.00	40.00	45.00	65.00	160.	335.	550.
1876-CC	17.00	30.00	60.00	75.00	135.	285.	650.	1450.
1876-S	16.00	24.00	40.00	45.00	65.00	175.	400.	900.
1877	16.00	24.00	40.00	45.00	65.00	160.	335.	550.
1877-CC	18.00	31.00	52.00	65.00	130.	260.	600.	1225.
1877-S	16.00	24.00	40.00	45.00	65.00	170.	350.	565.
1878	20.00	36.00	50.00	60.00	90.00	235.	435.	800.
1878-CC	265.	385.	550.	1050.	2000.	3050.	5750.	17500.
1878-S	6000.	7750.	10500.	13500.	18500.	23000.	35000.	70000.
1879	210.	225.	260.	290.	380.	465.	535.	800.
1880	195.	215.	250.	285.	360.	460.	550.	750.
1881	195.	215.	245.	280.	355.	455.	555.	850.
1882	215.	245.	285.	330.	405.	490.	565.	875.
1883	200.	220.	250.	310.	395.	475.	565.	900.
1884	255.	265.	290.	330.	425.	515.	570.	925.
1885	245.	255.	280.	325.	420.	505.	725.	975.
1886	285.	350.	415.	440.	475.	575.	765.	925.
1887	360.	410.	475.	525.	600.	700.	850.	1025.
1888	195.	220.	245.	270.	390.	455.	540.	850.
1889	195.	220.	245.	280.	400.	460.	545.	825.
1890	200.	225.	250.	300.	410.	470.	560.	925.
1891	40.00	55.00	85.00	100.	140.	250.	400.	725.

—— = Insufficient pricing data

Barber half dollar

Date of authorization: April 2, 1792
Dates of issue: 1892-1915
Designer/Engraver: Charles Barber
Diameter: 30.61 mm/1.21 inches
Weight: 12.50 grams/0.40 ounce
Metallic Content: 90% silver, 10% copper
Weight of pure silver: 11.25 grams/0.36 ounce
Edge: Reeded
Mint mark: Reverse below eagle

	G-4	VG-8	F-12	VF-20	EF-40	AU-50	AU-55	MS-60	MS-62	MS-63
1892	21.00	27.00	47.00	90.00	175.	280.	305.	380.	500.	675.
1892-O	125.	165.	270.	315.	425.	450.	525.	875.	975.	1375.
1892-O Micro O	1750.	2500.	3250.	4000.	5500.	8000.	11500.	15000.	20000.	30000.
1892-S	120.	155.	225.	290.	400.	600.	675.	900.	1225.	1850.
1893	14.00	20.00	45.00	80.00	160.	320.	380.	515.	650.	1000.
1893-O	23.00	33.00	70.00	135.	275.	375.	450.	565.	625.	1000.
1893-S	77.00	93.00	165.	305.	425.	550.	725.	1175.	1550.	2550.
1894	17.00	33.00	65.00	100.	225.	350.	400.	465.	575.	850.
1894-O	13.00	19.00	60.00	100.	235.	300.	375.	535.	600.	925.
1894-S	12.00	18.00	48.00	75.00	200.	350.	425.	475.	600.	1200.
1895	8.00	15.00	50.00	85.00	175.	310.	350.	570.	650.	975.
1895-O	12.00	22.00	55.00	100.	235.	375.	460.	600.	900.	1350.
1895-S	17.00	25.00	65.00	125.	265.	400.	425.	535.	725.	1325.
1896	16.00	22.50	55.00	90.00	210.	325.	350.	550.	650.	950.
1896-O	24.00	35.00	90.00	150.	360.	665.	850.	1300.	1650.	3000.
1896-S	65.00	80.00	120.	200.	375.	575.	950.	1250.	1650.	2550.
1897	7.50	9.75	32.00	75.00	135.	310.	350.	445.	550.	780.
1897-O	53.00	82.00	345.	725.	875.	1200.	1350.	1600.	2000.	2975.
1897-S	110.	125.	275.	425.	700.	1025.	1100.	1350.	1850.	3000.
1898	7.50	8.50	28.00	72.00	140.	315.	340.	410.	550.	780.
1898-O	18.00	35.00	95.00	185.	400.	500.	575.	975.	1250.	2500.
1898-S	9.00	17.00	42.00	85.00	205.	365.	405.	850.	1150.	2300.
1899	7.50	8.50	27.00	72.00	135.	305.	335.	410.	500.	780.
1899-O	8.00	13.00	45.00	90.00	225.	355.	380.	550.	650.	1050.
1899-S	12.00	20.00	49.00	85.00	220.	350.	375.	635.	800.	1600.
1900	6.50	8.50	28.00	72.00	135.	315.	340.	410.	470.	775.

	G-4	VG-8	F-12	VF-20	EF-40	AU-50	AU-55	MS-60	MS-62	MS-63
1900-O	7.00	10.50	39.00	90.00	250.	315.	400.	800.	1250.	2900.
1900-S	8.00	11.50	40.00	95.00	195.	320.	375.	625.	850.	1900.
1901	6.50	8.00	28.00	72.00	135.	315.	340.	410.	500.	750.
1901-O	7.50	14.00	52.00	115.	290.	475.	600.	1350.	1750.	3200.
1901-S	17.00	28.00	110.	225.	550.	900.	1050.	1600.	2500.	4100.
1902	6.50	8.50	28.00	65.00	135.	265.	300.	385.	450.	675.
1902-O	7.00	11.00	38.00	80.00	195.	360.	405.	725.	1250.	2350.
1902-S	7.75	13.00	48.00	90.00	200.	375.	440.	635.	925.	1800.
1903	7.50	9.00	38.00	80.00	170.	325.	365.	460.	625.	1375.
1903-O	7.00	12.00	44.00	78.00	185.	325.	375.	700.	800.	1350.
1903-S	7.00	12.50	44.00	78.00	215.	365.	425.	600.	750.	1625.
1904	6.50	9.00	30.00	72.00	130.	300.	325.	410.	525.	1100.
1904-O	9.50	17.00	52.00	115.	310.	500.	600.	1100.	1500.	2800.
1904-S	16.00	28.00	135.	335.	675.	1000.	1250.	1950.	2500.	4250.
1905	12.00	18.00	52.00	78.00	225.	325.	400.	550.	650.	1200.
1905-O	15.00	29.00	75.00	140.	260.	425.	525.	725.	1050.	1700.
1905-S	7.25	11.50	38.00	80.00	200.	350.	410.	625.	900.	1900.
1906	6.50	8.00	28.00	70.00	130.	310.	340.	410.	470.	775.
1906-D	6.50	8.50	29.00	72.50	130.	300.	340.	410.	470.	725.
1906-O	6.50	9.00	35.00	75.00	165.	325.	375.	600.	725.	1100.
1906-S	7.00	11.00	43.00	80.00	192.	325.	375.	600.	725.	1100.
1907	6.50	7.50	27.00	80.00	192.	325.	360.	410.	500.	675.
1907-D	6.50	9.00	28.00	80.00	140.	310.	350.	425.	525.	725.
1907-O	6.50	9.00	28.00	72.50	150.	310.	325.	510.	600.	825.
1907-S	7.00	12.00	75.00	110.	325.	525.	600.	925.	1400.	3100.
1907-S/S	13.00	20.00	100.	200.	425.	600.	675.	1025.	1500.	2850.
1908	6.50	8.00	30.00	72.00	155.	310.	340.	425.	525.	675.
1908-D	6.50	9.75	30.00	72.00	145.	310.	340.	425.	535.	675.
1908-O	6.50	8.00	29.00	72.00	145.	310.	350.	500.	585.	850.
1908-S	7.00	12.00	45.00	80.00	195.	340.	400.	750.	1250.	2100.
1909	6.50	8.00	28.00	72.00	130.	265.	300.	390.	475.	625.
1909-O	9.00	12.00	42.50	87.50	265.	500.	575.	750.	1000.	1550.
1909-S	6.50	9.00	30.00	72.50	180.	340.	400.	575.	700.	1200.
1910	11.00	19.00	65.00	125.	280.	425.	475.	600.	725.	1150.
1910-S	6.50	9.00	30.00	72.50	180.	340.	400.	625.	925.	1800.
1911	6.50	9.00	30.00	65.00	135.	310.	340.	425.	525.	750.
1911-D	6.50	11.00	40.00	85.00	195.	265.	325.	550.	650.	850.
1911-S	6.50	9.00	33.00	78.00	165.	340.	385.	560.	700.	1275.
1912	6.50	8.00	28.00	65.00	145.	310.	340.	410.	500.	675.
1912-D	6.50	8.50	28.00	72.00	130.	310.	340.	435.	525.	725.
1912-S	6.50	8.50	30.00	72.00	165.	325.	375.	525.	650.	1000.
1913	21.00	28.00	105.	185.	360.	700.	775.	950.	1175.	1650.
1913-D	6.50	10.50	36.00	72.50	180.	300.	340.	455.	550.	875.
1913-S	6.50	11.50	45.00	85.00	195.	350.	400.	600.	775.	1175.
1914	28.00	45.00	165.	325.	495.	750.	825.	975.	1100.	1500.
1914-S	6.50	9.50	35.00	72.50	180.	350.	400.	560.	675.	1050.
1915	22.00	30.00	87.50	200.	375.	725.	850.	1025.	1250.	1875.
1915-D	6.50	7.50	27.00	72.00	130.	265.	310.	390.	475.	675.
1915-S	6.50	7.50	29.00	72.00	145.	265.	310.	425.	500.	675.

Walking Liberty half dollar

Date of authorization: April 2, 1792
Dates of issue: 1916-1947
Designer: Adolph Weinman
Engraver: Charles Barber
Diameter: 30.61 mm/1.21 inches
Weight: 12.50 grams/0.40 ounce
Metallic Content: 90% silver, 10% copper
Weight of pure silver: 11.25 grams/0.32 ounce
Edge: Reeded
• Mint mark: (1916): Obverse below IN GOD WE TRUST
(1917): Obverse below IN GOD WE TRUST or reverse lower left

Obverse Mint mark

Reverse Mint mark

	VG-8	F-12	VF-20	EF-40	AU-50	MS-60	MS-62	MS-63	MS-64	MS-65
1916	33.00	57.00	110.	150.	200.	270.	310.	400.	600.	1330.
1916-D	27.00	35.00	72.00	132.	175.	255.	365.	500.	675.	1625.
1916-S	87.00	145.	310.	500.	625.	925.	1150.	1550.	2250.	4275.
1917	6.00	9.75	18.00	28.00	60.00	105.	120.	150.	275.	855.
1917-D Obverse Mint Mark	19.00	39.00	85.00	130.	250.	475.	575.	900.	2000.	5500.
1917-D Reverse Mint Mark	14.00	29.00	80.00	185.	400.	700.	1100.	2000.	4250.	15000.
1917-S Obverse Mint Mark	26.00	46.00	245.	650.	1075.	1950.	2450.	4250.	5500.	14250.

	VG-8	F-12	VF-20	EF-40	AU-50	MS-60	MS-62	MS-63	MS-64	MS-65
1917-S Reverse Mint Mark	7.50	15.00	26.00	45.00	135.	300.	675.	1550.	3250.	9450.
1918	8.50	16.00	45.00	125.	215.	450.	535.	850.	950.	3000.
1918-D	9.00	21.00	55.00	145.	350.	825.	1150.	1950.	5000.	19000.
1918-S	6.75	14.00	26.00	55.00	132.	365.	725.	1850.	3750.	15750.
1919	16.00	39.00	155.	400.	600.	1050.	1550.	2650.	3500.	4600.
1919-D	15.00	45.00	165.	575.	900.	2650.	3250.	5500.	15000.	85000.
1919-S	17.00	33.00	145.	725.	1500.	2300.	2700.	5500.	7500.	10950.
1920	7.50	12.00	25.00	60.00	115.	275.	400.	600.	1325.	6100.
1920-D	10.00	29.00	125.	360.	675.	1100.	1500.	3500.	5675.	8325.
1920-S	7.00	13.00	48.00	200.	385.	675.	900.	2275.	3975.	9250.
1921	115.	180.	575.	1400.	2200.	3000.	3250.	4350.	5000.	10500.
1921-D	165.	250.	700.	2000.	2600.	3250.	4000.	5150.	6000.	12600.
1921-S	27.00	65.00	540.	4050.	6500.	8700.	10000.	18000.	25000.	52500.
1923-S	11.00	21.00	57.50	205.	575.	1150.	1650.	3150.	4675.	11400.
1927-S	7.00	11.00	29.00	85.00	285.	675.	800.	1625.	2475.	8325.
1928-S	7.00	12.00	36.00	105.	300.	675.	900.	1850.	3300.	7200.
1929-D	8.00	11.00	23.00	75.00	150.	280.	375.	650.	1100.	1975.
1929-S	6.00	9.00	19.00	77.50	175.	325.	425.	800.	1000.	2150.
1933-S	6.50	8.00	13.00	42.00	195.	500.	675.	1000.	1400.	2850.
1934	3.00	3.50	4.00	10.00	25.00	50.00	65.00	88.00	125.	350.
1934-D	4.00	5.50	8.00	25.00	60.00	125.	150.	225.	405.	850.
1934-S	3.50	4.00	5.00	25.00	87.00	240.	325.	600.	1275.	2750.
1935	3.00	3.50	4.00	7.50	22.00	44.00	50.00	60.00	90.00	285.
1935-D	3.50	4.00	8.00	22.00	55.00	120.	150.	225.	300.	1175.
1935-S	3.25	3.50	5.75	23.00	87.00	160.	205.	370.	700.	1825.
1936	3.00	3.30	4.00	6.50	22.00	36.00	39.00	46.00	55.00	140.
1936-D	3.00	3.50	5.50	16.00	45.00	72.00	85.00	105.	125.	310.
1936-S	3.00	3.50	5.65	20.00	55.00	120.	135.	180.	225.	355.
1937	3.00	3.30	4.00	7.00	22.00	37.00	42.00	50.00	65.00	165.
1937-D	5.50	8.00	12.00	27.00	80.00	145.	160.	185.	225.	350.
1937-S	5.00	6.00	8.00	17.00	60.00	120.	140.	165.	225.	400.
1938	3.00	4.00	6.00	9.75	40.00	65.00	80.00	105.	120.	230.
1938-D	24.00	25.00	40.00	100.	250.	400.	435.	500.	575.	800.
1939	3.00	3.30	4.50	7.50	22.00	40.00	42.00	48.00	65.00	120.
1939-D	3.00	3.50	5.00	9.00	23.00	38.00	40.00	48.00	65.00	115.
1939-S	5.50	6.50	8.00	12.50	50.00	100.	110.	120.	135.	160.
1940	3.00	3.30	4.00	6.00	12.00	28.00	32.00	40.00	48.00	100.
1940-S	3.00	3.30	5.00	8.00	17.50	30.00	34.00	40.00	72.00	340.
1941	3.00	3.30	3.75	5.75	8.75	26.50	30.00	40.00	48.00	100.
1941-D	3.00	3.30	4.00	6.00	15.00	36.00	38.00	44.00	64.00	115.
1941-S	3.00	3.30	4.50	7.00	27.00	72.00	80.00	95.00	175.	1225.
1942	3.00	3.30	3.75	5.75	8.75	26.50	30.00	40.00	45.00	85.00
1942-D	3.00	3.30	4.00	6.00	17.00	36.00	42.00	60.00	90.00	190.
1942-D/S	——	——	67.50	80.00	200.	475.	550.	950.	1900.	3325.
1942-S	3.00	3.30	4.50	7.00	16.00	35.00	38.00	48.00	75.00	425.
1943	3.00	3.30	3.75	5.75	8.75	26.50	30.00	40.00	45.00	85.00

—— = Insufficient pricing data

	VG-8	F-12	VF-20	EF-40	AU-50	MS-60	MS-62	MS-63	MS-64	MS-65
1943-D	3.00	3.30	4.00	6.00	19.00	40.00	48.00	65.00	76.00	130.
1943-S	3.00	3.30	4.25	6.00	18.00	33.00	35.00	42.00	68.00	350.
1944	3.00	3.30	3.75	5.75	8.75	27.50	32.50	40.00	45.00	95.00
1944-D	3.00	3.30	4.00	6.00	16.00	31.00	35.00	46.00	60.00	105.
1944-S	3.00	3.30	4.00	6.00	16.00	31.00	33.00	42.50	65.00	400.
1945	3.00	3.30	3.75	5.75	8.75	26.50	30.00	40.00	45.00	86.00
1945-D	3.00	3.30	4.00	6.00	15.00	29.00	34.00	40.00	45.00	90.00
1945-S	3.00	3.30	4.00	6.00	15.00	30.00	34.00	40.00	45.00	135.
1946	3.00	3.30	4.00	6.00	11.00	26.50	30.00	40.00	45.00	120.
1946-D	4.25	5.75	9.00	10.00	19.00	30.00	32.50	40.00	45.00	85.00
1946-S	3.00	3.30	3.75	6.00	17.00	28.00	32.00	42.00	45.00	110.
1947	3.00	3.30	4.25	8.00	18.00	30.00	32.50	42.50	50.00	135.
1947-D	3.00	3.30	4.25	8.00	20.00	32.00	35.00	40.00	45.00	95.00

Franklin half dollar

Date of authorization: April 2, 1792
Dates of issue: 1948-1963
Designer: John Sinnock
Engraver: Gilroy Roberts
Diameter: 30.61 mm/1.21 inches
Weight: 12.50 grams/0.40 ounce
Metallic Content: 90% silver, 10% copper
Weight of pure silver: 11.25 grams/0.36 ounce
Edge: Reeded
Mint mark: Reverse above bell beam

NOTE: MS-65F refers to Full Bell Lines

	F-12	VF-20	EF-40	AU-50	MS-60	MS-63	MS-64	MS-65	MS-65F	PF-65
1948	3.50	3.75	4.25	5.50	14.00	20.00	25.00	65.00	185.	*
1948-D	3.50	3.75	4.75	5.50	10.00	14.00	25.00	160.	275.	*
1949	3.50	4.00	5.25	11.00	30.00	38.50	44.00	120.	235.	*
1949-D	3.25	4.00	7.00	15.00	30.00	45.00	90.00	925.	1800.	*
1949-S	4.00	5.75	11.00	25.00	45.00	53.00	60.00	145.	700.	*
1950	2.60	3.25	4.00	7.00	21.00	27.00	40.00	125.	275.	280.
1950-D	2.60	3.20	3.75	8.50	18.00	30.00	45.00	550.	950.	*

* = None issued

	F-12	VF-20	EF-40	AU-50	MS-60	MS-63	MS-64	MS-65	MS-65F	PF-65
1951	2.60	2.75	3.25	4.25	12.00	14.50	20.00	75.00	240.	180.
1951-D	2.85	3.00	4.25	12.50	18.00	27.00	42.00	275.	475.	*
1951-S	3.00	3.25	4.50	11.00	19.00	28.00	34.00	110.	500.	*
1952	2.60	2.75	3.00	4.75	7.00	14.00	35.00	85.00	250.	88.00
1952-D	2.60	2.75	2.90	4.50	7.00	10.00	27.00	225.	450.	*
1952-S	2.60	3.75	4.75	19.00	30.00	33.00	38.00	105.	1150.	*
1953	3.25	3.50	4.75	10.00	14.00	18.00	36.00	250.	900.	55.00
1953-D	2.60	2.75	2.90	4.50	6.00	10.00	21.00	160.	350.	*
1953-S	3.00	3.25	3.75	9.00	12.00	14.00	24.00	70.00	7250.	*
1954	2.60	2.75	2.90	3.50	5.00	10.00	21.00	85.00	175.	35.00
1954-D	2.60	2.75	2.90	3.50	5.00	10.00	21.00	145.	190.	*
1954-S	2.60	3.50	3.75	5.00	5.75	8.50	20.00	60.00	450.	*
1955	4.50	5.25	5.50	6.50	7.00	8.50	18.00	50.00	125.	21.00
1956	2.50	3.40	4.00	4.75	4.50	9.50	18.00	40.00	85.00	18.50
1957	2.50	2.90	3.15	3.50	5.00	9.50	15.00	40.00	100.	14.00
1957-D	2.50	2.75	2.85	3.25	4.50	8.50	17.00	40.00	125.	*
1958	2.50	3.00	3.25	3.50	4.75	8.50	15.00	45.00	95.00	14.00
1958-D	2.50	2.75	2.85	3.00	3.50	8.00	15.00	40.00	75.00	*
1959	2.50	2.75	2.85	3.00	3.75	7.00	15.00	125.	300.	9.00
1959-D	2.50	2.75	2.85	3.00	4.00	8.00	18.00	140.	250.	*
1960	2.50	2.75	2.85	3.00	3.50	6.50	14.00	160.	430.	9.00
1960-D	2.50	2.75	2.85	3.00	4.00	6.50	35.00	850.	1500.	*
1961	2.50	2.75	2.85	3.00	3.50	6.50	25.00	240.	1100.	9.00
1961-D	2.50	2.75	2.85	3.00	4.00	7.50	30.00	480.	850.	*
1962	2.50	2.75	2.85	3.00	3.50	7.50	18.00	320.	1500.	9.00
1962-D	2.50	2.75	2.85	3.00	3.50	7.50	26.00	400.	975.	*
1963	2.50	2.75	2.85	3.00	3.25	7.50	14.00	85.00	650.	9.00
1963-D	2.50	2.75	2.85	3.00	3.25	7.50	14.00	80.00	215.	*

* = None issued

Kennedy half dollar

Date of authorization: Dec. 30, 1963; July 23, 1965; Oct. 18, 1973
Dates of issue: 1964-present
Designer: Obverse: Gilroy Roberts
Reverse: Frank Gasparro
Bicentennial Obverse: Seth G. Huntington

Engraver: Gilroy Roberts
Bicentennial Obverse: Frank Gasparro
Diameter: 30.61 mm/1.21 inches
Weight: (1964, 1992-present silver Proof only): 12.50 grams/0.40 ounce
(1965-1970): 11.50 grams/0.37 ounce
(1971-present): 11.34 grams/0.36 ounce
(1976 Bicentennial Proof and Uncirculated): 11.50 grams/0.37 ounce
Metallic Content: (1964, 1992-present silver Proofs only): 90% silver, 10% copper
(1965-1970): 80% silver, 20% copper bonded to a core of 21.5% silver, 78.5% copper
(1971-present): 75% copper, 25% nickel bonded to pure copper core
(1976 Becentennial Proof and Uncirculated sets only): 80% silver, 20% copper bonded to a core of 21.5% silver, 78.5% copper
Weight of pure silver: (1964, 1992-present silver Proofs only) 11.25 grams/0.36 ounce
(1965-1970): 4.60 grams/0.15 ounce
(1976 Bicentennial Proof and Uncirculated sets only): 4.60 grams/0.15 ounce
Edge: Reeded
Mint mark: (1964): Reverse left near claw and laurel
(1968-present): Obverse below Kennedy

Bicentennial date, reverse

	MS-60	MS-63	MS-65	PF-63	PF-65
90 PERCENT SILVER					
1964	3.00	3.50	9.00	5.00	7.00
1964-D	3.00	3.50	12.00	*	*
40 PERCENT SILVER CLAD					
1965	1.20	1.25	9.50	*	*
1966	1.25	1.40	11.00	*	*
1967	1.25	1.50	9.50	*	*
1968-D	1.25	1.50	9.00	*	*
1968-S	*	*	*	2.25	3.00
1969-D	1.20	1.25	7.50	*	*
1969-S	*	*	*	2.25	2.50
1970-D	9.50	10.50	32.00	*	*
1970-S	*	*	*	5.50	8.00
COPPER-NICKEL CLAD					
1971	0.95	1.50	12.00	*	*
1971-D	0.95	1.25	5.00	*	*
1971-S	*	*	*	1.25	2.00
1972	1.00	1.50	9.00	*	*
1972-D	1.00	1.50	6.00	*	*
1972-S	*	*	*	1.00	1.50
1973	1.00	1.50	6.00	*	*
1973-D	0.95	1.25	5.50	*	*
1973-S	*	*	*	1.00	1.25
1974	0.90	1.00	4.75	*	*
1974-D	0.90	1.00	6.00	*	*
1974-S	*	*	*	0.90	1.10
DUAL DATE, BICENTENNIAL REVERSE					
1776-1976	0.90	1.00	10.00	*	*
1776-1976-D	0.90	1.00	4.75	*	*
1776-1976-S	*	*	*	0.80	1.00
1776-1976-S 40% silver	2.75	3.50	6.50	3.00	4.00
PRESIDENTIAL SEAL/EAGLE REVERSE RESUMED					
1977	1.10	1.40	6.75	*	*
1977-D	1.10	1.40	6.00	*	*
1977-S	*	*	*	0.90	1.35
1978	1.05	1.40	6.50	*	*
1978-D	1.00	1.25	6.50	*	*
1978-S	*	*	*	0.90	1.00
1979	0.95	1.00	5.50	*	*
1979-D	0.95	1.15	6.00	*	*
1979-S Filled S	*	*	*	0.75	1.00
1979-S Filled S	*	*	*	4.50	6.00
1980-P	0.90	1.00	5.00	*	*
1980-D	0.90	0.95	4.75	*	*
1980-S	*	*	*	1.00	1.50
1981-P	1.00	1.40	5.00	*	*
1981-D	0.95	1.40	4.50	*	*
1981-S Filled S	*	*	*	1.00	1.50
1982-P	1.10	1.65	5.00	*	*
1982-P No FG	7.00	10.00	——		*
1982-D	1.25	1.65	5.00	*	*
1982-S	*	*	*	0.90	1.10
1983-P	1.05	1.35	——	*	*
1983-D	1.05	1.35	5.00	*	*

—— = Insufficient pricing data * = None issued

	MS-60	MS-63	MS-65	PF-63	PF-65
1983-S	*	*	*	1.50	2.50
1984-P	1.25	1.45	5.00	*	*
1984-D	1.25	1.45	——	*	*
1984-S	*	*	*	2.50	4.00
1985-P	1.25	1.50	5.00	*	*
1985-D	1.25	1.50	5.00	*	*
1985-S	*	*	*	1.65	2.20
1986-P	2.75	3.00	9.00	*	*
1986-D	3.25	3.35	7.00	*	*
1986-S	*	*	*	8.00	12.00
1987-P	2.15	3.00	9.00	*	*
1987-D	2.15	3.00	9.00	*	*
1987-S	*	*	*	1.75	2.25
1988-P	0.90	1.00	9.00	*	*
1988-D	1.00	1.35	6.00	*	*
1988-S	*	*	*	2.50	3.50
1989-P	1.00	1.25	9.00	*	*
1989-D	0.90	1.10	9.50	*	*
1989-S	*	*	*	2.00	3.75
1990-P	0.90	1.10	15.00	*	*
1990-D	0.90	1.10	——	*	*
1990-S	*	*	*	5.00	8.00
1991-P	0.90	1.10	7.00	*	*
1991-D	0.90	1.10	11.00	*	*
1991-S	*	*	*	7.00	12.50
1992-P	0.90	1.10	6.00	*	*
1992-D	0.90	1.10	6.00	*	*
1992-S Clad	*	*	*	6.00	13.50
1992-S silver	*	*	*	5.50	13.00
1993-P	0.90	1.10	10.00	*	*
1993-D	0.90	1.10	9.00	*	*
1993-S Clad	*	*	*	5.50	13.00
1993-S silver	*	*	*	7.00	18.50
1994-P	0.90	1.10	6.00	*	*
1994-D	0.90	1.10	6.00	*	*
1994-S Clad	*	*	*	4.75	10.00
1994-S silver	*	*	*	5.75	14.50
1995-P	0.90	1.10	8.00	*	*
1995-D	0.90	1.10	6.00	*	*
1995-S Clad	*	*	*	4.75	11.00
1995-S silver	*	*	*	5.00	11.50
1996-P	0.90	1.10	9.00	*	*
1996-D	0.90	1.10	6.00	*	*
1996-S Clad	*	*	*	4.75	10.00
1996-S silver	*	*	*	5.25	11.50
1997-P	0.90	1.10	9.00	*	*
1997-D	0.90	1.10	6.00	*	*
1997-S Clad	*	*	*	5.00	10.00
1997-S silver	*	*	*	5.25	11.00
1998-P	0.90	1.10	9.00	*	*
1998-D	0.90	1.10	6.00	*	*
1998-S Clad	*	*	*	5.00	9.00
1998-S silver	*	*	*	10.00	15.00
1999-P	——	——	——	*	*
1999-D	——	——	——	*	*
1999-S Clad	——	——	——	——	——
1999-S silver	*	*	*	——	——

—— = Insufficient pricing data * = None issued

Flowing Hair dollar

Date of authorization: April 2, 1792
Dates of issue: 1794-1795
Designer/Engraver: Robert Scot
Diameter: 39.50 mm/1.56 inches
Weight: 26.96 grams/0.87 ounce
Metallic Content: 90% silver, 10% copper
Weight of pure silver: 24.26 grams/0.78 ounce
Edge: Lettered (HUNDRED CENTS ONE DOLLAR OR UNIT)
Mint mark: None

	AG-3	G-4	VG-8	F-12	VF-20	EF-40	EF-45	AU-50
1794	4500.	8250.	15500.	24000.	45000.	77500.	80000.	105000.
1795 2 leaves, Head of 1794	450.	775.	1000.	1475.	2150.	4450.	5600.	7500.
1795 3 leaves, Head of 1795	425.	725.	950.	1350.	1875.	4350.	5200.	7000.

Draped Bust dollar

Small Eagle

Heraldic Eagle

Date of authorization:	April 2, 1792
Dates of issue:	1795-1803
Designers:	Obverse: Gilbert Stuart-Robert Scot Reverse: (1795-1798): Scot-John Eckstein (1798-1803): Robert Scot
Engraver:	Robert Scot
Diameter:	39.50 mm/1.56 inches
Weight:	26.96 grams/0.87 ounce
Metallic Content:	89.25% silver, 10.75% copper
Weight of pure silver:	24.06 grams/0.77 ounce
Edge:	Lettered (HUNDRED CENTS ONE DOLLAR OR UNIT)
Mint mark:	None

	AG-3	G-4	VG-8	F-12	VF-20	EF-40	EF-45	AU-50
SMALL EAGLE								
1795	375.	600.	750.	1050.	1550.	3300.	4750.	6900.
1796 Small Date, Small Letters	425.	675.	825.	1150.	1600.	3400.	4750.	7300.
1796 Large Date, Small Letters	400.	625.	775.	1075.	1575.	3350.	4650.	6950.
1796 Small Date, Large Letters	375.	590.	750.	1000.	1500.	3300.	4600.	6900.
1797 Stars 9x7, Small Letters	700.	1150.	1650.	2350.	3250.	7500.	12500.	21000.
1797 Stars 9x7, Large Letters	275.	525.	700.	975.	1450.	3250.	4300.	6350.
1797 Stars 10x6	275.	525.	700.	975.	1450.	3200.	4750.	6500.
1798 13 Stars	400.	750.	900.	1200.	2000.	4000.	6250.	11000.
1798 15 Stars	550.	900.	1250.	1800.	2350.	4500.	7000.	13500.
HERALDIC EAGLE								
1798	185.	425.	475.	575.	775.	1275.	1625.	3375.
1799	185.	425.	475.	575.	775.	1325.	1600.	3200.
1799/8	185.	450.	500.	600.	785.	1425.	1725.	3650.
1799 Stars 8x5	185.	475.	525.	650.	900.	1600.	1875.	3750.
1800	185.	425.	475.	575.	780.	1300.	1625.	3350.
1800 AMERICAI	185.	450.	500.	575.	785.	1325.	1675.	3350.
1800 Dotted Date	185.	450.	500.	575.	800.	1350.	1800.	3600.
1801	200.	475.	525.	575.	800.	1800.	2250.	3700.
1802/1	185.	425.	475.	575.	785.	1600.	2100.	3750.
1801 Proof restrike, die crack links base of digits to first two stars.								
1802	170.	450.	500.	600.	780.	1325.	1625.	3200.
1802 Proof restrike with old-style 180, 1820s style 2 in date Prf 65 $175000.								
1803 Large 3	175.	425.	475.	575.	780.	1350.	1675.	3550.
1803 Small 3	175.	450.	500.	600.	785.	1400.	1700.	3600.
1803 Proof restrike with old-style digits Prf 65 $135000.								
1804 Three varieties struck in 1834-5 and 1858 Class I EF-40 $525,000; Proof 64 $650,000; Eliasberg now Proof 65 (PCGS) sold for $1.815 million.								

Gobrecht dollar

Date of authorization: April 2, 1792; Jan. 18, 1837
Dates of issue: 1836-1839
Designers: Obverse: Thomas Sully
Reverse: Titian Peale

Engraver: Christian Gobrecht
Diameter: 39.50 mm/1.56 inches
Weight: (1836): 26.96 grams/0.87 ounce
(1836, 1839, standard of 1837): 26.73 grams/0.86 ounce
Metallic Content: (1836): 89.25% silver, 10.75% copper
(1836, 1839, standard of 1837): 90% silver, 10% copper
Weight of pure silver: (1836): 24.06 grams/0.77 ounce
(1836, 1839, standard of 1837): 24.06 grams/0.77 ounce
Edge: (1836, standard of 1836): Plain
(1836, standard of 1837): Plain
(1839): Reeded
Mint mark: None

Note:
The series called the Gobrecht dollar contains patterns, coins struck for circulation and restrikes produced especially for collectors. Only three versions were issued for circulation, as listed above. The pattern and circulation pieces can be distinguished from the restrikes by a simple test. Orient the obverse normally, then rotate the coin as usual. If the eagle is flying level, the coin is a restrike; if the eagle is flying upward (as shown), it is an original pattern or circulation strike.

	VF-20	EF-40	EF-45	AU-50	AU-55	PF-60	PF-62	PF-63	PF-64	PF-65
1836 pattern, Die I (Proofs only)	——	——	——	13500.	15500.	19500.	25000.	47500.	68500.	135000.
1836 circulation, 416 grains, Die I	3600.	4500.	5750.	6350.	6850.	7500.	12000.	15000.	20000.	50000.
1836 circulation, 412.5 grains, Die II	4250.	5400.	6500.	7250.	8000.	9000.	13500.	18500.	30000.	65000.
1836 restrike, Name on Base, Coin turn, Eagle flying level, Die III						7750.	——	——	40000.	——
1836 restrike, Name on Base, Medal turn, Eagle flying level, Die IV						6500.	12000.	14750.	18500.	——
1838 pattern, original, Die I	4750.	5750.	7500.	8750.	10000.	13500.	19500.	28500.	67500.	125000.
1838 restrike, Reeded Edge	——	6500.	6750.	7750.	8500.	10000.	15500.	21000.	60000.	——
1839 Medal turn, Eagle flying level	——	——	——	——	——	9500.	14500.	20000.	39500.	——

—— = Insufficient pricing data

Seated Liberty dollar

Date of authorization: Jan. 18, 1837
Dates of issue: 1840-1873
Designers: Obverse: Robert Hughes-Christian Gobrecht-Thomas Sully
Reverse: John Reich-Christian Gobrecht
Engraver: Christian Gobrecht
Diameter: 38.10 mm/1.5 inches
Weight: 26.73 grams/0.86 ounce
Metallic Content: 90% silver, 10% copper
Weight of pure silver: 24.06 grams/0.77 ounce
Edge: Reeded
Mint mark: Reverse below eagle

	G-4	VG-8	F-12	VF-20	EF-40	AU-50	AU-55	MS-60	MS-63
1840	160.	200.	225.	275.	425.	750.	1075.	2400.	8250.
1841	100.	135.	170.	215.	300.	550.	675.	1725.	4500.
1842	100.	120.	170.	210.	290.	550.	600.	1000.	3000.
1843	100.	120.	170.	210.	290.	550.	750.	1950.	5300.
1844	135.	240.	290.	345.	475.	750.	1375.	3100.	8000.
1845	175.	215.	260.	300.	450.	785.	1500.	12000.	35000.
1846	100.	120.	170.	225.	320.	550.	625.	1450.	4500.
1846-O	135.	195.	255.	290.	475.	1125.	1800.	5000.	26500.
1847	100.	120.	170.	200.	290.	550.	625.	1400.	3250.
1848	275.	305.	425.	550.	700.	1175.	1775.	4650.	10500.
1849	120.	170.	200.	250.	375.	525.	850.	2100.	5250.
1850	325.	450.	575.	750.	1100.	2025.	2600.	5500.	16500.
1850-O	175.	250.	300.	585.	1300.	2975.	5750.	13000.	27500.
1851 Original MS-60 $22,000; MS-63 $40,000; MS-65 $90,000; Restrike Prf-62 $21,500; Prf-63 $25,000; Prf-64 $35,000									
1852 AU-55 $12,000; MS-60 $17,000; MS-63 $32,500; MS-65 $70,000; Restrike Prf-55 $20,500; Prf-63 $32,500									
1853	140.	200.	275.	350.	510.	750.	1275.	2450.	6500.
1854	725.	950.	1250.	1800.	3550.	4500.	5300.	6150.	8900.
1855	625.	825.	1025.	1575.	2950.	3700.	4950.	8000.	27500.

	G-4	VG-8	F-12	VF-20	EF-40	AU-50	AU-55	MS-60	MS-63
1856	250.	325.	400.	700.	1275.	1700.	2350.	3950.	7050.
1857	245.	320.	385.	600.	1150.	1450.	1650.	2300.	5350.
1858 Proofs only	*	*	2900.	3500.	4250.	5000.	5250.	5500.	8000.
1859	225.	260.	325.	375.	525.	1175.	1750.	3150.	5000.
1859-O	100.	120.	170.	210.	290.	525.	600.	925.	2450.
1859-S	240.	315.	385.	535.	1075.	3400.	4650.	8000.	47500.
1860	165.	225.	285.	375.	435.	540.	725.	1400.	3200.
1860-O	100.	120.	170.	210.	290.	525.	600.	900.	2400.
1861	500.	635.	725.	825.	1250.	1800.	2300.	2850.	5350.
1862	475.	625.	675.	775.	1000.	1700.	2250.	3100.	5500.
1863	200.	260.	350.	480.	750.	1300.	1650.	2550.	4500.
1864	190.	235.	325.	470.	625.	1400.	1750.	2800.	6000.
1865	175.	225.	300.	385.	565.	1100.	1600.	2650.	5500.
1866	——	——	——	——	*	*	*	*	*
MOTTO ABOVE EAGLE									
1866	155.	200.	265.	300.	475.	900.	1200.	1750.	3900.
1867	160.	210.	280.	340.	510.	950.	1350.	2150.	4850.
1868	150.	185.	240.	335.	475.	925.	1250.	2000.	5050.
1869	120.	155.	220.	280.	355.	850.	1150.	1550.	3600.
1870	100.	135.	170.	210.	325.	525.	675.	1225.	4750.
1870-CC	260.	350.	445.	675.	1450.	2750.	4250.	10000.	29500.
1870-S	——	——	60000.	82500.	125000.	200000.	——	300000.	600000.
1871	95.00	120.	170.	210.	285.	500.	625.	1150.	2500.
1871-CC	1650.	2450.	3650.	4500.	7500.	17500.	24000.	47500.	125000.
1872	95.00	120.	170.	210.	285.	525.	635.	1175.	2600.
1872-CC	750.	1200.	2050.	2750.	4400.	8500.	13500.	30000.	62500.
1872-S	225.	290.	380.	585.	1200.	2700.	4750.	9750.	28500.
1873	115.	155.	225.	240.	300.	575.	750.	1200.	2700.
1873-CC	3250.	4650.	6750.	9250.	18000.	33500.	45000.	75000.	——
1873-S Unknown in any collection									

—— = Insufficient pricing data * = None issued

Trade dollar

Date of authorization: Feb. 12, 1873
Dates of issue: 1973-1878
Designer/Engraver: William Barber
Diameter: 38.10 mm/1.5 inches
Weight: 27.22 grams/0.88 ounce
Metallic Content: 90% silver, 10% copper
Weight of pure silver: 24.49 grams/0.79 ounce
Edge: Reeded
Mint mark: Reverse below eagle

	F-12	VF-20	EF-40	AU-50	MS-60	MS-63	MS-64	MS-65	PF-63	PF-65
1873	100.	135.	185.	225.	600.	1600.	3850.	8750.	2100.	8250.
1873-CC	150.	300.	525.	1050.	2000.	——	——	——	*	*
1873-S	105.	140.	190.	315.	750.	2100.	3900.	13000.	*	*
1874	105.	135.	170.	225.	650.	1800.	3750.	12500.	2075.	8000.
1874-CC	100.	160.	225.	375.	1150.	5250.	8750.	17500.	*	*
1874-S	90.00	115.	135.	225.	400.	1400.	4250.	15000.	*	*
1875	300.	350.	565.	700.	1250.	2750.	4500.	13000.	2075.	7750.
1875-CC	110.	135.	200.	325.	750.	2650.	7000.	——	*	*
1875-S	100.	115.	135.	225.	380.	1175.	2750.	7750.	*	*
1875-S/CC	275.	385.	600.	1150.	2200.	10000.	19500.	——	*	*
1876	90.00	115.	135.	225.	390.	1250.	2900.	7750.	2100.	7350.
1876-CC	100.	155.	250.	500.	2500.	19000.	35000.	——	*	*
1876-S	90.00	115.	135.	225.	400.	1200.	3100.	9000.	*	*
1877	90.00	115.	135.	250.	425.	1300.	3750.	12500.	2100.	7350.
1877-CC	200.	240.	340.	600.	1200.	7000.	15000.	——	*	*
1877-S	90.00	115.	135.	225.	395.	1200.	2900.	8500.	*	*
1878	*	875.	1000.	1150.	*	*	*	*	2100.	7750.
1878-CC	600.	875.	1975.	3050.	6750.	15750.	27500.	——	*	*
1878-S	90.00	115.	135.	225.	415.	1400.	2900.	7750.	*	*
1879	*	800.	1000.	1100.	*	*	*	*	2000.	7250.
1880	*	750.	975.	1050.	*	*	*	*	2000.	7250.
1881	*	875.	1025.	1100.	*	*	*	*	2000.	7250.

—— = Insufficient pricing data   * = None issued

	F-12	VF-20	EF-40	AU-50	MS-60	MS-63	MS-64	MS-65	PF-63	PF-65
1882	*	875.	1050.	1125.	*	*	*	*	2000.	7250.
1883	*	*	*	*	*	*	*	*	2000.	7250.
1884	*	*	*	*	*	*	*	*	110000.	400000.
1885	*	*	*	*	*	*	*	*	——	900000.

Morgan dollar

Date of authorization: Feb.28, 1878
Dates of issue: 1878-1921
Designer/Engraver: George T. Morgan
Diameter: 38.10 mm/1.5 inches
Weight: 26.73 grams/0.86 ounce
Metallic Content: 90% silver, 10% copper
Weight of pure silver: 24.06 grams/0.77 ounce
Edge: Reeded
Mint mark: Reverse below eagle

Note: MS-64D, MS-65D refer to Deep Mirror Prooflike

	F-12	VF-20	EF-40	AU-50	MS-60	MS-63	MS-64	MS-64D	MS-65	MS-65D
1878 8 Tail Feathers	17.00	20.00	24.00	33.00	65.00	135.	250.	1100.	1425.	5400.
1878 7 Tail Feathers, Reverse of 1878	14.00	16.00	18.00	20.00	34.00	70.00	185.	350.	1375.	5500.
1878 7 Tail Feathers, Reverse of 1879	14.00	16.00	18.00	23.00	45.00	125.	300.	2650.	2550.	7250.
1878 Strongly Doubled Tailfeathers	16.00	21.00	28.00	45.00	95.00	150.	305.	1400.	2475.	——
1878-CC	40.00	45.00	50.00	70.00	110.	140.	225.	515.	1200.	3300.
1878-S	13.00	14.00	16.00	20.00	30.00	45.00	60.00	290.	240.	2150.
1879	12.00	13.00	14.00	16.00	25.00	50.00	100.	1000.	925.	6000.
1879-CC	68.00	120.	340.	750.	1400.	3250.	4950.	6500.	17250.	——

—— = Insufficient pricing data   * = None issued

	F-12	VF-20	EF-40	AU-50	MS-60	MS-63	MS-64	MS-64D	MS-65	MS-65D
1879-CC Large CC/Small CC	68.00	120.	280.	600.	1275.	2800.	4800.	11000.	——	——
1879-O	11.50	13.50	15.00	20.00	65.00	125.	350.	2350.	3050.	14000.
1879-S Reverse of 1878	15.00	16.00	18.00	35.00	90.00	350.	1275.	7000.	6500.	16000.
1879-S	12.00	13.00	15.00	17.00	21.00	33.00	55.00	125.	110.	400.
1880	11.00	11.50	14.00	16.00	20.00	50.00	85.00	750.	825.	3375.
1880/79-CC Reverse of 1878	60.00	72.00	95.00	135.	190.	300.	575.	1800.	2250.	12500.
1880-CC	60.00	72.00	95.00	125.	180.	240.	285.	525.	825.	2750.
1880-O	11.00	11.25	14.00	18.00	55.00	275.	1550.	4250.	15250.	50000.
1880-S	11.50	12.50	14.00	16.00	20.00	30.00	50.00	85.00	110.	400.
1881	11.00	11.25	14.00	16.00	20.00	40.00	85.00	1100.	825.	10000.
1881-CC	115.	125.	135.	145.	170.	210.	275.	425.	600.	1275.
1881-O	11.00	11.25	14.00	16.00	19.00	35.00	135.	850.	1750.	——
1881-S	11.50	12.00	14.00	16.00	19.00	30.00	50.00	100.	110.	400.
1882	11.00	11.25	14.00	16.00	19.00	35.00	55.00	500.	460.	3850.
1882-CC	36.00	42.00	52.00	55.00	75.00	95.00	110.	150.	400.	650.
1882-O	11.00	11.25	14.00	16.00	19.00	35.00	60.00	400.	750.	4500.
1882-O/S	17.00	19.00	23.00	50.00	150.	975.	2800.	——	——	——
1882-S	11.00	13.00	15.00	17.00	20.00	31.00	52.00	300.	110.	1150.
1883	11.00	12.00	14.00	16.00	19.00	34.00	55.00	250.	150.	675.
1883-CC	36.00	42.00	46.00	50.00	75.00	90.00	110.	155.	300.	550.
1883-O	11.00	11.25	14.00	16.00	19.00	31.00	50.00	160.	125.	650.
1883-S	12.50	14.00	23.00	100.	375.	1425.	4750.	——	23750.	——
1884	11.00	11.50	14.00	16.00	19.00	33.00	65.00	650.	235.	1900.
1884-CC	42.50	48.00	52.50	55.00	80.00	90.00	110.	145.	315.	625.
1884-O	11.00	11.25	14.00	16.00	19.00	31.00	50.00	100.	110.	525.
1884-S	13.00	16.00	34.00	195.	3200.	26000.	——	——	——	——
1885	11.00	11.25	14.00	16.00	19.00	31.00	50.00	120.	140.	500.
1885-CC	165.	175.	185.	200.	235.	250.	300.	400.	775.	1050.
1885-O	11.00	12.00	14.00	16.00	19.00	31.00	50.00	100.	115.	450.
1885-S	13.50	15.00	19.00	50.00	100.	190.	350.	5500.	2200.	——
1886	11.00	12.00	14.00	16.00	19.00	31.00	50.00	110.	110.	525.
1886-O	11.50	13.00	16.00	65.00	325.	2750.	10500.	40000.	——	——
1886-S	20.00	33.00	45.00	65.00	135.	265.	550.	2750.	3075.	——
1887/6	21.00	25.00	42.00	90.00	175.	800.	1100.	5750.	4250.	16500.
1887	11.00	11.25	14.00	16.00	19.00	30.00	50.00	100.	125.	500.
1887/6-O	22.00	27.00	48.00	120.	310.	2575.	14500.	——	27500.	——
1887-O	11.00	12.00	14.00	21.00	34.00	100.	275.	1350.	4950.	8500.
1887-S	14.50	16.00	18.00	32.00	67.50	155.	450.	2650.	3500.	——
1888	11.00	12.00	14.00	16.00	19.00	30.00	55.00	325.	185.	1600.
1888-O	11.00	12.00	14.00	16.00	19.00	35.00	60.00	400.	575.	1400.
1888-O Hot Lips, VAM-4	40.00	50.00	115.	525.	——	——	——		——	

—— = Insufficient pricing data * = None issued

MORGAN DOLLAR (CONTINUED)

	F-12	VF-20	EF-40	AU-50	MS-60	MS-63	MS-64	MS-64D	MS-65	MS-65D
1888-S	25.00	30.00	36.00	63.00	130.	250.	575.	1075.	4000.	9000.
1889	11.00	12.00	14.00	16.00	19.00	32.00	55.00	500.	360.	2500.
1889-CC	285.	440.	1025.	2550.	6850.	15000.	28000.	60000.	——	250000.
1889-O	11.00	12.00	14.00	29.00	80.00	225.	575.	1750.	5250.	12500.
1889-S	22.00	25.00	31.00	50.00	115.	195.	300.	2050.	1650.	6750.
1890	11.50	12.00	14.00	16.00	19.00	37.00	160.	975.	3550.	9500.
1890-CC	36.00	40.00	55.00	90.00	240.	400.	725.	1200.	7500.	7500.
1890-O	11.00	11.25	14.00	21.00	30.00	75.00	200.	825.	2100.	6500.
1890-S	12.50	13.50	14.00	21.00	37.00	85.00	175.	925.	1000.	7000.
1891	11.00	12.00	14.00	21.00	40.00	125.	650.	2800.	6900.	——
1891-CC	36.00	40.00	55.00	85.00	175.	315.	600.	2350.	3100.	——
1891-O	11.00	12.00	14.50	32.00	80.00	260.	625.	4000.	6500.	20000.
1891-S	12.00	13.00	14.00	21.00	38.00	95.00	235.	1250.	1550.	5750.
1892	12.50	14.50	21.00	60.00	120.	275.	625.	1925.	3850.	13500.
1892-CC	55.00	75.00	110.	210.	400.	650.	1350.	3500.	7500.	12000.
1892-O	12.00	13.00	17.00	48.00	85.00	215.	550.	5500.	6250.	——
1892-S	18.00	42.00	185.	1300.	12750.	40000.	50000.	100000.	80000.	135000.
1893	72.00	85.00	125.	195.	350.	775.	1275.	——	6500.	——
1893-CC	105.	185.	450.	750.	1350.	4250.	8250.	17500.	45000.	70000.
1893-O	95.00	125.	225.	485.	1600.	6250.	12000.	32500.	——	——
1893-S	1250.	2100.	4550.	14750.	30000.	75000.	130000.	——	260000.	——
1894	300.	325.	365.	575.	1125.	3175.	5250.	——	18750.	——
1894-O	23.00	38.00	50.00	150.	625.	3750.	6750.	——	45000.	——
1894-S	30.00	48.00	105.	210.	400.	675.	1525.	4500.	5400.	——
1895 Proof only										
	——	13500.	14500.	16000.	17000.	23000.	25000.	*	33000.	*
1895-O	115.	170.	250.	965.	9600.	33500.	62500.	——	200000.	——
1895-S	160.	215.	480.	700.	1450.	3550.	5750.	7500.	19500.	45000.
1896	11.00	11.25	14.00	16.00	19.00	35.00	55.00	145.	150.	660.
1896-O	14.00	15.00	19.50	110.	850.	7250.	30000.	——	——	——
1896-S	22.00	44.00	175.	385.	750.	1500.	2850.	11500.	8250.	20000.
1897	11.00	12.00	14.00	16.00	21.00	32.00	55.00	265.	285.	2750.
1897-O	13.00	14.00	21.00	95.00	625.	4500.	14500.	20500.	43500.	52500.
1897-S	12.00	13.00	15.00	21.00	37.00	80.00	120.	265.	575.	1750.
1898	12.00	13.00	15.00	18.00	20.00	32.00	55.00	190.	225.	1150.
1898-O	13.00	14.00	16.00	18.00	21.00	34.00	55.00	140.	110.	475.
1898-S	13.00	15.00	24.00	60.00	135.	245.	450.	1500.	2100.	——
1899	30.00	35.00	43.00	60.00	70.00	105.	170.	350.	600.	1925.
1899-O	11.00	12.50	14.00	16.00	21.00	31.00	55.00	250.	135.	700.
1899-S	15.00	18.00	30.00	65.00	140.	225.	425.	1300.	1900.	7000.
1900	12.00	11.25	14.00	16.00	19.00	35.00	55.00	3000.	165.	9000.
1900-O	12.50	12.00	14.00	16.00	21.00	35.00	55.00	560.	135.	2725.
1900-O/CC	25.00	35.00	47.50	95.00	180.	325.	500.	6250.	1550.	——
1900-S	14.00	19.00	29.00	48.00	100.	165.	325.	3300.	1450.	8000.
1901	18.00	30.00	59.00	250.	1875.	14500.	50000.	——	——	——

—— = Insufficient pricing data * = None issued

	F-12	VF-20	EF-40	AU-50	MS-60	MS-63	MS-64	MS-64D	MS-65	MS-65D
1901 Shifted Eagle, VAM-3	75.00	140.	250.	525.	——	——	——		——	
1901-O	11.00	11.25	14.00	16.00	20.00	32.00	50.00	775.	175.	3300.
1901-S	16.00	27.50	47.50	125.	275.	450.	725.	3850.	4000.	——
1902	11.00	12.00	14.00	21.00	37.50	75.00	125.	2350.	495.	16000.
1902-O	11.00	12.00	15.00	17.50	19.00	31.00	50.00	425.	150.	3700.
1902-S	35.00	60.00	85.00	115.	160.	250.	500.	——	3100.	——
1903	15.00	16.00	18.00	20.00	29.00	50.00	65.00	1850.	185.	8000.
1903-O	115.	120.	130.	150.	165.	200.	250.	765.	450.	4500.
1903-S	26.00	65.00	285.	900.	2450.	4250.	5000.	——	7150.	——
1904	12.50	13.00	15.00	32.00	67.50	150.	475.	——	3950.	——
1904-O	12.00	12.50	14.00	16.00	19.00	30.00	50.00	125.	110.	535.
1904-S	20.00	40.00	185.	500.	900.	1925.	2825.	6250.	6875.	——
1921	10.00	11.00	12.00	12.50	14.00	20.00	25.00	1600.	125.	8000.
1921-D	10.00	11.00	12.00	12.50	27.00	35.00	60.00	4500.	260.	——
1921-S	10.25	11.25	12.00	12.50	22.50	45.00	135.	7000.	1700.	——

Peace Dollar

Date of authorization: Feb.28, 1878
Dates of issue: 1921-1935
Designer: Anthony deFrancisci
Engraver: George T. Morgan
Diameter: 38.10 mm/1.5 inches
Weight: 26.73 grams/0.86 ounce
Metallic Content: 90% silver, 10% copper
Weight of pure silver: 24.06grams/0.77 ounce
Edge: Reeded
Mint mark: Reverse at lower tip of eagle's wing

	F-12	VF-20	EF-40	AU-50	MS-60	MS-63	MS-64	MS-65	MS-66
1921	35.00	42.50	50.00	92.50	130.	225.	575.	2750.	6750.

—— = Insufficient pricing data

	F-12	VF-20	EF-40	AU-50	MS-60	MS-63	MS-64	MS-65	MS-66
1922	9.50	10.50	11.25	11.50	12.00	22.00	45.00	160.	525.
1922-D	9.50	10.50	11.25	12.00	17.50	32.50	60.00	435.	2100.
1922-S	9.50	10.50	11.25	12.00	18.50	65.00	265.	2175.	5750.
1923	9.50	10.50	11.25	11.50	12.00	22.00	50.00	140.	500.
1923-D	9.50	10.50	11.25	12.00	28.50	82.50	200.	1275.	6750.
1923-S	9.50	10.50	11.25	12.00	19.00	65.00	225.	6000.	9500.
1924	9.50	10.50	11.25	12.00	12.00	25.00	60.00	145.	575.
1924-S	9.50	12.00	18.00	45.00	145.	400.	1050.	6500.	17500.
1925	9.50	10.50	11.25	12.00	13.00	25.00	50.00	150.	500.
1925-S	9.50	10.50	11.50	25.00	48.00	125.	575.	——	20000.
1926	9.50	10.50	11.50	17.00	22.00	35.00	75.00	370.	2300.
1926-D	9.50	10.50	12.50	27.50	48.00	110.	225.	600.	2200.
1926-S	9.50	10.50	11.25	16.50	30.00	50.00	165.	875.	3850.
1927	15.00	20.00	25.00	35.00	48.00	100.	250.	2650.	12500.
1927-D	14.00	17.00	25.00	65.00	120.	215.	600.	4400.	12500.
1927-S	14.00	18.00	22.00	55.00	95.00	275.	675.	7250.	12500.
1928	120.	135.	150.	170.	180.	290.	625.	2850.	6500.
1928-S	15.00	17.00	20.00	37.00	90.00	360.	1600.	18500.	26000.
1934	14.00	16.00	20.00	32.50	62.50	125.	275.	1100.	3750.
1934-D	14.00	15.00	18.00	32.50	75.00	185.	550.	1800.	4750.
1934-S	15.00	50.00	130.	425.	1000.	2150.	3600.	6250.	10250.
1935	12.50	13.00	16.00	24.00	42.00	70.00	150.	640.	2300.
1935-S	12.50	14.00	19.00	65.00	120.	250.	375.	975.	2900.

—— = Insufficient pricing data

Eisenhower dollar

Date of authorization: Dec. 31, 1970
Dates of issue: 1971-1978
Designers: Frank Gasparro
(Becentennial Reverse): Dennis R. Williams
Engraver: Frank Gasparro

Diameter: 38.10 mm/1.5 inches
Weight: (1971-1978): 22.68 grams/0.73 ounce
(1971-1976 Bicentennial Proof and Uncirculated sets only): 24.59 grams/0.79 ounce
Metallic Content: (1971-1978): 75% copper, 25% nickel bonded to a core of pure copper
(1971-1976 Becentennial Proof and Uncirculated sets only): 80% silver, 20% copper, bonded to a core of 21.5% silver, 78.5% copper
Weight of pure silver: (1971-1976 Bicentennial Proof and Uncirculated sets only): 9.84 grams/0.32 ounce
Edge: Reeded
Mint mark: Obverse above date

Bicentennial date, reverse

	MS-60	MS-63	MS-65	PF-63	PF-65
1971	2.75	3.00	95.00	*	*
1971-D	2.25	2.50	21.00	*	*
1971-S 40% silver	3.50	4.00	12.00	3.00	4.00
1972	2.25	2.50	150.	*	*
1972-D	2.25	2.75	45.00	*	*
1972-S 40% silver	3.50	4.00	9.00	3.25	4.00
1973	3.50	4.00	50.00	*	*
1973-D	3.50	4.00	42.00	*	*
1973-S copper-nickel clad	*	*	*	3.50	4.00
1973-S 40% silver	3.75	4.00	9.00	10.00	11.50
1974	2.00	2.50	60.00	*	*
1974-D	2.00	2.50	25.00	*	*
1974-S copper-nickel clad	*	*	*	3.50	4.00
1974-S 40% silver	3.50	3.75	8.00	4.25	4.75

* = None issued

DUAL DATE, BICENTENNIAL REVERSE

1776-1976 Bold Reverse Letters	3.00	3.50	150.	*	*
1776-1976 Thin Reverse Letters	2.25	2.50	35.00	*	*
1776-1976-D Bold Reverse Letters	2.50	2.75	55.00	*	*
1776-1976-D Thin Reverse Letters	2.25	2.50	15.00	*	*
1776-1976-S Bold Reverse Letters, copper-nickel clad	*	*	*	3.50	5.50
1776-1976-S Thin Reverse Letters, copper-nickel clad	*	*	*	3.50	4.25
1776-1976-S 40% silver	7.00	7.50	15.00	6.50	8.00

MOON LANDING REVERSE RESUMED

1977	2.25	2.50	35.00	*	*
1977-D	2.25	2.50	25.00	*	*
1977-S copper-nickel clad	*	*	*	3.25	3.75
1978	2.25	2.50	35.00	*	*
1978-D	2.25	2.50	25.00	*	*
1978-S copper-nickel clad	*	*	*	3.25	4.00

Anthony dollar

Date of authorization: Oct. 10, 1978
Dates of issue: 1979-1981, 1999
Designer/Engraver: Frank Gasparro
Diameter: 26.50 mm/1.05 inches
Weight: 8.10 grams/0.26 ounce
Metallic Content: 75% copper, 25% nickel bonded to a core of pure copper
Edge: Reeded
Mint mark: Obverse left of bust

	MS-60	MS-63	MS-65	PF-63	PF-65
1979-P Near Date	3.50	7.00	25.00	*	*
1979-P	1.15	1.75	9.00	*	*
1979-D	1.15	1.75	9.00	*	*
1979-S Filled S	1.20	1.75	6.00	3.00	3.75
1979-S Clear S	*	*	*	48.00	60.00
1980-P	1.15	1.75	9.00	*	*
1980-D	1.15	1.75	9.00	*	*
1980-S	1.20	1.75	6.00	4.00	5.00
1981-P	3.00	4.00	75.00	*	*
1981-D	2.50	2.75	30.00	*	*
1981-S Filled S	2.65	3.00	225.	4.00	5.00
1981-S Clear S	*	*	*	55.00	75.00
1999-P	——	——	——	*	*

—— = Insufficient pricing data   * = None issued

Coronet gold dollar

Enlarged to show detail

Date of authorization:	Jan. 18, 1837
Dates of issue:	1849-1954
Designer/Engraver:	James B. Longacre
Diameter:	13.00mm/0.51inch
Weight:	1.67 grams/0.05
Metallic Content:	90% gold, 10% copper and silver
Weight of pure gold:	1.50 grams/0.05 ounce
Edge:	Reeded
Mint mark:	Reverse below wreath

	F-12	VF-20	EF-40	AU-50	AU-55	MS-60	MS-62	MS-63	MS-64	MS-65
1849 Open Wreath, L, Small Head	120.	130.	155.	205.	235.	375.	775.	1700.	3200.	7750.
1849 Open Wreath, No L, Small Head	130.	150.	215.	285.	340.	750.	1325.	1900.	3750.	7900.
1849 Open Wreath, Large Head	120.	130.	155.	200.	230.	375.	510.	1450.	2775.	6500.
1849 Closed Wreath	120.	130.	150.	180.	220.	375.	510.	1450.	3000.	7250.
1849-C Closed Wreath	275.	525.	1100.	2750.	4000.	8400.	13250.	25000.	—	—
1849-C Open Wreath	135000.	225000.	—	—	—	—	—	—	—	—
1849-D	265.	500.	900.	1650.	2650.	4500.	6750.	11500.	20500.	41500.
1849-O	130.	165.	210.	325.	525.	1050.	1900.	3250.	6500.	18000.
1850	125.	145.	150.	175.	220.	375.	535.	1525.	4250.	8250.
1850-C	375.	650.	1300.	2500.	5500.	10000.	14500.	—	—	—
1850-D	345.	615.	1275.	2750.	5675.	10250.	17500.	27500.	—	—
1850-O	245.	290.	400.	800.	1450.	3750.	4250.	6500.	14500.	27500.
1851	120.	135.	150.	165.	210.	330.	460.	1250.	2750.	6000.
1851-C	275.	490.	775.	975.	1500.	2300.	3150.	5500.	15500.	30000.
1851-D	280.	505.	950.	2100.	3000.	5350.	8250.	11000.	20000.	41000.
1851-O	130.	160.	225.	265.	325.	675.	825.	2700.	5850.	16500.
1852	120.	130.	155.	165.	210.	330.	475.	1250.	2200.	6050.
1852-C	270.	500.	1050.	1950.	2250.	5000.	7000.	12650.	22500.	41000.
1852-D	340.	575.	1350.	2400.	3950.	9000.	20000.	—	—	—
1852-O	125.	170.	235.	430.	950.	1500.	2400.	4400.	11500.	26500.

—— = Insufficient pricing data

CORONET GOLD DOLLAR (CONTINUED)

	F-12	VF-20	EF-40	AU-50	AU-55	MS-60	MS-62	MS-63	MS-64	MS-65
1853	120.	130.	150.	165.	210.	265.	390.	1125.	2175.	5950.
1853-C	245.	535.	1100.	1900.	3000.	6000.	8800.	14500.	28000.	——
1853-D	340.	625.	1400.	2700.	5000.	10000.	22500.	35000.	——	——
1853-O	130.	160.	190.	275.	415.	700.	1275.	2950.	6500.	14000.
1854	120.	130.	150.	165.	210.	330.	475.	1250.	2200.	7000.
1854-D	550.	900.	2100.	4650.	9000.	15500.	——	——	——	——
1854-S	275.	350.	490.	650.	1100.	2300.	3350.	6750.	16500.	28000.

Indian Head gold dollar

Date of authorization: Jan. 18, 1837
Dates of issue: 1854-1889
Designer/Engraver: James B. Longacre
Diameter: 14.86mm/0.59inch
Weight: 1.67 grams/0.05 ounce
Metallic Content: 90% gold, 10% copper and silver
Weight of pure gold: 1.50 grams/0.95 ounce
Edge: Reeded
Mint mark: Reverse below wreath

Small Head

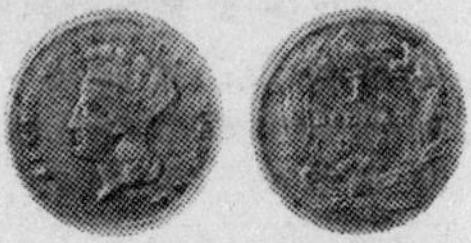

Large Head

	F-12	VF-20	EF-40	AU-50	AU-55	MS-60	MS-62	MS-63	MS-64	MS-65
SMALL HEAD										
1854	225.	325.	400.	675.	1100.	2650.	7000.	16750.	27500.	60000.
1855	225.	325.	405.	625.	1100.	2650.	7000.	18000.	27500.	60000.
1855-C	685.	1300.	2950.	6000.	12500.	20500.	——	——	——	——
1855-D	1400.	2400.	5750.	12500.	19500.	30000.	——	——	——	——
1855-O	300.	385.	675.	1075.	1750.	5400.	12500.	25000.	40000.	——
1856-S	350.	675.	1050.	1750.	2900.	6500.	15000.	——	——	——
LARGE HEAD										
1856 Upright 5	130.	140.	175.	300.	350.	650.	800.	1200.	1800.	4750.
1856 Slant 5	125.	130.	150.	185.	195.	265.	395.	1250.	1550.	3300.
1856-D	2450.	3750.	5000.	7150.	10750.	34000.	——	——	——	——
1857	115.	130.	145.	180.	195.	260.	475.	1100.	1550.	3150.
1857-C	300.	525.	1350.	3950.	6350.	12250.	——	——	——	——
1857-D	385.	900.	1800.	4400.	6500.	13250.	——	——	——	——
1857-S	300.	450.	575.	1100.	1850.	5500.	8750.	22000.	——	——
1858	115.	130.	160.	185.	205.	270.	550.	1050.	1500.	3650.
1858-D	515.	700.	1375.	3000.	4650.	10000.	21500.	30000.	47500.	82500.

—— = Insufficient pricing data

INDIAN HEAD GOLD DOLLAR (CONTINUED)

	F-12	VF-20	EF-40	AU-50	AU-55	MS-60	MS-62	MS-63	MS-64	MS-65
1858-S	275.	340.	450.	1150.	1600.	5250.	8850.	——	——	——
1859	125.	140.	155.	180.	210.	270.	515.	1075.	1650.	3800.
1859-C	305.	450.	1800.	4000.	8500.	17250.	26500.	37500.	60000.	125000.
1859-D	600.	700.	1400.	2700.	5150.	11500.	18500.	33500.	——	——
1859-S	200.	250.	450.	1350.	2100.	5850.	9750.	19000.	——	——
1860	135.	145.	165.	180.	235.	435.	585.	1125.	2025.	4050.
1860-D	1650.	2400.	3850.	6400.	10750.	27500.	——	——	——	——
1860-S	255.	300.	450.	625.	950.	2350.	3750.	7250.	14750.	27500.
1861	115.	130.	145.	160.	210.	255.	535.	1025.	1525.	3500.
1861-D	4250.	5750.	8500.	17500.	22500.	32000.	42500.	65000.	——	——
1862	115.	130.	145.	160.	205.	250.	450.	985.	1425.	2850.
1863	325.	425.	1000.	2150.	2750.	4000.	5000.	8000.	12000.	18000.
1864	260.	315.	335.	525.	675.	1050.	1600.	2350.	3650.	7600.
1865	275.	375.	425.	575.	775.	1550.	2400.	3300.	4500.	8750.
1866	260.	315.	375.	415.	550.	800.	1100.	2000.	2525.	5500.
1867	290.	380.	400.	575.	675.	875.	1075.	2050.	2625.	6000.
1868	245.	250.	300.	390.	545.	775.	1000.	1950.	2425.	5950.
1869	285.	325.	370.	525.	650.	775.	1200.	2300.	3050.	6250.
1870	220.	240.	285.	375.	435.	575.	975.	1775.	2225.	4500.
1870-S	270.	400.	675.	1100.	1450.	2750.	4250.	7750.	14500.	32500.
1871	220.	240.	280.	355.	425.	550.	950.	1750.	2175.	4050.
1872	225.	250.	325.	390.	475.	900.	1625.	2500.	3600.	5750.
1873 Closed 3	300.	375.	700.	1000.	1250.	1750.	2750.	5250.	10000.	22500.
1873 Open 3	115.	130.	140.	160.	185.	255.	535.	1050.	1375.	2350.
1874	115.	130.	140.	160.	185.	250.	450.	975.	1300.	2350.
1875	1700.	2200.	3450.	4100.	4750.	5250.	6500.	8250.	13000.	28000.
1876	185.	230.	275.	375.	455.	535.	710.	1150.	2025.	4100.
1877	140.	180.	250.	360.	440.	550.	660.	1050.	1925.	4250.
1878	175.	190.	270.	350.	455.	590.	625.	1125.	1975.	3600.
1879	140.	170.	215.	275.	300.	485.	645.	1075.	1500.	3250.
1880	130.	140.	170.	190.	205.	350.	485.	1100.	1425.	2350.
1881	130.	140.	170.	190.	205.	350.	485.	1025.	1325.	2650.
1882	140.	145.	180.	205.	220.	350.	485.	1050.	1350.	2350.
1883	130.	140.	170.	190.	205.	350.	485.	1025.	1325.	2350.
1884	130.	140.	170.	190.	205.	350.	485.	1025.	1350.	2350.
1885	130.	140.	170.	190.	205.	350.	485.	1025.	1325.	2350.
1886	130.	140.	170.	200.	210.	365.	485.	1050.	2025.	2850.
1887	130.	140.	170.	190.	200.	350.	475.	1000.	1325.	2350.
1888	130.	140.	170.	190.	200.	350.	475.	975.	1325.	2200.
1889	130.	140.	170.	190.	200.	325.	475.	975.	1300.	2100.

—— = Insufficient pricing data

Capped Bust $2.50 quarter eagle

No Stars obverse

With Stars obverse

Date of authorization: April 2, 1792
Dates of issue: 1796-1807
Designer/Engraver: Robert Scot
Diameter: 20.00mm/0.79 inch
Weight: 4.37 grams/0.14 ounce
Metallic Content: 91.67% gold, 8.33% copper and silver
Weight of pure gold: 4.01 grams/0.13 ounce
Edge: Reeded
Mint mark: None

	F-12	VF-20	EF-40	EF-45	AU-50	AU-55	AU-58	MS-60	MS-62	MS-63
1796 No Stars	10500.	19250.	38000.	45000.	57500.	75000.	120000.	150000.	180000.	——
1796 Stars	8750.	13500.	21000.	40000.	45000.	60000.	——	115000.	——	275000.
1797	8250.	10750.	13000.	16000.	30000.	47500.	——	125000.	——	——
1798	3400.	4250.	7500.	13500.	22500.	35000.	38000.	43500.	60000.	100000.
1802/1	2950.	3900.	5200.	6250.	7200.	13000.	15000.	19500.	30000.	55000.
1804 13 Stars	20000.	27500.	60000.	80000.	125000.	165000.	——	——	——	——
1804 14 Stars	3250.	4150.	5250.	6750.	8750.	14750.	17500.	25000.	37500.	——
1805	2950.	4200.	5450.	6500.	7500.	12000.	13500.	23500.	——	——
1806/4	3150.	4100.	5500.	——	7250.	11500.	13500.	22500.	——	——
1806/5	7000.	14000.	——	30000.	37500.	52500.	——	——	175000.	——
1807	2750.	3900.	5050.	6150.	7100.	11250.	12500.	19500.	29500.	52500.

—— = Insufficient pricing data

Capped Draped Bust $2.50 quarter eagle

Date of authorization: April 2, 1792
Dates of issue: 1808
Designer/Engraver: John Reich
Diameter: 20.00mm/0.79 inch
Weight: 4.37 grams/0.14 ounce
Metallic Content: 91.67% gold, 8.33% copper and silver
Weight of pure gold: 4.01 grams/0.13 ounce
Edge: Reeded
Mint mark: None

	F-12	VF-20	EF-40	EF-45	AU-50	AU-55	AU-58	MS-60	MS-62	MS-63
1808	8250.	14000.	20000.	25000.	32500.	40000.	52500.	65000.	——	——

—— = Insufficient pricing data

Capped Head $2.50 quarter eagle

Date of authorization: April 2, 1792
Dates of issue: 1821-1834
Designers: Obverse: John Reich-Robert Scot
Reverse: John Reich
Engravers: Obverse: Robert Scot
Reverse: John Reich
Diameter: (1821-1827): 18.50mm/0.73 inch
(1829-1834): 18.20mm/0.72 inch
Weight: 4.37 grams/0.14 ounce
Metallic Content: 91.67% gold, 8.33% copper and silver
Weight of pure gold: 4.01 grams/0.13 ounce
Edge: Reeded
Mint mark: None

	F-12	VF-20	EF-40	EF-45	AU-50	AU-55	AU-58	MS-60	MS-62	MS-63
1821	3000.	3425.	4650.	5400.	6750.	13500.	15000.	18750.	26500.	42500.
1824/1	2950.	3400.	4550.	4850.	6000.	9250.	10250.	16000.	20500.	31000.
1825	2900.	3450.	4450.	4800.	5500.	6700.	7500.	14500.	19000.	30000.
1826	3650.	4500.	5500.	6500.	11000.	19500.	25000.	37500.	—	—
1827	3750.	4450.	5150.	6000.	7500.	12000.	13500.	17500.	25000.	35000.
REDUCED DIAMETER										
1829	2700.	3250.	4325.	4700.	5300.	6450.	7500.	9500.	12250.	20500.
1830	2800.	3350.	4350.	4650.	5350.	6425.	7000.	9500.	12000.	19500.
1831	2850.	3375.	4400.	4700.	5400.	6500.	7500.	9750.	12500.	21000.
1832	2800.	3350.	4350.	4650.	5375.	6550.	9000.	12000.	15000.	25000.
1833	3050.	3500.	4500.	5050.	5600.	6650.	9250.	13000.	17000.	29000.
1834	6750.	10000.	16500.	21000.	26000.	—	—	35000.	—	—

—— = Insufficient pricing data

Classic Head $2.50 quarter eagle

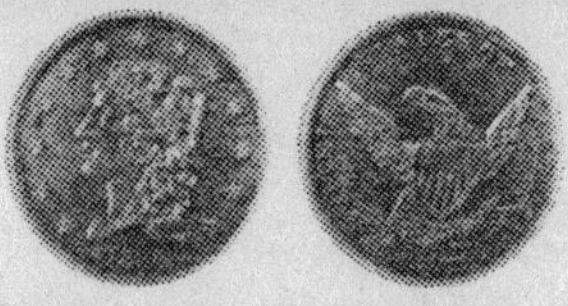

Date of authorization: June 28, 1834, Jan. 18, 1837
Dates of issue: 1834-1839
Designers: Obverse: William Kneass
Reverse: John Reich-William Kneass
Engraver: William Kneass
Diameter: 18.20mm/0.72 inch
Weight: 4.18 grams/0.13 ounce
Metallic Content: (1834-1836): 89.92% gold, 10.08% copper and silver
(1837-1839): 90% gold, 10% copper and silver
Weight of pure gold: (1834-1836): 3.758 grams/0.12 ounce
(1837-1839): 3.762 grams/0.12 ounce
Edge: Reeded
Mint mark: 1838-1839 only, obverse above

	F-12	VF-20	EF-40	EF-45	AU-50	AU-55	MS-60	MS-62	MS-63
1834 No Motto	225.	260.	400.	525.	625.	875.	1750.	2950.	5600.
1835	225.	260.	415.	550.	650.	925.	2200.	4250.	8750.
1836	225.	260.	400.	525.	600.	875.	1950.	3100.	5850.
1837	225.	260.	415.	575.	725.	1100.	2750.	4400.	10000.
1838	225.	260.	400.	550.	700.	1000.	2150.	3850.	6750.
1838-C	575.	1150.	2500.	3400.	7000.	13500.	27500.	35000.	57500.
1839/8	235.	270.	650.	850.	1750.	3100.	6000.	——	——
1839/8-C	475.	900.	1900.	2400.	4000.	9750.	22500.	36500.	50000.
1839/8-D	550.	1150.	2600.	3850.	5500.	10250.	24000.	35000.	47500.
1839-O	350.	450.	875.	1100.	1500.	2600.	5250.	11500.	22000.

—— = Insufficient pricing data

Coronet $2.50 quarter eagle

Date of authorization: Jan. 18, 1837
Dates of issue: 1840-1907
Designers: Obverse: Christian Gobrecht
Reverse: Christian Gobrecht-John Reich-William Kneass
Engraver: Christian Gobrecht
Diameter: 18.20mm/0.72 inch
Weight: 4.18 grams/0.13 ounce
Metallic Content: 90% gold, 10% copper
Weight of pure gold: 3.76 grams/0.12 ounce
Edge: Reeded
Mint mark: Reverse below eagle

	F-12	VF-20	EF-40	EF-45	AU-50	AU-55	MS-60	MS-62	MS-63
1840	160.	290.	775.	1500.	3850.	4500.	7000.	—	—
1840-C	355.	675.	1300.	2100.	5000.	10350.	16500.	34500.	—
1840-D	800.	2050.	8500.	12650.	17500.	27500.	—	—	—
1840-O	190.	330.	725.	1150.	1900.	3000.	8750.	17000.	—
1841	—	—	65000.	—	125000.	—	—	—	—
1841-C	325.	650.	1200.	1800.	3250.	8500.	21000.	52500.	—
1841-D	625.	1200.	3200.	5500.	10750.	16000.	25500.	47500.	—
1842	330.	800.	3100.	3800.	7000.	15000.	—	—	—
1842-C	575.	1150.	2350.	4100.	9750.	13750.	24000.	—	—
1842-D	700.	1400.	2800.	7400.	14250.	21000.	—	—	—
1842-O	250.	525.	1500.	1750.	2950.	6000.	16000.	—	—
1843	145.	160.	230.	265.	400.	700.	1800.	2750.	3650.
1843-C Large Date	500.	625.	1075.	1550.	3750.	5750.	8750.	—	—
1843-C Small Date	1075.	2000.	4500.	5500.	8750.	15000.	23500.	—	—
1843-D	415.	575.	1100.	1400.	2500.	4350.	9500.	22500.	—
1843-O Large Date	225.	325.	500.	1000.	2300.	4600.	9000.	—	28500.
1843-O Small Date	155.	190.	265.	325.	425.	750.	1825.	2750.	6000.
1844	275.	490.	900.	1225.	2250.	3950.	—	—	—
1844-C	400.	875.	1550.	2600.	6500.	14000.	22750.	—	—
1844-D	365.	600.	1175.	1350.	2100.	3600.	9500.	19250.	33500.
1845	150.	220.	290.	330.	475.	750.	1700.	2600.	4150.
1845-D	400.	700.	1200.	1650.	2900.	6250.	14000.	—	—
1845-O	550.	1150.	2375.	3050.	5750.	8500.	15000.	—	—
1846	215.	365.	525.	600.	1150.	2100.	6250.	—	—
1846-C	575.	950.	2350.	4150.	9250.	15500.	23000.	35000.	52500.
1846-D	445.	675.	1025.	1500.	2850.	6000.	11000.	—	—

— = Insufficient pricing data

	F-12	VF-20	EF-40	EF-45	AU-50	AU-55	MS-60	MS-62	MS-63
1846-O	160.	280.	480.	575.	1050.	1950.	5850.	17500.	——
1847	140.	235.	420.	525.	975.	1750.	5500.	6500.	11000.
1847-C	420.	590.	1075.	1475.	1950.	3400.	7500.	15250.	24250.
1847-D	430.	715.	1100.	1475.	2075.	4950.	11750.	18500.	——
1847-O	150.	275.	445.	590.	1050.	2200.	4650.	11500.	——
1848	300.	525.	950.	1200.	1650.	2750.	6250.	9000.	——
1848 CAL.	7000.	9000.	15000.	17000.	19000.	24500.	32500.	39000.	57500.
1848-C	400.	625.	1300.	1850.	3350.	7500.	17500.	35000.	——
1848-D	425.	600.	1150.	1700.	2650.	4250.	10250.	22500.	——
1849	145.	255.	450.	565.	1000.	1750.	3100.	4950.	——
1849-C	410.	700.	1550.	2950.	4750.	13500.	23000.	——	——
1849-D	430.	775.	1275.	1850.	3750.	6750.	17500.	35000.	——
1850	135.	160.	195.	225.	305.	600.	1250.	2200.	3350.
1850-C	375.	775.	1400.	2250.	3500.	7500.	21500.	60000.	——
1850-D	375.	700.	1300.	1850.	3600.	7000.	15000.	——	——
1850-O	160.	250.	350.	475.	1500.	2500.	5000.	7500.	14000.
1851	135.	150.	180.	190.	215.	265.	370.	775.	1850.
1851-C	350.	700.	1250.	1850.	3950.	7500.	17000.	38000.	——
1851-D	400.	800.	1400.	1950.	3450.	6950.	13500.	——	——
1851-O	145.	165.	325.	425.	975.	2900.	5050.	9500.	13750.
1852	135.	160.	190.	200.	240.	275.	375.	750.	1850.
1852-C	400.	700.	1450.	2400.	4200.	9250.	——	——	——
1852-D	485.	1050.	2800.	3750.	7750.	11250.	22000.	57500.	——
1852-O	145.	185.	300.	400.	1050.	1550.	5250.	——	15000.
1853	135.	150.	170.	180.	205.	255.	365.	775.	1800.
1853-D	625.	1400.	2500.	3000.	5250.	9500.	19500.	57500.	——
1854	135.	150.	170.	180.	205.	255.	380.	900.	2100.
1854-C	400.	825.	1800.	2950.	4250.	7750.	20250.	37500.	——
1854-D	1900.	2850.	7000.	8000.	14750.	19500.	36500.	70000.	——
1854-O	150.	200.	250.	285.	425.	735.	1650.	2650.	——
1854-S	——	——	——	——	——	——	——	——	——
1855	135.	150.	180.	190.	215.	265.	385.	850.	2450.
1855-C	620.	1350.	3250.	4250.	6000.	16750.	35000.	——	——
1855-D	1900.	3900.	7750.	10500.	21000.	38500.	——	——	——
1856	125.	150.	180.	190.	205.	250.	355.	800.	2250.
1856-C	490.	900.	2200.	2900.	4750.	10250.	19000.	27500.	——
1856-D	3950.	5500.	10100.	12650.	19500.	35000.	55000.	——	——
1856-O	175.	350.	675.	875.	1350.	3600.	7500.	——	——
1856-S	150.	205.	415.	650.	1275.	2000.	5850.	7250.	12500.
1857	135.	150.	185.	195.	205.	255.	360.	900.	2500.
1857-D	500.	1000.	2000.	2600.	3300.	7500.	17500.	27500.	——
1857-O	155.	180.	350.	525.	1175.	2150.	5400.	7950.	16000.
1857-S	150.	180.	375.	500.	950.	1900.	8250.	——	——
1858	135.	155.	220.	260.	350.	575.	1400.	2400.	3250.
1858-C	340.	600.	1250.	1750.	2950.	4300.	9750.	25250.	——
1859 Reverse of 1858	185.	225.	400.	475.	875.	1250.	3700.	6250.	12500.
1859 Reverse of 1859-1907	135.	155.	270.	350.	500.	565.	1250.	2300.	3400.

—— = Insufficient pricing data

	F-12	VF-20	EF-40	EF-45	AU-50	AU-55	MS-60	MS-62	MS-63
1859-D	550.	1250.	2350.	2600.	4200.	8750.	25500.	——	——
1859-S	225.	500.	825.	1200.	2700.	3675.	9500.	——	16500.
1860 Reverse of 1858	1750.	2100.	2650.	3250.	4350.	5500.	10500.	——	——
1860 Small Letters & Arrowhead, Reverse of 1859-1907	135.	155.	255.	345.	475.	525.	1100.	1850.	3050.
1860-C	375.	850.	1750.	2250.	3700.	9750.	26500.	——	60000.
1860-S	195.	300.	700.	875.	1225.	2150.	4200.	7500.	15000.
1861 Reverse of 1858	600.	1000.	1450.	1650.	2250.	2750.	5000.	8000.	12750.
1861 Reverse of 1859-1907	135.	150.	185.	195.	205.	240.	345.	625.	975.
1861-S	210.	425.	950.	1900.	3750.	5750.	——	——	——
1862	140.	170.	255.	350.	500.	600.	1500.	2550.	3450.
1862/1	600.	1000.	2200.	2750.	3500.	4500.	12000.	——	——
1862-S	485.	950.	2000.	2850.	4250.	8500.	19500.	——	——
1863 Proofs Only Prf 60 $17000 Prf 63(PCGS) $30800 Prf 64 $47500.									
1863-S	400.	650.	1700.	2900.	4450.	9500.	19000.	——	——
1864	2750.	5500.	14000.	21000.	27500.	——	——	——	——
1865	2200.	4250.	8500.	13500.	22000.	——	——	——	——
1865-S	180.	285.	625.	1250.	1600.	2350.	5750.	——	——
1866	650.	1350.	3500.	4400.	7000.	9750.	16500.	——	——
1866-S	195.	325.	950.	1350.	1950.	3600.	9750.	——	25500.
1867	200.	385.	575.	825.	1400.	1800.	3600.	4850.	8750.
1867-S	190.	270.	600.	850.	1650.	2250.	4950.	——	——
1868	160.	205.	345.	425.	615.	925.	2800.	——	10000.
1868-S	160.	190.	475.	650.	1100.	1850.	5750.	7500.	13500.
1869	165.	210.	375.	515.	700.	1400.	3500.	6400.	10500.
1869-S	175.	235.	450.	575.	1350.	1850.	5500.	——	14000.
1870	155.	195.	350.	475.	650.	1150.	3250.	5250.	10250.
1870-S	160.	200.	425.	500.	1000.	1650.	5150.	9500.	——
1871	160.	200.	300.	390.	500.	1000.	2250.	2700.	4250.
1871-S	155.	175.	340.	400.	510.	925.	2350.	2850.	4650.
1872	250.	425.	650.	800.	1250.	2600.	6000.	——	——
1872-S	165.	225.	490.	550.	1225.	1750.	5000.	7250.	12000.
1873 Closed 3	140.	165.	175.	200.	250.	350.	625.	1150.	2200.
1873 Open 3	135.	150.	165.	175.	190.	240.	345.	675.	1000.
1873-S	170.	220.	475.	525.	1200.	1550.	2600.	4250.	9000.
1874	180.	230.	365.	405.	725.	1150.	2650.	4200.	7850.
1875	2500.	3500.	4650.	5500.	7500.	9650.	19000.	——	——
1875-S	145.	190.	350.	425.	675.	1075.	4050.	5900.	11750.
1876	170.	320.	535.	625.	1100.	1950.	3550.	4250.	10500.
1876-S	145.	215.	525.	600.	1075.	2025.	3900.	5100.	11500.
1877	305.	385.	540.	625.	875.	1275.	2750.	3650.	7750.
1877-S	140.	155.	165.	175.	220.	280.	750.	1850.	2600.
1878	135.	150.	155.	165.	180.	210.	325.	550.	950.
1878-S	135.	150.	160.	170.	200.	235.	385.	900.	2400.
1879	135.	150.	155.	165.	185.	220.	345.	550.	1475.
1879-S	140.	170.	225.	375.	850.	1200.	2200.	2700.	5800.
1880	155.	225.	290.	350.	475.	675.	1300.	1800.	3500.

—— = Insufficient pricing data

	F-12	VF-20	EF-40	EF-45	AU-50	AU-55	MS-60	MS-62	MS-63
1881	725.	1650.	2450.	2900.	4450.	5600.	10500.	22500.	——
1882	180.	220.	255.	280.	390.	425.	725.	1500.	2750.
1883	180.	245.	475.	550.	800.	1100.	1900.	3250.	6250.
1884	180.	230.	385.	410.	525.	725.	1700.	2000.	3100.
1885	400.	750.	1500.	1750.	2250.	2650.	4200.	5750.	7250.
1886	165.	210.	275.	315.	450.	625.	1275.	1650.	3000.
1887	165.	190.	220.	245.	350.	400.	1050.	1500.	2850.
1888	165.	180.	195.	210.	255.	280.	500.	575.	1000.
1889	165.	180.	195.	205.	220.	250.	435.	550.	1000.
1890	165.	180.	195.	205.	230.	265.	530.	750.	1050.
1891	165.	180.	190.	200.	210.	240.	425.	625.	1100.
1892	165.	205.	275.	310.	485.	560.	950.	1250.	2600.
1893	145.	160.	185.	195.	205.	230.	400.	565.	1025.
1894	155.	180.	270.	295.	375.	425.	635.	1100.	1750.
1895	135.	145.	190.	200.	230.	255.	450.	525.	1100.
1896	135.	145.	155.	165.	175.	190.	325.	490.	1000.
1897	135.	150.	160.	170.	185.	200.	310.	480.	950.
1898	135.	145.	155.	165.	175.	190.	300.	475.	950.
1899	135.	145.	155.	170.	190.	205.	320.	490.	950.
1900	135.	145.	155.	165.	175.	190.	300.	450.	925.
1901	130.	140.	155.	165.	175.	190.	300.	450.	925.
1902	130.	140.	155.	165.	175.	190.	300.	450.	925.
1903	130.	140.	155.	165.	175.	190.	300.	435.	925.
1904	130.	140.	155.	165.	175.	190.	300.	435.	925.
1905	130.	140.	155.	165.	175.	190.	300.	435.	925.
1906	130.	140.	155.	165.	175.	190.	300.	435.	925.
1907	130.	140.	155.	165.	175.	190.	300.	435.	925.

—— = Insufficient pricing data

Indian Head $2.50 quarter eagle

Date of authorization: Jan. 18, 1837
Dates of issue: 1908-1929
Designer: Bela Lyon Pratt
Engraver: Charles Barber
Diameter: 17.78mm/0.70 inch
Weight: 4.18 grams/0.13 ounce
Metallic Content: 90% gold, 10% copper
Weight of pure gold: 3.76 grams/0.12 ounce
Edge: Reeded
Mint mark: Reverse lower left

	F-12	VF-20	EF-40	AU-50	AU-55	MS-60	MS-62	MS-63	MS-64	MS-65
1908	130.	145.	155.	170.	185.	260.	365.	765.	1275.	2975.
1909	130.	145.	155.	170.	185.	290.	365.	865.	1300.	3300.
1910	130.	145.	155.	170.	185.	265.	365.	850.	1750.	4350.
1911	130.	145.	155.	170.	185.	260.	365.	765.	1500.	4050.
1911-D	400.	600.	950.	1400.	1800.	3000.	4000.	6600.	9750.	45000.
1912	130.	145.	160.	180.	190.	300.	410.	910.	1650.	6000.
1913	130.	145.	155.	170.	185.	270.	380.	800.	1450.	3875.
1914	135.	150.	165.	185.	220.	475.	1400.	2800.	4250.	10250.
1914-D	130.	145.	160.	175.	200.	300.	650.	1275.	4500.	17500.
1915	130.	145.	155.	170.	185.	235.	310.	775.	1450.	3800.
1925-D	130.	140.	150.	165.	175.	235.	310.	700.	1300.	3050.
1926	130.	140.	150.	165.	175.	235.	310.	675.	1200.	2900.
1927	130.	140.	150.	165.	175.	235.	310.	675.	1300.	3300.
1928	130.	140.	150.	165.	175.	235.	310.	725.	1375.	3350.
1929	130.	140.	150.	165.	175.	235.	310.	735.	1375.	3300.

Indian Head $3 gold

Date of authorization:	Feb. 21, 1853
Dates of issue:	1854-1889
Designer/Engraver:	James B. Longacre
Diameter:	20.63mm/0.81 inch
Weight:	5.02 grams/0.16 ounce
Metallic Content:	(1854-1873): 90% gold, 10% copper and silver (1873-1889): 90% gold, 10% copper
Weight of pure gold:	4.51 grams/0.15 ounce
Edge:	Reeded
Mint mark:	Reverse below wreath

	F-12	VF-20	EF-40	AU-50	AU-55	MS-60	MS-62	MS-63	MS-64	MS-65
1854	420.	580.	630.	825.	975.	2000.	2975.	5700.	7750.	15000.
1854-D	4750.	7500.	13000.	29500.	46750.	80000.	125000.	——	——	——
1854-O	470.	775.	1150.	2500.	4250.	22500.	——	——	——	——
1855	420.	590.	640.	845.	1075.	2150.	3850.	6100.	9150.	18000.
1855-S	650.	1025.	1700.	4900.	7750.	21000.	——	——	——	——
1856	420.	580.	650.	850.	1000.	2150.	3900.	7200.	10500.	25250.
1856-S	525.	650.	1050.	1900.	3600.	9000.	——	22500.	45000.	——
1857	420.	585.	650.	950.	1500.	2650.	4250.	11000.	19000.	30000.
1857-S	675.	1075.	1850.	4250.	7750.	17000.	——	——	——	——
1858	625.	800.	1300.	2300.	3650.	6750.	8000.	16500.	——	——
1859	420.	600.	650.	875.	1225.	2200.	3900.	6250.	7850.	20500.
1860	420.	605.	665.	1050.	1450.	2250.	4000.	6050.	8400.	18000.
1860-S	550.	750.	1700.	4650.	9450.	——	——	——	——	——
1861	535.	650.	750.	1250.	1625.	2550.	4200.	9600.	16000.	22500.
1862	535.	650.	750.	1250.	1600.	2750.	4150.	9400.	16250.	26000.
1863	550.	665.	750.	1275.	1700.	2850.	4250.	9500.	15250.	19500.
1864	560.	675.	775.	1300.	1675.	2800.	4300.	9900.	16250.	25000.
1865	700.	1175.	2200.	3350.	5250.	11000.	16500.	22500.	30000.	40000.
1866	600.	685.	800.	1200.	1750.	2700.	4200.	9650.	15450.	22750.
1867	580.	680.	850.	1275.	1725.	2650.	4750.	9800.	15500.	22250.
1868	565.	660.	790.	1150.	1600.	2600.	4400.	8750.	15400.	22500.
1869	585.	690.	875.	1450.	1825.	4000.	5250.	10500.	18750.	26000.
1870	585.	690.	875.	1400.	1800.	4100.	5500.	11500.	21000.	37500.
1870-S unique										
1871	600.	700.	900.	1400.	1875.	3300.	4100.	9650.	16500.	24000.
1872	590.	685.	875.	1325.	1750.	3400.	4200.	9750.	17000.	25000.

—— = Insufficient pricing data

	F-12	VF-20	EF-40	AU-50	AU-55	MS-60	MS-62	MS-63	MS-64	MS-65
1873 Open 3 Proof Only				10750.	14500.	17000.	20000.	25000.	40000.	90000.
1873 Closed 3 originals	2200.	3500.	4500.	6750.	11750.	21000.	——	——	55000.	——
1874	410.	555.	625.	750.	900.	1950.	2950.	5250.	7550.	16500.
1875 Proof Only	——	——	——	——	30000.	40000.	50000.	67500.	100000.	215000.
1876 Proof Only	——	——	——	11000.	14000.	17500.	20000.	24500.	39000.	67500.
1877	745.	1125.	2650.	5750.	7850.	15500.	22000.	40000.	——	——
1878	405.	550.	620.	750.	875.	1750.	3175.	5600.	7500.	14750.
1879	460.	600.	825.	1100.	1400.	2150.	3900.	5600.	7850.	15500.
1880	470.	690.	1250.	2000.	2100.	2300.	3950.	5750.	7950.	15750.
1881	600.	1050.	2000.	3950.	4850.	6500.	8500.	12000.	22500.	40000.
1882	500.	665.	1075.	1600.	2000.	2300.	4500.	6450.	8500.	16500.
1883	505.	675.	1100.	1800.	2500.	3600.	4550.	6800.	9000.	18250.
1884	700.	950.	1300.	1850.	2450.	3400.	4700.	6700.	8900.	18750.
1885	650.	875.	1250.	1750.	2400.	3550.	4850.	6750.	9250.	19250.
1886	575.	800.	1200.	1800.	2550.	3650.	5250.	7500.	10000.	19500.
1887	470.	605.	725.	1050.	1200.	2150.	3000.	6000.	8150.	16250.
1888	470.	605.	725.	1050.	1200.	2150.	3000.	5600.	7900.	15750.
1889	470.	605.	725.	1050.	1200.	2150.	3000.	5600.	8300.	15000.

—— = Insufficient pricing data

Capped Bust $5 half eagle

Small Eagle — Heraldic Eagle

Date of authorization: April 2, 1792
Dates of issue: 1795-1807
Designer/Engraver: Robert Scot
Diameter: 25.00mm/0.99 inch
Weight: 8.75 grams/0.28 ounce
Metallic Content: 91.67% gold, 8.33% copper and silver
Weight of pure gold: 8.02 grams/0.26 ounce
Edge: Reeded
Mint mark: None

	F-12	VF-20	EF-40	AU-50	MS-60	MS-62	MS-63	MS-64	MS-65
SMALL EAGLE									
1795	5850.	7500.	11000.	16750.	36500.	75000.	120000.	—	—
1796/5	6750.	9000.	15500.	22000.	60000.	—	—	—	—
1797 15 Stars	8750.	14500.	29000.	50000.	—	—	—	—	—
1797 16 Stars	7750.	11000.	25500.	42500.	105000.	135000.	225000.	—	—
1798	—	—	250000.	—	—	—	—	—	—
HERALDIC EAGLE									
1795	6250.	10000.	18000.	38000.	100000.	130000.	—	—	—
1797/5	5000.	9500.	17500.	57500.	—	—	—	—	—
1797 16 Stars	—	—	—	—	—	—	—	—	—
1798 Small 8	1700.	2650.	5250.	11500.	20000.	—	—	—	—
1798 Large 8, 13 Stars	1550.	2250.	3050.	5750.	16500.	25000.	42500.	100000.	—
1798 Large 8, 14 Stars	1850.	2950.	7250.	18500.	—	—	—	—	—
1799 Small Stars	1600.	1850.	3750.	7000.	17000.	35000.	—	—	—
1799 Large Stars	1950.	2650.	5000.	10000.	25000.	47500.	—	—	—
1800	1325.	1600.	2300.	4025.	6150.	9775.	17500.	40500.	—
1802/1	1300.	1575.	2250.	3925.	5850.	7750.	14250.	31500.	—
1803/2	1300.	1575.	2250.	3775.	5750.	7600.	14750.	36000.	90000.
1804 Small 8	1400.	1635.	2250.	3800.	6000.	8250.	18250.	41500.	—
1804 Small 8/Large 8	1425.	1650.	2300.	3975.	6600.	9250.	24000.	55000.	—
1805	1350.	1625.	2250.	3975.	5650.	8000.	14750.	36000.	100000.
1806 Pointed 6, 8X5 Stars	1550.	1725.	2500.	4325.	9000.	14000.	25500.	—	—
1806 Round 6, 7X6 Stars	1300.	1550.	2250.	3775.	5350.	7600.	13500.	29000.	—
1807	1350.	1575.	2250.	3800.	5850.	8250.	14750.	35000.	—

—— = Insufficient pricing data

Capped Draped Bust $5 half eagle

Date of authorization: April 2, 1792
Dates of issue: 1807-1812
Designer/Engraver: John Reich
Diameter: 25.00mm/0.99 inch
Weight: 8.75 grams/0.28 ounce
Metallic Content: 91.67% gold, 8.33% copper and silver
Weight of pure gold: 8.02 grams/0.26 ounce
Edge: Reeded
Mint mark: None

	F-12	VF-20	EF-40	AU-50	MS-60	MS-62	MS-63	MS-64	MS-65
CAPPED DRAPED BUST									
1807	1375.	1625.	1950.	3050.	5150.	7350.	11750.	24500.	92500.
1808/7	1575.	1800.	2200.	5500.	11500.	15000.	19250.	47500.	——
1808	1325.	1575.	1925.	3050.	5100.	7300.	12500.	——	——
1809/8	1300.	1550.	1900.	3050.	5250.	8000.	12750.	25000.	——
1810 Small Date, Small 5	9500.	17500.	30000.	45000.	——	——	——	——	——
1810 Small Date, Tall 5	1700.	1900.	2150.	3350.	6350.	8350.	21000.	39500.	——
1810 Large Date, Small 5	——	——	——	——	——	——	——	——	——
1810 Large Date, Large 5	1375.	1600.	1975.	3000.	5000.	7150.	11500.	22500.	——
1811 Small 5	1325.	1575.	1950.	3000.	4950.	7700.	15000.	32500.	——
1811 Tall 5	1375.	1600.	2000.	3400.	6000.	9000.	24000.	50000.	——
1812	1275.	1525.	1900.	3000.	5000.	7200.	13000.	25000.	85000.

—— = Insufficient pricing data

Capped Head $5 half eagle

Date of authorization: April 2, 1792
Dates of issue: 1807-1812
Designer/Engraver: John Reich
Diameter: 25.00mm/0.99 inch
Weight: 8.75 grams/0.28 ounce
Metallic Content: 91.67% gold, 8.33% copper and silver
Weight of pure gold: 8.02 grams/0.26 ounce
Edge: Reeded
Mint mark: None

	F-12	VF-20	EF-40	AU-50	MS-60	MS-62	MS-63	MS-64	MS-65
1813	1500.	1750.	2200.	3100.	5900.	9000.	17500.	26000.	80000.
1814/3	1675.	2150.	2550.	3900.	8500.	19000.	30000.	57500.	——
1815	——	——	45000.	75000.	155000.	——	——	——	——
1818	1650.	1950.	2650.	4000.	8250.	18000.	27500.	——	——
1818 STATESOF	——	——	3750.	5900.	14250.	30000.	55000.	——	——
1818 5D/50	——	——	——	11500.	22500.	——	70000.	——	——
1819 Wide Date	——	——	25000.	55000.	——	——	——	——	——
1819 Close Date	——	15000.	22500.	50000.	——	——	——	——	——
1819 5D/50	——	12750.	17000.	35000.	——	——	90000.	——	——
1820 Curved Base 2, Small Letters	1775.	2150.	4600.	7000.	——	——	——	——	——
1820 Curved Base 2, Large Letters	1800.	2175.	4650.	7250.	——	——	32500.	——	——
1820 Square Base 2, Large Letters	1750.	2125.	2900.	5300.	9000.	14500.	21500.	30000.	87500.
1821	3750.	8500.	12500.	20250.	32500.	39000.	60000.	——	——
1822 3 known, 2 in Smithsonian Institution, Last sale 1982, $687,500, VF-30x									
1823	1825.	2750.	4250.	6900.	17500.	——	32500.	——	——
1824	3750.	7500.	12000.	20500.	34000.	45000.	60000.	75000.	——
1825/1	4000.	6000.	8250.	16500.	31500.	42500.	57500.	110000.	——
1825/4	——	——	265000.	——	——	——	——	——	——
1826	2900.	6000.	8050.	14000.	28000.	——	——	——	130000.
1827	——	——	——	——	25000.	40000.	57500.	87500.	——
1828/7	——	——	——	37500.	115000.	200000.	——	——	——
1828	——	——	——	32500.	65000.	——	——	——	——
1829 Large Planchet	——	——	——	——	——	——	——	300000.	——
SMALL PLANCHET									
1829 Small Planchet	——	——	75000.	175000.	——	——	——	475000.	——

—— = Insufficient pricing data

	F-12	VF-20	EF-40	AU-50	MS-60	MS-62	MS-63	MS-64	MS-65
1830 Small 5D	3500.	5550.	6500.	8400.	17500.	33000.	54000.	87500.	——
1830 Large 5D	3800.	5800.	7050.	9250.	19000.	39500.	65000.	——	——
1831 Small 5D	3950.	6000.	7900.	11750.	30000.	——	——	——	——
1831 Large 5D	3600.	5650.	6600.	8400.	18500.	30500.	46000.	90000.	175000.
1832 Curl Base 2, 12 Stars	——	100000.	150000.	——	——	——	400000.	——	——
1832 Square Base 2, 13 Stars	——	5900.	7150.	11500.	20000.	32500.	47500.	——	——
1833 Large Date	3450.	5550.	6400.	8250.	16000.	22000.	32500.	80000.	——
1833 Small Date	5750.	7750.	11000.	15250.	24000.	36000.	54000.	105000.	——
1834 Plain 4	3500.	5600.	6450.	10500.	22500.	30000.	42500.	87500.	——
1834 Crosslet 4	4250.	6100.	8750.	15000.	32000.	——	60000.	——	——

Classic Head $5 half eagle

Date of authorization: April 2, 1792
Dates of issue: 1834-1838
Designer: Obverse: William Kneass
Reverse: John Reich-William Kneass
Engraver: William Kneass
Diameter: 22.50mm/0.89 inch
Weight: 8.36 grams/0.27 ounce
Metallic Content: (1834-1836): 89.92% gold, 10.8% copper and silver
(1837-1838): 90% gold, 10% copper and silver
Weight of pure gold: (1834-1836): 7.516 grams/0.24 ounce
(1837-1838): 7.523 grams/0.24 ounce
Edge: Reeded
Mint mark: 1838 only, obverse above date

	F-12	VF-20	EF-40	EF-45	AU-50	AU-55	MS-60	MS-62	MS-63
1834 Plain 4	240.	300.	400.	490.	750.	1250.	2700.	3800.	7500.
1834 Crosslet 4	600.	1400.	3100.	4100.	5750.	8250.	16500.	31500.	45000.
1835	240.	295.	415.	500.	675.	1350.	2650.	4750.	9750.
1836	240.	295.	400.	490.	675.	1300.	2600.	3900.	7950.
1837	260.	310.	470.	585.	775.	1500.	3600.	——	17000.
1838	250.	305.	435.	525.	700.	1290.	3450.	4750.	15000.
1838-C	950.	1750.	4250.	7000.	14500.	23500.	37500.	70000.	——
1838-D	910.	1600.	3250.	4850.	6250.	13500.	27500.	50000.	——

—— = Insufficient pricing data

Coronet $5 half eagle

Date of authorization: Jan. 18, 1837
Dates of issue: 1839-1908
Designer: Obverse: Christian Gobrecht
Reverse: John Reich-William Kneass-Christian Gobrecht
Engraver: Christian Gobrecht
Diameter: (1839-1840): 22.50mm/0.89 inch
(1840-1908): 21.54mm/0.85 inch
Weight: 8.36 grams/0.27 ounce
Metallic Content: (1839-1849): 89.92% gold, 10.8% copper and silver
(1849-1908): 90% gold, 10% copper
Weight of pure gold: 7.52 grams/0.24 ounce
Edge: Reeded
Mint mark: Reverse below eagle

	F-12	VF-20	EF-40	EF-45	AU-50	AU-55	MS-60	MS-62	MS-63
1839	210.	250.	425.	775.	1100.	1600.	3150.	8500.	20000.
1839-C	575.	1200.	2700.	3750.	6500.	11750.	25000.	——	——
1839-D	500.	1050.	2450.	3550.	5700.	9750.	18750.	28000.	——
1840 Broad Mill	215.	245.	850.	1200.	2300.	3750.	8250.	——	25000.
1840 Narrow Mill	190.	210.	375.	585.	1350.	2200.	3850.	6250.	13000.
1840-C	435.	850.	2850.	4500.	8500.	17500.	30500.	——	——
1840-D	440.	775.	1600.	3350.	5600.	8750.	17500.	29000.	——
1840-O Broad Mill	325.	600.	1300.	1750.	2900.	——	——	——	——
1840-O Narrow Mill	235.	425.	975.	1275.	1700.	3000.	6750.	——	——
1841	245.	415.	975.	1250.	1600.	2350.	6000.	7000.	14500.
1841-C	400.	800.	1675.	2200.	2950.	6750.	21500.	33500.	——
1841-D	385.	725.	1550.	2750.	5050.	7500.	13500.	18500.	33500.
1842 Small Letters	180.	350.	1050.	1950.	3750.	7250.	——	——	——
1842 Large Letters	400.	825.	2000.	2800.	4250.	8750.	——	——	——
1842-C Large Date	390.	775.	1625.	2100.	3500.	6750.	19750.	29000.	40000.
1842-C Small Date	3250.	7500.	25500.	42500.	65000.	85000.	140000.	230000.	——
1842-D Large Date, Large Letters	1150.	2150.	4850.	8250.	15250.	25000.	47500.	——	——
1842-D Small Date, Small Letters	525.	800.	1375.	2300.	2750.	4100.	15000.	26000.	——
1842-O	375.	900.	3500.	6250.	13750.	——	——	——	42500.

—— = Insufficient pricing data

	F-12	VF-20	EF-40	EF-45	AU-50	AU-55	MS-60	MS-62	MS-63
1843	165.	185.	200.	235.	300.	525.	1500.	4450.	10750.
1843-C	400.	760.	1350.	2350.	4750.	7950.	21000.	30000.	40000.
1843-D	390.	650.	925.	1150.	2750.	4750.	9600.	17500.	26000.
1843-O Small Letters	365.	725.	1800.	2100.	3000.	—	30000.	—	—
1843-O Large Letters	180.	260.	1200.	1550.	2350.	4550.	13750.	—	—
1844	165.	190.	200.	235.	300.	500.	1500.	3900.	8500.
1844-C	675.	1100.	2850.	4950.	8750.	16500.	27500.	—	—
1844-D	500.	675.	1200.	1650.	2750.	5650.	13000.	20500.	36500.
1844-O	165.	215.	300.	375.	775.	1650.	4750.	7250.	14500.
1845	165.	195.	220.	255.	300.	545.	1700.	5750.	12000.
1845-D	535.	685.	1200.	1525.	1925.	4750.	13250.	19000.	26000.
1845-O	255.	400.	725.	1375.	3500.	6750.	14500.	19000.	27500.
1846 Small Date	165.	200.	230.	315.	700.	1600.	3250.	—	—
1846	165.	195.	225.	300.	350.	575.	1750.	4800.	12250.
1846-C	550.	1150.	2800.	4250.	6000.	13250.	25000.	40000.	77500.
1846-D/D	445.	650.	1075.	1750.	3800.	4500.	8750.	18500.	29000.
1846-O	235.	375.	1000.	1500.	4000.	6750.	11750.	17500.	25000.
1847	165.	185.	195.	250.	325.	400.	1400.	3900.	8100.
1847/7	190.	220.	265.	350.	550.	1200.	2400.	4750.	10000.
1847-C	450.	640.	1300.	1950.	3750.	6750.	17000.	24000.	32500.
1847-D	465.	625.	1200.	1650.	2375.	4350.	6650.	13500.	—
1847-O	600.	2500.	6600.	8750.	16000.	—	—	—	—
1848	165.	195.	205.	255.	425.	725.	1400.	2350.	9250.
1848-C	475.	700.	1050.	1700.	2500.	6350.	19500.	36000.	65000.
1848-D	440.	725.	1175.	1900.	2800.	5750.	13500.	25000.	—
1849	165.	190.	225.	365.	625.	1275.	2900.	6250.	16000.
1849-C	410.	600.	1150.	1500.	2200.	4875.	15000.	21750.	37500.
1849-D	425.	655.	1200.	1850.	2850.	6250.	15500.	24000.	—
1850	210.	275.	675.	775.	950.	1700.	3750.	7500.	12500.
1850-C	415.	600.	925.	1650.	2550.	4650.	15000.	25000.	35000.
1850-D	425.	850.	1350.	2250.	4300.	8650.	24000.	35000.	—
1851	165.	185.	210.	245.	300.	500.	1800.	4500.	9500.
1851-C	450.	660.	1200.	1700.	3000.	7500.	18000.	31000.	70000.
1851-D	400.	675.	1450.	2175.	3100.	8500.	14000.	22500.	37000.
1851-O	290.	575.	1250.	2500.	3800.	6750.	14000.	—	—
1852	165.	185.	195.	220.	300.	440.	1300.	3500.	8500.
1852-C	400.	625.	925.	1300.	2400.	3850.	7500.	13750.	26500.
1852-D	405.	625.	1050.	1975.	3500.	5500.	10500.	—	—
1853	165.	185.	200.	245.	300.	450.	1350.	3550.	7900.
1853-C	400.	600.	875.	1150.	1975.	3350.	7400.	14500.	34000.
1853-D	405.	610.	950.	1125.	1725.	3000.	5950.	12500.	29500.
1854	165.	215.	255.	355.	600.	1125.	1500.	4000.	11000.
1854-C	435.	800.	1300.	1625.	3475.	9000.	13250.	18000.	—
1854-D	390.	615.	1000.	1450.	2600.	4950.	9000.	16000.	26750.
1854-O	240.	300.	400.	825.	1450.	2200.	8000.	15500.	—
1854-S AU-55 $210000.									
1855	165.	185.	230.	255.	300.	625.	1500.	4200.	9500.

— = Insufficient pricing data

	F-12	VF-20	EF-40	EF-45	AU-50	AU-55	MS-60	MS-62	MS-63
1855-C	475.	850.	1650.	2150.	2700.	5500.	18000.	——	40000.
1855-D	500.	800.	1200.	1875.	3100.	6000.	17500.	26000.	36000.
1855-O	380.	700.	1800.	3000.	4750.	6000.	21000.	——	——
1855-S	215.	325.	1200.	1800.	3050.	5500.	——	——	——
1856	165.	185.	195.	230.	300.	575.	1550.	5250.	13500.
1856-C	425.	725.	1650.	2200.	2900.	7000.	21500.	——	——
1856-D	415.	775.	1375.	2100.	3100.	5750.	13000.	23500.	33000.
1856-O	400.	600.	1650.	2250.	5250.	7350.	19000.	——	——
1856-S	200.	285.	725.	875.	1200.	1950.	5500.	——	36500.
1857	165.	185.	195.	230.	305.	445.	1450.	4600.	9000.
1857-C	370.	625.	1400.	1950.	2650.	4600.	11500.	18500.	31000.
1857-D	415.	650.	1200.	2100.	3500.	8500.	16000.	26000.	——
1857-O	355.	675.	1125.	1850.	4250.	7500.	——	——	——
1857-S	205.	290.	700.	850.	1350.	2950.	7250.	——	——
1858	195.	240.	400.	525.	700.	1650.	3750.	6000.	13400.
1858-C	395.	700.	1175.	1650.	3150.	4600.	15250.	25000.	47500.
1858-D	425.	750.	1200.	1600.	2500.	4100.	11250.	22000.	——
1858-S	475.	875.	2500.	3300.	7250.	——	——	——	——
1859	200.	260.	400.	625.	775.	1700.	4750.	8000.	——
1859-C	390.	825.	1650.	2300.	3850.	6250.	18500.	32500.	52500.
1859-D	440.	785.	1200.	1775.	2750.	5250.	12500.	22500.	30000.
1859-S	600.	1650.	5050.	6250.	7750.	17000.	——	——	——
1860	190.	250.	350.	500.	875.	1750.	3750.	7000.	14250.
1860-C	425.	950.	1950.	2250.	3500.	8500.	14750.	——	——
1860-D	430.	925.	1800.	2350.	3450.	6000.	17000.	23500.	43500.
1860-S	550.	1050.	1700.	2900.	9000.	18000.	——	——	——
1861	165.	185.	195.	215.	290.	435.	1250.	2900.	7550.
1861-C	750.	2000.	4250.	5900.	8500.	17500.	37500.	75000.	115000.
1861-D	2750.	4000.	7000.	9500.	19500.	31000.	45000.	——	——
1861-S	525.	1200.	4250.	5750.	10000.	——	——	——	——
1862	455.	850.	1400.	1850.	3500.	——	——	——	——
1862-S	1300.	2950.	5600.	10000.	19000.	——	——	——	——
1863	450.	1175.	3500.	4750.	7750.	——	——	——	——
1863-S	625.	1450.	4250.	6500.	13500.	——	——	——	——
1864	360.	675.	1350.	1650.	3650.	7000.	15500.	——	——
1864-S	2900.	8000.	14250.	——	45000.	——	——	——	——
1865	500.	1400.	3250.	6000.	12500.	——	——	——	——
1865-S	525.	1475.	2025.	3500.	5850.	9000.	23500.	——	——
1866-S	775.	1750.	4350.	6500.	13750.	——	——	——	——
MOTTO ON REVERSE									
1866	375.	850.	1450.	1950.	3400.	5500.	——	——	——
1866-S	600.	900.	2850.	5250.	9250.	——	——	——	——
1867	275.	400.	1375.	1850.	3150.	4900.	——	——	——
1867-S	750.	1425.	2950.	5750.	14250.	——	——	——	——
1868	265.	500.	925.	2100.	3250.	5750.	12000.	——	——
1868-S	280.	375.	1475.	1600.	3600.	6250.	18000.	——	——

—— = Insufficient pricing data

	F-12	VF-20	EF-40	EF-45	AU-50	AU-55	MS-60	MS-62	MS-63
1869	425.	900.	1650.	2000.	4150.	—	—	—	—
1869-S	365.	525.	1800.	2900.	—	8250.	—	—	—
1870	350.	700.	1750.	2000.	3350.	5650.	—	—	—
1870-CC	1850.	4500.	14500.	19500.	27500.	—	—	—	—
1870-S	500.	1050.	2500.	4750.	11750.	—	—	—	—
1871	385.	725.	1500.	2000.	3375.	6250.	12000.	—	—
1871-CC	650.	1200.	3500.	9750.	—	—	—	—	—
1871-S	270.	355.	1150.	1800.	4150.	8500.	17000.	—	—
1872	400.	675.	1150.	1800.	2850.	4500.	12250.	15000.	21500.
1872-CC	575.	1100.	5250.	11500.	22500.	—	—	—	—
1872-S	275.	500.	775.	1000.	3250.	7000.	21000.	—	—
1873 Closed 3	150.	165.	190.	260.	500.	600.	1275.	4500.	9750.
1873 Open 3	150.	165.	185.	225.	300.	350.	665.	1800.	6250.
1873-CC	1250.	2750.	11500.	19500.	32500.	—	—	—	—
1873-S	340.	675.	975.	1600.	4000.	6500.	21000.	—	—
1874	315.	500.	1125.	1300.	2500.	4200.	—	—	—
1874-CC	410.	675.	2450.	4350.	11500.	16500.	34000.	—	—
1874-S	425.	800.	1725.	3600.	5000.	—	—	—	—
1875 EF-40 $47500 EF-45 $57500 AU-50 $75000 Prf 63 $50000 Prf 64 $100000									
1875-CC	700.	1600.	3600.	5500.	12250.	—	—	—	—
1875-S	500.	775.	2400.	3900.	6800.	9500.	27500.	—	—
1876	445.	825.	1950.	2350.	3550.	6250.	12500.	16000.	22500.
1876-CC	550.	1350.	4350.	5200.	12500.	16000.	—	—	—
1876-S	800.	1350.	3850.	7500.	—	—	—	—	—
1877	420.	825.	1750.	2250.	3500.	5000.	—	—	—
1877-CC	465.	1000.	3600.	4250.	8250.	—	—	—	—
1877-S	175.	275.	575.	975.	1850.	5100.	—	—	—
1878	150.	165.	170.	180.	230.	250.	450.	750.	2250.
1878-CC	1400.	3000.	6750.	10750.	22000.	—	—	—	—
1878-S	150.	165.	175.	190.	240.	535.	1075.	2000.	5000.
1879	150.	165.	170.	175.	200.	240.	400.	600.	1700.
1879-CC	345.	475.	1500.	1800.	2950.	5250.	—	—	—
1879-S	150.	165.	170.	180.	210.	270.	1050.	1850.	4250.
1880	150.	165.	170.	175.	200.	215.	245.	350.	1300.
1880-CC	270.	375.	725.	775.	1450.	4500.	11500.	—	—
1880-S	150.	165.	170.	175.	200.	215.	260.	340.	1100.
1881	150.	165.	170.	175.	200.	215.	240.	335.	925.
1881/0	250.	315.	600.	675.	800.	1000.	1350.	3100.	7000.
1881-CC	330.	450.	1600.	3750.	6500.	9250.	20000.	—	—
1881-S	150.	165.	170.	175.	200.	215.	255.	395.	1175.
1882	150.	165.	170.	175.	200.	215.	240.	345.	950.
1882-CC	250.	300.	450.	550.	725.	1850.	6750.	—	—
1882-S	150.	165.	170.	175.	200.	215.	265.	350.	1025.
1883	150.	165.	170.	175.	200.	215.	300.	575.	1700.
1883-CC	290.	385.	900.	1550.	3150.	7000.	18500.	—	—
1883-S	150.	165.	200.	210.	235.	330.	925.	1550.	3750.
1884	150.	165.	175.	185.	220.	325.	950.	1600.	3900.

—— = Insufficient pricing data

	F-12	VF-20	EF-40	EF-45	AU-50	AU-55	MS-60	MS-62	MS-63
1884-CC	315.	500.	950.	1800.	2550.	4500.	17500.	——	——
1884-S	150.	170.	180.	190.	220.	240.	325.	650.	1950.
1885	150.	165.	170.	175.	200.	215.	245.	500.	1200.
1885-S	150.	165.	170.	175.	200.	215.	240.	335.	875.
1886	150.	165.	170.	175.	200.	225.	270.	575.	1200.
1886-S	150.	165.	170.	175.	200.	225.	250.	345.	875.
1887 Proof Only - Prf 50 $17000;Prf 58 $18000; Prf 60 $25000; Prf 62 $32500; Prf 63(PCGS) $58000; Prf 64 $72500; Prf 65 $150000.									
1887-S	150.	165.	170.	175.	200.	215.	240.	400.	950.
1888	150.	165.	200.	225.	280.	350.	550.	1400.	2750.
1888-S	155.	175.	230.	240.	330.	750.	1100.	2500.	——
1889	165.	250.	330.	415.	525.	675.	950.	2400.	5000.
1890	215.	325.	485.	565.	675.	900.	1600.	4200.	11500.
1890-CC	185.	245.	320.	350.	450.	600.	1000.	2200.	4500.
1891	150.	165.	190.	200.	225.	275.	500.	900.	1900.
1891-CC	175.	240.	290.	330.	380.	435.	700.	1325.	3350.
1892	150.	165.	170.	175.	200.	215.	240.	350.	1400.
1892-CC	180.	240.	315.	375.	450.	875.	1550.	3100.	7750.
1892-O	360.	460.	750.	825.	1200.	1700.	2700.	6000.	12500.
1892-S	150.	165.	180.	190.	230.	430.	675.	1200.	3750.
1893	150.	165.	170.	175.	200.	215.	245.	335.	765.
1893-CC	185.	245.	325.	385.	550.	775.	1575.	3800.	8000.
1893-O	150.	185.	215.	240.	275.	450.	1075.	2300.	6100.
1893-S	150.	165.	175.	185.	200.	275.	350.	525.	1250.
1894	150.	165.	170.	175.	200.	215.	240.	335.	815.
1894-O	150.	175.	260.	280.	350.	750.	1450.	2650.	5500.
1894-S	165.	200.	325.	360.	600.	1000.	2400.	3250.	9750.
1895	150.	165.	170.	175.	200.	215.	240.	335.	815.
1895-S	150.	195.	280.	290.	500.	1100.	3000.	4000.	——
1896	150.	165.	175.	185.	200.	225.	350.	515.	1650.
1896-S	150.	190.	285.	315.	400.	700.	1450.	2950.	——
1897	150.	165.	170.	175.	200.	215.	240.	335.	865.
1897-S	150.	170.	225.	240.	275.	360.	875.	1500.	6900.
1898	150.	165.	170.	175.	200.	215.	240.	345.	840.
1898-S	150.	165.	170.	175.	200.	215.	250.	390.	1175.
1899	150.	165.	170.	175.	200.	215.	240.	335.	775.
1899-S	150.	170.	170.	170.	200.	215.	240.	350.	865.
1900	150.	165.	170.	175.	200.	215.	240.	335.	750.
1900-S	150.	170.	190.	200.	230.	250.	375.	500.	1150.
1901	150.	165.	170.	175.	200.	215.	240.	335.	775.
1901-S	150.	165.	170.	175.	200.	215.	240.	335.	750.
1901/0-S	150.	170.	210.	220.	265.	310.	360.	475.	890.
1902	150.	165.	170.	175.	200.	215.	240.	350.	865.
1902-S	150.	165.	170.	175.	200.	215.	240.	340.	790.
1903	150.	165.	170.	175.	200.	215.	240.	350.	865.
1903-S	150.	165.	170.	175.	200.	215.	240.	340.	790.
1904	150.	165.	170.	175.	200.	215.	240.	335.	790.

—— = Insufficient pricing data

	F-12	VF-20	EF-40	EF-45	AU-50	AU-55	MS-60	MS-62	MS-63
1904-S	150.	165.	185.	195.	270.	475.	1050.	1850.	3500.
1905	150.	165.	170.	175.	200.	215.	250.	345.	1050.
1905-S	150.	165.	170.	180.	225.	325.	600.	1150.	2600.
1906	150.	165.	170.	175.	200.	215.	240.	350.	1100.
1906-D	150.	165.	170.	175.	200.	215.	240.	335.	775.
1906-S	150.	165.	170.	170.	200.	215.	320.	490.	1500.
1907	150.	165.	170.	175.	200.	215.	240.	335.	750.
1907-D	150.	165.	170.	175.	200.	215.	240.	335.	790.
1908	150.	165.	170.	175.	200.	215.	240.	325.	750.

—— = Insufficient pricing data

Indian Head $5 half eagle

Date of authorization: Jan. 18, 1837
Dates of issue: 1908-1929
Designer: Bela Lyon Pratt
Engraver: Charles Barber
Diameter: 21.54mm/0.85 inch
Weight: 8.36 grams/0.27 ounce
Metallic Content: 90% gold, 10% copper
Weight of pure gold: 7.52 grams/0.24 ounce
Edge: Reeded
Mint mark: Reverse lower left

	F-12	VF-20	EF-40	AU-50	AU-55	MS-60	MS-62	MS-63	MS-64	MS-65
1908	160.	175.	200.	240.	265.	345.	600.	1700.	3900.	13750.
1908-D	160.	175.	200.	240.	265.	340.	625.	1775.	4150.	25000.
1908-S	180.	300.	375.	475.	725.	1150.	1650.	2750.	5500.	14500.
1909	160.	175.	200.	240.	265.	365.	650.	1825.	4400.	14500.
1909-D	160.	175.	200.	240.	265.	340.	560.	1550.	4025.	14500.
1909-O	350.	650.	1000.	1850.	2900.	6500.	14500.	30000.	—	—
1909-S	185.	195.	225.	295.	385.	1250.	2450.	6250.	15000.	41500.
1910	160.	175.	200.	240.	265.	350.	625.	1775.	4350.	20000.
1910-D	165.	180.	205.	265.	275.	420.	675.	2200.	11500.	—
1910-S	180.	195.	220.	300.	485.	1100.	3950.	7200.	23500.	—
1911	160.	175.	200.	240.	265.	340.	650.	1650.	3750.	13500.
1911-D	250.	325.	450.	625.	1025.	2950.	6750.	14500.	54500.	—
1911-S	180.	195.	210.	255.	290.	485.	750.	2800.	22000.	—
1912	160.	175.	200.	245.	265.	340.	610.	1675.	4450.	14500.
1912-S	180.	195.	210.	315.	525.	1350.	4100.	9000.	27500.	—
1913	160.	175.	200.	250.	265.	340.	650.	1650.	4250.	14500.
1913-S	185.	210.	230.	385.	600.	1400.	3250.	12500.	40000.	—
1914	165.	180.	200.	250.	265.	365.	625.	1925.	4250.	14500.
1914-D	165.	180.	205.	255.	270.	365.	675.	2350.	5250.	34500.
1914-S	180.	185.	210.	315.	525.	1450.	2800.	10000.	34000.	—
1915	165.	180.	200.	250.	265.	335.	625.	1600.	4500.	14500.
1915-S	185.	225.	350.	465.	675.	1850.	4600.	13000.	40000.	—
1916-S	180.	190.	250.	280.	350.	550.	1050.	2750.	7750.	20000.
1929	—	—	3800.	4300.	4850.	5750.	6400.	7300.	9150.	29500.

— = Insufficient pricing data

Capped Bust $10 eagle

Small Eagle reverse

Heraldic Eagle reverse

Date of authorization:	April 2, 1792
Dates of issue:	1795-1804
Designer/Engraver:	Robert Scot
Diameter:	33.00mm/1.30 inches
Weight:	17.50 grams/0.56 ounce
Metallic Content:	91.67% gold, 8.33% copper and silver
Weight of pure gold:	16.04 grams/0.52 ounce
Edge:	Reeded
Mint mark:	None

	F-12	VF-20	EF-40	EF-45	AU-50	AU-55	MS-60	MS-63	MS-64	MS-65
SMALL EAGLE										
1795 13 Leaves	6250.	8500.	15000.	16500.	21000.	30000.	50000.	100000.	175000.	—
1795 9 Leaves	16500.	32500.	42500.	47500.	62500.	80000.	165000.	—	—	—
1796	6850.	9500.	16500.	20000.	24000.	35000.	57500.	—	—	—
1797	8000.	13750.	27500.	38500.	52500.	72500.	—	—	—	—
HERALDIC EAGLE										
1797	2550.	3500.	4800.	6250.	8500.	11500.	18000.	—	—	—
1798/7 9 X 4 Stars	6250.	12500.	25000.	29000.	37500.	47500.	72500.	—	—	—

—— = Insufficient pricing data

	F-12	VF-20	EF-40	EF-45	AU-50	AU-55	MS-60	MS-63	MS-64	MS-65
1798/7 7 X 6 Stars	21500.	37500.	57500.	72500.	95000.	137500.	225000.	——	——	——
1799	2250.	2750.	4250.	4650.	6000.	7250.	10000.	25000.	45000.	150000.
1800	2600.	3550.	4600.	5400.	6500.	7500.	17500.	43000.	——	——
1801	2275.	2775.	4275.	4700.	6000.	7250.	10250.	27500.	50000.	——
1803 Small Stars	2400.	3050.	4400.	5150.	6250.	7500.	12000.	42500.	65000.	——
1803 Large Stars	2450.	3350.	4500.	5250.	6250.	7500.	12500.	47500.	67500.	——
1803 14 Reverse Stars	——	——	4700.	5500.	6500.	9000.	19000.	——	——	——
1804	3750.	4500.	5750.	7000.	9750.	13000.	28500.	——	——	——

Coronet $10 eagle

Date of authorization: Jan. 18, 1837
Dates of issue: 1838-1907
Designers: Obverse: Christian Gobrecht
Reverse: John Reich-William Kneass-Christian Gobrecht
Engraver: Christian Gobrecht
Diameter: 27.00mm/1.07 inches
Weight: 16.72 grams/.54 ounce
Metallic Content: (1838-1873)90% gold,10% copper and silver
(1873-1907): 90% gold, 10% copper
Weight of pure gold: 15.05 grams/0.48 ounce
Edge: Reeded
Mint mark: Reverse below eagle

	F-12	VF-20	EF-40	EF-45	AU-50	AU-55	MS-60	MS-62	MS-63
1838	600.	1150.	2900.	4025.	6250.	11000.	27500.	55000.	——
1839 Old Portrait	535.	900.	1650.	2350.	3850.	7000.	21500.	——	47500.
1839 New Portrait	850.	1750.	3200.	4500.	6750.	11500.	——	——	——
1840	305.	360.	575.	850.	1600.	3000.	12000.	——	——
1841	300.	325.	550.	700.	1375.	2450.	8500.	20000.	——
1841-O	1250.	2200.	4500.	5750.	11500.	19500.	——	——	——
1842 Small Date	270.	330.	400.	700.	2050.	3150.	8250.	——	——

—— = Insufficient pricing data

	F-12	VF-20	EF-40	EF-45	AU-50	AU-55	MS-60	MS-62	MS-63
1842 Large Date	280.	340.	450.	700.	1250.	3000.	8250.	——	27500.
1842-O	285.	375.	625.	1000.	2550.	6250.	29000.	——	——
1843 Doubled Date	295.	425.	575.	750.	3050.	——	——	——	——
1843	280.	330.	400.	625.	1700.	5450.	——	——	——
1843-O	275.	320.	375.	600.	1375.	3500.	16000.	18000.	——
1844	575.	1500.	2700.	3400.	6000.	——	18000.	——	——
1844-O	265.	330.	440.	775.	1650.	3250.	17000.	38500.	——
1845	400.	525.	750.	1300.	2000.	3150.	12500.	21500.	——
1845-O	280.	360.	700.	1100.	1800.	7500.	19000.	40000.	——
1846	450.	575.	1025.	2500.	5250.	11000.	——	——	——
1846-O	290.	425.	700.	2400.	5250.	——	——	——	——
1846/5-O	320.	625.	1050.	1400.	3100.	7750.	——	——	——
1847	245.	290.	340.	390.	525.	825.	3500.	7500.	17000.
1847-O	265.	300.	375.	450.	625.	1100.	4500.	9000.	16500.
1848	270.	320.	400.	500.	700.	1300.	5300.	10000.	15000.
1848-O	320.	500.	1100.	1900.	3750.	9250.	15000.	23500.	——
1849	255.	290.	350.	450.	600.	900.	3550.	5900.	12500.
1849/1848	450.	700.	975.	1300.	1800.	3500.	——	——	——
1849-O	385.	750.	1700.	2900.	5500.	8500.	——	——	——
1850 Large Date	255.	290.	370.	435.	650.	950.	3950.	6300.	12500.
1850 Small Date	320.	375.	925.	1450.	2350.	——	9500.	——	——
1850-O	295.	425.	1000.	1600.	2550.	6000.	——	——	——
1851	255.	290.	395.	525.	925.	1400.	4650.	——	23000.
1851-O	250.	290.	500.	700.	1150.	2950.	6000.	——	——
1852	255.	290.	335.	440.	600.	1100.	4050.	7000.	12750.
1852-O	370.	685.	1125.	2300.	3550.	9500.	19500.	37500.	——
1853	255.	290.	335.	415.	560.	850.	3750.	6250.	12500.
1853/2	420.	600.	800.	950.	1650.	3650.	——	——	——
1853-O	290.	320.	415.	575.	1000.	1900.	——	——	——
1854	295.	315.	385.	515.	775.	1400.	5700.	16500.	——
1854-O Small Date	270.	350.	675.	900.	1400.	——	——	——	——
1854-O Large Date	365.	500.	800.	1100.	1800.	3700.	8500.	19500.	41500.
1854-S	275.	305.	425.	560.	1275.	1900.	10750.	——	——
1855	260.	290.	360.	430.	575.	1100.	4500.	9500.	24000.
1855-O	315.	575.	1300.	2450.	5950.	9250.	——	——	——
1855-S	750.	1150.	2350.	3000.	5500.	7750.	——	——	——
1856	270.	290.	350.	430.	575.	1100.	4650.	6150.	13500.
1856-O	415.	625.	975.	2150.	3750.	7500.	——	——	——
1856-S	250.	290.	525.	675.	1100.	2600.	8750.	——	——
1857	290.	525.	925.	1250.	2200.	3500.	——	——	——
1857 overdate	600.	1400.	2850.	3750.	7500.	——	——	——	——
1857-O	600.	1100.	1850.	2300.	3200.	6500.	22500.	——	——
1857-S	315.	415.	1100.	1400.	2200.	4500.	——	——	——
1858	——	4750.	8000.	10250.	13500.	——	——	——	——
1858-O	270.	330.	625.	775.	1650.	3250.	9500.	19000.	——
1858-S	800.	1600.	3250.	3500.	5500.	15000.	——	——	——
1859	285.	365.	700.	900.	1250.	2350.	7750.	10500.	——

—— = Insufficient pricing data

	F-12	VF-20	EF-40	EF-45	AU-50	AU-55	MS-60	MS-62	MS-63
1859-O	1800.	3750.	7700.	12500.	17000.	——	——	——	——
1859-S	1100.	1650.	4100.	8000.	14750.	——	——	——	——
1860	260.	415.	650.	1050.	1500.	2800.	5800.	——	——
1860-O	375.	550.	1050.	1300.	1825.	4000.	——	——	——
1860-S	1850.	3400.	5500.	8250.	15750.	——	——	——	——
1861	250.	300.	355.	440.	525.	875.	3900.	7000.	15500.
1861-S	625.	1650.	2600.	3925.	7000.	10500.	——	——	——
1862	255.	600.	975.	1450.	2000.	2750.	——	——	——
1862-S	650.	1750.	2800.	3500.	6500.	——	——	——	——
1863	——	3650.	7500.	11000.	17000.	23000.	52500.	——	——
1863-S	675.	1725.	3600.	5000.	9750.	——	31500.	——	——
1864	725.	1600.	2750.	3800.	6000.	——	19000.	——	——
1864-S	2750.	5250.	12500.	17000.	26000.	——	——	——	——
1865	700.	1750.	3450.	4000.	6350.	——	——	——	——
1865-S	2250.	6750.	12000.	——	——	——	——	——	——
1865-S Inverted 865/186	1100.	2300.	6250.	9250.	17000.	——	——	——	——
1866-S	1350.	2400.	3400.	4100.	9500.	16500.	——	——	——
MOTTO ON REVERSE									
1866	515.	850.	1700.	2550.	3950.	8250.	——	——	——
1866-S	575.	1550.	3375.	4100.	7250.	——	——	——	——
1867	600.	1475.	2550.	3450.	5000.	7250.	——	——	——
1867-S	1100.	2150.	4750.	6950.	10250.	16500.	——	——	——
1868	440.	475.	725.	1200.	1900.	3400.	17500.	——	——
1868-S	600.	1300.	2250.	2800.	4250.	——	——	——	——
1869	750.	1200.	2600.	3200.	6750.	12500.	24500.	——	——
1869-S	825.	1800.	2650.	3350.	7000.	14750.	27500.	——	——
1870	435.	600.	1100.	1375.	2675.	6250.	——	——	——
1870-CC	4500.	10500.	28500.	——	——	——	——	——	——
1870-S	675.	1250.	2650.	3500.	7250.	14500.	——	——	——
1871	——	1050.	1925.	2400.	3800.	6750.	16500.	——	——
1871-CC	1350.	2100.	4950.	7950.	19000.	——	——	——	——
1871-S	625.	1100.	1800.	2150.	5500.	12500.	——	——	——
1872	1300.	1900.	3450.	5500.	12500.	——	27000.	35000.	——
1872-CC	1600.	3450.	10750.	——	——	——	——	——	——
1872-S	400.	585.	950.	1125.	1750.	5000.	——	——	——
1873	——	4500.	9500.	——	——	——	——	——	——
1873-CC	2000.	6750.	12750.	——	——	——	——	——	——
1873-S	585.	950.	2300.	3250.	4750.	6000.	——	——	——
1874	240.	265.	280.	290.	350.	425.	1850.	5200.	10000.
1874-CC	560.	875.	2400.	5000.	8750.	——	——	——	——
1874-S	600.	1200.	3500.	4250.	7350.	11750.	——	——	——
1875	——	42000.	60000.	80000.	90000.	——	——	——	——
1875-CC	1900.	3500.	9000.	13750.	——	——	——	——	——
1876	——	3100.	6000.	12000.	17500.	——	——	——	——
1876-CC	1650.	3150.	6250.	8000.	19500.	29000.	——	——	——
1876-S	625.	1000.	1950.	2750.	5600.	——	——	——	——

—— = Insufficient pricing data

	F-12	VF-20	EF-40	EF-45	AU-50	AU-55	MS-60	MS-62	MS-63
1877	——	1950.	3400.	5500.	9000.	——	——	——	——
1877-CC	1550.	2500.	5000.	7000.	——	——	——	——	——
1877-S	325.	475.	700.	1200.	2200.	3200.	——	——	——
1878	230.	250.	290.	300.	355.	500.	1300.	2350.	4750.
1878-CC	2550.	4300.	7850.	12500.	20000.	——	——	——	——
1878-S	300.	400.	600.	1150.	1975.	3150.	——	——	——
1879	225.	250.	265.	280.	340.	425.	775.	1450.	3600.
1879/8	290.	350.	400.	500.	750.	850.	1200.	1900.	——
1879-CC	3100.	7500.	14000.	——	——	——	——	——	——
1879-O	2050.	2400.	3800.	5500.	9000.	14750.	——	——	——
1879-S	225.	250.	260.	270.	290.	650.	1200.	3500.	——
1880	220.	250.	260.	270.	290.	295.	345.	700.	2250.
1880-CC	340.	450.	725.	1000.	1500.	3900.	12500.	——	——
1880-O	265.	385.	750.	800.	1000.	2100.	9000.	——	——
1880-S	225.	265.	285.	300.	350.	375.	465.	1300.	3500.
1881	215.	250.	260.	270.	290.	295.	310.	490.	975.
1881-CC	315.	360.	475.	625.	875.	1150.	6750.	12000.	——
1881-O	250.	375.	650.	825.	1225.	2050.	7750.	——	——
1881-S	215.	250.	260.	270.	290.	300.	400.	825.	——
1882	215.	250.	260.	270.	290.	295.	315.	485.	925.
1882-CC	475.	650.	1100.	1850.	2800.	6750.	——	——	——
1882-O	260.	300.	525.	750.	1025.	2000.	8250.	——	——
1882-S	225.	250.	270.	280.	305.	325.	450.	1550.	5000.
1883	225.	250.	260.	270.	290.	295.	360.	650.	1900.
1883-CC	340.	400.	650.	1150.	2250.	4500.	11500.	——	——
1883-O	1350.	3550.	7000.	——	10250.	13000.	——	——	——
1883-S	235.	270.	350.	365.	400.	550.	1350.	3250.	——
1884	225.	250.	260.	270.	290.	375.	875.	1750.	4250.
1884-CC	395.	600.	900.	1350.	2200.	4100.	10000.	——	——
1884-S	225.	250.	270.	280.	315.	375.	650.	1650.	——
1885	220.	250.	265.	275.	290.	320.	410.	675.	3750.
1885-S	220.	250.	260.	270.	290.	300.	375.	1500.	4200.
1886	230.	250.	265.	275.	290.	325.	385.	525.	2400.
1886-S	215.	250.	260.	270.	290.	300.	370.	455.	950.
1887	220.	250.	260.	270.	330.	475.	825.	2050.	4250.
1887-S	225.	250.	260.	270.	290.	295.	355.	625.	2500.
1888	230.	250.	265.	275.	325.	515.	825.	4850.	——
1888-O	215.	250.	260.	270.	320.	400.	550.	1850.	7500.
1888-S	215.	250.	260.	270.	290.	295.	350.	1100.	3250.
1889	275.	355.	500.	580.	900.	1750.	3150.	——	——
1889-S	215.	250.	260.	270.	290.	295.	315.	460.	1950.
1890	235.	250.	270.	280.	330.	500.	875.	2650.	4650.
1890-CC	310.	350.	475.	510.	725.	950.	2400.	6000.	16000.
1891	220.	250.	260.	270.	290.	300.	335.	650.	2700.
1891-CC	275.	335.	385.	415.	475.	525.	725.	1325.	4750.
1892	225.	250.	260.	270.	290.	295.	310.	430.	1550.
1892-CC	295.	325.	400.	475.	625.	1000.	3200.	5000.	9500.

—— = Insufficient pricing data

	F-12	VF-20	EF-40	EF-45	AU-50	AU-55	MS-60	MS-62	MS-63
1892-O	230.	255.	270.	280.	300.	340.	400.	2350.	—
1892-S	235.	260.	265.	275.	290.	310.	385.	825.	2350.
1893	215.	250.	260.	270.	290.	295.	310.	395.	925.
1893-CC	325.	400.	600.	800.	1450.	2600.	—	—	—
1893-O	225.	250.	290.	300.	325.	410.	600.	2450.	5250.
1893-S	235.	260.	265.	285.	300.	390.	525.	1400.	3975.
1894	215.	250.	260.	270.	290.	295.	310.	420.	950.
1894-O	215.	250.	285.	310.	375.	550.	1000.	2350.	5000.
1894-S	250.	295.	415.	500.	875.	—	3250.	—	—
1895	215.	250.	260.	270.	290.	295.	310.	425.	925.
1895-O	220.	250.	275.	290.	320.	360.	485.	1300.	3650.
1895-S	255.	305.	365.	400.	825.	1250.	2500.	5000.	—
1896	220.	250.	260.	270.	290.	295.	310.	525.	2000.
1896-S	235.	255.	325.	350.	500.	600.	2750.	—	10000.
1897	215.	250.	260.	270.	290.	295.	310.	420.	925.
1897-O	220.	250.	295.	305.	355.	375.	775.	1300.	2150.
1897-S	235.	265.	300.	315.	370.	400.	850.	1800.	3400.
1898	215.	250.	260.	270.	290.	295.	310.	430.	1000.
1898-S	225.	250.	265.	275.	295.	305.	400.	635.	1550.
1899	215.	250.	260.	270.	290.	295.	310.	415.	925.
1899-O	235.	265.	285.	295.	320.	385.	500.	1150.	2250.
1899-S	235.	250.	260.	270.	290.	295.	335.	600.	1600.
1900	220.	250.	260.	270.	290.	295.	310.	415.	925.
1900-S	230.	270.	295.	325.	375.	525.	975.	2100.	3900.
1901	215.	250.	260.	270.	290.	295.	310.	415.	800.
1901-O	220.	250.	265.	275.	305.	350.	410.	650.	1850.
1901-S	215.	250.	260.	270.	290.	295.	310.	410.	775.
1902	220.	250.	260.	270.	290.	310.	345.	575.	1125.
1902-S	215.	250.	260.	270.	290.	295.	310.	415.	900.
1903	220.	250.	260.	270.	290.	295.	330.	445.	925.
1903-O	215.	250.	265.	275.	300.	315.	375.	800.	1950.
1903-S	230.	250.	260.	270.	290.	300.	335.	455.	925.
1904	220.	250.	260.	270.	290.	295.	310.	420.	925.
1904-O	230.	250.	260.	270.	290.	295.	385.	650.	1750.
1905	220.	250.	260.	270.	290.	295.	310.	415.	925.
1905-S	230.	250.	270.	280.	330.	450.	1250.	3900.	5000.
1906	220.	250.	260.	270.	290.	295.	310.	420.	1000.
1906-D	215.	250.	260.	270.	290.	295.	310.	470.	950.
1906-O	235.	265.	280.	290.	350.	390.	575.	950.	2150.
1906-S	230.	250.	260.	270.	290.	345.	485.	1100.	3900.
1907	215.	250.	260.	270.	290.	295.	310.	410.	800.
1907-D	230.	250.	260.	270.	290.	295.	345.	455.	925.
1907-S	235.	250.	265.	275.	300.	325.	725.	1175.	2650.

— = Insufficient pricing data

Indian Head $10 eagle

Date of authorization: Jan. 18, 1837
Dates of issue: 1907-1933
Designer: Augustus Saint-Gaudens
Engraver: Charles Barber
Diameter: 27.00mm/1.07 inches
Weight: 16.72 grams0/.54 ounce
Metallic Content: 90% gold,10% copper
Weight of pure gold: 15.05 grams/0.48 ounce
Edge: Starred
Mint mark: Reverse left of TEN DOLLARS

	F-12	VF-20	EF-40	AU-50	AU-55	MS-60	MS-62	MS-63	MS-64	MS-65
1907 Wire Rim, Periods	——	——	4500.	5850.	6150.	7400.	9000.	14000.	20000.	50000.
1907 Rolled Rim, Periods	——	——	13500.	21000.	25000.	32500.	37000.	46000.	62500.	105000.
1907 No Periods	350.	370.	385.	405.	450.	575.	900.	1675.	2750.	7250.
1908	360.	390.	415.	500.	525.	725.	1150.	2400.	5250.	12000.
1908-D	360.	390.	400.	440.	475.	825.	1400.	6500.	11000.	38500.
MOTTO ON REVERSE										
1908	355.	370.	380.	390.	435.	500.	590.	1150.	2400.	5800.
1908-D	370.	390.	405.	415.	485.	725.	1150.	3500.	9500.	25000.
1908-S	385.	395.	415.	440.	700.	1950.	3100.	4750.	10000.	22500.
1909	350.	375.	380.	390.	435.	510.	650.	1800.	3500.	8900.
1909-D	360.	380.	390.	400.	535.	790.	1300.	2650.	11000.	45000.
1909-S	370.	385.	395.	405.	480.	650.	1150.	2100.	4800.	12750.
1910	355.	370.	375.	385.	410.	485.	580.	1030.	2200.	5950.
1910-D	355.	365.	370.	380.	405.	480.	575.	975.	2050.	6000.
1910-S	355.	385.	395.	405.	500.	775.	1300.	3650.	16500.	75000.
1911	335.	355.	365.	375.	400.	475.	570.	925.	2025.	5600.
1911-D	400.	450.	650.	875.	1450.	4050.	7750.	12500.	65000.	——
1911-S	360.	390.	475.	600.	650.	1000.	1825.	3000.	5950.	12500.
1912	345.	360.	375.	385.	405.	490.	595.	1090.	2300.	6500.
1912-S	350.	365.	390.	425.	525.	950.	1350.	2350.	6400.	55000.
1913	335.	345.	365.	375.	400.	475.	570.	925.	2125.	5950.
1913-S	365.	405.	650.	900.	1750.	4150.	10000.	20000.	57500.	——
1914	335.	355.	370.	380.	415.	495.	600.	1000.	2750.	8000.

—— = Insufficient pricing data

	F-12	VF-20	EF-40	AU-50	AU-55	MS-60	MS-62	MS-63	MS-64	MS-65
1914-D	335.	355.	365.	375.	405.	495.	625.	1150.	3000.	11500.
1914-S	350.	370.	385.	425.	480.	725.	1750.	3750.	14000.	45000.
1915	335.	360.	375.	385.	410.	485.	565.	1250.	2200.	5950.
1915-S	370.	390.	550.	800.	1250.	2750.	6600.	9500.	31500.	65000.
1916-S	365.	385.	415.	430.	450.	700.	1550.	2600.	6250.	15000.
1920-S	4750.	5750.	7000.	9100.	11250.	15000.	19000.	41000.	65000.	170000.
1926	335.	355.	365.	375.	390.	460.	550.	825.	1725.	4850.
1930-S	——	——	——	5500.	6250.	7500.	8250.	11500.	15500.	30000.
1932	335.	345.	355.	365.	385.	450.	490.	790.	1575.	4500.
1933	——	——	——	——	——	65000.	80000.	107500.	150000.	325000.

Coronet $20 double eagle

Date of authorization: March 3, 1849
Dates of issue: 1850-1907
Designer/Engraver: James B. Longacre
Diameter: 34.29mm/1.35 inches
Weight: 33.44 grams/1.07 ounce
Metallic Content: (1850-1873): 90% gold, 10% copper and silver
(1873-1907): 90% gold, 10% copper
Weight of pure gold: 30.09 grams/0.97 ounce
Edge: Reeded
Mint mark: Reverse below eagle

	F-12	VF-20	EF-40	EF-45	AU-50	AU-55	MS-60	MS-62	MS-63
NO MOTTO ON REVERSE									
1849 One Specimen U.S. Mint collection									
1850	485.	625.	675.	750.	1500.	1900.	3650.	15000.	37500.
1850-O	625.	725.	1600.	2500.	6000.	12000.	30000.	——	——
1851	470.	550.	600.	650.	850.	1250.	3750.	9000.	19000.
1851-O	510.	585.	740.	925.	1625.	5750.	17500.	30000.	48000.
1852	475.	530.	650.	620.	750.	1200.	2700.	6500.	14000.
1852-O	500.	565.	660.	900.	1600.	4400.	15000.	22500.	34000.

—— = Insufficient pricing data

	F-12	VF-20	EF-40	EF-45	AU-50	AU-55	MS-60	MS-62	MS-63
1853	470.	530.	575.	700.	900.	1500.	4900.	11500.	26000.
1853/2	515.	615.	900.	1650.	3375.	5500.	35000.	—	—
1853-O	580.	615.	950.	1400.	2600.	4400.	25000.	—	—
1854	490.	530.	575.	635.	900.	1500.	4750.	12250.	—
1854-O	—	20000.	38500.	50000.	65000.	—	—	—	—
1854-S	495.	650.	1000.	1500.	1800.	2750.	7500.	10000.	—
1855	490.	530.	625.	660.	1100.	2100.	7000.	11000.	40000.
1855-O	1900.	2750.	5000.	8400.	16500.	31000.	60000.	—	—
1855-S	475.	750.	1000.	1500.	1800.	2750.	—	—	—
1856	475.	550.	585.	615.	900.	2200.	8000.	14500.	38500.
1856-O	—	22000.	42500.	50000.	72500.	—	—	—	—
1856-S	475.	600.	1000.	1500.	2000.	—	—	—	—
1857	485.	530.	575.	600.	825.	1475.	4000.	7500.	29000.
1857-O	685.	850.	1450.	1850.	3600.	6250.	—	—	—
1857-S	475.	700.	1200.	2000.	2750.	—	—	—	—
1858	490.	640.	725.	800.	1300.	2750.	4200.	16500.	32000.
1858-O	825.	1050.	1725.	2100.	4025.	8000.	—	—	—
1858-S	475.	650.	1000.	1750.	2500.	—	—	16500.	—
1859	685.	950.	1950.	2500.	3800.	6100.	—	—	—
1859-O	1800.	2850.	6250.	9500.	15500.	20500.	—	—	—
1859-S	550.	700.	1200.	1600.	2100.	3500.	—	15000.	—
1860	490.	530.	575.	600.	725.	1150.	3500.	8750.	17500.
1860-O	2500.	3500.	6500.	10350.	15000.	20000.	—	—	—
1860-S	950.	1100.	1650.	1825.	2250.	4750.	—	—	—
1861	475.	530.	575.	600.	725.	1025.	3500.	6500.	—
1861-O	750.	1450.	3100.	4000.	6500.	13800.	—	—	—
1861-S	650.	1000.	1500.	1700.	2000.	3750.	10000.	—	34000.
1861 Paquet Reverse MS-67 (NGC - Norweb specimen) sold for $660,000									
1861-S Paquet Reverse	—	5250.	11500.	14500.	23500.	37500.	—	—	—
1862	535.	725.	1400.	2250.	2750.	4650.	10000.	16000.	40000.
1862-S	600.	800.	1400.	1800.	2475.	4750.	14000.	—	—
1863	480.	600.	850.	1200.	1800.	3800.	13000.	17500.	37500.
1863-S	600.	750.	1200.	1700.	2100.	3000.	8500.	14000.	35000.
1864	465.	530.	680.	975.	1550.	3600.	8650.	—	—
1864-S	600.	750.	1200.	1950.	2750.	4000.	9750.	17500.	32500.
1865	475.	530.	640.	725.	850.	1475.	5500.	13500.	29500.
1865-S	465.	535.	675.	740.	1265.	3250.	6000.	8500.	12500.
1866-S	775.	1600.	2300.	3850.	8750.	—	—	—	—
MOTTO ON REVERSE									
1866	470.	520.	655.	920.	1300.	1900.	5100.	—	32000.
1866-S	480.	530.	655.	725.	2025.	4950.	18000.	—	—
1867	460.	515.	600.	625.	725.	1100.	1800.	5000.	19000.
1867-S	465.	515.	665.	725.	1500.	3500.	15500.	—	—
1868	520.	545.	950.	1150.	1625.	2850.	8000.	—	32500.
1868-S	470.	515.	645.	675.	1250.	2500.	11000.	24000.	—
1869	470.	515.	640.	675.	1000.	2500.	4850.	7500.	18000.

— = Insufficient pricing data

	F-12	VF-20	EF-40	EF-45	AU-50	AU-55	MS-60	MS-62	MS-63
1869-S	460.	515.	560.	725.	950.	1875.	4500.	——	27500.
1870	475.	515.	740.	1050.	1450.	1900.	7500.	——	——
1870-CC	19500.	40000.	80000.	115000.	——	——	——	——	——
1870-S	460.	515.	575.	615.	725.	1150.	5200.	——	25000.
1871	485.	530.	675.	825.	1375.	1875.	3600.	8250.	21000.
1871-CC	1200.	2250.	4650.	6500.	11000.	17250.	——	——	——
1871-S	470.	515.	540.	565.	660.	1100.	3550.	11000.	20000.
1872	460.	515.	525.	550.	650.	1075.	2300.	10500.	21000.
1872-CC	750.	1000.	1400.	2300.	3825.	9250.	24500.	——	——
1872-S	460.	515.	530.	550.	615.	1000.	2300.	——	24000.
1873 Closed 3	530.	575.	675.	725.	800.	1150.	2550.	8000.	——
1873 Open 3	460.	515.	525.	535.	545.	575.	735.	3100.	9750.
1873-CC	640.	775.	1275.	1950.	3250.	8800.	22500.	42500.	——
1873-S Closed 3	465.	515.	565.	570.	575.	800.	1600.	4900.	21500.
1873-S Open 3	535.	565.	615.	700.	950.	2000.	4700.	——	——
1874	465.	515.	525.	535.	560.	670.	1400.	8000.	18500.
1874-CC	545.	575.	630.	675.	1425.	2100.	7500.	——	——
1874-S	465.	515.	525.	535.	565.	670.	1500.	8000.	22000.
1875	460.	515.	525.	535.	550.	620.	825.	3750.	10000.
1875-CC	550.	575.	575.	700.	825.	1075.	2100.	6750.	19500.
1875-S	460.	515.	525.	535.	550.	625.	950.	4300.	17500.
1876	460.	515.	525.	535.	550.	600.	735.	3750.	10250.
1876-CC	540.	580.	600.	675.	950.	2025.	4750.	12000.	39000.
1876-S	460.	515.	525.	535.	550.	620.	735.	3200.	10650.
TWENTY DOLLARS REVERSE									
1877	475.	480.	500.	525.	560.	605.	700.	2000.	4500.
1877-CC	575.	650.	825.	925.	1275.	2500.	16000.	30000.	46500.
1877-S	460.	470.	485.	515.	555.	605.	675.	1825.	8000.
1878	465.	485.	495.	515.	545.	575.	645.	1600.	5000.
1878-CC	675.	800.	1250.	1900.	3350.	6500.	20000.	——	——
1878-S	460.	485.	505.	555.	570.	640.	935.	3650.	18000.
1879	470.	490.	510.	535.	555.	615.	950.	4800.	8500.
1879-CC	725.	1050.	1400.	1650.	4100.	9750.	22500.	——	——
1879-O	1950.	3100.	4150.	5600.	9000.	13750.	28500.	——	75000.
1879-S	465.	485.	505.	540.	560.	620.	1100.	10250.	19500.
1880	475.	500.	545.	580.	665.	900.	2900.	5500.	18500.
1880-S	470.	490.	515.	545.	570.	615.	950.	2975.	8000.
1881	2250.	3600.	7000.	8500.	11500.	16000.	——	——	——
1881-S	470.	485.	505.	525.	540.	565.	925.	2200.	7250.
1882	——	8500.	16000.	24000.	29500.	42500.	——	——	——
1882-CC	560.	585.	675.	775.	1100.	2500.	6150.	11500.	25000.
1882-S	465.	480.	495.	515.	535.	555.	750.	1700.	——
1883 Proofs Only - Prf 60 $30000 Prf 63 $44000 Prf 64 $75000 Prf 65 $195000.									
1883-CC	560.	580.	660.	740.	800.	1950.	3950.	7250.	22000.
1883-S	465.	475.	485.	505.	535.	550.	650.	1200.	4500.
1884 Proofs Only - Prf 60 $35000 Prf 63 $48500 Prf 64 $85000.									
1884-CC	535.	575.	620.	700.	875.	1675.	2450.	6200.	20000.

—— = Insufficient pricing data

	F-12	VF-20	EF-40	EF-45	AU-50	AU-55	MS-60	MS-62	MS-63
1884-S	460.	470.	480.	495.	535.	550.	610.	1300.	3600.
1885	——	——	6250.	7250.	9000.	13500.	34000.	40000.	——
1885-CC	750.	900.	1350.	1600.	3450.	4650.	10750.	25000.	45000.
1885-S	460.	475.	485.	505.	535.	550.	665.	1125.	3900.
1886	——	5750.	11000.	14000.	18500.	24000.	40000.	47500.	67500.
1887 Proofs Only - Prf 60 $16500 Prf 63 $29500 Prf 64 $55000.									
1887-S	460.	490.	500.	520.	555.	570.	650.	1000.	7000.
1888	465.	485.	510.	530.	550.	620.	700.	1100.	4900.
1888-S	460.	475.	490.	500.	505.	535.	650.	975.	3500.
1889	465.	480.	505.	525.	575.	630.	725.	1200.	6000.
1889-CC	590.	655.	750.	825.	1200.	1500.	3400.	7500.	15500.
1889-S	460.	480.	500.	515.	530.	545.	650.	1075.	3800.
1890	470.	480.	505.	525.	550.	580.	635.	1400.	4500.
1890-CC	555.	590.	650.	725.	850.	1225.	2750.	7750.	15750.
1890-S	470.	480.	505.	520.	535.	550.	625.	900.	4500.
1891	——	2950.	4000.	5000.	7750.	11750.	——	——	——
1891-CC	1150.	1650.	2500.	3000.	4600.	6500.	12500.	27500.	——
1891-S	450.	460.	480.	485.	500.	520.	600.	685.	2400.
1892	725.	900.	1350.	1550.	2000.	3050.	4900.	9500.	19000.
1892-CC	625.	650.	650.	745.	1050.	1600.	2650.	8000.	21000.
1892-S	450.	460.	485.	505.	520.	535.	580.	645.	2400.
1893	450.	460.	480.	500.	530.	545.	590.	775.	2000.
1893-CC	615.	650.	750.	925.	1150.	1400.	2000.	5950.	10000.
1893-S	450.	460.	480.	490.	510.	525.	575.	725.	2500.
1894	450.	460.	480.	485.	505.	520.	565.	595.	1375.
1894-S	450.	460.	485.	495.	525.	540.	580.	700.	1750.
1895	450.	460.	480.	485.	495.	510.	550.	560.	1100.
1895-S	450.	460.	485.	495.	510.	525.	570.	700.	1500.
1896	450.	460.	480.	485.	505.	515.	550.	585.	1250.
1896-S	450.	460.	485.	495.	510.	535.	600.	800.	1725.
1897	450.	460.	480.	485.	500.	515.	550.	600.	1100.
1897-S	450.	460.	480.	485.	510.	525.	565.	640.	1250.
1898	450.	460.	490.	500.	525.	555.	700.	1650.	5850.
1898-S	450.	460.	480.	490.	495.	500.	540.	625.	1200.
1899	450.	460.	480.	490.	495.	500.	540.	585.	1050.
1899-S	450.	460.	480.	485.	505.	520.	575.	625.	1475.
1900	450.	460.	480.	485.	490.	500.	540.	550.	675.
1900-S	450.	460.	480.	485.	505.	535.	590.	625.	1975.
1901	450.	460.	470.	480.	490.	520.	570.	595.	750.
1901-S	450.	480.	485.	495.	515.	530.	575.	800.	1950.
1902	450.	480.	505.	540.	665.	735.	900.	1400.	3250.
1902-S	450.	475.	490.	500.	510.	525.	555.	600.	2300.
1903	450.	460.	480.	485.	490.	500.	540.	550.	725.
1903-S	450.	460.	485.	495.	510.	525.	565.	595.	1350.
1904	450.	460.	470.	480.	490.	495.	525.	550.	625.
1904-S	450.	460.	470.	480.	490.	500.	545.	565.	750.
1905	450.	485.	535.	560.	615.	825.	1100.	5000.	18000.

—— = Insufficient pricing data

	F-12	VF-20	EF-40	EF-45	AU-50	AU-55	MS-60	MS-62	MS-63
1905-S	450.	480.	500.	510.	525.	540.	585.	645.	1900.
1906	450.	485.	520.	525.	560.	600.	750.	975.	——
1906-D	450.	460.	470.	480.	505.	545.	630.	645.	2000.
1906-S	450.	460.	470.	480.	495.	510.	550.	725.	1650.
1907	450.	460.	470.	480.	490.	500.	540.	555.	950.
1907-D	450.	460.	470.	480.	500.	515.	550.	670.	1250.
1907-S	450.	460.	470.	480.	490.	510.	555.	610.	1600.

Saint-Gaudens $20 double eagle

Date of authorization: March 3, 1849
Dates of issue: 1907-1933
Designer: Augustus Saint-Gaudens
Engraver: Charles Barber
Diameter: 34.29mm/1.35 inches
Weight: 33.47 grams/1.07 ounce
Metallic Content: 90% gold, 10% copper
Weight of pure gold: 30.09 grams/0.97 ounce
Edge: Lettered (E PLURIBUS UNUM, with stars dividing words)
Mint mark: Obverse above date

	F-12	VF-20	EF-40	AU-50	AU-55	MS-60	MS-62	MS-63	MS-64	MS-65
1907 Extremely High Relief Proofs Only		*	*	*	*	*	*	*	*	350000.
1907 High Relief, Roman Numerals, Wire Rim	2400.	2850.	3400.	4750.	5700.	7400.	8500.	10750.	14850.	23500.
1907 High Relief, Roman Numerals, Flat Rim	2450.	2900.	3450.	4800.	5750.	7500.	8650.	11000.	15250.	24000.
1907	490.	500.	515.	550.	560.	575.	650.	775.	1350.	2750.
1908	490.	500.	515.	535.	560.	575.	625.	700.	825.	1250.
1908-D	515.	520.	540.	565.	575.	600.	725.	750.	1625.	14000.
MOTTO ON REVERSE										
1908	490.	510.	530.	555.	560.	580.	675.	950.	3750.	16000.
1908-D	505.	530.	550.	565.	575.	600.	700.	660.	1300.	4250.

—— = Insufficient pricing data * = None issued

	F-12	VF-20	EF-40	AU-50	AU-55	MS-60	MS-62	MS-63	MS-64	MS-65
1908-S	535.	645.	850.	1350.	2250.	3700.	7900.	12000.	22500.	57500.
1909/8	510.	535.	575.	690.	875.	1250.	2450.	5400.	13750.	31500.
1909	505.	515.	545.	580.	600.	700.	1075.	2650.	7750.	75000.
1909-D	515.	540.	595.	735.	825.	1375.	1700.	2600.	5650.	35000.
1909-S	490.	500.	515.	540.	560.	575.	650.	625.	1250.	4750.
1910	490.	500.	515.	540.	560.	575.	590.	625.	1325.	6250.
1910-D	490.	500.	515.	540.	560.	575.	590.	625.	775.	2475.
1910-S	490.	500.	515.	540.	560.	575.	650.	775.	1600.	9500.
1911	490.	500.	525.	575.	600.	615.	750.	1025.	2400.	13500.
1911-D	490.	500.	520.	540.	560.	575.	590.	625.	775.	1650.
1911-S	490.	500.	525.	550.	565.	575.	675.	750.	1100.	4900.
1912	490.	505.	530.	580.	600.	615.	725.	1250.	2450.	12500.
1913	490.	500.	520.	550.	565.	610.	800.	1875.	3400.	22500.
1913-D	490.	500.	515.	535.	560.	575.	650.	775.	1300.	5000.
1913-S	500.	520.	565.	615.	650.	1100.	1900.	3300.	8500.	50000.
1914	475.	500.	545.	580.	600.	615.	750.	1300.	2500.	12000.
1914-D	475.	500.	520.	545.	560.	575.	590.	625.	850.	2200.
1914-S	475.	500.	515.	535.	560.	575.	590.	625.	825.	2050.
1915	490.	510.	530.	585.	600.	610.	800.	1350.	3250.	12500.
1915-S	475.	500.	525.	545.	560.	575.	590.	625.	825.	1800.
1916-S	475.	500.	520.	545.	560.	575.	590.	675.	825.	1700.
1920	475.	500.	525.	550.	570.	585.	675.	900.	3000.	——
1920-S	——	——	8000.	13000.	17000.	26500.	32500.	55000.	90000.	——
1921	——	——	10000.	15500.	21500.	38000.	50000.	80000.	125000.	225000.
1922	465.	490.	505.	520.	535.	550.	590.	625.	725.	3700.
1922-S	500.	530.	580.	660.	700.	825.	900.	1700.	4850.	32500.
1923	465.	490.	505.	520.	535.	550.	590.	625.	900.	6500.
1923-D	475.	490.	505.	520.	535.	550.	590.	625.	725.	1200.
1924	465.	490.	505.	520.	535.	550.	590.	625.	725.	1175.
1924-D	——	——	850.	1200.	1450.	2200.	2750.	4400.	15500.	50000.
1924-S	——	——	——	1050.	1400.	2050.	2600.	4750.	14500.	49500.
1925	465.	490.	505.	520.	535.	550.	590.	625.	725.	1150.
1925-D	——	——	——	1350.	1800.	2600.	3400.	6750.	19750.	52500.
1925-S	800.	900.	1050.	1650.	2200.	5500.	7750.	19500.	32500.	67500.
1926	465.	490.	505.	520.	535.	550.	590.	625.	725.	1200.
1926-D	——	——	——	2650.	4500.	7000.	13500.	24500.	41500.	62500.
1926-S	——	——	825.	1150.	1475.	1750.	2100.	2650.	5200.	36000.
1927	465.	490.	505.	520.	535.	550.	590.	625.	725.	1150.
1927-D	——	——	——	——	——	——	——	225000.	300000.	650000.
1927-S	——	——	3750.	6250.	7000.	12000.	22000.	29500.	41000.	105000.
1928	465.	490.	505.	520.	535.	550.	590.	625.	725.	1150.
1929	——	——	——	7000.	7500.	8750.	10000.	13000.	20500.	52500.
1930-S	——	——	——	14000.	15500.	19500.	25000.	36000.	46500.	80000.
1931	——	——	——	12750.	14000.	16000.	20000.	24000.	37500.	55000.
1931-D	——	——	——	10500.	11500.	12500.	16000.	18500.	28000.	52500.
1932	——	——	——	——	10000.	12000.	15000.	16500.	27000.	45000.

1933 Not officially issued; at least three survive, all in government hands.

—— = Insufficient pricing data

Commemorative coins 1892-1954

	EF-40	AU-50	MS-60	MS-63	MS-64	MS-65	MS-66
WORLD'S COLUMBIAN EXPOSITION							
1892 silver half dollar	10.00	13.00	32.00	85.00	150.	675.	1600.
1893 silver half dollar	10.00	13.00	32.00	80.00	150.	800.	2000.
1893 Isabella quarter dollar	180.	230.	300.	525.	975.	2400.	4000.
LAFAYETTE MONUMENT							
1900 silver dollar	240.	300.	550.	1450.	2500.	9000.	13000.
LOUISIANA PURCHASE EXPOSITION							
1903 Jefferson gold dollar	315.	360.	445.	750.	1300.	1950.	3300.
1903 McKinley gold dollar	300.	330.	400.	700.	1250.	2250.	3350.
LEWIS & CLARK EXPOSITION							
1904 gold dollar	430.	525.	800.	1875.	3000.	5750.	8900.
1905 gold dollar	430.	500.	975.	3000.	4750.	13500.	25000.
PANAMA-PACIFIC EXPOSITION							
1915-S silver half dollar	160.	190.	335.	675.	1050.	2100.	3300.
1915-S gold dollar	300.	360.	400.	550.	850.	2000.	3200.
1915-S gold $2.50	1050.	1250.	1650.	3000.	3750.	4850.	6000.
1915-S gold $50 Round	22000.	24000.	28000.	41000.	58000.	120000.	185000.
1915-S gold $50 Octagonal	18500.	20000.	24000.	37500.	55000.	110000.	150000.
MCKINLEY MEMORIAL							
1916 gold dollar	265.	295.	360.	590.	850.	1875.	3375.
1917 gold dollar	305.	375.	525.	1075.	1350.	2750.	4850.
ILLINOIS CENTENNIAL							
1918 silver half dollar	58.00	72.00	85.00	95.00	175.	550.	1175.
MAINE CENTENNIAL							
1920 silver half dollar	60.00	72.00	90.00	160.	200.	575.	1425.
PILGRIM TERCENTENARY							
1920 silver half dollar	46.00	52.50	65.00	85.00	110.	450.	1500.
1921 silver half dollar	85.00	100.	120.	150.	240.	660.	2000.
MISSOURI CENTENNIAL							
1921 silver half dollar, No 2*4	175.	220.	465.	640.	1100.	6300.	13000.
1921 silver half dollar, 2*4	285.	385.	490.	925.	1400.	6250.	15500.
ALABAMA CENTENNIAL							
1921 silver half dollar, 2x2	115.	165.	325.	525.	900.	2550.	6500.
1921 silver half dollar, No 2x2	65.00	88.00	210.	500.	800.	2200.	8500.
GRANT MEMORIAL							
1922 silver half dollar, No Star	62.00	72.00	85.00	175.	300.	775.	1650.
1922 silver half dollar, Star	465.	650.	1050.	1650.	2400.	7700.	14500.
1922 gold dollar, Star	1075.	1250.	1450.	1850.	2250.	2650.	3175.
1922 gold dollar, No Star	1075.	1200.	1325.	1650.	1800.	2675.	3250.
MONROE DOCTRINE CENTENNIAL							
1923-S silver half dollar	25.00	30.00	45.00	120.	350.	2400.	5000.
HUGUENOT-WALLOON TERCENTENARY							
1924 silver half dollar	65.00	80.00	95.00	110.	135.	550.	1400.
LEXINGTON-CONCORD SESQUICENTENNIAL							
1925 silver half dollar	52.00	60.00	72.00	105.	125.	630.	1800.
STONE MOUNTAIN MEMORIAL							
1925 silver half dollar	30.00	33.00	42.00	55.00	70.00	200.	625.

	EF-40	AU-50	MS-60	MS-63	MS-64	MS-65	MS-66
CALIFORNIA DIAMOND JUBILEE							
1925-S silver half dollar	80.00	100.	115.	175.	235.	775.	1750.
FORT VANCOUVER CENTENNIAL							
1925 silver half dollar	200.	235.	280.	375.	400.	1200.	2100.
AMERICAN INDEPENDENCE SESQUICENTENNIAL							
1926 silver half dollar	45.00	55.00	75.00	150.	400.	4750.	19500.
1926 gold $2.50	240.	265.	300.	575.	900.	3600.	21000.
OREGON TRAIL MEMORIAL							
1926 silver half dollar	80.00	90.00	100.	120.	135.	195.	435.
1926-S silver half dollar	80.00	90.00	100.	120.	135.	195.	350.
1928 silver half dollar	130.	150.	165.	180.	210.	295.	425.
1933-D silver half dollar	220.	230.	245.	275.	300.	425.	625.
1934-D silver half dollar	120.	135.	150.	165.	180.	285.	600.
1936 silver half dollar	100.	110.	120.	130.	145.	210.	275.
1936-S silver half dollar	100.	120.	130.	160.	200.	260.	385.
1937-D silver half dollar	110.	125.	140.	150.	170.	190.	260.
1938 silver half dollar PDS set	——	——	575.	650.	700.	800.	950.
1939 silver half dollar PDS set	——	——	1175.	1325.	1450.	2000.	2400.
VERMONT-BENNINGTON SESQUICENTENNIAL							
1927 silver half dollar	125.	140.	155.	200.	260.	810.	2000.
HAWAII DISCOVERY SESQUICENTENNIAL							
1928 silver half dollar	900.	1050.	1350.	1950.	2500.	4800.	7250.
MARYLAND TERCENTENARY							
1934 silver half dollar	105.	115.	125.	140.	160.	360.	1000.
TEXAS INDEPENDENCE CENTENNIAL							
1934 silver half dollar	78.00	85.00	90.00	95.00	105.	145.	225.
1935 silver half dollar PDS set	——	——	300.	315.	345.	435.	765.
1936 silver half dollar PDS set	——	——	300.	315.	345.	435.	575.
1937 silver half dollar PDS set	——	——	300.	315.	345.	435.	700.
1938 silver half dollar PDS set	——	——	600.	750.	835.	1000.	1800.
DANIEL BOONE BICENTENNIAL							
1934 silver half dollar	62.00	70.00	82.00	88.00	95.00	145.	300.
1935 silver half dollar PDS set, Small 1934	——	——	600.	800.	1100.	1800.	3500.
1935 silver half dollar PDS set	——	——	255.	300.	330.	455.	1050.
1936 silver half dollar PDS set	——	——	255.	285.	330.	480.	1200.
1937 silver half dollar PDS set	——	——	625.	720.	800.	1150.	2100.
1938 silver half dollar PDS set	——	——	800.	1025.	1150.	1500.	3350.
CONNECTICUT TERCENTENNARY							
1935 silver half dollar	145.	165.	195.	205.	250.	550.	975.
ARKANSAS CENTENNIAL							
1935 silver half dollar PDS set	——	——	230.	270.	335.	720.	3900.
1936 silver half dollar PDS set	——	——	235.	270.	335.	1000.	3300.
1936 silver half dollar single	55.00	62.00	65.00	72.00	90.00	230.	850.
1937 silver half dollar PDS set	——	——	240.	300.	345.	1050.	6600.
1938 silver half dollar PDS set	——	——	360.	440.	480.	2000.	8000.
1939 silver half dollar PDS set	——	——	660.	900.	1100.	2800.	9500.
ARKANSAS-ROBINSON							
1936 silver half dollar	63.00	72.00	80.00	85.00	100.	265.	1150.

—— = Insufficient pricing data

	EF-40	AU-50	MS-60	MS-63	MS-64	MS-65	MS-66
HUDSON, NY, SESQUICENTENNIAL							
1935 silver half dollar	380.	450.	500.	515.	615.	1325.	2450.
CALIFORNIA-PACIFIC EXPOSITION (San Diego)							
1935-S silver half dollar	48.00	55.00	60.00	63.00	80.00	90.00	200.
1936-D silver half dollar	56.00	60.00	65.00	70.00	80.00	100.	250.
OLD SPANISH TRAIL							
1935 silver half dollar	735.	765.	800.	850.	875.	1025.	1250.
PROVIDENCE, RI, TERCENTENNARY							
1936 silver half dollar single	60.00	65.00	72.00	80.00	95.00	200.	675.
1936 silver half dollar PDS set	——	——	230.	260.	310.	700.	3500.
CLEVELAND CENTENNIAL & GREAT LAKES EXPOSITION							
1936 silver half dollar	52.00	60.00	65.00	65.00	85.00	210.	725.
WISCONSIN TERRITORIAL CENTENNIAL							
1936 silver half dollar	140.	150.	170.	180.	200.	225.	290.
CINCINNATI MUSIC CENTER							
1936 silver half dollar PDS set	——	——	745.	785.	880.	1775.	7200.
1936 silver half dollar single	190.	220.	235.	240.	265.	480.	1400.
LONG ISLAND TERCENTENARY							
1936 silver half dollar	60.00	65.00	68.00	72.00	87.00	400.	1150.
YORK COUNTY, MAINE, TERCENTENARY							
1936 silver half dollar	130.	135.	145.	160.	170.	200.	230.
BRIDGEPORT, CT, CENTENNIAL							
1936 silver half dollar	90.00	100.	105.	115.	120.	270.	700.
LYNCHBURG, VA, SESQUICENTENNIAL							
1936 silver half dollar	135.	145.	155.	170.	185.	315.	875.
ALBANY, NY, CHARTER 250TH ANNIVERSARY							
1936 silver half dollar	180.	195.	205.	215.	235.	350.	765.
ELGIN, IL, PIONEER MEMORIAL							
1936 silver half dollar	150.	160.	165.	180.	190.	230.	575.
SAN FRANCISCO-OAKLAND BAY BRIDGE							
1936-S silver half dollar	80.00	90.00	110.	125.	145.	300.	500.
COLUMBIA, SC, SESQUICENTENNIAL							
1936 silver half dollar 150th PDS set	——	——	500.	525.	550.	650.	1050.
1936 silver half dollar 150th single	135.	150.	155.	170.	175.	210.	290.
DELAWARE TERCENTENARY							
1936 silver half dollar	170.	200.	210.	220.	230.	350.	950.
BATTLE OF GETTYSBURG 75TH ANNIVERSARY							
1936 silver half dollar	225.	250.	270.	275.	320.	535.	1050.
NORFOLK, VA, BICENTENNIAL & TERCENTENARY							
1936 silver half dollar	325.	340.	350.	360.	375.	400.	420.
ROANOKE COLONIZATION 350TH ANNIVERSARY							
1937 silver half dollar	145.	155.	170.	185.	195.	240.	275.
BATTLE OF ANTIETAM 75TH ANNIVERSARY							
1937 silver half dollar	365.	400.	445.	450.	500.	600.	700.

—— = Insufficient pricing data

	EF-40	AU-50	MS-60	MS-63	MS-64	MS-65	MS-66
NEW ROCHELLE, NY, 250TH ANNIVERSARY							
1938 silver half dollar	245.	265.	275.	295.	300.	375.	725.
IOWA STATEHOOD CENTENNIAL							
1946 silver half dollar	60.00	72.00	77.00	80.00	85.00	105.	145.
BOOKER T WASHINGTON MEMORIAL							
1946 silver half dollar PDS set	——	——	38.00	50.00	72.00	130.	630.
1946 silver half dollar single	10.00	10.50	12.00	16.00	20.00	35.00	135.
1947 silver half dollar PDS set	——	——	50.00	80.00	110.	275.	1375.
1948 silver half dollar PDS set	——	——	100.	115.	150.	185.	950.
1949 silver half dollar PDS set	——	——	180.	220.	240.	290.	720.
1950 silver half dollar PDS set	——	——	90.00	115.	125.	165.	1325.
1951 silver half dollar PDS set	——	——	110.	140.	160.	175.	775.
BOOKER T WASHINGTON - GEORGE WASHINGTON CARVER							
1951 silver half dollar PDS set	——	——	80.00	100.	125.	500.	1750.
1951 silver half dollar single	10.00	11.50	12.50	18.00	22.00	50.00	325.
1952 silver half dollar PDS set	——	——	56.00	125.	185.	400.	1675.
1953 silver half dollar PDS set	——	——	57.50	120.	160.	510.	1675.
1954 silver half dollar PDS set	——	——	72.00	90.00	110.	475.	1675.

Commemorative coins 1982-1999

	MS-60	MS-63	MS-64	MS-65	PF-65
WASHINGTON'S BIRTH 250TH ANNIVERSARY					
1982-D silver half dollar	4.00	4.50	5.00	5.75	*
1982-S silver half dollar	*	*	*	*	5.75
GAMES OF XXIII OLYMPIAD, LOS ANGELES					
1983-P silver dollar	8.00	8.50	8.75	10.00	*
1983-D silver dollar	9.00	10.00	11.00	12.00	*
1983-S silver dollar	8.00	8.25	8.50	9.00	10.00
1984-P silver dollar	13.00	13.50	14.00	14.50	*
1984-D silver dollar	22.00	22.50	23.00	24.50	*
1984-S silver dollar	23.00	23.50	24.00	25.00	11.50
1984-P gold $10 eagle	*	*	*	*	275.
1984-D gold $10 eagle	*	*	*	*	245.
1984-S gold $10 eagle	*	*	*	*	210.
1984-W gold $10 eagle	——	——	200.	225.	225.
STATUE OF LIBERTY - ELLIS ISLAND CENTENNIAL					
1986-D clad half dollar	4.00	4.25	4.50	5.50	*
1986-S clad half dollar	*	*	*	*	5.50
1986-P silver dollar	9.00	9.50	10.50	12.00	*
1986-S silver dollar	*	*	*	*	11.00
1986-W gold half eagle	——	——	108.	115.	125.
CONSTITUTION BICENTENNIAL					
1987-P silver dollar	7.50	7.75	8.00	8.50	*
1987-S silver dollar	*	*	*	*	8.50
1987-W gold half eagle	——	——	102.	104.	98.00
GAMES OF XXIV OLYMPIAD, CALGARY, SEOUL					
1988-D silver dollar	9.75	10.00	10.25	10.50	*
1988-S silver dollar	*	*	*	*	8.50
1988-W gold half eagle	——	——	107.	110.	104.

—— = Insufficient pricing data　　* = None issued

	MS-60	MS-63	MS-64	MS-65	PF-65
BICENTENNIAL OF CONGRESS					
1989-D clad half dollar	9.00	9.50	9.75	10.00	*
1989-S clad half dollar	*	*	*	*	6.00
1989-D silver dollar	14.00	14.50	14.75	15.00	*
1989-S silver dollar	*	*	*	*	12.00
1989-W gold half eagle	——	——	110.	115.	107.
EISENHOWER BIRTH CENTENNIAL					
1990-W silver dollar	11.00	12.00	13.00	13.50	*
1990-P silver dollar	*	*	*	*	16.00
MOUNT RUSHMORE 50TH ANNIVERSARY					
1991-D clad half dollar	12.00	13.00	13.50	14.00	*
1991-S clad half dollar	*	*	*	*	13.00
1991-P silver dollar	23.00	23.50	24.00	26.00	*
1991-S silver dollar	*	*	*	*	26.00
1991-W gold half eagle	——	——	130.	135.	124.
KOREAN WAR 38TH ANNIVERSARY					
1991-D silver dollar	15.00	15.50	15.75	16.00	*
1991-P silver dollar	*	*	*	*	16.50
UNITED SERVICE ORGANIZATIONS 50TH ANNIVERSARY					
1991-D silver dollar	15.50	16.00	16.25	16.50	*
1991-S silver dollar	*	*	*	*	15.00
GAMES OF XXV OLYMPIAD, ALBERTVILLE, BARCELONA					
1992-P clad half dollar	5.75	6.00	6.25	6.50	*
1992-S clad half dollar	*	*	*	*	8.00
1992-D silver dollar	22.50	23.00	23.50	24.00	*
1992-S silver dollar	*	*	*	*	29.00
1992-W gold half eagle	——	——	130.	135.	117.
WHITE HOUSE BICENTENNIAL					
1992-D silver dollar	25.00	25.50	26.00	26.50	*
1992-W silver dollar	*	*	*	*	27.50
COLUMBUS DISCOVERY QUINCENTENNIAL					
1992-D clad half dollar	12.00	12.50	13.00	13.50	*
1992-S clad half dollar	*	*	*	*	13.00
1992-P silver dollar	*	*	*	*	26.50
1992-D silver dollar	18.00	18.50	19.00	20.00	*
1992-W gold half eagle	——	——	130.	135.	140.
BILL OF RIGHTS - JAMES MADISON					
1993-W silver half dollar	11.00	12.50	13.00	14.00	*
1993-S silver half dollar	*	*	*	*	13.00
1993-D silver dollar	14.50	15.00	15.50	16.00	*
1993-S silver dollar	*	*	*	*	16.00
1993-W gold half eagle	——	——	165.	180.	117.
WORLD WAR II 50TH ANNIVERSARY, DUAL DATES 1991-1995					
(1993)-P WWII clad half dollar	9.00	9.50	10.00	10.50	12.00
(1993)-D silver dollar	20.50	21.50	22.50	23.50	*
(1993)-W silver dollar	*	*	*	*	25.00
(1993)-W WWII gold half eagle	——	——	175.	190.	139.

—— = Insufficient pricing data   * = None issued

	MS-60	MS-63	MS-64	MS-65	PF-65
SOCCER WORLD CUP					
1994-D clad half dollar	6.50	7.00	7.50	8.5	*
1994-P clad half dollar	*	*	*	*	11.50
1994-D silver dollar	21.50	22.00	22.50	23.00	*
1994-S silver dollar	*	*	*	*	27.50
1994-W gold half eagle	——	——	145.	150.	135.
THOMAS JEFFERSON 250TH ANNIVERSARY OF BIRTH, dual date 1743-1993					
(1994)-P silver dollar	29.50	30.00	30.50	31.00	*
(1994)-S silver dollar	*	*	*	*	28.00
WOMEN IN MILITARY SERVICE MEMORIAL					
1994-W silver dollar	26.00	26.50	27.00	27.00	*
1994-P silver dollar	*	*	*	*	28.00
VIETNAM VETERANS' MEMORIAL					
1994-W silver dollar	26.00	26.25	26.50	27.00	*
1994-P silver dollar	*	*	*	*	29.00
PRISONER OF WAR MUSEUM					
1994-W silver dollar	26.00	26.25	26.50	27.00	*
1994-P silver dollar	*	*	*	*	29.00
UNITED STATES CAPITOL BICENTENNIAL					
1994-D silver dollar	25.50	26.00	26.25	26.50	*
1994-S silver dollar	*	*	*	*	25.00
CIVIL WAR BATTLEFIELDS					
1995-D clad half dollar	10.50	10.75	11.00	11.50	*
1995-S clad half dollar	*	*	*	*	12.00
1995-P silver dollar	25.00	25.50	26.00	27.00	*
1995-S silver dollar	*	*	*	*	32.00
1995-W gold half eagle	——	——	225.	260.	175.
SPECIAL OLYMPICS WORLD GAMES					
1995-W silver dollar	29.00	29.50	30.00	31.00	*
1995-P silver dollar	*	*	*	*	27.00
GAMES OF THE XXVI OLYMPIAD, ATLANTA					
1995-S Basketball clad half dollar	12.00	12.50	13.00	13.50	13.00
1995-S Baseball clad half dollar	12.00	12.50	13.00	13.50	13.00
1995-D Gymnastics silver dollar	29.00	29.50	30.00	31.00	*
1995-P Gymnastics silver dollar	*	*	*	*	34.00
1995-D Cycling silver dollar	29.00	29.50	30.00	31.00	*
1995-P Cycling silver dollar	*	*	*	*	34.00
1995-D Track & Field silver dollar	29.00	29.50	30.00	31.00	*
1995-P Track & Field silver dollar	*	*	*	*	34.00
1995-D Paralympic, blind runner silver dollar	29.00	29.50	30.00	31.00	*
1995-P Paralympic, blind runner silver dollar	*	*	*	*	35.00
1995-W Torch Runner gold half eagle	——	——	180.	195.	169.
1995-W Atlanta Stadium gold half eagle	——	——	180.	195.	179.
1996-S Swimming clad half dollar	12.00	12.50	13.00	13.50	13.00
1996-S Soccer clad half dollar	12.00	12.50	13.00	13.50	13.00
1996-D Tennis silver dollar	30.00	31.00	31.50	32.00	*
1996-P Tennis silver dollar	*	*	*	*	37.00
1996-D Rowing silver dollar	30.00	31.00	31.50	32.00	*
1996-P Rowing silver dollar	*	*	*	*	37.00
1996-D High Jump silver dollar	30.00	31.00	31.50	32.00	*
1996-P High Jump silver dollar	*	*	*	*	37.00
1996-D Paralympic, wheelchair athlete silver dollar	30.00	31.00	31.50	32.00	*

—— = Insufficient pricing data   * = None issued

	MS-60	MS-63	MS-64	MS-65	PF-65
1996-P Paralympic, wheelchair athlete silver dollar	*	*	*	*	37.00
1996-W Olympic Flame brazier gold half eagle	——	——	215.	220.	199.
1996-W Flagbearer gold half eagle	——	——	215.	220.	199.
NATIONAL COMMUNITY SERVICE					
1996-S silver dollar	52.00	55.00	58.00	70.00	37.00
NATIONAL LAW ENFORCEMENT OFFICERS MEMORIAL					
1997-P	——	——	35.00	40.00	45.00
SMITHSONIAN INSTITUTION 150TH ANNIVERSARY					
1996-D silver dollar	31.00	32.00	33.00	34.00	*
1996-P silver dollar	*	*	*	*	37.00
1996-W gold half eagle	——	——	195.	210.	210.
U.S. BOTANIC GARDEN					
1997-P silver dollar	32.50	33.00	33.50	38.00	39.00
U.S. BOTANIC GARDEN COINAGE & CURRENCY SET					
1997-P Unc. dollar, 1997-P Matte Finish Jefferson 5-cent coin & Series 1995 $1 FRN					215.
JACKIE ROBINSON					
1997-S silver dollar	——	——	——	32.00	37.00
1997-W gold half eagle	——	——	——	190.	190.
BLACK REVOLUTIONAL WAR PATRIOTS					
1998-S silver dollar	——	——	——	45.00	50.00
ROBERT F. KENNEDY					
1998-S dollar	——	——	——	45.00	50.00
GEORGE WASHINGTON					
1999-W gold half eagle	——	——	——	——	——
YELLOWSTONE NATIONAL PARK					
1999-P silver dollar	——	——	——	——	——
DOLLEY MADISON					
1999-P silver dollar	——	——	——	——	——

—— = Insufficient pricing data   * = None issued

Proof Sets

Year	Price	Range
1936	2900.	4250.
1937	1900.	2800.
1938	775.	1175.
1939	715.	1025.
1940	600.	925.
1941	465.	725.
1942 5-piece	475.	725.
1942 6-piece	500.	775.
1950	300.	485.
1951	190.	275.
1952	100.	190.
1953	87.50	130.
1954	45.00	65.00
1955 Flat	45.00	55.00
1956	23.00	28.00
1957	10.00	12.50
1958	18.00	22.00
1959	12.00	14.00
1960	9.00	11.00
1960 Small Date cent	15.00	20.00
1961	6.25	7.00
1962	6.25	7.00
1963	6.25	7.00
1964	6.25	7.00
1968-S	4.50	5.50
1969-S	4.50	5.50
1970-S	8.00	9.50
1970-S Level 7 (Small Date)	50.00	60.00
1971-S	4.00	5.00
1972-S	4.50	5.00
1973-S	6.00	7.00
1974-S	6.00	7.00
1975-S	6.25	7.50
1976-S	6.00	7.00
1976-S Bicentennial 3-piece	11.00	14.00
1977-S	5.25	6.75
1978-S	5.50	7.00
1979-S Filled S	5.50	7.00
1979-S Clear S	55.00	65.00
1980-S	4.00	5.50
1981-S Filled S	5.25	6.50
1981-S Clear S	170.	200.
1982-S	3.75	4.75
1983-S	4.00	5.25
1983-S Prestige	70.00	85.00
1984-S	6.25	8.00
1984-S Prestige	20.00	25.00
1985-S	4.00	5.00
1986-S	11.00	14.00
1986-S Prestige	22.00	28.00
1987-S	3.60	5.25
1987-S Prestige	18.00	21.00
1988-S	5.00	6.75
1988-S Prestige	26.00	32.00
1989-S	4.50	6.00
1989-S Prestige	26.00	33.00
1990-S	7.00	9.50
1990-S No S Lincoln cent	1200.	1400.
1990-S Prestige	17.50	24.00
1991-S	12.50	17.50
1991-S Prestige	44.00	55.00
1992-S	12.50	15.50
1992-S Prestige	42.50	50.00
1992-S Silver	12.50	16.50
1992-S Silver Premier	16.00	19.50
1993-S	20.00	24.00
1993-S Prestige	40.00	45.00
1993-S Silver	27.00	33.00
1993-S Silver Premier	26.00	31.00
1994-S	13.00	17.50
1994-S Prestige	50.00	65.00
1994-S Silver	30.00	35.00
1994-S Silver Premier	25.00	30.00
1995-S	28.00	35.00
1995-S Prestige	110.	125.
1995-S Silver	30.00	36.00
1995-S Silver Premier	28.00	34.00
1996-S	8.00	11.00
1996-S Prestige	100.	120.
1996-S Silver	23.00	28.00
1996-S Silver Premier	27.00	33.00
1997-S	20.00	22.00
1997-S Prestige	170.	205.
1997-S Silver	22.00	27.00
1997-S Silver Premier	31.00	37.00
1998-S	10.00	12.00
1998-S Silver	20.00	25.00
1998-S Silver Premier	33.00	38.00
1999-S Five-coin 25¢	——	——
1999-S Nine-coin	——	——
1999-S Silver nine-coin	——	——

—— = Insufficient pricing data * = None issued

Uncirculated Mint sets

	Phila.	Denver	San Fr.	Price	Range
1947 Double set	240.	240.	70.00	500.	550.
1948 Double set	150.	145.	45.00	250.	300.
1949 Double set	150.	160.	190.	400.	500.
1950 No Sets Issued					
1951 Double set	40.00	165.	120.	245.	350.
1952 Double set	22.50	57.50	170.	190.	275.
1953 Double set	90.00	35.00	75.00	175.	225.
1954 Double set	30.00	25.00	35.00	70.00	90.00
1955 Double set	41.00	19.50	5.50	50.00	75.00
1956 Double set	27.50	22.50	*	50.00	65.00
1957 Double set	42.50	42.50	*	75.00	100.
1958 Double set	43.00	39.00	*	70.00	85.00
1959 Single set	7.00	7.50	*	15.00	20.00
1960	7.50	7.50	*	14.00	18.00
1961	7.00	7.00	*	15.00	20.00
1962	5.25	5.25	*	9.00	10.00
1963	5.00	5.00	*	10.00	12.00
1964	5.00	5.00	*	8.00	10.00

Year	Price	Range
1965 Special Mint Sets	3.00	4.00
1966 Special Mint Sets	3.00	4.00
1967 Special Mint Sets	5.00	6.00
1968 (PD&S)	2.25	3.25
1969 (PD&S)	4.00	5.00
1970 (PD&S)	8.00	10.00
1971 (PD&S)	3.00	4.00
1972 (PD&S)	2.00	3.00
1973 (PD&S)	6.50	8.50
1974 (PD&S)	4.25	6.25
1975	6.00	8.00
1976-S 3-piece 40% silver	10.00	14.00
1976	7.00	8.00
1977	7.00	8.00
1978	7.00	8.00
1979	4.00	5.00
1980	5.00	6.00
1981	10.00	12.00
1984	4.00	5.00
1985	4.00	5.00
1986	7.50	10.00
1987	4.25	6.00
1988	4.00	5.00
1989	5.00	6.00
1990	3.00	4.00
1991	7.50	9.00
1992	7.00	10.00
1993	5.00	8.00
1994	7.00	11.00
1995	19.00	25.00
1996	8.75	10.00
1997	10.00	12.50
1998	8.00	10.00
1999	—	—

— = Insufficient pricing data * = None issued

Year sets

	Phila.	Denver	San Fr.	Price Range	
1940	190.	90.00	185.	360.	465.
1941	115.	165.	225.	400.	505.
1942	95.00	160.	175.	340.	430.
1943	105.	180.	170.	350.	455.
1944	85.00	120.	105.	250.	310.
1945	92.50	115.	110.	235.	320.
1946	50.00	45.00	80.00	140.	175.

Brilliant Uncirculated rolls

Date	1¢	5¢	10¢	25¢	50¢
1¢	5¢	10¢	25¢	50¢	
1934	225.	1600.	1200.	1100.	1450.
1934-D	800.	4250.	2750.	5750.	——
1935	90.00	975.	825.	875.	1250.
1935-D	205.	2250.	2900.	6000.	3950.
1935-S	400.	1650.	1350.	3250.	6250.
1936	64.00	775.	575.	775.	1200.
1936-D	130.	1175.	1700.	——	1500.
1936-S	120.	1550.	1175.	3650.	3250.
1937	37.00	675.	575.	675.	1250.
1937-D	73.00	800.	1250.	1475.	4000.
1937-S	77.00	925.	1225.	5000.	3300.
1938	73.00	60.00	950.	2050.	1750.
1938-D	85.00	120.	1000.	*	——
1938-D Bison	*	500.	*	*	*
1938-S	52.00	125.	1100.	2250.	*
1939	37.00	52.00	575.	650.	1200.
1939-D	86.00	1500.	450.	1050.	1250.
1939-S	69.00	625.	1400.	2500.	2500.
1940	37.00	29.00	340.	475.	950.
1940-D	37.00	65.00	500.	2450.	*
1940-S	40.00	90.00	475.	525.	1000.
1941	42.00	30.00	325.	205.	850.
1941-D	100.	100.	600.	700.	1000.
1941-S	88.00	100.	350.	800.	3250.
1942	22.00	195.	220.	125.	875.
1942-P	*	215.	*	*	*
1942-D	14.00	600.	525.	325.	1300.
1942-S	140.	156.	575.	1800.	1450.
1943	39.00	87.00	215.	120.	700.
1943-D	40.00	85.00	375.	525.	1650.
1943-S	77.00	105.	515.	875.	1200.
1944	10.00	120.	220.	110.	850.
1944-D	16.00	200.	325.	245.	975.
1944-S	15.00	85.00	320.	240.	1400.
1945	27.00	115.	230.	77.00	700.
1945-D	12.00	85.00	225.	170.	875.
1945-S	10.00	65.00	250.	130.	850.
1946	11.00	11.00	30.00	105.	800.
1946-D	11.00	16.00	37.00	95.00	725.
1946-S	12.00	11.00	49.00	80.00	900.
1947	39.00	28.00	48.00	160.	850.
1947-D	12.00	28.00	82.00	120.	725.

Date	1¢	5¢	10¢	25¢	50¢
1947-S	16.00	19.00	60.00	95.00	*
1948	19.00	12.00	135.	83.00	225.
1948-D	13.00	34.00	105.	110.	180.
1948-S	18.00	17.00	97.00	105.	*
1949	30.00	14.00	500.	540.	575.
1949-D	23.00	23.00	165.	250.	675.
1949-S	42.00	33.00	825.	*	1000.
1950	25.00	35.00	83.00	69.00	390.
1950-D	22.00	210.	115.	73.00	425.
1950-S	27.00	*	425.	195.	*
1951	29.00	37.00	47.00	95.00	215.
1951-D	9.00	25.00	50.00	74.00	250.
1951-S	22.00	47.00	260.	435.	375.
1952	16.00	22.00	59.00	88.00	145.
1952-D	9.00	44.00	41.00	62.00	130.
1952-S	55.00	18.00	190.	300.	700.
1953	5.50	7.25	41.00	70.00	230.
1953-D	5.00	7.00	30.00	58.00	115.
1953-S	10.00	12.00	27.00	69.00	190.
1954	8.00	6.00	27.00	56.00	85.00
1954-D	5.00	6.00	27.00	56.00	80.00
1954-S	4.00	6.00	27.00	56.00	105.
1955	5.00	10.00	28.00	56.00	135.
1955-D	3.00	6.00	27.00	60.00	*
1955-S	11.00	*	27.00	*	*
1956	4.00	4.00	27.00	56.00	79.00
1956-D	4.00	4.00	27.00	56.00	*
1957	3.00	4.75	27.00	56.00	81.00
1957-D	3.00	4.00	27.00	56.00	65.00
1958	3.00	3.75	28.00	56.00	69.00
1958-D	3.00	3.75	27.00	56.00	60.00
1959	1.20	3.50	27.00	56.00	60.00
1959-D	1.20	3.50	27.00	56.00	68.00
1960	1.10	3.75	27.00	56.00	60.00
1960-D	1.10	3.55	27.00	56.00	65.00
1960 Small Date	68.00	*	*	*	*
1960-D Small Date	3.00	*	*	*	*
1961	1.30	3.80	27.00	56.00	60.00
1961-D	1.25	3.70	27.00	56.00	61.00
1962	1.50	3.50	27.00	56.00	60.00
1962-D	1.25	3.95	27.00	56.00	60.00
1963	1.30	3.45	27.00	56.00	60.00

—— = Insufficient pricing data   * = None issued

BRILLIANT UNCIRCULATED ROLLS (CONTINUED)

Date	1¢	5¢	10¢	25¢	50¢
1963-D	1.25	3.45	27.00	56.00	60.00
1964	1.10	4.00	27.00	56.00	60.00
1964-D	1.50	4.25	27.00	56.00	60.00
1965	1.90	3.25	7.25	20.00	21.00
1966	3.90	3.75	10.00	21.00	20.00
1967	3.00	4.25	9.00	22.50	20.00
1968	1.90	*	7.50	23.00	*
1968-D	1.50	4.50	7.50	29.00	20.00
1968-S	1.20	3.75	*	*	*
1969	5.75	*	26.00	25.50	*
1969-D	1.15	4.00	9.50	24.00	20.00
1969-S	1.35	3.65	*	*	*
1970	2.00	*	8.00	21.00	*
1970-D	1.45	3.75	7.75	19.00	190.
1970-S	1.15	4.25	*	*	*
1971	6.50	14.00	13.50	25.00	14.50
1971-D	5.00	4.00	9.00	23.50	14.00
1971-S	4.75	*	*	*	*
1972	2.50	4.25	9.50	13.75	15.00
1972-D	2.50	4.00	8.50	20.00	15.00
1972-S	1.75	*	*	*	*
1973	1.50	6.00	10.00	17.00	16.00
1973-D	1.25	5.00	8.00	17.50	15.75
1973-S	1.25	*	*	*	*
1974	1.10	4.25	8.00	18.00	14.50
1974-D	1.10	6.25	7.75	22.00	15.25
1974-S	3.30	*	*	*	*
1975	1.50	5.50	10.00	*	*
1975-D	1.75	4.85	9.25	*	*
1976	1.50	11.50	14.00	17.50	15.50
1976-D	3.25	13.00	12.00	18.00	15.00
1976-S 40% silver BU	*	*	*	50.00	55.00
1976-S 40% silver Proof	*	*	*	65.00	70.00
1977	1.35	5.00	7.25	16.00	19.00
1977-D	1.20	10.50	8.50	16.00	21.50
1978	1.80	3.75	8.00	15.00	20.00
1978-D	1.10	4.25	8.25	15.00	22.00
1979	1.45	3.75	7.25	21.00	14.50
1979-D	1.05	4.50	7.00	19.00	19.00
1980	1.60	4.25	7.50	16.00	15.00
1980-D	1.50	4.00	7.50	16.00	13.50
1981	1.50	3.25	7.00	15.00	18.00
1981-D	1.50	3.75	7.00	15.00	16.50
1982	3.50	21.00	52.50	110.	24.00
1982 Small Date Zinc	15.00	*	*	*	*
1982-D	2.75	42.50	12.50	23.00	30.00
1982-D Large Date Zinc	5.25	*	*	*	*
1983	1.60	40.00	31.00	180.	29.00
1983-D	1.65	32.50	28.50	110.	24.00
1984	4.50	10.00	11.50	24.00	17.50
1984-D	12.00	5.00	12.50	55.00	17.00
1985	2.75	5.00	15.00	50.00	17.00
1985-D	2.25	6.25	10.50	85.00	16.50
1986	11.00	5.50	13.75	95.00	35.00
1986-D	4.00	6.50	13.75	85.00	41.00
1987	3.75	3.75	7.00	16.50	45.00
1987-D	2.10	4.00	7.00	16.50	43.00
1988	2.00	3.75	9.00	25.00	17.50
1988-D	1.75	4.00	8.00	17.00	17.00
1989	1.25	3.75	7.50	19.00	17.00
1989-D	1.25	3.75	7.50	18.00	17.00
1990	1.50	3.75	7.00	21.00	17.00
1990-D	1.50	3.75	7.00	16.00	17.00
1991	1.50	5.00	8.00	18.00	18.00
1991-D	1.50	5.00	8.00	18.00	22.00
1992	1.50	5.00	8.00	18.50	17.00
1992-D	1.50	5.00	8.00	17.50	20.00
1993	1.60	3.75	7.50	16.00	15.00
1993-D	1.50	3.75	7.50	16.00	15.00
1994	1.50	3.75	7.50	16.00	15.00
1994-D	1.50	3.75	7.50	16.00	15.00
1995	1.50	3.50	7.25	14.25	15.00
1995-D	1.50	3.50	7.50	14.00	15.00
1996	1.40	3.50	7.25	14.00	15.00
1996-D	1.40	3.50	7.50	14.00	15.00
1997	1.40	3.50	7.25	15.00	15.00
1997-D	1.40	3.75	7.50	15.00	15.00
1998	1.40	3.75	7.50	15.00	22.00
1998-D	1.40	3.75	7.50	15.00	15.00
1999	1.40	3.75	7.50	16.00	——
1999-D	1.40	3.75	7.50	16.00	——

—— = Insufficient pricing data   * = None issued

Proof 65 coins

	1¢	5¢	10¢	25¢	50¢	$1.00
1859 Copper-nickel 1¢	4950.	*	3750.	4750.	5600.	12000.
1860	3500.	*	1300.	4750.	5700.	14000.
1861	4500.	*	1425.	4750.	6250.	13000.
1862	2200.	*	1900.	4750.	5300.	14500.
1863	2650.	*	1325.	4750.	5400.	12000.
1864 Copper-nickel 1¢	3025.	*	*	*	*	*
1864 Bronze 1¢	9500.	*	1375.	4750.	5100.	11000.
1865	7000.	*	1350.	4750.	5500.	11250.
1866 Motto	3750.	4500.	1350.	2275.	3400.	10500.
1867 Rays 5¢	*	70000.	*	*	*	*
1867 No Rays 5¢	3500.	2600.	1375.	2100.	3750.	9250.
1868	3350.	1300.	1325.	2300.	3400.	9300.
1869	1950.	1075.	1375.	2200.	3250.	9500.
1870	2200.	1150.	1300.	2250.	3200.	9450.
1871	2100.	1000.	1450.	2200.	3150.	10000.
1872	3500.	1075.	1500.	2250.	3200.	9350.
1873 No Arrows	2850.	925.	1300.	2250.	3500.	9000.
1873 With Arrows	*	*	5500.	5750.	8750.	*
1874	2300.	1250.	4250.	5750.	8000.	*
1875	6000.	1775.	1300.	2000.	3100.	*
1876	2600.	950.	1375.	2000.	3075.	*
1877	8500.	2200.	1400.	2000.	3125.	*
1878	900.	800.	1275.	2000.	3600.	*
1878 8 Tail Feathers	*	*	*	*	*	5500.
1878 7 Tail Feathers 2nd Reverse	*	*	*	*	*	14000.
1879	675.	700.	1300.	2000.	2800.	5000.
1880	625.	575.	1250.	2000.	2850.	5000.
1881	600.	575.	1225.	2000.	3100.	5000.
1882	650.	600.	1275.	2000.	2850.	5000.
1883 Shield 5¢	725.	560.	1300.	2000.	2800.	5000.
1883 With CENTS Liberty 5¢	*	530.	*	*	*	*
1883 No CENTS Liberty 5¢	*	785.	*	*	*	*
1884	650.	500.	1225.	2000.	3050.	5000.
1885	625.	925.	1225.	2000.	2950.	5000.
1886	1750.	600.	1250.	2000.	2950.	5000.
1887	3500.	530.	1275.	2000.	2850.	5000.
1888	4350.	530.	1250.	2000.	2900.	5000.
1889	650.	550.	1250.	2000.	2950.	5000.
1890	1750.	575.	1250.	2000.	2750.	5000.
1891	1850.	575.	1250.	2000.	2750.	5000.
1892	600.	575.	1200.	1775.	3100.	5000.
1893	675.	575.	1200.	1775.	3100.	5800.
1894	975.	585.	1200.	1775.	3100.	5000.
1895	600.	600.	1325.	1775.	3100.	33000.
1896	1250.	600.	1200.	1775.	3100.	5000.
1897	650.	520.	1200.	1775.	3100.	5000.
1898	650.	520.	1200.	1775.	3100.	5000.
1899	650.	520.	1200.	1775.	3150.	5000.
1900	600.	520.	1200.	1775.	3100.	5000.
1901	600.	495.	1200.	1775.	3100.	5500.
1902	600.	520.	1200.	1775.	3100.	5000.
1903	600.	500.	1200.	1775.	3150.	5000.
1904	725.	650.	1200.	1775.	3100.	5000.
1905	600.	600.	1200.	1775.	3100.	*
1906	600.	550.	1200.	1775.	3100.	*
1907	950.	540.	1200.	1775.	3100.	*

* = None issued

	1¢	5¢	10¢	25¢	50¢	$1.00
1908	600.	485.	1200.	1775.	3100.	*
1909 Indian 1¢	600.	485.	1200.	1775.	3100.	*
1909 Lincoln VDB 1¢	7500.	*	*	*	*	*
1909 Lincoln 1¢	1250.	*	*	*	*	*
1910	1150.	485.	1200.	1775.	3000.	*
1911	1100.	490.	1225.	1775.	3100.	*
1912	4000.	490.	1225.	1775.	3100.	*
1913 Bison on Mound 5¢	1500.	2350.	1250.	1775.	3150.	*
1913 Bison on Plain 5¢	*	1200.	*	*	*	*
1914	1100.	1175.	1250.	1775.	3100.	*
1915	2500.	1225.	1275.	1900.	3100.	*
1916	10000.	2100.	——	*	*	*
1921 Morgan Zerbe Proof	*	*	*	*	*	9250.
1936	850.	850.	825.	1000.	2600.	*
1937	110.	750.	360.	335.	685.	*
1938	100.	80.00	285.	220.	525.	*
1939	95.00	60.00	230.	167.	470.	*
1940	90.00	60.00	200.	145.	375.	*
1941	75.00	55.00	140.	138.	350.	*
1942	77.50	50.00	140.	125.	330.	*
1942 Wartime Alloy 5¢	*	80.00	*	*	*	*

—— = Insufficient pricing data * = None issued

American Eagle silver bullion

Date of authorization:	Dec. 17, 1985
Dates of issue:	1986-present
Designers:	Obverse: Adolph A. Weinman Reverse: John Mercanti
Engravers:	Obverse: Edgar Steever Reverse: John Mercanti
Diameter:	40.10mm/1.58 inches
Weight:	31.10 grams/1.00 ounce
Metallic Content:	100% silver (.999 fine)
Weight of pure gold:	31.10 grams/1.00 ounce
Edge:	Reeded
Mint mark:	Proofs only, reverse left of eagle's tail

Values for all American Eagles appear at the end of the bullion section of this chapter. Silver spot at time of writing: about $5.40.

American Eagle gold bullion

Date of authorization:	Dec. 17, 1985
Dates of issue:	1986-present
Designers:	Obverse: Augustus Saint-Gaudens Reverse: Miley Busiek
Engravers:	Obverse: Matthew Peloso Reverse: Sheri Winter
Diameter:	\$50: 32.70mm/1.29 inches \$25: 27.00mm/1.07 inches \$10: 22.00mm/0.87 inch \$5: 16.50mm/0.65 inch
Weight:	\$50: 33.93 grams/1.09 ounce \$25: 16.97 grams/0.55 ounce \$10: 8.48 grams/0.27 ounce \$5: 3.39 grams/0.11 ounce
Metallic Content:	91.67% gold, 5.33% copper, 3% silver
Weight of pure gold:	\$50: 1.00 ounce \$25: 0.50 ounce \$10: 0.25 ounce \$5: 0.10 ounce
Edge:	Reeded
Mint mark:	Proofs only, obverse below date

Values for all American Eagles appear at the end of the bullion section of this chapter. Gold spot at time of writing: about $260.30.

American Eagle platinum bullion

Date of authorization:	Dec. 17, 1985
Dates of issue:	1997-present
Designers/Engravers:	Obverse: John Mercanti Reverse: Thomas D. Rogers Sr.
Diameter:	$100: 32.70mm/1.29 inches $50: 27.00mm/1.07 inches $25: 22.00mm/0.87 inch $10: 16.50mm/0.65 inch
Weight:	$100: 31.10 grams/1.00 ounce $50: 15.55 grams/0.50 ounce $25: 7.78 grams/0.25 ounce $10: 3.11 grams/0.10 ounce
Metallic Content:	100% platinum (.9995 fine)
Weight of pure platinum:	$100: 1.00 ounce $50: 0.50 ounce $25: 0.25 ounce $10: 0.10 ounce
Edge:	Reeded
Mint mark:	Proofs only, left, between rays

Values for all American Eagles appear at the end of the bullion section of this chapter. Pllatinum spot at time of writing: about $352.50.

Market values for American Eagle Bullion Coins

	$5 gold	$10 gold	$25 gold	$50 gold	gold set	$1 silver
1986 Unc.	45.00	100.	190.	325.	660.	10.00
1986 Proof ($1 silver - S, $50 gold - W)			*	575.	*	20.00
1987 Unc.	46.00	100.	225.	325.	696.	9.00
1987 Proof ($1 silver - S, gold $25 - P, $50 - W)	*	*	300.	575.	910.	20.00
1988 Unc.	45.00	110.	315.	325.	795.	9.00
1988 Proof ($1 silver - S; gold $5, $10, $25 - P, $50 - W)	60.00	150.	300.	575.	1128.	32.00
1989 Unc.	50.00	110.	400.	325.	885.	9.00
1989 Proof ($1 silver - S; gold $5, $10, $25 - P, $50 - W)	60.00	150.	300.	575.	848.	20.00
1990 Unc.	46.00	110.	385.	325.	866.	9.00
1990 Proof ($1 silver - S; gold $5, $10, $25 - P, $50 - W)	55.00	150.	300.	575.	1128.	20.00
1991 Unc.	48.00	135.	410.	325.	918.	9.00
1991 Proof ($1 silver - S; gold $5, $10, $25 - P, $50 - W)	60.00	145.	300.	575.	1123.	20.00
1992 Unc.	35.00	115.	270.	350.	770.	9.00
1992 Proof ($1 silver - S; gold $5, $10, $25 - P, $50 - W)	72.50	150.	300.	575.	1141.	20.00
1993 Unc.	35.00	125.	200.	325.	685.	9.00
1993 Proof ($1 silver - P; gold $5, $10, $25 - P, $50 - W)	70.00	150.	300.	575.	1139.	42.00
1994 Unc.	35.00	85.00	160.	325.	605.	8.50
1994 Proof ($1 silver - P; gold $5, $10, $25 - P, $50 - W)	60.00	150.	300.	575.	848.	40.00
1995 Unc.	35.00	95.00	220.	325.	675.	8.50
1995 Proof ($1 silver, gold $5, $10, $25, $50 - W, 10th Anniversary set)	62.50	150.	300.	575.	1600.	750.
1995 Proof ($1 silver - P; gold $5, $10, $25, $50 - W)	*	*	*	*	1131.	37.00
1996 Unc.	34.00	82.50	315.	325.	757.	8.50
1996 Proof ($1 silver - P; gold $5, $10, $25, $50 - W)	80.00	150.	300.	575.	1149.	30.00
1997 Unc.	34.00	100.	190.	315.	639.	8.25
1997 Proof ($1 silver - P; gold $5, $10, $25, $50 - W)	90.00	175.	300.	575.	1186.	25.00
1998 Unc.	34.00	82.50	160.	300.	577.	8.00
1998 Proof ($1 silver - P; gold $5, $10, $25, $50 - W)	65.00	150.	300.	575.	1134.	23.00
1999 Unc.	—	—	—	—	—	—
1999 Proof ($1 silver - P; gold $5, $10, $25, $50 - W)	—	—	—	—	—	—

	$10 platinum	$25 platinum	$50 platinum	$100 platinum	platinum set
1997 Unc.	55.00	205.	525.	495.	1331.
1997 Proof	125.	200.	400.	775.	1560.
1998 Unc.	42.50	170.	300.	410.	959.
1998 Proof	115.	200.	400.	700.	1472.
1999 Unc.	—	—	—	—	—
1999 Proof	—	—	—	—	—

* = None issued

U.S Type Coin Trend Values

	AG-3	G-4	VG-8	F-12	VF-20	EF-40	AU-50	MS-60	MS-63	MS-64	MS-65	PF-60	PF-63	PF-65
HALF CENTS														
Flowing Hair 1793	800.	1425.	2200.	3600.	5200.	10750.	15500.	25500.	55000.	115000.	—	—	—	—
Liberty Cap 1794-1797	85.00	225.	350.	625.	1100.	2900.	5000.	7250.	16500.	37500.	82500.	—	—	—
Draped Bust 1800-1808	14.50	35.00	42.50	55.00	80.00	180.	385.	975.	2500.	3850.	12500.	—	—	—
Classic Head 1809-1835	14.00	30.00	35.00	44.00	55.00	70.00	125.	200.	425.	725.	7500.	2500.	4750.	25000.
Coronet 1849-1857	15.00	29.00	35.00	40.00	50.00	75.00	125.	180.	365.	650.	4500.	2000.	3850.	8500.
CENTS - (Large)														
Flowing Hair, Chain 1793	1025.	2450.	3850.	6000.	8500.	19000.	35000.	55000.	110000.	160000.	—	—	—	—
Flowing Hair, Wreath 1793	450.	850.	1250.	2500.	3550.	7250.	12250.	19000.	42500.	77500.	185000.	—	—	—
Liberty Cap 1793-1796	85.00	150.	235.	450.	700.	1850.	3150.	4750.	6500.	12500.	62500.	—	—	—
Draped Bust 1796-1807	11.50	38.00	57.50	115.	255.	675.	1300.	2100.	5750.	11500.	60000.	—	—	—
Classic Head 1808-1814	15.00	34.00	72.50	200.	425.	825.	1800.	2750.	7250.	15000.	55000.	—	—	—
Coronet 1816-1839	4.50	10.00	11.00	20.00	50.00	85.00	150.	275.	475.	700.	7500.	3500.	12000.	—
Coronet 1839-1857	4.25	9.00	10.50	12.50	18.00	42.00	90.00	175.	285.	390.	2350.	2150.	5800.	19500.
CENTS - (Small)														
Flying Eagle 1856-1858	5.50	17.00	19.00	24.00	32.50	85.00	150.	220.	525.	950.	2450.	1650.	5500.	21500.
Indian copper-nickel 1859	3.75	8.00	10.00	15.00	35.00	80.00	130.	220.	410.	900.	2450.	410.	1575.	4950.
Indian copper-nickel, Shield 1860-64	1.75	5.50	6.00	7.00	10.00	21.00	40.00	65.00	150.	270.	685.	285.	650.	2200.
Indian Bronze 1864-1909	0.65	1.30	1.45	1.90	2.25	6.00	12.50	20.00	37.00	55.00	270.	85.00	135.	600.
TWO CENTS														
1864-1873	3.75	7.25	11.50	22.00	24.00	30.00	50.00	90.00	145.	215.	935.	275.	450.	1775.
THREE CENT NICKEL														
1865-1889	4.00	7.00	7.15	14.00	15.00	18.00	35.00	80.00	120.	230.	665.	150.	250.	490.

U.S Type Coin Trend Values (continued)

	AG-3	G-4	VG-8	F-12	VF-20	EF-40	AU-50	MS-60	MS-63	MS-64	MS-65	PF-60	PF-63	PF-65
THREE CENT SILVER														
1851-1853 One Outline of Star	6.50	13.00	20.00	23.00	29.00	58.00	125.	145.	250.	380.	925.	——	——	——
1854-1858 Three Outlines of Star	8.00	15.50	19.00	23.00	40.00	85.00	165.	260.	550.	1275.	3375.	1350.	2100.	7500.
1859-1873 Two Outlines of Star	6.75	13.25	18.00	23.00	35.00	60.00	125.	160.	250.	415.	925.	325.	450.	1300.
NICKEL FIVE CENT														
Shield, With Rays 1866-1867	10.00	17.50	19.00	22.00	38.00	100.	145.	200.	390.	600.	2300.	875.	1850.	4500.
Shield, No Rays 1867-1883	4.50	12.50	14.00	15.00	16.00	32.00	57.00	90.00	150.	260.	650.	140.	245.	560.
Liberty Head, No CENTS 1883	1.50	2.00	4.50	5.00	6.00	7.50	11.00	22.50	45.00	70.00	235.	155.	240.	530.
Liberty Head, With CENTS 1883-1912	0.55	1.05	1.75	3.75	7.00	20.00	42.50	55.00	85.00	170.	475.	110.	170.	485.
Indian Head, Bison on Mound 1913	2.25	4.75	5.50	6.00	8.00	12.00	20.00	30.00	40.00	55.00	100.	700.	900.	2350.
Indian Head, Bison on Plain 1913-38	0.45	0.60	0.65	0.70	1.00	2.10	6.50	11.00	16.00	21.00	40.00	375.	475.	750.
HALF DIMES														
Flowing Hair 1794-1795	315.	515.	675.	900.	1325.	2100.	2925.	4350.	7000.	10000.	27000.	——	——	——
Draped Bust, Small Eagle 1796-1797	350.	625.	800.	1200.	1825.	3150.	3900.	7250.	12000.	32500.	75000.	——	——	——
Draped Bust, Heraldic Eagle 1800-05	200.	425.	575.	750.	1175.	2300.	3300.	4650.	6950.	13000.	26500.	——	——	——
Capped Bust 1829-1837	8.50	17.00	25.00	29.00	55.00	115.	180.	280.	575.	1000.	2425.	3500.	7250.	30000.
Seated Liberty, No Stars 1837-1838	16.00	24.00	33.00	48.00	90.00	180.	340.	575.	825.	1450.	3100.	4350.	11500.	40000.
Seated Liberty, No Drapery 1838-1840	3.50	9.00	10.00	12.50	22.00	60.00	125.	240.	375.	625.	1625.	——	——	25000.
Seated Liberty, Drapery 1840-1859	3.50	9.00	10.00	12.00	18.00	40.00	77.00	120.	225.	475.	950.	500.	1050.	4250.
Seated Liberty, Arrows 1853-1855	3.25	9.00	10.00	12.00	15.00	45.00	80.00	160.	285.	600.	1725.	2650.	6000.	16000.
Seated Liberty, Legend 1860-1873	3.25	9.00	8.25	12.00	13.50	29.00	60.00	105.	170.	295.	875.	240.	425.	1400.
DIMES														
Draped Bust, Small Eagle 1796-1797	425.	950.	1400.	1700.	2850.	4400.	5650.	7750.	15000.	20500.	45000.	——	——	——

—— = Insufficient pricing data

U.S Type Coin Trend Values (continued)

	AG-3	G-4	VG-8	F-12	VF-20	EF-40	AU-50	MS-60	MS-63	MS-64	MS-65	PF-60	PF-63	PF-65
Draped Bust, Heraldic Eagle 1798-1807	190.	375.	450.	600.	775.	1450.	1925.	3750.	5950.	12000.	24000.	——	——	——
Capped Bust, Large Planchet 1809-27	9.00	18.00	25.00	35.00	85.00	260.	490.	850.	1750.	3350.	7500.	4000.	9000.	37500.
Capped Bust, Small Planchet 1828-37	8.00	16.00	18.00	25.00	52.50	175.	275.	600.	1150.	2075.	5500.	2900.	8750.	23500.
Seated Liberty, No Stars 1837-1838	14.00	25.00	35.00	70.00	250.	475.	650.	950.	1850.	3450.	6250.	5000.	17500.	37500.
Seated Liberty, No Drapery 1838-1840	5.00	9.25	10.75	14.00	25.00	52.50	135.	270.	675.	1200.	3250.	——	——	——
Seated Liberty, Drapery 1840-1860	3.50	8.50	9.50	11.50	13.00	35.00	100.	225.	600.	925.	2400.	550.	1150.	3750.
Seated Liberty, Arrows 1853-1855	3.50	8.50	9.00	10.50	16.00	38.00	120.	275.	650.	1200.	3150.	2750.	3500.	40500.
Seated Liberty, Legend 1860-1891	3.25	7.75	9.00	11.00	12.00	20.00	65.00	120.	205.	360.	1050.	280.	310.	1225.
Seated Liberty, Arrows 1873-1874	4.00	9.50	12.50	20.00	40.00	135.	235.	425.	925.	1700.	4500.	675.	1025.	4250.
Barber 1892-1916	1.00	1.50	1.90	4.00	7.50	20.00	50.00	85.00	140.	235.	725.	250.	325.	1200.
Winged Liberty Head 1916-1945	0.40	0.45	0.50	0.85	1.00	1.25	2.00	5.00	9.00	12.50	17.00	95.00	110.	140.
TWENTY CENT PIECE														
Seated Liberty 1875-1878	30.00	42.00	48.00	70.00	100.	160.	275.	460.	1050.	1675.	5000.	925.	1800.	8000.
QUARTERS														
Draped Bust, Small Eagle 1796	2250.	4250.	6250.	8250.	9750.	14000.	16750.	24500.	35000.	60000.	105000.	——	——	——
Draped Bust, Heraldic Eagle 1804-07	95.00	175.	245.	360.	675.	1475.	2100.	3850.	7500.	21500.	47500.	——	——	——
Capped Bust, Large Planchet 1815-28	23.00	48.00	60.00	90.00	250.	640.	950.	1950.	3500.	4950.	15000.	6500.	18500.	52500.
Capped Bust, Small Planchet 1831-38	19.00	39.00	45.00	55.00	85.00	200.	525.	775.	1975.	4150.	11750.	5000.	15000.	45000.
Seated Liberty, No Motto 1838-65	5.00	13.00	16.00	21.50	27.00	50.00	120.	280.	550.	950.	3400.	440.	850.	4750.
Seated Liberty, Arrows & Rays 1853	6.75	12.50	16.00	23.50	37.00	130.	300.	775.	2025.	4400.	16500.	26500.	62500.	——
Seated Liberty, Arrows 1854-55	5.00	12.50	16.00	21.50	28.00	70.00	235.	475.	1175.	2100.	7000.	6250.	8500.	24000.
Seated Liberty, Motto 1866-91	5.00	13.00	16.00	21.25	27.00	50.00	110.	225.	405.	700.	1525.	360.	625.	2000.
Seated Liberty, Arrows 1873-74	6.50	14.50	18.50	29.00	55.00	185.	360.	675.	1450.	1925.	3250.	675.	1150.	5750.
Barber 1892-1916	2.00	3.50	4.00	16.00	29.00	60.00	110.	160.	250.	500.	1375.	375.	575.	1775.

—— = Insufficient pricing data

U.S Type Coin Trend Values (continued)

	AG-3	G-4	VG-8	F-12	VF-20	EF-40	AU-50	MS-60	MS-63	MS-64	MS-65	PF-60	PF-63	PF-65
Standing Liberty, Bared Breast 1916-17	3.00	15.00	18.00	27.00	43.00	60.00	115.	150.	240.	325.	700.	——	——	——
Standing Liberty, Mailed Breast 1917-30	1.75	3.00	3.75	4.50	12.50	25.00	50.00	95.00	150.	250.	450.	——	——	——
HALF DOLLARS														
Flowing Hair 1794-1795	290.	385.	600.	850.	1400.	4350.	8750.	23000.	50000.	90000.	——	——	——	——
Draped Bust, Small Eagle 1796-1797	7500.	10000.	14000.	18750.	22500.	43000.	63500.	97500.	135000.	175000.	——	——	——	——
Draped Bust, Heraldic Eagle 1801-07	37.00	125.	160.	210.	330.	650.	1650.	4300.	11000.	19500.	39000.	——	——	——
Capped Bust, Lettered Edge 1807-36	16.00	35.00	38.00	45.00	50.00	75.00	175.	425.	1250.	2400.	6250.	4000.	16000.	85000.
Capped Bust, Reeded Edge 1836-39	18.00	32.00	36.00	45.00	75.00	120.	250.	600.	1650.	4000.	12500.	15000.	35000.	——
Seated Liberty, No Motto 1839-66	7.65	15.50	24.00	40.00	48.00	70.00	160.	375.	740.	1700.	4500.	525.	825.	5100.
Seated Liberty, Arrows & Rays 1853	8.25	18.00	29.00	44.00	80.00	225.	450.	1275.	3550.	6250.	19000.	25000.	60000.	——
Seated Liberty, Arrows 1854-55	7.75	16.00	25.00	40.00	45.00	90.00	250.	475.	1450.	2500.	7600.	10500.	13000.	29000.
Seated Liberty, Motto 1866-91	7.50	16.00	24.00	40.00	45.00	65.00	160.	335.	540.	1200.	3000.	400.	625.	2750
Seated Liberty, Arrows 1873-74	9.50	18.00	27.00	40.00	70.00	190.	350.	875.	2000.	3700.	14500.	825.	1400.	8000.
Barber 1892-1915	4.35	6.50	7.50	27.00	65.00	130.	265.	380.	625.	1025.	2650.	450.	650.	3000.
Walking Liberty 1916-1947	2.10	2.50	3.00	3.30	3.75	5.75	8.75	26.50	40.00	45.00	85.00	190.	225.	330.
DOLLARS														
Flowing Hair 1794-1795	425.	725.	950.	1350.	1875.	4350.	7000.	16000.	45000.	100000.	225000.	——	——	——
Draped Bust, Small Eagle 1795-1798	275.	525.	700.	975.	1450.	3200.	6350.	16000.	46000.	90000.	150000.	——	——	——
Draped Bust, Heraldic Eagle 1798-1803	170.	425.	475.	575.	775.	1275.	3200.	8500.	25000.	37500.	80000.	37500.	72500.	200000.
Gobrecht 1836-1839	1150.	2100.	2500.	2850.	3600.	4500.	6350.	——	——	——	——	6500.	14750.	50000.
Seated Liberty, No Motto 1840-66	60.00	100.	120.	170.	200.	290.	525.	900.	2400.	5750.	16000.	1350.	2800.	11000.
Seated Liberty, Motto 1866-73	60.00	95.00	120.	170.	210.	285.	500.	1150.	2500.	5300.	24500.	1150.	2600.	9000.
Morgan 1878-1921	7.75	9.00	10.00	10.00	11.00	12.00	12.50	14.00	20.00	25.00	110.	775.	1500.	5000.
Peace 1921-1935	6.50	7.50	9.00	9.50	10.50	11.25	11.50	12.00	22.00	45.00	140.	——	——	——

—— = Insufficient pricing data

U.S Type Coin Trend Values (continued)

	AG-3	G-4	VG-8	F-12	VF-20	EF-40	AU-50	MS-60	MS-63	MS-64	MS-65	PF-60	PF-63	PF-65
Trade 1873-1885	27.50	40.00	55.00	90.00	115.	135.	225.	380.	1175.	2750.	7750.	1125.	2000.	7250.

U.S Gold Type Coin Trend Values

	F-12	VF-20	EF-40	AU-50	MS-60	MS-63	MS-64	MS-65	PF-60	PF-63	PF-64	PF-65
GOLD DOLLARS												
Coronet 1849-1854	120.	130.	150.	165.	265.	1125.	2175.	5950.	——	——	——	——
Indian Head Small Head 1854-1856	225.	325.	400.	625.	2650.	16750.	27500.	60000.	——	——	85000.	175000.
Indian Head Large Head 1856-1889	115.	130.	140.	160.	250.	975.	1300.	2100.	2350.	3750.	5350.	9000.
QUARTER EAGLES												
Capped Bust, No Stars 1796	10500.	19250.	38000.	57500.	150000.	——	——	——	——	——	——	——
Capped Bust 1796-1807	2750.	3900.	5050.	7100.	19500.	52500.	——	——	——	——	——	——
Capped Draped Bust 1808	8250.	14000.	20000.	32500.	65000.	——	——	——	——	——	——	——
Capped Head 1821-1834	2700.	3250.	4325.	5300.	9500.	19500.	33500.	62500.	——	——	——	——
Classic Head 1834-1839	225.	260.	400.	600.	1750.	5600.	11500.	28500.	35000.	75000.	150000.	300000.
Coronet 1840-1907	125.	140.	155.	175.	300.	925.	1275.	2175.	2500.	4800.	7500.	13250.
Indian Head 1908-1929	130.	140.	150.	165.	235.	675.	1200.	2900.	3250.	6250.	10250.	15000.
THREE DOLLARS												
Indian Head 1854-1889	405.	550.	620.	750.	1750.	5250.	7500.	14750.	5750.	9100.	11250.	26000.
FOUR DOLLAR (Stella)												
Flowing Hair - 1879-1880	16000.	18000.	20000.	22000.	——	——	——	——	32500.	50000.	72500.	89500.
Coiled Hair - 1879-1880	——	——	——	——	——	——	——	——	75000.	130000.	185000.	350000.

—— = Insufficient pricing data

U.S Gold Type Coin Trend Values (continued)

	F-12	VF-20	EF-40	AU-50	MS-60	MS-63	MS-64	MS-65	PF-60	PF-63	PF-64	PF-65
HALF EAGLES												
Capped Bust, Small Eagle 1795-1798	5850.	7500.	11000.	16750.	36500.	120000.	——	——	——	——	——	——
Capped Bust, Heraldic Eagle 1795-1807	1300.	1550.	2250.	3775.	5350.	13500.	29000.	90000.	——	——	——	——
Capped Draped Bust 1807-1812	1275.	1525.	1900.	3000.	4950.	11500.	22500.	85000.	——	——	——	——
Capped Head 1813-1834	1500.	1750.	2200.	3100.	5900.	17500.	26000.	80000.	——	130000.	——	——
Classic Head 1834-1838	240.	295.	400.	675.	2600.	7500.	17500.	62500.	36000.	85000.	——	——
Coronet, No Motto 1839-1866	165.	185.	195.	290.	1250.	7550.	17500.	42000.	8250.	18500.	30000.	72500.
Coronet, Motto 1866-1908	150.	165.	170.	200.	240.	750.	1575.	4250.	3150.	8500.	14000.	24500.
Indian Head 1908-1929	160.	175.	200.	240.	335.	1550.	3750.	13500.	3800.	8000.	12000.	25000.
EAGLES												
Capped Bust, Small Eagle 1795-1797	6250.	8500.	15000.	21000.	50000.	100000.	175000.	——	——	——	——	——
Capped Bust, Heraldic Eagle 1797-1804	2250.	2750.	4250.	6000.	10000.	25000.	45000.	150000.	——	——	——	——
Coronet, No Motto 1838-1866	245.	290.	335.	525.	3500.	12500.	28000.	75000.	14500.	28000.	37500.	67500.
Coronet, Motto 1866-1907	215.	250.	260.	290.	310.	775.	1750.	4500.	3650.	10000.	17000.	35000.
Indian Head, No Motto 1907-1908	350.	370.	385.	405.	575.	1675.	2750.	7250.	——	——	——	——
Indian Head, 1908-1933	335.	345.	355.	365.	450.	790.	1575.	4500.	4000.	11500.	15750.	30000.
DOUBLE EAGLES												
Coronet, No Motto 1849-1866	465.	530.	575.	725.	2700.	12500.	17500.	32500.	22500.	37500.	70000.	175000.
Coronet, TWENTY D. 1866-1876	460.	515.	525.	545.	735.	9750.	24000.	65000.	14000.	30000.	52500.	130000.
Coronet, TWENTY DOLLARS 1877-1907	450.	460.	470.	490.	525.	625.	1150.	3450.	6800.	15000.	25000.	55000.
Saint-Gaudens, Roman Numerals, High Relief 1907	2400.	2850.	3400.	4750.	7400.	10750.	14850.	23500.	9000.	22500.	35000.	60000.
Saint-Gaudens, Arabic Numerals, No Motto 1907-08	490.	500.	515.	535.	575.	700.	825.	1250.	——	——	——	——
Saint-Gaudens, Motto 1908-1933	465.	490.	505.	520.	550.	625.	725.	1150.	6750.	15500.	26000.	38500.

—— = Insufficient pricing data

5 Mintages

The mintage figures that follow are based on years of study by various numismatists, including *Coin World* staff members. The figures were compiled from official Mint Reports, data from the National Archives, conversations with other experts and in some cases, an educated guess. In many instances, the figures given are based on the best information available to researchers today. Prior to 1950, the generally accepted source of mintage figures was the Annual Report of the Director of the Mint. Since the Mint Report for many years was simply a bookkeeper's record of how many coins were issued in a given year, the figures given often had no relation to the actual number of coins struck with each date. Particularly for many 18th century and early 19th century coins, mintage figures here reflect the number of coins struck during the year, no matter the date on the coin.

Mintage figures should not be mistaken for survival figures. For example, 12,000 1895 Morgan dollars were recorded as having been struck, but none are known today; it is likely that all were melted before any entered circulation. Similarly, some coins' survival rates may suggest higher mintages than are recorded.

The mintage figures in this book differ from those in other works, particularly for coins struck since 1965. A coinage shortage in the mid-1960s led Mint officials to suspend the use of Mint marks from 1965-67. Three facilities — the Philadelphia and Denver Mints and the San Francisco Assay Office — struck coins but their separate products are indistinguishable from each other. For that reason, price guides traditionally have combined mintages despite the confusion this may cause future numismatists. For example, many collectors refer to the 40 percent silver Kennedy half dollars without Mint marks, struck between 1965 and 1970, as "Philadelphia" strikes. However, not a single 40 percent silver half dollar was ever struck at the Philadelphia Mint during that period.

This book also clarifies mintage figures of more recent years, particularly for coins struck at the former San Francisco Assay Office and West Point Bullion Depository (both received Mint status in 1988). Like most Philadelphia coins struck until 1979-80, none have Mint marks.

For various reasons, in most price guides and other numismatic works, mintages for coins struck at the West Point and San Francisco facilities have been added to the Philadelphia mintages, since no Mint marks were used on any of the coins.

This book differs. Separate mintage figures are given for all coins by striking facility; we have not combined mintage figures just because the coins have no Mint marks. To indicate those coins that do not have Mint marks, the Mint mark letter is enclosed in parentheses [a coin indicated by a P has a P Mint mark; one indicated by (P) does not have a Mint mark but was struck at the Philadelphia Mint].

Since the Mint has altered its bookkeeping practices several times in recent years, some mintage figures for circulation coins include the pieces struck for assay purposes and those business strikes struck for Uncirculated Mint sets, while other figures may not include those pieces.

In years prior to 1860, when Proof mintages were small and were not recorded, a delta (Δ) marks those issues that are known or are thought to exist. In many instances from 1860 to 1922 the figures shown are approximate, the result of incomplete records, restrikes and the melting of unsold Proofs. Where a delta is followed by an R in parentheses [Δ(R)], the original Proof mintage is unknown, but original specimens are believed to exist, and restrikes are known.

Since 1950, Proof coins have been available from the Mint in sets only (designated by ‹§› in the Notes column). Therefore, Proof mintages since 1950 listed here represent the official tally of Proof sets sold, distributed across the coins included in the set. Proof coins sold as part of a special set, such as a Prestige Proof set, are also included.

Where [——] appears under a mintage column, no coins of that date/Mint were issued.

DATE	NOTE	BUSINESS	PROOF
Liberty Cap, Left half cent			
1793		35,334	—
Liberty Cap, Right half cent			
1794		81,600	—
1795		139,690	—
1796		1,390	—
1797		127,840	—
Draped Bust half cent			
1800		202,908	—
1802		20,266	—
1803		92,000	—
1804		1,055,312	—
1805		814,464	—
1806		356,000	—
1807		476,000	—
1808		400,000	—
Classic Head half cent			
1809		1,154,572	—
1810		215,000	—
1811	‹1›	63,140	—
1825		63,000	Δ
1826		234,000	Δ
1828		606,000	Δ
1829		487,000	Δ
1831		2,200	Δ (R)
1832	‹2›	154,000	Δ
1833	‹2›	120,000	Δ
1834	‹2›	141,000	Δ
1835	‹2›	398,000	Δ
1836		—	Δ (R)
Coronet half cent			
1840 (P)		—	Δ (R)
1841 (P)		—	Δ (R)
1842 (P)		—	Δ (R)
1843 (P)		—	Δ (R)
1844 (P)		—	Δ (R)
1845 (P)		—	Δ (R)
1846 (P)		—	Δ (R)
1847 (P)		—	Δ (R)
1848 (P)		—	Δ (R)
1849 (P)		43,364	Δ (R)
1850 (P)		39,812	Δ
1851 (P)		147,672	Δ
1852 (P)		—	Δ (R)
1853 (P)		129,694	—
1854 (P)		55,358	Δ
1855 (P)		56,500	Δ
1856 (P)		40,430	Δ (R)
1857 (P)		35,180	Δ (R)
Flowing Hair, Chain cent			
1793		36,103	—
Flowing Hair, Wreath cent			
1793		63,353	—
Liberty Cap cent			
1793		11,056	—
1794		918,521	—

DATE	NOTE	BUSINESS	PROOF
1795		538,500	—
1796		109,825	—
Draped Bust cent			
1796		363,375	—
1797		897,510	—
1798		1,841,745	—
1799		42,540	—
1800		2,822,175	—
1801		1,362,837	—
1802		3,435,100	—
1803		3,131,691	—
1804	‹1›	96,500	—
1805		941,116	—
1806		348,000	—
1807		829,221	—
Classic Head cent			
1808		1,007,000	—
1809		222,867	—
1810		1,458,500	—
1811		218,025	—
1812		1,075,500	—
1813		418,000	—
1814		357,830	—
Coronet cent			
1816		2,820,982	—
1817		3,948,400	Δ
1818		3,167,000	Δ
1819		2,671,000	Δ
1820		4,407,550	Δ
1821		389,000	Δ
1822		2,072,339	Δ
1823	‹1, 3›	68,061	Δ
1824		1,193,939	—
1825		1,461,100	Δ
1826		1,517,425	Δ
1827		2,357,732	Δ
1828		2,260,624	Δ
1829		1,414,500	Δ
1830		1,711,500	Δ
1831		3,539,260	Δ
1832		2,362,000	Δ
1833		2,739,000	Δ
1834		1,855,100	Δ
1835		3,878,400	Δ
1836		2,111,000	Δ
1837		5,558,300	Δ
1838 (P)		6,370,200	Δ
1839 (P)		3,128,661	Δ
1840 (P)		2,462,700	Δ
1841 (P)		1,597,367	Δ
1842 (P)		2,383,390	Δ
1843 (P)		2,425,342	Δ
1844 (P)		2,398,752	Δ
1845 (P)		3,894,804	Δ
1846 (P)		4,120,800	Δ
1847 (P)		6,183,669	Δ
1848 (P)		6,415,799	Δ
1849 (P)		4,178,500	Δ

DATE	NOTE	BUSINESS	PROOF
1850 (P)		4,426,844	Δ
1851 (P)		9,889,707	——
1852 (P)		5,063,094	Δ
1853 (P)		6,641,131	——
1854 (P)		4,236,156	Δ
1855 (P)		1,574,829	Δ
1856 (P)	‹4›	2,690,463	Δ
1857 (P)		333,456	Δ

Flying Eagle cent

DATE	NOTE	BUSINESS	PROOF
1857 (P)		17,450,000	Δ
1858 (P)		24,600,000	Δ

Indian Head cent

DATE	NOTE	BUSINESS	PROOF
1859 (P)		36,400,000	Δ
1860 (P)		20,566,000	1,000
1861 (P)		10,100,000	1,000
1862 (P)		28,075,000	550
1863 (P)		49,840,000	460
1864 (P)			
C-N	‹5›	13,740,000	300
bronze	‹5›	39,233,714	170
1865 (P)		35,429,286	500
1866 (P)		9,826,500	725
1867 (P)		9,821,000	625
1868 (P)		10,266,500	600
1869 (P)		6,420,000	600
1870 (P)		5,275,000	1,000
1871 (P)		3,929,500	960
1872 (P)		4,042,000	950
1873 (P)	‹6›	11,676,500	1,100
1874 (P)		14,187,500	700
1875 (P)		13,528,000	700
1876 (P)		7,944,000	1,150
1877 (P)	‹7›	852,500	510
1878 (P)		5,797,500	2,350
1879 (P)		16,228,000	3,200
1880 (P)		38,961,000	3,955
1881 (P)		39,208,000	3,575
1882 (P)		38,578,000	3,100
1883 (P)		45,591,500	6,609
1884 (P)		23,257,800	3,942
1885 (P)		11,761,594	3,790
1886 (P)		17,650,000	4,290
1887 (P)		45,223,523	2,960
1888 (P)		37,489,832	4,582
1889 (P)		48,866,025	3,336
1890 (P)		——	2,740
1891 (P)		——	2,350
1892 (P)		37,647,087	2,745
1893 (P)		46,640,000	2,195
1894 (P)		16,749,500	2,632
1895 (P)		38,341,574	2,062
1896 (P)		39,055,431	1,862
1897 (P)		50,464,392	1,938
1898 (P)		49,821,284	1,795
1899 (P)		53,598,000	2,031
1900 (P)		66,821,284	2,262
1901 (P)		79,609,158	1,985
1902 (P)		87,374,704	2,018
1903 (P)		85,092,703	1,790

DATE	NOTE	BUSINESS	PROOF
1904 (P)		61,326,198	1,817
1905 (P)		80,717,011	2,152
1906 (P)		96,020,530	1,725
1907 (P)		108,137,143	1,475
1908 (P)		32,326,367	1,620
1908-S		1,115,000	——
1909 (P)		14,368,470	2,175
1909-S		309,000	——

Lincoln cent

DATE	NOTE	BUSINESS	PROOF
1909 (P)			
VDB		27,994,580	420
No VDB		72,700,420	2,198
1909-S			
VDB		484,000	——
No VDB		1,825,000	——
1910 (P)		146,798,813	2,405
1910-S		6,045,000	——
1911 (P)		101,176,054	1,733
1911-D		12,672,000	——
1911-S		4,026,000	——
1912 (P)		68,150,915	2,145
1912-D		10,411,000	——
1912-S		4,431,000	——
1913 (P)		76,529,504	2,848
1913-D		15,804,000	——
1913-S		6,101,000	——
1914 (P)		75,237,067	1,365
1914-D		1,193,000	——
1914-S		4,137,000	——
1915 (P)		29,090,970	1,150
1915-D		22,050,000	——
1915-S		4,833,000	——
1916 (P)		131,832,627	1,050
1916-D		35,956,000	——
1916-S		22,510,000	——
1917 (P)		196,429,785	Δ
1917-D		55,120,000	——
1917-S		32,620,000	——
1918 (P)		288,104,634	——
1918-D		47,830,000	——
1918-S		34,680,000	——
1919 (P)		392,021,000	——
1919-D		57,154,000	——
1919-S		139,760,000	——
1920 (P)		310,165,000	——
1920-D		49,280,000	——
1920-S		46,220,000	——
1921 (P)		39,157,000	——
1921-S		15,274,000	——
1922-D	‹8›	7,160,000	——
1923 (P)		74,723,000	——
1923-S		8,700,000	——
1924 (P)		75,178,000	——
1924-D		2,520,000	——
1924-S		11,696,000	——
1925 (P)		139,949,000	——
1925-D		22,580,000	——
1925-S		26,380,000	——
1926 (P)		157,088,000	——

DATE	NOTE	BUSINESS	PROOF
1926-D		28,020,000	—
1926-S		4,550,000	—
1927 (P)		144,440,000	—
1927-D		27,170,000	—
1927-S		14,276,000	—
1928 (P)		134,116,000	—
1928-D		31,170,000	—
1928-S		17,266,000	—
1929 (P)		185,262,000	—
1929-D		41,730,000	—
1929-S		50,148,000	—
1930 (P)		157,415,000	—
1930-D		40,100,000	—
1930-S		24,286,000	—
1931 (P)		19,396,000	—
1931-D		4,480,000	—
1931-S		866,000	—
1932 (P)		9,062,000	—
1932-D		10,500,000	—
1933 (P)		14,360,000	—
1933-D		6,200,000	—
1934 (P)		219,080,000	—
1934-D		28,446,000	—
1935 (P)		245,388,000	—
1935-D		47,000,000	—
1935-S		38,702,000	—
1936 (P)		309,632,000	5,569
1936-D		40,620,000	—
1936-S		29,130,000	—
1937 (P)		309,170,000	9,320
1937-D		50,430,000	—
1937-S		34,500,000	—
1938 (P)		156,682,000	14,734
1938-D		20,010,000	—
1938-S		15,180,000	—
1939 (P)		316,466,000	13,520
1939-D		15,160,000	—
1939-S		52,070,000	—
1940 (P)		586,810,000	15,872
1940-D		81,390,000	—
1940-S		112,940,000	—
1941 (P)		887,018,000	21,100
1941-D		128,700,000	—
1941-S		92,360,000	—
1942 (P)		657,796,000	32,600
1942-D		206,698,000	—
1942-S		85,590,000	—
1943 (P)	‹9›	684,628,670	—
1943-D	‹9›	217,660,000	—
1943-S	‹9›	191,550,000	—
1944 (P)		1,435,400,000	—
1944-D		430,578,000	—
1944-S		282,760,000	—
1945 (P)		1,040,515,000	—
1945-D		226,268,000	—
1945-S		181,770,000	—
1946 (P)		991,655,000	—
1946-D		315,690,000	—
1946-S		198,100,000	—
1947 (P)		190,555,000	—

DATE	NOTE	BUSINESS	PROOF
1947-D		194,750,000	—
1947-S		99,000,000	—
1948 (P)		317,570,000	—
1948-D		172,637,500	—
1948-S		81,735,000	—
1949 (P)		217,775,000	—
1949-D		153,132,500	—
1949-S		64,290,000	—
1950 (P)	‹§›	272,635,000	51,386
1950-D		334,950,000	—
1950-S		118,505,000	—
1951 (P)	‹§›	294,576,000	57,500
1951-D		625,355,000	—
1951-S		136,010,000	—
1952 (P)	‹§›	186,765,000	81,980
1952-D		746,130,000	—
1952-S		137,800,004	—
1953 (P)	‹§›	256,755,000	128,800
1953-D		700,515,000	—
1953-S		181,835,000	—
1954 (P)	‹§›	71,640,050	233,300
1954-D		251,552,500	—
1954-S		96,190,000	—
1955 (P)	‹§›	330,580,000	378,200
1955-D		563,257,500	—
1955-S		44,610,000	—
1956 (P)	‹§›	420,745,000	669,384
1956-D		1,098,210,100	—
1957 (P)	‹§›	282,540,000	1,247,952
1957-D		1,051,342,000	—
1958 (P)	‹§›	252,525,000	875,652
1958-D		800,953,300	—
1959 (P)	‹§›	609,715,000	1,149,291
1959-D		1,279,760,000	—
1960 (P)	‹§, 10›	586,405,000	1,691,602
1960-D		1,580,884,000	—
1961 (P)	‹§›	753,345,000	3,028,244
1961-D		1,753,266,700	—
1962 (P)	‹§›	606,045,000	3,218,019
1962-D		1,793,148,400	—
1963 (P)	‹§›	754,110,000	3,075,645
1963-D		1,774,020,400	—
1964 (P)	‹§, 11›	2,648,575,000	3,950,762
1964-D	‹11›	3,799,071,500	—
1965 (P)	‹11›	301,470,000	—
1965 (D)	‹11›	973,364,900	—
1965 (S)	‹11›	220,030,000	—
1966 (P)	‹11›	811,100,000	—
1966 (D)	‹11›	991,431,200	—
1966 (S)	‹11›	383,355,000	—
1967 (P)	‹11›	907,575,000	—
1967 (D)	‹11›	1,327,377,100	—
1967 (S)	‹11›	813,715,000	—
1968 (P)		1,707,880,970	—
1968-D		2,886,269,600	—
1968-S	‹§›	258,270,001	3,041,506
1969 (P)		1,136,910,000	—
1969-D		4,002,832,200	—
1969-S	‹§›	544,375,000	2,934,631
1970 (P)		1,898,315,000	—

DATE	NOTE	BUSINESS	PROOF
1970-D		2,891,438,900	——
1970-S	‹§›	690,560,004	2,632,810
1971 (P)		1,919,490,000	——
1971-D		2,911,045,600	——
1971-S	‹§›	525,130,054	3,220,733
1972 (P)		2,933,255,000	——
1972-D		2,655,071,400	——
1972-S	‹§›	380,200,104	3,260,996
1973 (P)		3,728,245,000	——
1973-D		3,549,576,588	——
1973-S	‹§›	319,937,634	2,760,339
1974 (P)		4,232,140,523	——
1974-D		4,235,098,000	——
1974-S	‹§›	409,421,878	2,612,568
1975 (P)		3,874,182,000	——
1975-D		4,505,275,300	——
1975-S	‹§›	——	2,845,450
1975 (W)		1,577,294,142	——
1976 (P)		3,133,580,000	——
1976-D		4,221,592,455	——
1976-S		——	——
1976 (W)		1,540,695,000	——
1977 (P)		3,074,575,000	——
1977-D		4,194,062,300	——
1977-S	‹§›	——	3,236,798
1977 (W)		1,395,355,000	——
1978 (P)		3,735,655,000	——
1978-D		4,280,233,400	——
1978 (S)		291,700,000	——
1978-S	‹§›	——	3,120,285
1978 (W)		1,531,250,000	——
1979 (P)		3,560,940,000	——
1979-D		4,139,357,254	——
1979 (S)		751,725,000	——
1979-S	‹§›	——	3,677,175
1979 (W)		1,705,850,000	——
1980 (P)		6,230,115,000	——
1980-D		5,140,098,660	——
1980 (S)		1,184,590,000	——
1980-S	‹§›	——	3,554,806
1980 (W)		1,576,200,000	——
1981 (P)		6,611,305,000	——
1981-D		5,373,235,677	——
1981 (S)		880,440,000	——
1981-S	‹§›	——	4,063,083
1981 (W)		1,882,400,000	——
1982 (P)	‹12›	7,135,275,000	——
1982-D	‹12›	6,012,979,368	——
1982 (S)	‹12›	1,587,245,000	——
1982-S	‹§›	——	3,857,479
1982 (W)	‹12›	1,990,005,000	——
1983 (P)		5,567,190,000	——
1983-D		6,467,199,428	——
1983 (S)		180,765,000	——
1983-S	‹§›	——	3,279,126
1983 (W)		2,004,400,000	——
1984 (P)		6,114,864,000	——
1984-D		5,569,238,906	——
1984-S	‹§›	——	3,065,110
1984 (W)		2,036,215,000	——

DATE	NOTE	BUSINESS	PROOF
1985 (P)		4,951,904,887	——
1985-D		5,287,399,926	——
1985-S	‹§›	——	3,362,821
1985 (W)		696,585,000	——
1986 (P)		4,490,995,493	——
1986-D		4,442,866,698	——
1986-S	‹§›	——	3,010,497
1986 (W)		400,000	——
1987 (P)		4,682,466,931	——
1987-D		4,879,389,514	——
1987-S	‹§›	——	3,792,233
1988 (P)		6,092,810,000	——
1988-D		5,253,740,443	——
1988-S	‹§›	——	3,262,948
1989 (P)		7,261,535,000	——
1989-D		5,345,467,711	——
1989-S	‹§›	——	3,220,914
1990 (P)		6,851,765,000	——
1990-D		4,922,894,553	——
1990-S	‹§›	——	3,299,559
1991 (P)		5,165,940,000	——
1991-D		4,158,442,076	——
1991-S	‹§›	——	2,867,787
1992 (P)		4,648,905,000	——
1992-D		4,448,673,300	——
1992-S	‹§›	——	4,176,544
1993 (P)		5,684,705,000	——
1993-D		6,426,650,571	——
1993-S	‹§›	——	3,360,876
1994 (P)		6,500,850,000	——
1994-D		7,131,765,000	——
1994-S	‹§›	——	3,222,140
1995 (P)		6,411,440,000	——
1995-D		7,128,560,000	——
1995-S	‹§›	——	2,791,067
1996 (P)		6,612,465,000	——
1996-D		6,510,795,000	——
1996-S	‹§›	——	2,920,158
1997 (P)		4,622,800,000	——
1997-D		4,576,555,000	——
1997-S	‹§›	——	2,796,194
1998 (P)		5,032,200,000	——
1998-D		5,225,200,000	——
1998-S	‹§›	——	2,965,503

Two cents

1864 (P)	‹13›	19,847,500	100
1865 (P)		13,640,000	500
1866 (P)		3,177,000	725
1867 (P)		2,938,750	625
1868 (P)		2,803,750	600
1869 (P)		1,546,500	600
1870 (P)		861,250	1,000
1871 (P)		721,250	960
1872 (P)		65,000	950
1873 (P)	‹6, 14›	——	1,100

Copper-nickel 3 cents

1865 (P)		11,382,000	400
1866 (P)		4,801,000	725
1867 (P)		3,915,000	625

DATE	NOTE	BUSINESS	PROOF
1868 (P)		3,252,000	600
1869 (P)		1,604,000	600
1870 (P)		1,335,000	1,000
1871 (P)		604,000	960
1872 (P)		862,000	950
1873 (P)	‹6›	1,173,000	1,100
1874 (P)		790,000	700
1875 (P)		228,000	700
1876 (P)		162,000	1,150
1877 (P)	‹7›	——	510
1878 (P)		——	2,350
1879 (P)		38,000	3,200
1880 (P)		21,000	3,955
1881 (P)		1,077,000	3,575
1882 (P)		22,200	3,100
1883 (P)		4,000	6,609
1884 (P)		1,700	3,942
1885 (P)		1,000	3,790
1886 (P)		——	4,290
1887 (P)	‹15›	5,001	2,960
1888 (P)		36,501	4,582
1889 (P)		18,125	3,336
Silver 3 cents			
1851 (P)		5,447,400	Δ
1851-O		720,000	Δ
1852 (P)		18,663,500	——
1853 (P)	‹16›	11,400,000	——
1854 (P)		671,000	Δ
1855 (P)		139,000	Δ
1856 (P)		1,458,000	Δ
1857 (P)		1,042,000	Δ
1858 (P)		1,604,000	Δ
1859 (P)		365,000	Δ
1860 (P)		286,000	1,000
1861 (P)		497,000	1,000
1862 (P)		343,000	550
1863 (P)	‹17›	21,000	460
1864 (P)	‹18›	12,000	470
1865 (P)		8,000	500
1866 (P)		22,000	725
1867 (P)		4,000	625
1868 (P)		3,500	600
1869 (P)		4,500	600
1870 (P)		3,000	1,000
1871 (P)		3,400	960
1872 (P)		1,000	950
1873 (P)	‹6›	——	600
Shield 5 cents			
1866 (P)		14,742,500	125
1867 (P)	‹19›	30,909,500	625
1868 (P)		28,817,000	600
1869 (P)		16,395,000	600
1870 (P)		4,806,000	1,000
1871 (P)		561,000	960
1872 (P)		6,036,000	950
1873 (P)	‹6›	4,550,000	1,100
1874 (P)		3,538,000	700
1875 (P)		2,097,000	700
1876 (P)		2,530,000	1,150

DATE	NOTE	BUSINESS	PROOF
1877 (P)	‹7›	——	510
1878 (P)		——	2,350
1879 (P)		25,900	3,200
1880 (P)		16,000	3,955
1881 (P)		68,800	3,575
1882 (P)		11,473,500	3,100
1883 (P)		1,451,500	5,419
Liberty Head 5 cents			
1883 (P)			
No CENTS		5,474,300	5,219
CENTS		16,026,200	6,783
1884 (P)		11,270,000	3,942
1885 (P)		1,472,700	3,790
1886 (P)		3,326,000	4,290
1887 (P)		15,260,692	2,960
1888 (P)		10,715,901	4,582
1889 (P)		15,878,025	3,336
1890 (P)		16,256,532	2,740
1891 (P)		16,832,000	2,350
1892 (P)		11,696,897	2,745
1893 (P)		13,368,000	2,195
1894 (P)		5,410,500	2,632
1895 (P)		9,977,822	2,062
1896 (P)		8,841,058	1,862
1897 (P)		20,426,797	1,938
1898 (P)		12,530,292	1,795
1899 (P)		26,027,000	2,031
1900 (P)		27,253,733	2,262
1901 (P)		26,478,228	1,985
1902 (P)		31,487,561	2,018
1903 (P)		28,004,935	1,790
1904 (P)		21,401,350	1,817
1905 (P)		29,825,124	2,152
1906 (P)		38,612,000	1,725
1907 (P)		39,213,325	1,475
1908 (P)		22,684,557	1,620
1909 (P)		11,585,763	4,763
1910 (P)		30,166,948	2,405
1911 (P)		39,557,639	1,733
1912 (P)		26,234,569	2,145
1912-D		8,474,000	——
1912-S		238,000	——
1913 (P)	‹20›	——	——
Indian Head 5 cents			
1913 (P)			
Mound		30,992,000	1,520
Plain		29,857,186	1,514
1913-D			
Mound		5,337,000	——
Plain		4,156,000	——
1913-S			
Mound		2,105,000	——
Plain		1,209,000	——
1914 (P)		20,664,463	1,275
1914-D		3,912,000	——
1914-S		3,470,000	——
1915 (P)		20,986,220	1,050
1915-D		7,569,500	——
1915-S		1,505,000	——

DATE	NOTE	BUSINESS	PROOF
1916 (P)		63,497,466	600
1916-D		13,333,000	—
1916-S		11,860,000	—
1917 (P)		51,424,029	Δ
1917-D		9,910,800	—
1917-S		4,193,000	—
1918 (P)		32,086,314	—
1918-D		8,362,000	—
1918-S		4,882,000	—
1919 (P)		60,868,000	—
1919-D		8,006,000	—
1919-S		7,521,000	—
1920 (P)		63,093,000	—
1920-D		9,418,000	—
1920-S		9,689,000	—
1921 (P)		10,663,000	—
1921-S		1,557,000	—
1923 (P)		35,715,000	—
1923-S		6,142,000	—
1924 (P)		21,620,000	—
1924-D		5,258,000	—
1924-S		1,437,000	—
1925 (P)		35,565,100	—
1925-D		4,450,000	—
1925-S		6,256,000	—
1926 (P)		44,693,000	—
1926-D		5,638,000	—
1926-S		970,000	—
1927 (P)		37,981,000	—
1927-D		5,730,000	—
1927-S		3,430,000	—
1928 (P)		23,411,000	—
1928-D		6,436,000	—
1928-S		6,936,000	—
1929 (P)		36,446,000	—
1929-D		8,370,000	—
1929-S		7,754,000	—
1930 (P)		22,849,000	—
1930-S		5,435,000	—
1931-S		1,200,000	—
1934 (P)		20,213,003	—
1934-D		7,480,000	—
1935 (P)		58,264,000	—
1935-D		12,092,000	—
1935-S		10,300,000	—
1936 (P)		118,997,000	4,420
1936-D		24,814,000	—
1936-S		14,930,000	—
1937 (P)		79,480,000	5,769
1937-D		17,826,000	—
1937-S		5,635,000	—
1938-D		7,020,000	—

Jefferson 5 cents

DATE	NOTE	BUSINESS	PROOF
1938 (P)		19,496,000	19,365
1938-D		5,376,000	—
1938-S		4,105,000	—
1939 (P)		120,615,000	12,535
1939-D		3,514,000	—
1939-S		6,630,000	—
1940 (P)		176,485,000	14,158
1940-D		43,540,000	—
1940-S		39,690,000	—
1941 (P)		203,265,000	18,720
1941-D		53,432,000	—
1941-S		43,445,000	—
1942 (P)	‹21›	49,789,000	29,600
1942-P	‹21›	57,873,000	27,600
1942-D	‹21›	13,938,000	—
1942-S	‹21›	32,900,000	—
1943-P	‹21›	271,165,000	—
1943-D	‹21›	15,294,000	—
1943-S	‹21›	104,060,000	—
1944-P	‹21, 22›	119,150,000	—
1944-D	‹21›	32,309,000	—
1944-S	‹21›	21,640,000	—
1945-P	‹21›	119,408,100	—
1945-D	‹21›	37,158,000	—
1945-S	‹21›	58,939,000	—
1946 (P)		161,116,000	—
1946-D		45,292,200	—
1946-S		13,560,000	—
1947 (P)		95,000,000	—
1947-D		37,822,000	—
1947-S		24,720,000	—
1948 (P)		89,348,000	—
1948-D		44,734,000	—
1948-S		11,300,000	—
1949 (P)		60,652,000	—
1949-D		36,498,000	—
1949-S		9,716,000	—
1950 (P)	‹§›	9,796,000	51,386
1950-D		2,630,030	—
1951 (P)	‹§›	28,552,000	57,500
1951-D		20,460,000	—
1951-S		7,776,000	—
1952 (P)	‹§›	63,988,000	81,980
1952-D		30,638,000	—
1952-S		20,572,000	—
1953 (P)	‹§›	46,644,000	128,800
1953-D		59,878,600	—
1953-S		19,210,900	—
1954 (P)	‹§›	47,684,050	233,300
1954-D		117,136,560	—
1954-S		29,384,000	—
1955 (P)	‹§›	7,888,000	378,200
1955-D		74,464,100	—
1956 (P)	‹§›	35,216,000	669,384
1956-D		67,222,640	—
1957 (P)	‹§›	38,408,000	1,247,952
1957-D		136,828,900	—
1958 (P)	‹§›	17,088,000	875,652
1958-D		168,249,120	—
1959 (P)	‹§›	27,248,000	1,149,291
1959-D		160,738,240	—
1960 (P)	‹§›	55,416,000	1,691,602
1960-D		192,582,180	—
1961 (P)	‹§›	73,640,000	3,028,244
1961-D		229,342,760	—
1962 (P)	‹§›	97,384,000	3,218,019

DATE	NOTE	BUSINESS	PROOF
1962-D		280,195,720	—
1963 (P)	‹§›	175,776,000	3,075,645
1963-D		276,829,460	—
1964 (P)	‹§, 11›	1,024,672,000	3,950,762
1964-D	‹11›	1,787,297,160	—
1965 (P)	‹11›	12,440,000	—
1965 (D)	‹11›	82,291,380	—
1965 (S)	‹11›	39,040,000	—
1966 (P)	‹11, 23›	—	Δ
1966 (D)	‹11›	103,546,700	—
1966 (S)	‹11›	50,400,000	—
1967 (P)	‹11›	—	—
1967 (D)	‹11›	75,993,800	—
1967 (S)	‹11›	31,332,000	—
1968 (P)		—	—
1968-D		91,227,880	—
1968-S	‹§›	100,396,004	3,041,506
1969 (P)		—	—
1969-D		202,807,500	—
1969-S	‹§›	120,165,000	2,934,631
1970-D		515,485,380	—
1970-S	‹§›	238,832,004	2,632,810
1971 (P)		106,884,000	—
1971-D		316,144,800	—
1971-S	‹24›	—	3,220,733
1972 (P)		202,036,000	—
1972-D		351,694,600	—
1972-S	‹§›	—	3,260,996
1973 (P)		384,396,000	—
1973-D		261,405,400	—
1973-S	‹§›	—	2,760,339
1974 (P)		601,752,000	—
1974-D		277,373,000	—
1974-S	‹§›	—	2,612,568
1975 (P)		181,772,000	—
1975-D		401,875,300	—
1975-S	‹§›	—	2,845,450
1976 (P)		367,124,000	—
1976-D		563,964,147	—
1976-S		—	—
1977 (P)		585,376,000	—
1977-D		297,313,422	—
1977-S	‹§›	—	3,236,798
1978 (P)		391,308,000	—
1978-D		313,092,780	—
1978-S	‹§›	—	3,120,285
1979 (P)		463,188,000	—
1979-D		325,867,672	—
1979-S	‹§›	—	3,677,175
1980-P	‹25›	593,004,000	—
1980-D		502,323,448	—
1980-S	‹§›	—	3,554,806
1981-P		657,504,000	—
1981-D		364,801,843	—
1981-S	‹§›	—	4,063,083
1982-P		292,355,000	—
1982-D		373,726,544	—
1982-S	‹§›	—	3,857,479
1983-P		561,615,000	—
1983-D		536,726,276	—
1983-S	‹§›	—	3,279,126
1984-P		746,769,000	—
1984-D		517,675,146	—
1984-S	‹§›	—	3,065,110
1985-P		647,114,962	—
1985-D		459,747,446	—
1985-S	‹§›	—	3,362,821
1986-P		536,883,493	—
1986-D		361,819,144	—
1986-S	‹§›	—	3,010,497
1987-P		371,499,481	—
1987-D		410,590,604	—
1987-S	‹§›	—	3,792,233
1988-P		771,360,000	—
1988-D		663,771,652	—
1988-S	‹§›	—	3,262,948
1989-P		898,812,000	—
1989-D		570,842,474	—
1989-S	‹§›	—	3,220,914
1990-P		661,636,000	—
1990-D		663,938,503	—
1990-S	‹§›	—	3,299,559
1991-P		614,104,000	—
1991-D		436,496,678	—
1991-S	‹§›	—	2,867,787
1992-P		399,552,000	—
1992-D		450,565,113	—
1992-S	‹§›	—	4,176,544
1993-P		412,076,000	—
1993-D		406,084,135	—
1993-S	‹§›	—	3,360,876
1994-P	<116>	722,160,000	—
1994-D		715,762,110	—
1994-S	‹§›	—	3,222,140
1995-P		774,156,000	—
1995-D		888,112,000	—
1995-S	‹§›	—	2,791,067
1996-P		829,332,000	—
1996-D		817,736,000	—
1996-S	‹§›	—	2,920,158
1997-P		470,972,000	—
1997-D		466,640,000	—
1997-S	‹§›	—	2,796,194
1998-P		688,292,000	—
1998-D		635,380,000	—
1998-S	‹§›	—	2,965,503

Flowing Hair half dime

1794		7,756	—
1795		78,660	—

Draped Bust half dime

1796		10,230	—
1797		44,527	—
1800		40,000	—
1801		33,910	—
1802		13,010	—
1803		37,850	—
1805		15,600	—

Capped Bust half dime

DATE	NOTE	BUSINESS	PROOF
1829		1,230,000	Δ
1830		1,240,000	Δ
1831		1,242,700	Δ
1832		965,000	Δ
1833		1,370,000	Δ
1834		1,480,000	Δ
1835		2,760,000	Δ
1836		1,900,000	Δ
1837		871,000	Δ

Seated Liberty half dime

DATE	NOTE	BUSINESS	PROOF
1837		1,405,000	—
1838 (P)		2,255,000	Δ
1838-O	‹26›	115,000	—
1839 (P)		1,069,150	Δ
1839-O		981,550	—
1840 (P)		1,344,085	Δ
1840-O		935,000	—
1841 (P)		1,150,000	Δ
1841-O		815,000	—
1842 (P)		815,000	Δ
1842-O		350,000	—
1843 (P)		1,165,000	Δ
1844 (P)		430,000	Δ
1844-O		220,000	—
1845 (P)		1,564,000	Δ
1846 (P)		27,000	Δ
1847 (P)		1,274,000	Δ
1848 (P)		668,000	Δ
1848-O		600,000	—
1849 (P)		1,309,000	Δ
1849-O		140,000	—
1850 (P)		955,000	Δ
1850-O		690,000	—
1851 (P)		781,000	Δ
1851-O		860,000	—
1852 (P)		1,000,500	Δ
1852-O		260,000	—
1853 (P)			
No Arrows	‹16›	135,000	—
Arrows	‹16›	13,210,020	Δ
1853-O			
No Arrows	‹16›	160,000	—
Arrows	‹16›	2,200,000	—
1854 (P)		5,740,000	Δ
1854-O		1,560,000	—
1855 (P)		1,750,000	Δ
1855-O		600,000	—
1856 (P)		4,880,000	Δ
1856-O		1,100,000	—
1857 (P)		7,280,000	Δ
1857-O		1,380,000	—
1858 (P)		3,500,000	Δ
1858-O		1,660,000	—
1859 (P)		340,000	Δ
1859-O		560,000	—
1860 (P)	‹28›	798,000	1,000
1860-O	‹28, 29›	1,060,000	Δ
1861 (P)		3,360,000	1,000
1862 (P)		1,492,000	550
1863 (P)		18,000	460
1863-S		100,000	—
1864 (P)	‹18›	48,000	470
1864-S		90,000	—
1865 (P)		13,000	500
1865-S		120,000	—
1866 (P)		10,000	725
1866-S		120,000	—
1867 (P)		8,000	625
1867-S		120,000	—
1868 (P)		88,600	600
1868-S		280,000	—
1869 (P)		208,000	600
1869-S		230,000	—
1870 (P)		535,600	1,000
1871 (P)		1,873,000	960
1871-S		161,000	—
1872 (P)		2,947,000	950
1872-S		837,000	—
1873 (P)	‹6›	712,000	600
1873-S	‹6›	324,000	—

Draped Bust dime

DATE	NOTE	BUSINESS	PROOF
1796		22,135	—
1797		25,261	—
1798		27,550	—
1800		21,760	—
1801		34,640	—
1802		10,975	—
1803		33,040	—
1804		8,265	—
1805		120,780	—
1807		165,000	—

Capped Bust dime

DATE	NOTE	BUSINESS	PROOF
1809		51,065	—
1811		65,180	—
1814		421,500	—
1820		942,587	Δ
1821		1,186,512	Δ
1822		100,000	Δ
1823	‹3›	440,000	Δ
1824		100,000	Δ
1825		410,000	Δ
1827		1,215,000	Δ
1828		125,000	Δ
1829		770,000	Δ
1830		510,000	Δ
1831		771,350	Δ
1832		522,500	Δ
1833		485,000	Δ
1834		635,000	Δ
1835		1,410,000	Δ
1836		1,190,000	Δ
1837		359,500	Δ

Seated Liberty dime

DATE	NOTE	BUSINESS	PROOF
1837		682,500	—
1838 (P)		1,992,500	Δ
1838-O	‹26›	406,034	—

DATE	NOTE	BUSINESS	PROOF
1839 (P)		1,0,115	Δ
1839-O		1,323,000	——
1840 (P)		1,358,580	Δ
1840-O		1,175,000	——
1841 (P)		1,622,500	Δ
1841-O		2,007,500	——
1842 (P)		1,887,500	Δ
1842-O		2,020,000	——
1843 (P)		1,370,000	Δ
1843-O		50,000	——
1844 (P)		72,500	Δ
1845 (P)		1,755,000	Δ
1845-O		230,000	——
1846 (P)		31,300	Δ
1847 (P)		245,000	Δ
1848 (P)		451,500	Δ
1849 (P)		839,000	Δ
1849-O		300,000	——
1850 (P)		1,931,500	Δ
1850-O		510,000	——
1851 (P)		1,026,500	Δ
1851-O		400,000	——
1852 (P)		1,535,500	Δ
1852-O		430,000	——
1853 (P)			
No Arrows	‹16›	95,000	——
With Arrows	‹16›	12,078,010	Δ
1853-O		1,100,000	——
1854 (P)		4,470,000	Δ
1854-O		1,770,000	——
1855 (P)		2,075,000	Δ
1856 (P)		5,780,000	Δ
1856-O		1,180,000	——
1856-S		70,000	——
1857 (P)		5,580,000	Δ
1857-O		1,540,000	——
1858 (P)		1,540,000	——
1858-O		290,000	Δ
1858-S		60,000	——
1859 (P)		430,000	Δ
1859-O		480,000	——
1859-S		60,000	——
1860 (P)	‹28›	606,000	1,000
1860-O	‹28›	40,000	——
1860-S	‹28›	140,000	——
1861 (P)		1,883,000	1,000
1861-S		172,500	——
1862 (P)		847,000	550
1862-S		180,750	——
1863 (P)		14,000	460
1863-S		157,500	——
1864 (P)	‹18›	11,000	470
1864-S		230,000	——
1865 (P)		10,000	500
1865-S		175,000	——
1866 (P)		8,000	725
1866-S		135,000	——
1867 (P)		6,000	625
1867-S		140,000	——
1868 (P)		464,000	600

DATE	NOTE	BUSINESS	PROOF
1868-S		260,000	——
1869 (P)		256,000	600
1869-S		450,000	——
1870 (P)		470,500	1,000
1870-S		50,000	——
1871 (P)		906,750	960
1871-CC		20,100	——
1871-S		320,000	——
1872 (P)		2,395,500	950
1872-CC		35,480	——
1872-S		190,000	——
1873 (P)			
No Arrows	‹6›	1,568,000	600
With Arrows	‹6›	2,377,700	800
1873-CC			
No Arrows	‹6, 30›	12,400	——
With Arrows	‹6›	18,791	——
1873-S			
With Arrows	‹6›	455,000	——
1874 (P)		2,940,000	700
1874-CC		10,817	——
1874-S		240,000	——
1875 (P)		10,350,000	700
1875-CC		4,645,000	——
1875-S		9,070,000	——
1876 (P)		11,460,000	1,150
1876-CC		8,270,000	——
1876-S		10,420,000	——
1877 (P)		7,310,000	510
1877-CC		7,700,000	——
1877-S		2,340,000	——
1878 (P)		1,678,000	800
1878-CC		200,000	——
1879 (P)		14,000	1,100
1880 (P)		36,000	1,355
1881 (P)		24,000	975
1882 (P)		3,910,000	1,100
1883 (P)		7,674,673	1,039
1884 (P)		3,365,505	875
1884-S		564,969	——
1885 (P)		2,532,497	930
1885-S		43,690	——
1886 (P)		6,376,684	886
1886-S		206,524	——
1887 (P)		11,283,229	710
1887-S		4,454,450	——
1888 (P)		5,495,655	832
1888-S		1,720,000	——
1889 (P)		7,380,000	711
1889-S		972,678	——
1890 (P)		9,910,951	590
1890-S		1,423,076	——
1891 (P)		15,310,000	600
1891-O		4,540,000	——
1891-S		3,196,116	——
Barber dime			
1892 (P)		12,120,000	1,245
1892-O		3,841,700	——
1892-S		990,710	——

DATE	NOTE	BUSINESS	PROOF
1893 (P)		3,340,000	792
1893-O		1,760,000	—
1893-S		2,491,401	—
1894 (P)		1,330,000	972
1894-O		720,000	—
1894-S	‹31›	—	—
1895 (P)		690,000	880
1895-O		440,000	—
1895-S		1,120,000	—
1896 (P)		2,000,000	762
1896-O		610,000	—
1896-S		575,056	—
1897 (P)		10,868,533	731
1897-O		666,000	—
1897-S		1,342,844	—
1898 (P)		16,320,000	735
1898-O		2,130,000	—
1898-S		1,702,507	—
1899 (P)		19,580,000	846
1899-O		2,650,000	—
1899-S		1,867,493	—
1900 (P)		17,600,000	912
1900-O		2,010,000	—
1900-S		5,168,270	—
1901 (P)		18,859,665	813
1901-O		5,620,000	—
1901-S		593,022	—
1902 (P)		21,380,000	777
1902-O		4,500,000	—
1902-S		2,070,000	—
1903 (P)		19,500,000	755
1903-O		8,180,000	—
1903-S		613,300	—
1904 (P)		14,600,357	670
1904-S		800,000	—
1905 (P)		14,551,623	727
1905-O		3,400,000	—
1905-S		6,855,199	—
1906 (P)		19,957,731	675
1906-D	‹32›	4,060,000	Δ
1906-O		2,610,000	—
1906-S		3,136,640	—
1907 (P)		22,220,000	575
1907-D		4,080,000	—
1907-O		5,058,000	—
1907-S		3,178,470	—
1908 (P)		10,600,000	545
1908-D		7,490,000	—
1908-O		1,789,000	—
1908-S		3,220,000	—
1909 (P)		10,240,000	650
1909-D		954,000	—
1909-O		2,287,000	—
1909-S		1,000,000	—
1910 (P)		11,520,000	551
1910-D		3,490,000	—
1910-S		1,240,000	—
1911 (P)		18,870,000	543
1911-D		11,209,000	—
1911-S		3,520,000	—
1912 (P)		19,350,000	700
1912-D		11,760,000	—
1912-S		3,420,000	—
1913 (P)		19,760,000	622
1913-S		510,000	—
1914 (P)		17,360,230	—
1914-D		11,908,000	425
1914-S		2,100,000	—
1915 (P)		5,620,000	450
1915-S		960,000	—
1916 (P)		18,490,000	Δ
1916-S		5,820,000	—

Winged Liberty Head dime

DATE	NOTE	BUSINESS	PROOF
1916 (P)		22,180,080	—
1916-D		264,000	—
1916-S		10,450,000	—
1917 (P)		55,230,000	—
1917-D		9,402,000	—
1917-S		27,330,000	—
1918 (P)		26,680,000	—
1918-D		22,674,800	—
1918-S		19,300,000	—
1919 (P)		35,740,000	—
1919-D		9,939,000	—
1919-S		8,850,000	—
1920 (P)		59,030,000	—
1920-D		19,171,000	—
1920-S		13,820,000	—
1921 (P)		1,230,000	—
1921-D		1,080,000	—
1923 (P)	‹22›	50,130,000	—
1923-S		6,440,000	—
1924 (P)		24,010,000	—
1924-D		6,810,000	—
1924-S		7,120,000	—
1925 (P)		25,610,000	—
1925-D		5,117,000	—
1925-S		5,850,000	—
1926 (P)		32,160,000	—
1926-D		6,828,000	—
1926-S		1,520,000	—
1927 (P)		28,080,000	—
1927-D		4,812,000	—
1927-S		4,770,000	—
1928 (P)		19,480,000	—
1928-D		4,161,000	—
1928-S		7,400,000	—
1929 (P)		25,970,000	—
1929-D		5,034,000	—
1929-S		4,730,000	—
1930 (P)	‹22›	6,770,000	—
1930-S		1,843,000	—
1931 (P)		3,150,000	—
1931-D		1,260,000	—
1931-S		1,800,000	—
1934 (P)		24,080,000	—
1934-D		6,772,000	—
1935 (P)		58,830,000	—
1935-D		10,477,000	—

DATE	NOTE	BUSINESS	PROOF
1935-S		15,840,000	——
1936 (P)		87,500,000	4,130
1936-D		16,132,000	——
1936-S		9,210,000	——
1937 (P)		56,860,000	5,756
1937-D		14,146,000	——
1937-S		9,740,000	——
1938 (P)		22,190,000	8,728
1938-D		5,537,000	——
1938-S		8,090,000	——
1939 (P)		67,740,000	9,321
1939-D		24,394,000	——
1939-S		10,540,000	——
1940 (P)		65,350,000	11,827
1940-D		21,198,000	——
1940-S		21,560,000	——
1941 (P)		175,090,000	16,557
1941-D		45,634,000	——
1941-S		43,090,000	——
1942 (P)		205,410,000	22,329
1942-D		60,740,000	——
1942-S		49,300,000	——
1943 (P)		191,710,000	——
1943-D		71,949,000	——
1943-S		60,400,000	——
1944 (P)		231,410,000	——
1944-D		62,224,000	——
1944-S		49,490,000	——
1945 (P)		159,130,000	——
1945-D		40,245,000	——
1945-S		41,920,000	——
Roosevelt dime			
1946 (P)		255,250,000	——
1946-D		61,043,500	——
1946-S		27,900,000	——
1947 (P)		121,520,000	——
1947-D		46,835,000	——
1947-S		34,840,000	——
1948 (P)		74,950,000	——
1948-D		52,841,000	——
1948-S		35,520,000	——
1949 (P)		30,940,000	——
1949-D		26,034,000	——
1949-S		13,510,000	——
1950 (P)	‹§›	50,130,114	51,386
1950-D		46,803,000	——
1950-S		20,440,000	——
1951 (P)	‹§›	102,880,102	57,500
1951-D		56,529,000	——
1951-S		31,630,000	——
1952 (P)	‹§›	99,040,093	81,980
1952-D		122,100,000	——
1952-S		44,419,500	——
1953 (P)	‹§›	53,490,120	128,800
1953-D		136,433,000	——
1953-S		39,180,000	——
1954 (P)	‹§›	114,010,203	233,300
1954-D		106,397,000	——
1954-S		22,860,000	——

DATE	NOTE	BUSINESS	PROOF
1955 (P)	‹§›	12,450,181	378,200
1955-D		13,959,000	——
1955-S		18,510,000	——
1956 (P)	‹§›	108,640,000	669,384
1956-D		108,015,100	——
1957 (P)	‹§›	160,160,000	1,247,952
1957-D		113,354,330	——
1958 (P)	‹§›	31,910,000	875,652
1958-D		136,564,600	——
1959 (P)	‹§›	85,780,000	1,149,291
1959-D		164,919,790	——
1960 (P)	‹§›	70,390,000	1,691,602
1960-D		200,160,400	——
1961 (P)	‹§›	93,730,000	3,028,244
1961-D		209,146,550	——
1962 (P)	‹§›	72,450,000	3,218,019
1962-D		334,948,380	——
1963 (P)	‹§›	123,650,000	3,075,645
1963-D		421,476,530	——
1964 (P)	‹§, 11›	929,360,000	3,950,762
1964-D	‹11›	1,357,517,180	——
1965 (P)	‹11›	845,130,000	——
1965 (D)	‹11›	757,472,820	——
1965 (S)	‹11›	47,177,750	——
1966 (P)	‹11›	622,550,000	——
1966 (D)	‹11›	683,771,010	——
1966 (S)	‹11›	74,151,947	——
1967 (P)	‹11›	1,030,110,000	——
1967 (D)	‹11›	1,156,277,320	——
1967 (S)	‹11›	57,620,000	——
1968 (P)		424,470,400	——
1968-D		480,748,280	——
1968-S	‹§, 33›	——	3,041,506
1969 (P)		145,790,000	——
1969-D		563,323,870	——
1969-S	‹§›	——	2,934,631
1970 (P)		345,570,000	——
1970-D		754,942,100	——
1970-S	‹§, 34›	——	2,632,810
1971 (P)		162,690,000	——
1971-D		377,914,240	——
1971-S	‹§›	——	3,220,733
1972 (P)		431,540,000	——
1972-D		330,290,000	——
1972-S	‹§›	——	3,260,996
1973 (P)		315,670 ,000	——
1973-D		455,032,426	——
1973-S	‹§›	——	2,760,339
1974 (P)		470,248,000	——
1974-D		571,083,000	——
1974-S	‹§›	——	2,612,568
1975 (P)		513,682,000	——
1975-D		313,705,300	——
1975 (S)		71,991,900	——
1976 (P)		568,760,000	——
1976-D		695,222,774	——
1976-S		——	——
1977 (P)		796,930,000	——
1977-D		376,607,228	——
1977-S	‹§›	——	3,236,798

DATE	NOTE	BUSINESS	PROOF
1978 (P)		663,980,000	——
1978-D		282,847,540	——
1978-S	‹§›	——	3,120,285
1979 (P)		315,440,000	——
1979-D		390,921,184	——
1979-S	‹§›	——	3,677,175
1980-P	‹25›	735,170,000	——
1980-D		719,354,321	——
1980-S	‹§›	——	3,554,806
1981-P		676,650,000	——
1981-D		712,284,143	——
1981-S	‹§›	——	4,063,083
1982-P	‹35›	519,475,000	——
1982-D		542,713,584	——
1982-S	‹§›	——	3,857,479
1983-P		647,025,000	——
1983-D		730,129,224	——
1983-S	‹§›	——	3,279,126
1984-P		856,669,000	——
1984-D		704,803,976	——
1984-S	‹§›	——	3,065,110
1985-P		705,200,962	——
1985-D		587,979,970	——
1985-S	‹§›	——	3,362,821
1986-P		682,649,693	——
1986-D		473,326,974	——
1986-S	‹§›	——	3,010,497
1987-P		762,709,481	——
1987-D		653,203,402	——
1987-S	‹§›	——	3,792,233
1988-P		1,030,550,000	——
1988-D		962,385,488	——
1988-S	‹§›	——	3,262,948
1989-P		1,298,400,000	——
1989-D		896,535,597	——
1989-S	‹§›	——	3,220,914
1990-P		1,034,340,000	——
1990-D		839,995,824	——
1990-S	‹§›	——	3,299,559
1991-P		927,220,000	——
1991-D		601,241,114	——
1991-S	‹§›	——	2,867,787
1992-P		593,500,000	——
1992-D		616,273,932	——
1992-S	‹§›		
Clad		——	2,858,903
90% silver		——	1,317,641
1993-P		766,180,000	——
1993-D		750,110,166	——
1993-S	‹§›		
Clad		——	2,569,882
90% silver		——	790,994
1994-P		1,189,000,000	——
1994-D		1,303,268,110	——
1994-S	‹§›		
Clad		——	2,443,590
90% silver		——	778,550
1995-P		1,125,500,000	——
1995-D		1,274,890,000	——

DATE	NOTE	BUSINESS	PROOF
1995-S	‹§›		
Clad		——	2,124,790
90% silver		——	666,277
1996-P		1,421,630,000	——
1996-D		1,400,300,000	——
1996-S	‹§›		
Clad		——	2,145,077
90% silver		——	775,081
1996-W	<118>	1,450,440	——
1997-P		991,640,000	——
1997-D		979,810,000	——
1997-S	‹§›		
Clad		——	2,055,000
90% silver		——	741,194
1998-P	1,163,000,000	——	
1998-D		1,172,300,000	——
1998-S	‹§›		
Clad		——	2,086,507
90% silver		——	878,996

Twenty cents

DATE	NOTE	BUSINESS	PROOF
1875 (P)		38,500	1,200
1875-CC		133,290	——
1875-S	‹36›	1,155,000	Δ
1876 (P)		14,750	1,150
1876-CC	‹37›	10,000	——
1877 (P)		——	510
1878 (P)		——	600

Draped Bust quarter dollar

DATE	NOTE	BUSINESS	PROOF
1796		6,146	——
1804		6,738	——
1805		121,394	——
1806		286,424	——
1807		140,343	——

Capped Bust quarter dollar

DATE	NOTE	BUSINESS	PROOF
1815		89,235	——
1818		361,174	Δ
1819		144,000	——
1820		127,444	Δ
1821		216,851	Δ
1822		64,080	Δ
1823	‹3›	17,800	Δ
1824		24,000	Δ
1825		148,000	Δ
1827	‹38›	——	Δ (R)
1828		102,000	Δ
1831		398,000	Δ
1832		320,000	Δ
1833		156,000	Δ
1834		286,000	Δ
1835		1,952,000	Δ
1836		472,000	Δ
1837		252,400	Δ
1838 (P)		366,000	Δ

Seated Liberty quarter dollar

DATE	NOTE	BUSINESS	PROOF
1838 (P)		466,000	——
1839 (P)		491,146	Δ
1840 (P)		188,127	Δ
1840-O		425,200	——

DATE	NOTE	BUSINESS	PROOF
1841 (P)		120,000	Δ
1841-O		452,000	——
1842 (P)		88,000	Δ
1842-O		769,000	——
1843 (P)		645,600	Δ
1843-O		968,000	——
1844 (P)		421,200	Δ
1844-O		740,000	——
1845 (P)		922,000	Δ
1846 (P)		510,000	Δ
1847 (P)		734,000	Δ
1847-O		368,000	——
1848 (P)		146,000	Δ
1849 (P)		340,000	Δ
1849-O		16,000	——
1850 (P)		190,800	Δ
1850-O		396,000	——
1851 (P)		160,000	Δ
1851-O		88,000	——
1852 (P)		177,060	Δ
1852-O		96,000	——
1853 (P)			
No Arr. & Rays	‹16›	44,200	——
Arrows & Rays	‹16›	15,210,020	Δ
1853-O		1,332,000	——
1854 (P)		12,380,000	Δ
1854-O		1,484,000	——
1855 (P)		2,857,000	Δ
1855-O		176,000	——
1855-S	‹39›	396,400	Δ
1856 (P)		7,264,000	Δ
1856-O		968,000	——
1856-S		286,000	——
1857 (P)		9,644,000	Δ
1857-O		1,180,000	——
1857-S		82,000	——
1858 (P)		7,368,000	Δ
1858-O		520,000	——
1858-S		121,000	——
1859 (P)		1,344,000	Δ
1859-O		260,000	——
1859-S		80,000	——
1860 (P)		804,400	1,000
1860-O		388,000	——
1860-S		56,000	——
1861 (P)		4,853,600	1,000
1861-S		96,000	——
1862 (P)		932,000	550
1862-S		67,000	——
1863 (P)		191,600	460
1864 (P)		93,600	470
1864-S		20,000	——
1865 (P)		58,800	500
1865-S		41,000	——
1866 (P)	‹40›	16,800	725
1866-S	‹40›	28,000	——
1867 (P)		20,000	625
1867-S		48,000	——
1868 (P)		29,400	600
1868-S		96,000	——

DATE	NOTE	BUSINESS	PROOF
1869 (P)		16,000	600
1869-S		76,000	——
1870 (P)		86,400	1,000
1870-CC		8,340	——
1871 (P)		118,200	960
1871-CC		10,890	——
1871-S		30,900	——
1872 (P)		182,000	950
1872-CC		22,850	——
1872-S		83,000	——
1873 (P)			
No Arrows	‹6›	212,000	600
With Arrows	‹6›	1,271,160	540
1873-CC			
No Arrows	‹6›	4,000	——
With Arrows	‹6›	12,462	——
1873-S			
With Arrows	‹6›	156,000	——
1874 (P)		471,200	700
1874-S		392,000	——
1875 (P)		4,292,800	700
1875-CC		140,000	——
1875-S		680,000	——
1876 (P)		17,816,000	1,150
1876-CC		4,944,000	——
1876-S		8,596,000	——
1877 (P)		10,911,200	510
1877-CC		4,192,000	——
1877-S		8,996,000	——
1878 (P)		2,260,000	800
1878-CC		996,000	——
1878-S		140,000	——
1879 (P)	‹41›	14,450	250
1880 (P)		13,600	1,355
1881 (P)		12,000	975
1882 (P)		15,200	1,100
1883 (P)		14,400	1,039
1884 (P)		8,000	875
1885 (P)		13,600	930
1886 (P)		5,000	886
1887 (P)		10,000	710
1888 (P)		10,001	832
1888-S		1,216,000	——
1889 (P)		12,000	711
1890 (P)		80,000	590
1891 (P)		3,920,000	600
1891-O	‹42›	68,000	Δ
1891-S		2,216,000	——

Barber quarter dollar

DATE	NOTE	BUSINESS	PROOF
1892 (P)		8,236,000	1,245
1892-O		2,640,000	——
1892-S		964,079	——
1893 (P)		5,444,023	792
1893-O		3,396,000	——
1893-S		1,454,535	——
1894 (P)		3,432,000	972
1894-O		2,852,000	——
1894-S		2,648,821	——
1895 (P)		4,440,000	880

DATE	NOTE	BUSINESS	PROOF
1895-O		2,816,000	—
1895-S		1,764,681	—
1896 (P)		3,874,000	762
1896-O		1,484,000	—
1896-S		188,039	—
1897 (P)		8,140,000	731
1897-O		1,414,800	—
1897-S		542,229	—
1898 (P)		11,100,000	735
1898-O		1,868,000	—
1898-S		1,020,592	—
1899 (P)		12,624,000	846
1899-O		2,644,000	—
1899-S		708,000	—
1900 (P)		10,016,000	912
1900-O		3,416,000	—
1900-S		1,858,585	—
1901 (P)		8,892,000	813
1901-O		1,612,000	—
1901-S		72,664	—
1902 (P)		12,196,967	777
1902-O		4,748,000	—
1902-S		1,524,612	—
1903 (P)		9,669,309	755
1903-O		3,500,000	—
1903-S		1,036,000	—
1904 (P)		9,588,143	670
1904-O		2,456,000	—
1905 (P)		4,967,523	727
1905-O		1,230,000	—
1905-S		1,884,000	—
1906 (P)		3,655,760	675
1906-D		3,280,000	—
1906-O		2,056,000	—
1907 (P)		7,192,000	575
1907-D		2,484,000	—
1907-O		4,560,000	—
1907-S		1,360,000	—
1908 (P)		4,232,000	545
1908-D		5,788,000	—
1908-O		6,244,000	—
1908-S		784,000	—
1909 (P)		9,268,000	650
1909-D		5,114,000	—
1909-O		712,000	—
1909-S		1,348,000	—
1910 (P)		2,244,000	551
1910-D		1,500,000	—
1911 (P)		3,720,000	543
1911-D		933,600	—
1911-S		988,000	—
1912 (P)		4,400,000	700
1912-S		708,000	—
1913 (P)		484,000	613
1913-D		1,450,800	—
1913-S		40,000	—
1914 (P)		6,244,230	380
1914-D		3,046,000	—
1914-S		264,000	—
1915 (P)		3,480,000	450
1915-D		3,694,000	—
1915-S		704,000	—
1916 (P)		1,788,000	—
1916-D		6,540,800	—
Standing Liberty quarter dollar			
1916 (P)		52,000	—
1917 (P)			
Bare Breast		8,740,000	Δ
Mailed Breast		13,880,000	—
1917-D			
Bare Breast		1,509,200	—
Mailed Breast		6,224,400	—
1917-S			
Bare Breast		1,952,000	—
Mailed Breast		5,552,000	—
1918 (P)		14,240,000	—
1918-D		7,380,000	—
1918-S		11,072,000	—
1919 (P)		11,324,000	—
1919-D		1,944,000	—
1919-S		1,836,000	—
1920 (P)		27,860,000	—
1920-D		3,586,400	—
1920-S		6,380,000	—
1921 (P)		1,916,000	—
1923 (P)		9,716,000	—
1923-S		1,360,000	—
1924 (P)		10,920,000	—
1924-D		3,112,000	—
1924-S		2,860,000	—
1925 (P)		12,280,000	—
1926 (P)		11,316,000	—
1926-D		1,716,000	—
1926-S		2,700,000	—
1927 (P)		11,912,000	—
1927-D		976,400	—
1927-S		396,000	—
1928 (P)		6,336,000	—
1928-D		1,627,600	—
1928-S		2,644,000	—
1929 (P)		11,140,000	—
1929-D		1,358,000	—
1929-S		1,764,000	—
1930 (P)		5,632,000	—
1930-S		1,556,000	—
Washington quarter dollar			
1932 (P)		5,404,000	—
1932-D		436,800	—
1932-S		408,000	—
1934 (P)		31,912,052	—
1934-D		3,527,200	—
1935 (P)		32,484,000	—
1935-D		5,780,000	—
1935-S		5,660,000	—
1936 (P)		41,300,000	3,837
1936-D		5,374,000	—
1936-S		3,828,000	—
1937 (P)		19,696,000	5,542
1937-D		7,189,600	—

DATE	NOTE	BUSINESS	PROOF
1937-S		1,652,000	——
1938 (P)		9,472,000	8,045
1938-S		2,832,000	——
1939 (P)		33,540,000	8,795
1939-D		7,092,000	——
1939-S		2,628,000	——
1940 (P)		35,704,000	11,246
1940-D		2,797,600	——
1940-S		8,244,000	——
1941 (P)		79,032,000	15,287
1941-D		16,714,800	——
1941-S		16,080,000	——
1942 (P)		102,096,000	21,123
1942-D		17,487,200	——
1942-S		19,384,000	——
1943 (P)		99,700,000	——
1943-D		16,095,600	——
1943-S		21,700,000	——
1944 (P)		104,956,000	——
1944-D		14,600,800	——
1944-S		12,560,000	——
1945 (P)		74,372,000	——
1945-D		12,341,600	——
1945-S		17,004,001	——
1946 (P)		53,436,000	——
1946-D		9,072,800	——
1946-S		4,204,000	——
1947 (P)		22,556,000	——
1947-D		15,338,400	——
1947-S		5,532,000	——
1948 (P)		35,196,000	——
1948-D		16,766,800	——
1948-S		15,960,000	——
1949 (P)		9,312,000	——
1949-D		10,068,400	——
1950 (P)	‹§›	24,920,126	51,386
1950-D		21,075,600	——
1950-S		10,284,004	——
1951 (P)	‹§›	43,448,102	57,500
1951-D		35,354,800	——
1951-S		9,048,000	——
1952 (P)	‹§›	38,780,093	81,980
1952-D		49,795,200	——
1952-S		13,707,800	——
1953 (P)	‹§›	18,536,120	128,800
1953-D		56,112,400	——
1953-S		14,016,000	——
1954 (P)	‹§›	54,412,203	233,300
1954-D		42,305,500	——
1954-S		11,834,722	——
1955 (P)	‹§›	18,180,181	378,200
1955-D		3,182,400	——
1956 (P)	‹§›	44,144,000	669,384
1956-D		32,334,500	——
1957 (P)	‹§›	46,532,000	1,247,952
1957-D		77,924,160	——
1958 (P)	‹§›	6,360,000	875,652
1958-D		78,124,900	——
1959 (P)	‹§›	24,384,000	1,149,291
1959-D		62,054,232	——

DATE	NOTE	BUSINESS	PROOF
1960 (P)	‹§›	29,164,000	1,691,602
1960-D		63,000,324	——
1961 (P)	‹§›	37,036,000	3,028,244
1961-D		83,656,928	——
1962 (P)	‹§›	36,156,000	3,218,019
1962-D		127,554,756	——
1963 (P)	‹§›	74,316,000	3,075,645
1963-D		135,288,184	——
1964 (P)	‹§, 11›	560,390,585	3,950,762
1964-D	‹11›	704,135,528	——
1965 (P)	‹11›	1,082,216,000	——
1965 (D)	‹11›	673,305,540	——
1965 (S)	‹11›	61,836,000	——
1966 (P)	‹11›	404,416,000	——
1966 (D)	‹11›	367,490,400	——
1966 (S)	‹11›	46,933,517	——
1967 (P)	‹11›	873,524,000	——
1967 (D)	‹11›	632,767,848	——
1967 (S)	‹11›	17,740,000	——
1968 (P)		220,731,500	——
1968-D		101,534,000	——
1968-S	‹§›	——	3,041,506
1969 (P)		176,212,000	——
1969-D		114,372,000	——
1969-S	‹§›	——	2,934,631
1970 (P)		136,420,000	——
1970-D		417,341,364	——
1970-S	‹§›	——	2,632,810
1971 (P)		109,284,000	——
1971-D		258,634,428	——
1971-S	‹§›	——	3,220,733
1972 (P)		215,048,000	——
1972-D		311,067,732	——
1972-S	‹§›	——	3,260,996
1973 (P)		346,924,000	——
1973-D		232,977,400	——
1973-S	‹§›	——	2,760,339
1974 (P)	‹43›	801,456,000	——
1974-D	‹43›	353,160,300	——
1974-S	‹§, 43›	——	2,612,568
1976 (P)	‹43›	809,408,016	——
1976-D	‹43›	860,118,839	——
1976-S	‹43›	——	——
1976 (W)	‹43›	376,000	——
1977 (P)		461,204,000	——
1977-D		256,524,978	——
1977-S	‹§›	——	3,236,798
1977 (W)		7,352,000	——
1978 (P)		500,652,000	——
1978-D		287,373,152	——
1978-S	‹§›	——	3,120,285
1978 (W)		20,800,000	——
1979 (P)		493,036,000	——
1979-D		489,789,780	——
1979-S	‹§›	——	3,677,175
1979 (W)		22,672,000	——
1980-P	‹25›	635,832,000	——
1980-D		518,327,487	——
1980-S	‹§›	——	3,554,806
1981-P		601,716,000	——

DATE	NOTE	BUSINESS	PROOF
1981-D		575,722,833	——
1981-S	‹§›	——	4,063,083
1982-P		500,931,000	——
1982-D		480,042,788	——
1982-S	‹§›	——	3,857,479
1983-P		673,535,000	——
1983-D		617,806,446	——
1983-S	‹§›	——	3,279,126
1984-P		676,545,000	——
1984-D		546,483,064	——
1984-S	‹§›	——	3,065,110
1985-P		775,818,962	——
1985-D		519,962,888	——
1985-S	‹§›	——	3,362,821
1986-P		551,199,333	——
1986-D		504,298,660	——
1986-S	‹§›	——	3,010,497
1987-P		582,499,481	——
1987-D		655,595,696	——
1987-S	‹§›	——	3,792,233
1988-P		562,052,000	——
1988-D		596,810,688	——
1988-S	‹§›	——	3,262,948
1989-P		512,868,000	——
1989-D		896,733,858	——
1989-S	‹§›	——	3,220,914
1990-P		613,792,000	——
1990-D		927,638,181	——
1990-S	‹§›	——	3,299,559
1991-P		570,960,000	——
1991-D		630,966,693	——
1991-S	‹§›	——	2,867,787
1992-P		384,764,000	——
1992-D		389,777,107	——
1992-S	‹§›		
Clad		——	2,858,903
90% silver		——	1,317,641
1993-P		639,276,000	——
1993-D		645,476,128	——
1993-S	‹§›		
Clad		——	2,569,882
90% silver		——	790,994
1994-P		825,600,000	——
1994-D		880,034,110	——
1994-S	‹§›		
Clad		——	2,443,590
90% silver		——	778,550
1995-P		1,004,336,000	——
1995-D		1,103,216,000	——
1995-S	‹§›		
Clad		——	2,124,790
90% silver		——	666,277
1996-P		925,040,000	——
1996-D		906,868,000	——
1996-S	‹§›		
Clad		——	2,145,077
90% silver		——	775,081
1997-P		595,740,000	——
1997-D		599,680,000	——
1997-S	‹§›		
Clad		——	2,055,000
90% silver		——	741,194
1998-P		960,400,000	——
1998-D		907,000,000	——
1998-S	‹§›		
Clad		——	2,086,507
90% silver		——	878,996
1999-P Delaware		373,400,000	——
1999-D Delaware		400,832,000	——
1999-P Pennsylvania		349,000,000	——
1999-D Pennsylvania		357,800,000	——

Flowing Hair half dollar

DATE	NOTE	BUSINESS	PROOF
1794		23,464	——
1795		299,680	——

Draped Bust, Small Eagle half dollar

DATE	NOTE	BUSINESS	PROOF
1796		934	——
1797		2,984	——

Draped Bust, Heraldic Eagle half dollar

DATE	NOTE	BUSINESS	PROOF
1801		30,289	——
1802		29,890	——
1803		188,234	——
1805		211,722	——
1806		839,576	——
1807		301,076	——

Capped Bust half dollar

DATE	NOTE	BUSINESS	PROOF
1807		750,500	——
1808		1,368,600	——
1809		1,405,810	——
1810		1,276,276	——
1811		1,203,644	——
1812		1,628,059	——
1813		1,241,903	——
1814		1,039,075	——
1815		47,150	——
1817	‹44›	1,215,567	Δ
1818		1,960,322	Δ
1819		2,208,000	Δ
1820		751,122	Δ
1821		1,305,797	Δ
1822		1,559,573	Δ
1823		1,694,200	Δ
1824		3,504,954	Δ
1825		2,943,166	Δ
1826		4,004,180	Δ
1827		5,493,400	Δ
1828		3,075,200	Δ
1829		3,712,156	Δ
1830		4,764,800	Δ
1831		5,873,660	Δ
1832		4,797,000	Δ
1833		5,206,000	Δ (R)
1834		6,412,004	Δ (R)
1835		5,352,006	Δ (R)
1836			
Lettered Edge		6,545,000	Δ
Reeded Edge	‹45›	1,200	Δ
1837		3,629,820	Δ
1838 (P)		3,546,000	Δ

DATE	NOTE	BUSINESS	PROOF
1838-O	‹46›	——	Δ
1839 (P)		1,362,160	Δ
1839-O	‹47›	178,976	Δ

Seated Liberty half dollar

DATE	NOTE	BUSINESS	PROOF
1839 (P)	‹48›	1,972,400	Δ
1840 (P)		1,435,008	Δ
1840-O		855,100	——
1841 (P)		310,000	Δ
1841-O		401,000	——
1842 (P)		2,012,764	Δ
1842-O		957,000	——
1843 (P)		3,844,000	Δ
1843-O		2,268,000	——
1844 (P)		1,766,000	Δ
1844-O		2,005,000	——
1845 (P)		589,000	Δ
1845-O		2,094,000	——
1846 (P)		2,210,000	Δ
1846-O		2,304,000	——
1847 (P)		1,156,000	Δ
1847-O		2,584,000	——
1848 (P)		580,000	Δ
1848-O		3,180,000	——
1849 (P)		1,252,000	Δ
1849-O		2,310,000	——
1850 (P)		227,000	Δ
1850-O		2,456,000	——
1851 (P)		200,750	——
1851-O		402,000	——
1852 (P)		77,130	Δ
1852-O		144,000	——
1853 (P)	‹16, 49›	3,532,708	Δ
1853-O	‹49›	1,328,000	——
1854 (P)		2,982,000	Δ
1854-O		5,240,000	——
1855 (P)		759,500	Δ
1855-O		3,688,000	——
1855-S	‹50›	129,950	Δ
1856 (P)		938,000	Δ
1856-O		2,658,000	——
1856-S		211,000	——
1857 (P)		1,988,000	Δ
1857-O		818,000	——
1857-S		158,000	——
1858 (P)		4,226,000	Δ
1858-O		7,294,000	——
1858-S		476,000	——
1859 (P)		748,000	Δ
1859-O		2,834,000	——
1859-S		566,000	——
1860 (P)		302,700	1,000
1860-O		1,290,000	——
1860-S		472,000	——
1861 (P)		2,887,400	1,000
1861-O	‹51›	2,532,633	Δ
1861-S		939,500	——
1862 (P)		253,000	550
1862-S		1,352,000	——
1863 (P)		503,200	460
1863-S		916,000	——
1864 (P)		379,100	470
1864-S		658,000	——
1865 (P)		511,400	500
1865-S		675,000	——
1866 (P)	‹40›	744,900	725
1866-S			
No Motto	‹40›	60,000	——
Motto	‹40›	994,000	——
1867 (P)		449,300	625
1867-S		1,196,000	——
1868 (P)		417,600	600
1868-S		1,160,000	——
1869 (P)		795,300	600
1869-S		656,000	——
1870 (P)		633,900	1,000
1870-CC		54,617	——
1870-S		1,004,000	——
1871 (P)		1,203,600	960
1871-CC		153,950	——
1871-S		2,178,000	——
1872 (P)		880,600	950
1872-CC		257,000	——
1872-S		580,000	——
1873 (P)			
No Arrows	‹6›	801,200	600
With Arrows	‹6›	1,815,150	550
1873-CC			
No Arrows	‹6, 52›	122,500	——
With Arrows	‹6›	214,560	——
1873-S			
No Arrows	‹6›	5,000	——
With Arrows	‹6›	228,000	——
1874 (P)		2,359,600	700
1874-CC		59,000	——
1874-S		394,000	——
1875 (P)		6,026,800	700
1875-CC		1,008,000	——
1875-S		3,200,000	——
1876 (P)		8,418,000	1,150
1876-CC		1,956,000	——
1876-S		4,528,000	——
1877 (P)		8,304,000	510
1877-CC		1,420,000	——
1877-S		5,356,000	——
1878 (P)		1,377,600	800
1878-CC		62,000	——
1878-S		12,000	——
1879 (P)		4,800	1,100
1880 (P)		8,400	1,355
1881 (P)		10,000	975
1882 (P)		4,400	1,100
1883 (P)		8,000	1,039
1884 (P)		4,400	875
1885 (P)		5,200	930
1886 (P)		5,000	886
1887 (P)		5,000	710
1888 (P)		12,001	832
1889 (P)		12,000	711

DATE	NOTE	BUSINESS	PROOF
1890 (P)		12,000	590
1891 (P)		200,000	600

Barber half dollar

DATE	NOTE	BUSINESS	PROOF
1892 (P)		934,245	1,245
1892-O		390,000	—
1892-S		1,029,028	—
1893 (P)		1,826,000	792
1893-O		1,389,000	—
1893-S		740,000	—
1894 (P)		1,148,000	972
1894-O		2,138,000	—
1894-S		4,048,690	—
1895 (P)		1,834,338	880
1895-O	‹53›	1,766,000	Δ
1895-S		1,108,086	—
1896 (P)		950,000	762
1896-O		924,000	—
1896-S		1,140,948	—
1897 (P)		2,480,000	731
1897-O		632,000	—
1897-S		933,900	—
1898 (P)		2,956,000	735
1898-O		874,000	—
1898-S		2,358,550	—
1899 (P)		5,538,000	846
1899-O		1,724,000	—
1899-S		1,686,411	—
1900 (P)		4,762,000	912
1900-O		2,744,000	—
1900-S		2,560,322	—
1901 (P)		4,268,000	813
1901-O		1,124,000	—
1901-S		847,044	—
1902 (P)		4,922,000	777
1902-O		2,526,000	—
1902-S		1,460,670	—
1903 (P)		2,278,000	755
1903-O		2,100,000	—
1903-S		1,920,772	—
1904 (P)		2,992,000	670
1904-O		1,117,600	—
1904-S		553,038	—
1905 (P)		662,000	727
1905-O		505,000	—
1905-S		2,494,000	—
1906 (P)		2,638,000	675
1906-D		4,028,000	—
1906-O		2,446,000	—
1906-S		1,740,154	—
1907 (P)		2,598,000	575
1907-D		3,856,000	—
1907-O		3,946,600	—
1907-S		1,250,000	—
1908 (P)		1,354,000	545
1908-D		3,280,000	—
1908-O		5,360,000	—
1908-S		1,644,828	—
1909 (P)		2,368,000	650
1909-O		925,400	—
1909-S		1,764,000	—
1910 (P)		418,000	551
1910-S		1,948,000	—
1911 (P)		1,406,000	543
1911-D		695,080	—
1911-S		1,272,000	—
1912 (P)		1,550,000	700
1912-D		2,300,800	—
1912-S		1,370,000	—
1913 (P)		188,000	627
1913-D		534,000	—
1913-S		604,000	—
1914 (P)		124,230	380
1914-S		992,000	—
1915 (P)		138,000	450
1915-D		1,170,400	—
1915-S		1,604,000	—

Walking Liberty half dollar

DATE	NOTE	BUSINESS	PROOF
1916 (P)		608,000	Δ
1916-D		1,014,400	—
1916-S		508,000	—
1917 (P)		12,292,000	—
1917-D			
Obv. Mint Mark		765,400	—
Rev. Mint Mark		1,940,000	—
1917-S			
Obv. Mint Mark		952,000	—
Rev. Mint Mark		5,554,000	—
1918 (P)		6,634,000	—
1918-D		3,853,040	—
1918-S		10,282,000	—
1919 (P)		962,000	—
1919-D		1,165,000	—
1919-S		1,552,000	—
1920 (P)		6,372,000	—
1920-D		1,551,000	—
1920-S		4,624,000	—
1921 (P)		246,000	—
1921-D		208,000	—
1921-S		548,000	—
1923-S		2,178,000	—
1927-S		2,392,000	—
1928-S		1,940,000	—
1929-D		1,001,200	—
1929-S		1,902,000	—
1933-S		1,786,000	—
1934 (P)		6,964,000	—
1934-D		2,361,400	—
1934-S		3,652,000	—
1935 (P)		9,162,000	—
1935-D		3,003,800	—
1935-S		3,854,000	—
1936 (P)		12,614,000	3,901
1936-D		4,252,400	—
1936-S		3,884,000	—
1937 (P)		9,522,000	5,728
1937-D		1,676,000	—
1937-S		2,090,000	—
1938 (P)		4,110,000	8,152

DATE	NOTE	BUSINESS	PROOF
1938-D		491,600	——
1939 (P)		6,812,000	8,808
1939-D		4,267,800	——
1939-S		2,552,000	——
1940 (P)		9,156,000	11,279
1940-S		4,550,000	——
1941 (P)		24,192,000	15,412
1941-D		11,248,400	——
1941-S		8,098,000	——
1942 (P)		47,818,000	21,120
1942-D		10,973,800	——
1942-S		12,708,000	——
1943 (P)		53,190,000	——
1943-D		11,346,000	——
1943-S		13,450,000	——
1944 (P)		28,206,000	——
1944-D		9,769,000	——
1944-S		8,904,000	——
1945 (P)		31,502,000	——
1945-D		9,996,800	——
1945-S		10,156,000	——
1946 (P)		12,118,000	——
1946-D		2,151,000	——
1946-S		3,724,000	——
1947 (P)		4,094,000	——
1947-D		3,900,600	——

Franklin half dollar

DATE	NOTE	BUSINESS	PROOF
1948 (P)		3,006,814	——
1948-D		4,028,600	——
1949 (P)		5,614,000	——
1949-D		4,120,600	——
1949-S		3,744,000	——
1950 (P)	‹§›	7,742,123	51,386
1950-D		8,031,600	——
1951 (P)	‹§›	16,802,102	57,500
1951-D		9,475,200	——
1951-S		13,696,000	——
1952 (P)	‹§›	21,192,093	81,980
1952-D		25,395,600	——
1952-S		5,526,000	——
1953 (P)	‹§›	2,668,120	128,800
1953-D		20,900,400	——
1953-S		4,148,000	——
1954 (P)	‹§›	13,188,203	233,300
1954-D		25,445,580	——
1954-S		4,993,400	——
1955 (P)	‹§›	2,498,181	378,200
1956 (P)	‹§›	4,032,000	669,384
1957 (P)	‹§›	5,114,000	1,247,952
1957-D		19,966,850	——
1958 (P)	‹§›	4,042,000	875,652
1958-D		23,962,412	——
1959 (P)	‹§›	6,200,000	1,149,291
1959-D		13,0,750	——
1960 (P)	‹§›	6,024,000	1,691,602
1960-D		18,215,812	——
1961 (P)	‹§›	8,290,000	3,028,244
1961-D		20,276,442	——
1962 (P)	‹§›	9,714,000	3,218,019
1962-D		35,473,281	——
1963 (P)	‹§›	22,164,000	3,075,645
1963-D		67,069,292	——

Kennedy half dollar

DATE	NOTE	BUSINESS	PROOF
1964 (P)	‹§, 11›	273,304,004	3,950,762
1964-D	‹11›	156,205,446	——
1965 (P)	‹11›	——	——
1965 (D)	‹11›	63,049,366	——
1965 (S)	‹11, 54›	470,000	——
1966 (P)	‹11›	——	——
1966 (D)	‹11›	106,439,312	——
1966 (S)	‹11, 54›	284,037	——
1967 (P)	‹11›	——	——
1967 (D)	‹11›	293,183,634	——
1967 (S)	‹11, 54›	——	——
1968-D		246,951,930	——
1968-S	‹§›	——	3,041,506
1969-D		129,881,800	——
1969-S	‹§›	——	2,934,631
1970-D	‹55›	2,150,000	——
1970-S	‹§›	——	2,632,810
1971 (P)		155,164,000	——
1971-D		302,097,424	——
1971-S	‹§›	——	3,220,733
1972 (P)		153,180,000	——
1972-D		141,890,000	——
1972-S	‹§›	——	3,260,996
1973 (P)		64,964,000	——
1973-D		83,171,400	——
1973-S	‹§›	——	2,760,339
1974 (P)	‹43›	201,596,000	——
1974-D	‹43›	79,066,300	——
1974-S	‹§, 43›	——	2,612,568
1976 (P)	‹43›	234,308,000	——
1976-D	‹43›	287,565,248	——
1976-S	‹43›	——	——
1977 (P)		43,598,000	——
1977-D		31,449,106	——
1977-S	‹§›	——	3,236,798
1978 (P)		14,350,000	——
1978-D		13,765,799	——
1978-S	‹§›	——	3,120,285
1979 (P)		68,312,000	——
1979-D		15,815,422	——
1979-S	‹§›	——	3,677,175
1980-P	‹25›	44,134,000	——
1980-D		33,456,449	——
1980-S	‹§›	——	3,554,806
1981-P		29,544,000	——
1981-D		27,839,533	——
1981-S	‹§›	——	4,063,083
1982-P		10,819,000	——
1982-D		13,140,102	——
1982-S	‹§›	——	3,857,479
1983-P		34,139,000	——
1983-D		32,472,244	——
1983-S	‹§›	——	3,279,126
1984-P		26,029,000	——
1984-D		26,262,158	——

DATE	NOTE	BUSINESS	PROOF
1984-S	‹§›	——	3,065,110
1985-P		18,706,962	——
1985-D		19,814,034	——
1985-S	‹§›	——	3,362,821
1986-P		13,107,633	——
1986-D		15,366,145	——
1986-S	‹§›	——	3,010,497
1987-P	‹55›	——	——
1987-D	‹55›	——	——
1987-S	‹§›	——	3,792,233
1988-P		13,626,000	——
1988-D		12,000,096	——
1988-S	‹§›	——	3,262,948
1989-P		24,542,000	——
1989-D		23,000,216	——
1989-S	‹§›	——	3,220,914
1990-P		22,278,000	——
1990-D		20,096,242	——
1990-S	‹§›	——	3,299,559
1991-P		14,874,000	——
1991-D		15,054,678	——
1991-S	‹§›	——	2,867,787
1992-P		17,628,000	——
1992-D		17,000,106	——
1992-S	‹§›		
Clad		——	2,858,903
90% Silver		——	1,317,641
1993-P		15,510,000	——
1993-D		15,000,006	——
1993-S	‹§›		
Clad		——	2,569,882
90% Silver		——	790,994
1994-P		23,718,000	——
1994-D		23,828,110	——
1994-S	‹§›		
Clad		——	2,443,590
90% Silver		——	778,550
1995-P		26,496,000	——
1995-D		26,288,000	——
1995-S	‹§›		
Clad		——	2,124,790
90% Silver		——	666,277
1996-P		24,442,000	——
1996-D		24,744,000	——
1996-S	‹§›		
Clad		——	2,145,077
90% silver		——	775,081
1997-P		20,882,000	——
1997-D		19,876,000	——
1997-S	‹§›		
Clad		——	2,055,000
90% silver		——	741,194
1998-P		15,646,000	——
1998-D		15,064,000	——
1998-S	‹§›		
Clad		——	2,086,507
90% silver		——	878,996

Flowing Hair silver dollar

DATE	NOTE	BUSINESS	PROOF
1794		1,758	——
1795		160,295	——

Draped Bust silver dollar

DATE	NOTE	BUSINESS	PROOF
1795		42,738	——
1796		72,920	——
1797		7,776	——
1798	‹56›	327,536	——
1799		423,515	——
1800		220,920	——
1801	‹57›	54,454	——
1802	‹57›	41,650	——
1803	‹57›	85,634	——
1804	‹58›	——	——
1805	‹59›	——	——

Gobrecht silver dollar

DATE	NOTE	BUSINESS	PROOF
1836	‹60›	1,600	Δ
1838	‹60›	——	Δ
1839 (P)	‹60›	300	Δ

Seated Liberty silver dollar

DATE	NOTE	BUSINESS	PROOF
1840 (P)		61,005	Δ (R)
1841 (P)		173,000	Δ (R)
1842 (P)		184,618	Δ (R)
1843 (P)		165,100	Δ (R)
1844 (P)		20,000	Δ (R)
1845 (P)		24,500	Δ (R)
1846 (P)		110,600	Δ (R)
1846-O		59,000	—— (R)
1847 (P)		140,750	Δ (R)
1848 (P)		15,000	Δ (R)
1849 (P)		62,600	Δ (R)
1850 (P)		7,500	Δ (R)
1850-O		40,000	—— (R)
1851 (P)		1,300	Δ (R)
1852 (P)		1,100	Δ (R)
1853 (P)	‹16, 61›	46,110	—— (R)
1854 (P)		33,140	Δ
1855 (P)		26,000	Δ
1856 (P)		63,500	Δ
1857 (P)		94,000	Δ
1858 (P)	‹62›	——	Δ
1859 (P)		256,500	Δ
1859-O		360,000	——
1859-S		20,000	——
1860 (P)		217,600	1,330
1860-O		515,000	——
1861 (P)		77,500	1,000
1862 (P)		11,540	550
1863 (P)		27,200	460
1864 (P)		30,700	470
1865 (P)		46,500	500
1866 (P)	‹40›	48,900	725
1867 (P)		46,900	625
1868 (P)		162,100	600
1869 (P)		423,700	600
1870 (P)		415,000	1,000
1870-CC	‹63›	12,462	Δ
1870-S	‹64›	——	——
1871 (P)		1,073,800	960
1871-CC		1,376	——

DATE	NOTE	BUSINESS	PROOF
1872 (P)		1,105,500	950
1872-CC		3,150	—
1872-S		9,000	—
1873 (P)	‹6›	293,000	600
1873-CC	‹6›	2,300	—
1873-S	‹6, 65›	700	—

Morgan silver dollar

DATE	NOTE	BUSINESS	PROOF
1878 (P)	‹66›	10,508,550	1,000
1878-CC		2,212,000	—
1878-S		9,774,000	—
1879 (P)		14,806,000	1,100
1879-CC		756,000	—
1879-O	‹67›	2,887,000	Δ
1879-S		9,110,000	—
1880 (P)		12,600,000	1,355
1880-CC		591,000	—
1880-O		5,305,000	—
1880-S		8,900,000	—
1881 (P)		9,163,000	975
1881-CC		296,000	—
1881-O		5,708,000	—
1881-S		12,760,000	—
1882 (P)		11,100,000	1,100
1882-CC	‹68›	1,133,000	Δ
1882-O		6,090,000	—
1882-S		9,250,000	—
1883 (P)		12,290,000	1,039
1883-CC	‹69›	1,204,000	Δ
1883-O	‹70›	8,725,000	Δ
1883-S		6,250,000	—
1884 (P)		14,070,000	875
1884-CC	‹71›	1,136,000	Δ
1884-O		9,730,000	—
1884-S		3,200,000	—
1885 (P)		17,786,837	930
1885-CC		228,000	—
1885-O		9,185,000	—
1885-S		1,497,000	—
1886 (P)		19,963,000	886
1886-O		10,710,000	—
1886-S		750,000	—
1887 (P)		20,290,000	710
1887-O		11,550,000	—
1887-S		1,771,000	—
1888 (P)		19,183,000	832
1888-O		12,150,000	—
1888-S		657,000	—
1889 (P)		21,726,000	811
1889-CC		350,000	—
1889-O		11,875,000	—
1889-S		700,000	—
1890 (P)		16,802,000	590
1890-CC		2,309,041	—
1890-O		10,701,000	—
1890-S		8,230,373	—
1891 (P)		8,693,556	650
1891-CC		1,618,000	—
1891-O		7,954,529	—
1891-S		5,296,000	—

DATE	NOTE	BUSINESS	PROOF
1892 (P)		1,036,000	1,245
1892-CC		1,352,000	—
1892-O		2,744,000	—
1892-S		1,200,000	—
1893 (P)		389,000	792
1893-CC	‹72›	677,000	Δ
1893-O		300,000	—
1893-S		100,000	—
1894 (P)		110,000	972
1894-O		1,723,000	—
1894-S		1,260,000	—
1895 (P)	‹73›	12,000	880
1895-O		450,000	—
1895-S		400,000	—
1896 (P)		9,976,000	762
1896-O		4,900,000	—
1896-S		5,000,000	—
1897 (P)		2,822,000	731
1897-O		4,004,000	—
1897-S		5,825,000	—
1898 (P)		5,884,000	735
1898-O		4,440,000	—
1898-S		4,102,000	—
1899 (P)		330,000	846
1899-O		12,290,000	—
1899-S		2,562,000	—
1900 (P)		8,830,000	912
1900-O		12,590,000	—
1900-S		3,540,000	—
1901 (P)		6,962,000	813
1901-O		13,320,000	—
1901-S		2,284,000	—
1902 (P)		7,994,000	777
1902-O		8,636,000	—
1902-S		1,530,000	—
1903 (P)		4,652,000	755
1903-O		4,450,000	—
1903-S		1,241,000	—
1904 (P)		2,788,000	650
1904-O		3,720,000	—
1904-S		2,304,000	—
1921 (P)		44,690,000	Δ
1921-D		20,345,000	—
1921-S		21,695,000	—

Peace silver dollar

DATE	NOTE	BUSINESS	PROOF
1921 (P)	‹74›	1,006,473	—
1922 (P)		51,737,000	Δ
1922-D		15,063,000	—
1922-S		17,475,000	—
1923 (P)		30,800,000	—
1923-D		6,811,000	—
1923-S		19,020,000	—
1924 (P)		11,811,000	—
1924-S		1,728,000	—
1925 (P)		10,198,000	—
1925-S		1,610,000	—
1926 (P)		1,939,000	—
1926-D		2,348,700	—
1926-S		6,980,000	—

DATE	NOTE	BUSINESS	PROOF
1927 (P)		848,000	—
1927-D		1,268,900	—
1927-S		866,000	—
1928 (P)		360,649	—
1928-S		1,632,000	—
1934 (P)		954,057	—
1934-D		1,569,500	—
1934-S		1,011,000	—
1935 (P)		1,576,000	—
1935-S		1,964,000	—

Trade dollar

DATE	NOTE	BUSINESS	PROOF
1873 (P)	‹6, 75›	396,635	865
1873-CC	‹6›	124,500	—
1873-S	‹6›	703,000	—
1874 (P)		987,100	700
1874-CC		1,373,200	—
1874-S		2,549,000	—
1875 (P)		218,200	700
1875-CC		1,573,700	—
1875-S		4,487,000	—
1876 (P)		455,000	1,150
1876-CC		509,000	—
1876-S		5,227,000	—
1877 (P)		3,039,200	510
1877-CC		534,000	—
1877-S		9,519,000	—
1878 (P)		—	900
1878-CC		97,000	—
1878-S		4,162,000	—
1879 (P)		—	1,541
1880 (P)		—	1,987
1881 (P)		—	960
1882 (P)		—	1,097
1883 (P)		—	979
1884 (P)	‹76›	—	10
1885 (P)	‹76›	—	5

Eisenhower dollar

DATE	NOTE	BUSINESS	PROOF
1971 (P)		47,799,000	—
1971-D		68,587,424	—
1971-S			
40% silver	‹§, 77›	6,868,530	4,265,234
1972 (P)		75,890,000	—
1972-D		92,548,511	—
1972-S			
40% silver	‹77›	2,193,056	1,811,631
1973 (P)	‹78›	2,000,056	—
1973-D	‹78›	2,000,000	—
1973-S			
copper-nickel	‹§›	—	2,760,339
40% silver	‹77›	1,883,140	1,013,646
1974 (P)	‹43›	27,366,000	—
1974-D	‹43›	45,517,000	—
1974-S			
copper-nickel	‹§, 43›	—	2,612,568
40% silver	‹43, 77›	1,900,156	1,306,579
1976 (P)	‹43›	117,337,000	—
1976-D	‹43›	103,228,274	—
1976-S	‹43, 77›	—	—
1977 (P)		12,596,000	—

DATE	NOTE	BUSINESS	PROOF
1977-D		32,983,006	—
1977-S	‹§›	—	3,236,798
1978 (P)		25,702,000	—
1978-D		33,012,890	—
1978-S	‹§›	—	3,120,285

Anthony dollar

DATE	NOTE	BUSINESS	PROOF
1979-P	‹25›	360,222,000	—
1979-D		288,015,744	—
1979-S	‹§›	109,576,000	3,677,175
1980-P		27,610,000	—
1980-D		41,628,708	—
1980-S	‹§›	20,422,000	3,554,806
1981-P	‹79›	3,000,000	—
1981-D	‹79›	3,250,000	—
1981-S	‹§, 79›	3,492,000	4,063,083

Coronet gold dollar

DATE	NOTE	BUSINESS	PROOF
1849 (P)		688,567	Δ
1849-C		11,634	—
1849-D		21,588	—
1849-O		215,000	—
1850 (P)		481,953	—
1850-C		6,966	—
1850-D		8,382	—
1850-O		14,000	—
1851 (P)		3,317,671	—
1851-C		41,267	—
1851-D		9,882	—
1851-O		290,000	—
1852 (P)		2,045,351	—
1852-C		9,434	—
1852-D		6,360	—
1852-O		140,000	—
1853 (P)		4,076,051	—
1853-C		11,515	—
1853-D		6,583	—
1853-O		290,000	—
1854 (P)		736,709	Δ
1854-D		2,935	—
1854-S		14,632	—

Indian Head gold dollar

DATE	NOTE	BUSINESS	PROOF
1854 (P)		902,736	Δ
1855 (P)		758,269	Δ
1855-C		9,803	—
1855-D		1,811	—
1855-O		55,000	—
1856 (P)			
Large Head		1,762,936	Δ
1856-D			
Large Head		1,460	—
1856-S			
Small Head		24,600	—
1857 (P)		774,789	Δ
1857-C		13,280	—
1857-D		3,533	—
1857-S		10,000	—
1858 (P)		117,995	Δ
1858-D		3,477	—
1858-S		10,000	—

DATE	NOTE	BUSINESS	PROOF
1859 (P)		168,244	Δ
1859-C		5,235	——
1859-D		4,952	——
1859-S		15,000	——
1860 (P)		36,514	154
1860-D		1,566	——
1860-S		13,000	——
1861 (P)		527,150	349
1861-D	‹80›	——	——
1862 (P)		1,361,365	35
1863 (P)		6,200	50
1864 (P)		5,900	50
1865 (P)		3,700	25
1866 (P)		7,100	30
1867 (P)		5,200	50
1868 (P)		10,500	25
1869 (P)		5,900	25
1870 (P)		6,300	35
1870-S	‹81›	3,000	——
1871 (P)		3,900	30
1872 (P)		3,500	30
1873 (P)	‹6›	125,100	25
1874 (P)		198,800	20
1875 (P)		400	20
1876 (P)		3,200	45
1877 (P)		3,900	20
1878 (P)		3,000	20
1879 (P)		3,000	30
1880 (P)		1,600	36
1881 (P)		7,620	87
1882 (P)		5,000	125
1883 (P)		10,800	207
1884 (P)		5,230	1,006
1885 (P)		11,156	1,105
1886 (P)		5,000	1,016
1887 (P)		7,500	1,043
1888 (P)		15,501	1,079
1889 (P)		28,950	1,779
Capped Bust $2.50 quarter eagle			
1796		1,395	——
1797		427	——
1798		1,094	——
1802		3,035	——
1804		3,327	——
1805		1,781	——
1806		1,616	——
1807		6,812	——
Capped Draped Bust quarter eagle			
1808		2,710	——
Capped Head $2.50 quarter eagle			
1821		6,448	Δ
1824		2,600	Δ
1825		4,434	Δ
1826		760	Δ
1827		2,800	Δ
1829		3,403	Δ
1830		4,540	Δ
1831		4,520	Δ
1832		4,400	Δ
1833		4,160	Δ
1834	‹82›	4,000	Δ
Classic Head $2.50 quarter eagle			
1834		113,370	Δ
1835		131,402	Δ
1836		547,986	Δ
1837		45,080	Δ
1838 (P)		47,030	——
1838-C		7,908	——
1839 (P)		27,021	——
1839-C		18,173	——
1839-D		13,674	——
1839-O		17,781	——
Coronet $2.50 quarter eagle			
1840 (P)		18,859	Δ
1840-C		12,838	——
1840-D		3,532	——
1840-O		33,580	——
1841 (P)	‹83›	——	Δ
1841-C		10,297	——
1841-D		4,164	——
1842 (P)		2,823	Δ
1842-C		6,737	——
1842-D		4,643	——
1842-O		19,800	——
1843 (P)		100,546	Δ
1843-C		26,096	——
1843-D		36,209	——
1843-O		368,002	——
1844 (P)		6,784	Δ
1844-C		11,622	——
1844-D		17,332	——
1845 (P)		91,051	Δ
1845-D		19,460	——
1845-O		4,000	——
1846 (P)		21,598	Δ
1846-C		4,808	——
1846-D		19,303	——
1846-O		62,000	——
1847 (P)		29,814	Δ
1847-C		23,226	——
1847-D		15,784	——
1847-O		124,000	——
1848 (P)		7,497	Δ
CAL.	‹84›	1,389	——
1848-C		16,788	——
1848-D		13,771	——
1849 (P)		23,294	Δ
1849-C		10,220	——
1849-D		10,945	——
1850 (P)		252,923	——
1850-C		9,148	——
1850-D		12,148	——
1850-O		84,000	——
1851 (P)		1,372,748	——
1851-C		14,923	——
1851-D		11,264	——
1851-O		148,000	——

DATE	NOTE	BUSINESS	PROOF
1852 (P)		1,159,681	—
1852-C		9,772	—
1852-D		4,078	—
1852-O		140,000	—
1853 (P)		1,404,668	—
1853-D		3,178	—
1854 (P)		596,258	Δ
1854-C		7,295	—
1854-D		1,760	—
1854-O		153,000	—
1854-S		246	—
1855 (P)		235,480	Δ
1855-C		3,677	—
1855-D		1,123	—
1856 (P)		384,240	Δ
1856-C		7,913	—
1856-D		874	—
1856-O		21,100	—
1856-S		71,120	—
1857 (P)		214,130	Δ
1857-D		2,364	—
1857-O		34,000	—
1857-S		69,200	—
1858 (P)		47,377	Δ
1858-C		9,056	—
1859 (P)		39,444	Δ
1859-D		2,244	—
1859-S		15,200	—
1860 (P)		22,563	112
1860-C		7,469	—
1860-S		35,600	—
1861 (P)		1,272,428	90
1861-S		24,000	—
1862 (P)		98,508	35
1862-S		8,000	—
1863 (P)		—	30
1863-S		10,800	—
1864 (P)		2,824	50
1865 (P)		1,520	25
1865-S		23,376	—
1866 (P)		3,080	30
1866-S		38,960	—
1867 (P)		3,200	50
1867-S		28,000	—
1868 (P)		3,600	25
1868-S		34,000	—
1869 (P)		4,320	25
1869-S		29,500	—
1870 (P)		4,520	35
1870-S		16,000	—
1871 (P)		5,320	30
1871-S		22,000	—
1872 (P)		3,000	30
1872-S		18,000	—
1873 (P)	‹6›	178,000	25
1873-S	‹6›	27,000	—
1874 (P)		3,920	20
1875 (P)		400	20
1875-S		11,600	—
1876 (P)		4,176	45
1876-S		5,000	—
1877 (P)		1,632	20
1877-S		35,400	—
1878 (P)		286,240	20
1878-S		178,000	—
1879 (P)		88,960	30
1879-S		43,500	—
1880 (P)		2,960	36
1881 (P)		640	51
1882 (P)		4,000	67
1883 (P)		1,920	82
1884 (P)		1,950	73
1885 (P)		800	87
1886 (P)		4,000	88
1887 (P)		6,160	122
1888 (P)		16,006	92
1889 (P)		17,600	48
1890 (P)		8,720	93
1891 (P)		10,960	80
1892 (P)		2,440	105
1893 (P)		30,000	106
1894 (P)		4,000	122
1895 (P)		6,000	119
1896 (P)		19,070	132
1897 (P)		29,768	136
1898 (P)		24,000	165
1899 (P)		27,200	150
1900 (P)		67,000	205
1901 (P)		91,100	223
1902 (P)		133,540	193
1903 (P)		201,060	197
1904 (P)		160,790	170
1905 (P)		217,800	144
1906 (P)		176,330	160
1907 (P)		336,294	154

Indian Head $2.50 quarter eagle

DATE	NOTE	BUSINESS	PROOF
1908 (P)		564,821	236
1909 (P)		441,760	139
1910 (P)		492,000	682
1911 (P)		704,000	191
1911-D		55,680	—
1912 (P)		616,000	197
1913 (P)		722,000	165
1914 (P)		240,000	117
1914-D		448,000	—
1915 (P)		606,000	100
1925-D		578,000	—
1926 (P)		446,000	—
1927 (P)		388,000	—
1928 (P)		416,000	—
1929 (P)		532,000	—

Three dollar gold

DATE	NOTE	BUSINESS	PROOF
1854 (P)		138,618	Δ
1854-D		1,120	—
1854-O		24,000	—
1855 (P)		50,555	Δ
1855-S		6,600	—
1856 (P)		26,010	Δ
1856-S		34,500	—

DATE	NOTE	BUSINESS	PROOF
1857 (P)		20,891	Δ
1857-S		14,000	—
1858 (P)		2,133	Δ
1859 (P)		15,638	Δ
1860 (P)		7,036	119
1860-S	‹85›	4,408	—
1861 (P)		5,959	113
1862 (P)		5,750	35
1863 (P)		5,000	39
1864 (P)		2,630	50
1865 (P)		1,140	25
1866 (P)		4,000	30
1867 (P)		2,600	50
1868 (P)		4,850	25
1869 (P)		2,500	25
1870 (P)		3,500	35
1870-S	‹86›	—	—
1871 (P)		1,300	30
1872 (P)		2,000	30
1873 (P)	‹6, 87›	—	25 (R)
1874 (P)		41,800	20
1875 (P)		—	20 (R)
1876 (P)		—	45
1877 (P)		1,468	20
1878 (P)		82,304	20
1879 (P)		3,000	30
1880 (P)		1,000	36
1881 (P)		500	54
1882 (P)		1,500	76
1883 (P)		900	89
1884 (P)		1,000	106
1885 (P)		800	110
1886 (P)		1,000	142
1887 (P)		6,000	160
1888 (P)		5,000	291
1889 (P)		2,300	129

Capped Bust $5 half eagle

DATE	NOTE	BUSINESS	PROOF
1795		8,707	—
1796		6,196	—
1797		3,609	—
1798	‹88›	24,867	—
1799		7,451	—
1800		37,628	—
1802		53,176	—
1803		33,506	—
1804		30,475	—
1805		33,183	—
1806		64,093	—
1807		32,488	—

Capped Draped Bust $5 half eagle

DATE	NOTE	BUSINESS	PROOF
1807		51,605	—
1808		55,578	—
1809		33,875	—
1810		100,287	—
1811		99,581	—
1812		58,087	—

Capped Head $5 half eagle

DATE	NOTE	BUSINESS	PROOF
1813		95,428	—
1814		15,454	—
1815		635	—
1818		48,588	—
1819		51,723	—
1820		263,806	Δ
1821		34,641	Δ
1822	‹89›	17,796	—
1823		14,485	Δ
1824		17,340	Δ
1825	‹90›	29,060	Δ
1826		18,069	Δ
1827		24,913	Δ
1828	‹91›	28,029	Δ
1829		57,442	Δ
1830		126,351	Δ
1831		140,594	Δ
1832		157,487	Δ
1833		193,630	Δ
1834		50,141	Δ

Classic Head $5 half eagle

DATE	NOTE	BUSINESS	PROOF
1834		657,460	Δ
1835		371,534	Δ
1836		553,147	Δ
1837		207,121	Δ
1838 (P)		286,588	Δ
1838-C		19,145	—
1838-D		20,583	—

Coronet $5 half eagle

DATE	NOTE	BUSINESS	PROOF
1839 (P)		118,143	Δ
1839-C		17,235	—
1839-D		18,939	—
1840 (P)		137,382	Δ
1840-C		19,028	—
1840-D		22,896	—
1840-O		38,700	—
1841 (P)		15,833	Δ
1841-C		21,511	—
1841-D		30,495	—
1841-O		50	—
1842 (P)		27,578	Δ
1842-C		27,480	—
1842-D		59,608	—
1842-O		16,400	—
1843 (P)		611,205	Δ
1843-C		44,353	—
1843-D		98,452	—
1843-O		101,075	—
1844 (P)		340,330	Δ
1844-C		23,631	—
1844-D		88,982	—
1844-O	‹92›	364,600	Δ
1845 (P)		417,099	Δ
1845-D		90,629	—
1845-O		41,000	—
1846 (P)		395,942	Δ
1846-C		12,995	—
1846-D		80,294	—
1846-O		58,000	—

DATE	NOTE	BUSINESS	PROOF
1847 (P)		915,981	Δ
1847-C		84,151	——
1847-D		64,405	——
1847-O		12,000	——
1848 (P)		260,775	Δ
1848-C		64,472	——
1848-D		47,465	——
1849 (P)		133,070	——
1849-C		64,823	——
1849-D		39,036	——
1850 (P)		64,491	——
1850-C		63,591	——
1850-D		43,984	——
1851 (P)		377,505	——
1851-C		49,176	——
1851-D		62,710	——
1851-O		41,000	——
1852 (P)		573,901	——
1852-C		72,574	——
1852-D		91,584	——
1853 (P)		305,770	——
1853-C		65,571	——
1853-D		89,678	——
1854 (P)		160,675	——
1854-C		39,283	——
1854-D		56,413	——
1854-O		46,000	——
1854-S		268	——
1855 (P)		117,098	Δ
1855-C		39,788	——
1855-D		22,432	——
1855-O		11,100	——
1855-S		61,000	——
1856 (P)		197,990	Δ
1856-C		28,457	——
1856-D		19,786	——
1856-O		10,000	——
1856-S		105,100	——
1857 (P)		98,188	Δ
1857-C		31,360	——
1857-D		17,046	——
1857-O		13,000	——
1857-S		87,000	——
1858 (P)		15,136	Δ
1858-C		38,856	——
1858-D		15,362	——
1858-S		18,600	——
1859 (P)		16,814	Δ
1859-C		31,847	——
1859-D		10,366	——
1859-S		13,220	——
1860 (P)		19,763	62
1860-C		14,813	——
1860-D		14,635	——
1860-S		21,200	——
1861 (P)		688,084	66
1861-C	‹93›	6,879	——
1861-D		1,597	——
1861-S		18,000	——
1862 (P)		4,430	35

DATE	NOTE	BUSINESS	PROOF
1862-S		9,500	——
1863 (P)		2,442	30
1863-S		17,000	——
1864 (P)		4,220	50
1864-S		3,888	——
1865 (P)		1,270	25
1865-S		27,612	——
1866 (P)	‹40›	6,700	30
1866-S			
No Motto	‹40›	9,000	——
Motto	‹40›	34,920	——
1867 (P)		6,870	50
1867-S		29,000	——
1868 (P)		5,700	25
1868-S		52,000	——
1869 (P)		1,760	25
1869-S		31,000	——
1870 (P)		4,000	35
1870-CC		7,675	——
1870-S		17,000	——
1871 (P)		3,200	30
1871-CC		20,770	——
1871-S		25,000	——
1872 (P)		1,660	30
1872-CC		16,980	——
1872-S		36,400	——
1873 (P)	‹6›	112,480	25
1873-CC	‹6›	7,416	——
1873-S	‹6›	31,000	——
1874 (P)		3,488	20
1874-CC		21,198	——
1874-S		16,000	——
1875 (P)		200	20
1875-CC		11,828	——
1875-S		9,000	——
1876 (P)		1,432	45
1876-CC		6,887	——
1876-S		4,000	——
1877 (P)		1,132	20
1877-CC		8,680	——
1877-S		26,700	——
1878 (P)		131,720	20
1878-CC		9,054	——
1878-S		144,700	——
1879 (P)		301,920	30
1879-CC		17,281	——
1879-S		426,200	——
1880 (P)		3,166,400	36
1880-CC		51,017	——
1880-S		1,348,900	——
1881 (P)		5,708,760	42
1881-CC		13,886	——
1881-S		969,000	——
1882 (P)		2,514,520	48
1882-CC		82,817	——
1882-S		969,000	——
1883 (P)		233,400	61
1883-CC		12,958	——
1883-S		83,200	——
1884 (P)		191,030	48

DATE	NOTE	BUSINESS	PROOF
1884-CC		16,402	——
1884-S		177,000	——
1885 (P)		601,440	66
1885-S		1,211,500	——
1886 (P)		388,360	72
1886-S		3,268,000	——
1887 (P)		——	87
1887-S		1,912,000	——
1888 (P)		18,202	94
1888-S		293,900	——
1889 (P)		7,520	45
1890 (P)		4,240	88
1890-CC		53,800	——
1891 (P)		61,360	53
1891-CC		208,000	——
1892 (P)		753,480	92
1892-CC		82,968	——
1892-O		10,000	——
1892-S		298,400	——
1893 (P)		1,528,120	77
1893-CC		60,000	——
1893-O		110,000	——
1893-S		224,000	——
1894 (P)		957,880	75
1894-O		16,600	——
1894-S		55,900	——
1895 (P)		1,345,855	81
1895-S		112,000	——
1896 (P)		58,960	103
1896-S		155,400	——
1897 (P)		867,800	83
1897-S		354,000	——
1898 (P)		633,420	75
1898-S		1,397,400	——
1899 (P)		1,710,630	99
1899-S	‹94›	1,545,000	Δ
1900 (P)		1,405,500	230
1900-S		329,000	——
1901 (P)		615,900	140
1901-S		3,648,000	——
1902 (P)		172,400	162
1902-S		939,000	——
1903 (P)		226,870	154
1903-S		1,855,000	——
1904 (P)		392,000	136
1904-S		97,000	——
1905 (P)		302,200	108
1905-S		880,700	——
1906 (P)		348,735	85
1906-D	‹95›	320,000	——
1906-S		598,000	——
1907 (P)		626,100	92
1907-D	‹95›	888,000	——
1908 (P)		421,874	——
Indian Head $5 half eagle			
1908 (P)		577,845	167
1908-D		148,000	——
1908-S		82,000	——
1909 (P)		627,060	78
1909-D		3,423,560	——
1909-O		34,200	——
1909-S		297,200	——
1910 (P)		604,000	250
1910-D		193,600	——
1910-S		770,200	——
1911 (P)		915,000	139
1911-D		72,500	——
1911-S		1,416,000	——
1912 (P)		790,000	144
1912-S		392,000	——
1913 (P)		916,000	99
1913-S		408,000	——
1914 (P)		247,000	125
1914-D		247,000	——
1914-S		263,000	——
1915 (P)		588,000	75
1915-S		164,000	——
1916-S		240,000	——
1929 (P)		662,000	——
Capped Bust $10 eagle			
1795		5,583	——
1796		4,146	——
1797	‹96›	14,555	——
1798		1,742	——
1799		37,449	——
1800		5,999	——
1801		44,344	——
1803		15,017	——
1804		3,757	——
Coronet $10 eagle			
1838 (P)		7,200	Δ
1839 (P)	‹97›	38,248	Δ
1840 (P)		47,338	Δ
1841 (P)		63,131	Δ
1841-O		2,500	——
1842 (P)		81,507	Δ
1842-O		27,400	——
1843 (P)		75,462	Δ
1843-O		175,162	——
1844 (P)		6,361	Δ
1844-O	‹98›	118,700	Δ
1845 (P)		26,153	Δ
1845-O		47,500	——
1846 (P)		20,095	Δ
1846-O		81,780	——
1847 (P)		862,258	Δ
1847-O		571,500	——
1848 (P)		145,484	Δ
1848-O		35,850	——
1849 (P)		653,618	——
1849-O		23,900	——
1850 (P)		291,451	——
1850-O		57,500	——
1851 (P)		176,328	——
1851-O		263,000	——
1852 (P)		263,106	——
1852-O	‹99›	18,000	Δ
1853 (P)		201,253	——

DATE	NOTE	BUSINESS	PROOF
1853-O	‹100›	51,000	Δ
1854 (P)		54,250	—
1854-O		52,500	—
1854-S		123,826	—
1855 (P)		121,701	Δ
1855-O		18,000	—
1855-S		9,000	—
1856 (P)		60,490	Δ
1856-O		14,500	—
1856-S		68,000	—
1857 (P)		16,606	Δ
1857-O		5,500	—
1857-S		26,000	—
1858 (P)		2,521	Δ
1858-O		20,000	—
1858-S		11,800	—
1859 (P)		16,093	Δ
1859-O		2,300	—
1859-S		7,000	—
1860 (P)		15,055	50
1860-O		11,100	—
1860-S		5,000	—
1861 (P)		113,164	69
1861-S		15,500	—
1862 (P)		10,960	35
1862-S		12,500	—
1863 (P)		1,218	30
1863-S		10,000	—
1864 (P)		3,530	50
1864-S		2,500	—
1865 (P)		3,980	25
1865-S		16,700	—
1866 (P)	‹40›	3,750	30
1866-S			
No Motto	‹40›	8,500	—
Motto	‹40›	11,500	—
1867 (P)		3,090	50
1867-S		9,000	—
1868 (P)		10,630	25
1868-S		13,500	—
1869 (P)		1,830	25
1869-S		6,430	—
1870 (P)		3,990	35
1870-CC		5,908	—
1870-S		8,000	—
1871 (P)		1,790	30
1871-CC		8,085	—
1871-S		16,500	—
1872 (P)		1,620	30
1872-CC		4,600	—
1872-S		17,300	—
1873 (P)	‹6›	800	25
1873-CC	‹6›	4,543	—
1873-S	‹6›	12,000	—
1874 (P)		53,140	20
1874-CC		16,767	—
1874-S		10,000	—
1875 (P)		100	20
1875-CC		7,715	—
1876 (P)		687	45

DATE	NOTE	BUSINESS	PROOF
1876-CC		4,696	—
1876-S		5,000	—
1877 (P)		797	20
1877-CC		3,332	—
1877-S		17,000	—
1878 (P)		73,780	20
1878-CC		3,244	—
1878-S		26,100	—
1879 (P)		384,740	30
1879-CC		1,762	—
1879-O		1,500	—
1879-S		224,000	—
1880 (P)		1,644,840	36
1880-CC		11,190	—
1880-O		9,200	—
1880-S		506,250	—
1881 (P)		3,877,220	42
1881-CC		24,015	—
1881-O		8,350	—
1881-S		970,000	—
1882 (P)		2,324,440	44
1882-CC		6,764	—
1882-O		10,820	—
1882-S		132,000	—
1883 (P)		208,700	49
1883-CC		12,000	—
1883-O		800	—
1883-S		38,000	—
1884 (P)		76,890	45
1884-CC		9,925	—
1884-S		124,250	—
1885 (P)		253,462	67
1885-S		228,000	—
1886 (P)		236,100	60
1886-S		826,000	—
1887 (P)		53,600	80
1887-S		817,000	—
1888 (P)		132,924	72
1888-O		21,335	—
1888-S		648,700	—
1889 (P)		4,440	45
1889-S		425,400	—
1890 (P)		57,980	63
1890-CC		17,500	—
1891 (P)		91,820	48
1891-CC		103,732	—
1892 (P)		797,480	72
1892-CC		40,000	—
1892-O		28,688	—
1892-S		115,500	—
1893 (P)		1,840,840	55
1893-CC		14,000	—
1893-O		17,000	—
1893-S		141,350	—
1894 (P)		2,470,735	43
1894-O		107,500	—
1894-S		25,000	—
1895 (P)		567,770	56
1895-O		98,000	—
1895-S		49,000	—

DATE	NOTE	BUSINESS	PROOF
1896 (P)		76,270	78
1896-S		123,750	——
1897 (P)		1,000,090	69
1897-O		42,500	——
1897-S		234,750	——
1898 (P)		812,130	67
1898-S		473,600	——
1899 (P)		1,262,219	86
1899-O		37,047	——
1899-S		841,000	——
1900 (P)		293,840	120
1900-S		81,000	——
1901 (P)		1,718,740	85
1901-O		72,041	——
1901-S		2,812,750	——
1902 (P)		82,400	113
1902-S		469,500	——
1903 (P)		125,830	96
1903-O		112,771	——
1903-S		538,000	——
1904 (P)		161,930	108
1904-O		108,950	——
1905 (P)		200,992	86
1905-S		369,250	——
1906 (P)		165,420	77
1906-D	‹101›	981,000	Δ
1906-O		86,895	——
1906-S		457,000	——
1907 (P)		1,203,899	74
1907-D		1,030,000	——
1907-S		210,500	——

Indian Head $10 eagle

DATE	NOTE	BUSINESS	PROOF
1907 (P)	‹102›	239,406	——
1908 (P)			
Without Motto		33,500	——
With Motto		341,370	116
1908-D			
Without Motto		210,000	——
With Motto836,500		——	
1908-S			
With Motto		59,850	——
1909 (P)		184,789	74
1909-D		121,540	——
1909-S		292,350	——
1910 (P)		318,500	204
1910-D		2,356,640	——
1910-S		811,000	——
1911 (P)		505,500	95
1911-D		30,100	——
1911-S		51,000	——
1912 (P)		405,000	83
1912-S		300,000	——
1913 (P)		442,000	71
1913-S		66,000	——
1914 (P)		151,000	50
1914-D		343,500	——
1914-S		208,000	——
1915 (P)		351,000	75
1915-S		59,000	——
1916-S		138,500	——
1920-S		126,500	——
1926 (P)		1,014,000	——
1930-S		96,000	——
1932 (P)		4,463,000	——
1933 (P)	‹103›	312,500	——

Coronet $20 double eagle

DATE	NOTE	BUSINESS	PROOF
1849 (P)	‹104›	——	Δ
1850 (P)	‹105›	1,170,261	Δ
1850-O		141,000	——
1851 (P)		2,087,155	——
1851-O		315,000	——
1852 (P)		2,053,026	——
1852-O		190,000	——
1853 (P)		1,261,326	——
1853-O		71,000	——
1854 (P)		757,899	——
1854-O		3,250	——
1854-S	‹106›	141,468	Δ
1855 (P)		364,666	——
1855-O		8,000	——
1855-S		879,675	——
1856 (P)		329,878	Δ
1856-O		2,250	——
1856-S		1,189,780	——
1857 (P)		439,375	——
1857-O		30,000	——
1857-S		970,500	——
1858 (P)		211,714	Δ
1858-O		35,250	——
1858-S		846,710	——
1859 (P)		43,597	Δ
1859-O		9,100	——
1859-S		636,445	——
1860 (P)		577,611	59
1860-O		6,600	——
1860-S		544,950	——
1861 (P)	‹107›	2,976,387	66
1861-O	‹108›	17,741	——
1861-S	‹109›	768,000	——
1862 (P)		92,098	35
1862-S		854,173	——
1863 (P)		142,760	30
1863-S		966,570	——
1864 (P)		204,235	50
1864-S		793,660	——
1865 (P)		351,175	25
1865-S		1,042,500	——
1866 (P)	‹40, 110›	698,745	30
1866-S			
No Motto	‹40, 110›	120,000	——
With Motto	‹40, 110›	722,250	——
1867 (P)		251,015	50
1867-S		920,750	——
1868 (P)		98,575	25
1868-S		837,500	——
1869 (P)		175,130	25
1869-S		686,750	——
1870 (P)		155,150	35

DATE	NOTE	BUSINESS	PROOF
1870-CC		3,789	——
1870-S		982,000	——
1871 (P)		80,120	30
1871-CC		17,387	——
1871-S		928,000	——
1872 (P)		251,850	30
1872-CC		26,900	——
1872-S		780,000	——
1873 (P)	‹6›	1,709,800	25
1873-CC	‹6›	22,410	——
1873-S	‹6›	1,040,600	——
1874 (P)		366,780	20
1874-CC		115,000	——
1874-S		1,214,000	——
1875 (P)		295,720	20
1875-CC		111,151	——
1875-S		1,230,000	——
1876 (P)		583,860	45
1876-CC		138,441	——
1876-S		1,597,000	——
1877 (P)	‹111›	397,650	20
1877-CC		42,565	——
1877-S		1,735,000	——
1878 (P)		543,625	20
1878-CC		13,180	——
1878-S		1,739,000	——
1879 (P)		207,600	30
1879-CC		10,708	——
1879-O		2,325	——
1879-S		1,223,800	——
1880 (P)		51,420	36
1880-S		836,000	——
1881 (P)		2,220	61
1881-S		727,000	——
1882 (P)		590	59
1882-CC		39,140	——
1882-S		1,125,000	——
1883 (P)		——	92
1883-CC		59,962	——
1883-S		1,189,000	——
1884 (P)		——	71
1884-CC		81,139	——
1884-S		916,000	——
1885 (P)		751	77
1885-CC		9,450	——
1885-S		683,500	——
1886 (P)		1,000	106
1887 (P)		——	121
1887-S		283,000	——
1888 (P)		226,164	102
1888-S		859,600	——
1889 (P)		44,070	41
1889-CC		30,945	——
1889-S		774,700	——
1890 (P)		75,940	55
1890-CC		91,209	——
1890-S		802,750	——
1891 (P)		1,390	52
1891-CC		5,000	——
1891-S		1,288,125	——
1892 (P)		4,430	93
1892-CC		27,265	——
1892-S		930,150	——
1893 (P)		344,280	59
1893-CC		18,402	——
1893-S		996,175	——
1894 (P)		1,368,940	50
1894-S		1,048,550	——
1895 (P)		1,114,605	51
1895-S		1,143,500	——
1896 (P)		792,535	128
1896-S		1,403,925	——
1897 (P)		1,383,175	86
1897-S		1,470,250	——
1898 (P)		170,395	75
1898-S		2,575,175	——
1899 (P)		1,669,300	84
1899-S		2,010,300	——
1900 (P)		1,874,460	124
1900-S		2,459,500	——
1901 (P)		111,430	96
1901-S		1,596,000	——
1902 (P)		31,140	114
1902-S		1,753,625	——
1903 (P)		287,270	158
1903-S		954,000	——
1904 (P)		6,256,699	98
1904-S		5,134,175	——
1905 (P)		58,919	90
1905-S		1,813,000	——
1906 (P)		69,596	94
1906-D	‹112›	620,250	Δ
1906-S		2,065,750	——
1907 (P)		1,451,786	78
1907-D	‹113›	842,250	Δ
1907-S		2,165,800	——

Saint-Gaudens $20 double eagle

DATE	NOTE	BUSINESS	PROOF
1907 (P)			
Roman Numerals	‹114›	11,250	——
Arabic Numerals		361,667	——
1908 (P)			
No Motto		4,271,551	——
With Motto		156,258	101
1908-D			
No Motto		663,750	——
With Motto		349,500	——
1908-S			
With Motto		22,000	——
1909 (P)		161,215	67
1909-D		52,500	——
1909-S		2,774,925	——
1910 (P)		482,000	167
1910-D		429,000	——
1910-S		2,128,250	——
1911 (P)		197,250	100
1911-D		846,500	——
1911-S		775,750	——
1912 (P)		149,750	74
1913 (P)		168,780	58

DATE	NOTE	BUSINESS	PROOF
1913-D		393,500	——
1913-S		34,000	——
1914 (P)		95,250	70
1914-D		453,000	——
1914-S		1,498,000	——
1915 (P)		152,000	50
1915-S		567,500	——
1916-S		796,000	——
1920 (P)		228,250	——
1920-S		558,000	——
1921 (P)		528,500	——
1922 (P)		1,375,500	——
1922-S		2,658,000	——
1923 (P)		566,000	——
1923-D		1,702,250	——
1924 (P)		4,323,500	——
1924-D		3,049,500	——
1924-S		2,927,500	——
1925 (P)		2,831,750	——
1925-D		2,938,500	——
1925-S		3,776,500	——
1926 (P)		816,750	——
1926-D		481,000	——
1926-S		2,041,500	——
1927 (P)		2,946,750	——
1927-D		180,000	——
1927-S		3,107,000	——
1928 (P)		8,816,000	——
1929 (P)		1,779,750	——
1930-S		74,000	——
1931 (P)		2,938,250	——
1931-D		106,500	——
1932 (P)		1,101,750	——
1933 (P)	<115>	445,000	——

American Eagle 1-oz silver $1

DATE	NOTE	BUSINESS	PROOF
1986 (S)		5,393,005	——
1986-S		——	1,446,778
1987 (S)		11,442,335	——
1987-S		——	904,732
1988 (S)		5,004,646	——
1988-S		——	557,370
1989 (S or W)		5,203,327	——
1989-S		——	617,694
1990 (S or W)		5,840,110	——
1990-S		——	695,510
1991 (S or W)		7,191,066	——
1991-S		——	511,924
1992 (S or W)		5,540,068	——
1992-S		——	498,543
1993 (S or W)		6,763,762	——
1993-P		——	405,913
1994 (S or W)		4,227,319	——
1994-P		——	372,168
1995 (S or W)		4,672,051	——
1995-P		——	438,511
1995-W	<119>	——	30,125
1996 (S or W)		3,603,386	——
1996-P	<120>	——	500,000
1997 (S or W)		4,295,004	——
1997-P		——	435,368
1998 (S or W)		4,847,549	——
1998-P		——	Pending

American Eagle 1/10-oz gold $5

DATE	NOTE	BUSINESS	PROOF
1986 (W)	<117>	912,609	——
1987 (W)	<117>	580,266	——
1988 (W)	<117>	159,500	——
1988-P	<117>	——	143,881
1989 (W)	<117>	264,790	——
1989-P	<117>	——	84,647
1990 (W)	<117>	210,210	——
1990-P	<117>	——	99,349
1991 (W)	<117>	165,200	——
1991-P	<117>	——	70,334
1992 (W)		209,300	——
1992-P		——	64,874
1993 (W)		210,709	——
1993-P		——	58,649
1994 (W)		206,380	——
1994-P		——	62,849
1995 (W)		223,025	——
1995-W		——	62,673
1996 (W)		401,964	——
1996-W		——	56,700
1997 (S or W)		528,266	——
1997-P		——	34,984
1998 (S or W)		1,344,520	——
1998-P		——	39,625

American Eagle 1/4-oz gold $10

DATE	NOTE	BUSINESS	PROOF
1986 (W)	<117>	726,031	——
1987 (W)	<117>	269,255	——
1988 (W)	<117>	49,000	——
1988-P	<117>	——	98,028
1989 (W)	<117>	81,789	——
1989-P	<117>	——	54,170
1990 (W)	<117>	41,000	——
1990-P	<117>	——	62,674
1991 (W)	<117>	36,100	——
1991-P	<117>	——	50,839
1992 (W)		59,546	——
1992-P		——	46,269
1993 (W)		71,864	——
1993-P		——	46,464
1994 (W)		72,650	——
1994-P		——	48,172
1995 (W)		83,752	——
1995-W		——	47,484
1996 (W)		60,318	——
1996-W		——	37,900
1997 (S or W)		108,805	——
1997-P		——	29,808
1998 (S or W)		309,829	——
1998-P		——	29,733

American Eagle 1/2-oz gold $25

DATE	NOTE	BUSINESS	PROOF
1986 (W)	<117>	599,566	——
1987 (W)	<117>	131,255	——
1987-P	<117>	——	143,398
1988 (W)	<117>	45,000	——

DATE	NOTE	BUSINESS	PROOF
1988-P	<117>	——	76,528
1989 (W)	<117>	44,829	——
1989-P	<117>	——	44,798
1990 (W)	<117>	31,000	——
1990-P	<117>	——	51,636
1991 (W)	<117>	24,100	——
1991-P	<117>	——	53,125
1992 (W)		54,404	——
1992-P		——	40,976
1993 (W)		73,324	——
1993-P		——	43,319
1994 (W)		62,400	——
1994-P		——	44,584
1995 (W)		53,474	——
1995-W		——	45,442
1996 (W)		39,287	——
1996-W		——	34,700
1997 (S or W)		79,605	——
1997-P		——	26,340
1998 (S or W)		169,029	——
1998-P		——	26,625
American Eagle 1-Oz gold $50			
1986 (W)	<117>	1,362,650	——
1986-W	<117>	——	446,290
1987 (W)	<117>	1,045,500	——
1987-W	<117>	——	147,498
1988 (W)	<117>	465,500	——
1988-W	<117>	——	87,133
1989 (W)	<117>	415,790	——
1989-W	<117>	——	54,570
1990 (W)	<117>	373,210	——
1990-W	<117>	——	62,401
1991 (W)	<117>	243,100	——
1991-W	<117>	——	50,411
1992 (W)		275,000	——
1992-W		——	44,826
1993 (W)		480,192	——
1993-W		——	34,389
1994 (W)		221,633	——
1994-W		——	46,674
1995 (W)		200,636	——
1995-W		——	46,484
1996 (W)		189,148	——
1996-W		——	36,000
1997 (S or W)		664,508	——
1997-W		——	27,554
1998 (S or W)		1,468,530	——
1998-P		——	28,067
American Eagle 1/10-Oz Platinum $10			
1997 (W)		70,250	——
1997-W		——	37,025
1998 (W)		39,525	——
1998-W		——	19,920
American Eagle 1/4-Oz Platinum $25			
1997 (W)		27,100	——
1997-W		——	18,661
1998 (W)		38,887	——
1998-W		——	14,920
American Eagle 1/2-Oz Platinum $50			
1997 (W)		20,500	——
1997-W		——	15,463
1998 (W)		32,419	——
1998-W		——	13,929
American Eagle 1-Oz Platinum $100			
1997 (W)		56,000	——
1997-W		——	18,000
1998 (W)		133,002	——
1998-W		——	14,665

MINTAGE NOTES

Many different Proof issues before 1880 were restruck in Proof one or more times. In some instances, as with the 1873 $3 gold piece, there are more coins of this date known than were "officially" struck.

KEY

(R): Known to have been restruck at least once.

(§): Proofs originally sold in sets only.

——: None issued.

Δ: Specimens known or believed to exist; no official mintage reported.

U: Final, official mintages unreported by the U.S. Mint.

NOTES

1. 1804, 1823 cent, and 1811 half cent: Counterfeits, called restrikes, exist which were made outside the Mint, using old, genuine but mismatched Mint dies.
2. 1832-35 half cent: The figures shown are listed in the Mint Report for 1833-36 instead, but are assumed to be misplaced.
3. 1823 cent, dime, quarter dollar: Proofs exist with overdate, 1823/2.
4. 1856 cent: More than 1,000 1856 Flying Eagle cents were struck in Proof and Uncirculated, in this and later years. As they were patterns they are not included in the Mint Report or this figure.
5. 1864 cent: Proof breakdown by varieties thought to be about 300 to 350 copper-nickel and about 100 to 150 bronze coins without the designer's initial L. Perhaps 20 or fewer Proofs with initial L were struck. Business strike bronze coins with designer's initial L are also rarer.
6. 1873 coinage: Early in the year a relatively closed style of 3 was used in the date on all denominations. In response to complaints that the 3 looked like an 8, a new, more open 3 was introduced. Most types were struck with both styles, except for those which were created or discontinued by the Coinage Act of Feb. 12, 1873. This law created the Trade dollar and eliminated the standard silver dollar, the

silver 5-cent piece, the 3-cent piece and the 2-cent piece. The weight of the dime, quarter dollar and half dollar were slightly increased, and the heavier coins were marked by arrows for the remainder of 1873 and all of 1874. All Proofs are of the relatively Closed 3 variety.

7. 1877 minor coinages: Proof estimates for this year vary considerably, usually upwards. For lack of any records, the number shown is that of the silver Proofs of this year, conforming with the method used in the preceding years. These figures may be considerably low.

8. 1922 "Plain" cent: No cents were struck in Philadelphia in 1922. Some 1922-D cents are found with the Mint mark missing due to obstructed dies. Beware of altered coins.

9. 1943-(P), D, S cent: All 1943 cents were made of zinc-plated steel. A few 1943 bronze and 1944 steel cents were made by accident. Many fakes of these have been produced. Test any suspected off-metal 1943 or 1944 cent with a magnet to see if it has been plated, and check the date for alterations. Cents struck on steel planchets produced in 1942 weigh 41.5 grains, while those struck on planchets produced later in 1943 weigh 42.5 grains.

10. 1960 cent: Includes Large Date and Small Date varieties. The Small Date is the scarcer for both Proof and business strikes.

11. 1964-67 coinage: All coins dated 1965-67 were made without Mint marks. Many coins dated 1964-66 were struck in later years.

12. 1982 cent: The composition of the cent changed from 95 percent copper, 5 percent zinc to 97.5 percent zinc, 2.5 percent copper (composed of a planchet of 99.2 percent zinc, 0.8 percent copper, plated with pure copper). Some 1982 cents were struck in late 1981.

13. 1864 2 cents: Struck with Large and Small Motto IN GOD WE TRUST. The Small Motto in Proof is rare.

14. 1873 2 cents: Originally struck in Proof only early in 1873 with a Closed 3. An estimated 500 restrikes in Proof with an Open 3.

15. 1887 copper-nickel 3 cents: Many Proofs struck from an overdated die, 1887/6.

16. 1853 silver coinage: In early 1853 the weight of all fractional silver coins was reduced by about 7 percent, to prevent hoarding and melting. To distinguish between the old and new weights, arrows were placed on either side of the date on the half dime through half dollar, and rays were put around the eagle on the quarter and half dollar. The rays were removed after 1853, and the arrows after 1855. Much of the old silver was withdrawn from circulation and melted. The exception to all this was the silver 3-cent piece, which was decreased in weight but increased in fineness, making it intrinsically worth more than before and proportionate with the other fractional silver coins. No coins of the new weight were struck until 1854, at which time an olive branch and a cluster of arrows was added to the reverse.

17. 1863 silver 3 cents: It is possible that all of these non-Proofs were dated 1862. Proof coins dated 1863/2 were struck in 1864. Obviously these were hard times at the Mint.

18. 1864-(P) silver 3 cents, half dime, and dime: These figures, like many others in the years 1861-1871, are highly controversial due to extraordinary bookkeeping methods used in the Mint in this era.

19. 1867 copper-nickel 5 cents: Struck with rays on reverse (type of 1866) and without rays (type of 1868-83). Approximately 25 Proofs struck With Rays on reverse (type of 1866), and 600 Without Rays (type of 1868-83).

20. 1913 Liberty Head copper-nickel 5 cents: Five unauthorized pieces were struck by person or persons unknown, using Mint machinery and dies.Only four pieces can be accounted for. Beware of forgeries.

21. 1942-1945-(P), P, D, S 5 cents: To conserve nickel during the war, the composition of the 5-cent piece was changed to a 56 percent copper, 35 percent silver, and 9 percent manganese alloy. Coins of this alloy were marked with a large Mint mark over the dome of Monticello, including those from Philadelphia. They consist of some 1942-P, all 1942-S, and all 1943-45 coins. The 1942 Philadelphia coins were made either way. Many wartime alloy 5-cent coins have been melted for their silver content.

22. 1944 copper-nickel 5 cents, 1923-D and 1930-D dimes: Coins without a Mint mark are counterfeits made for circulation. Not all counterfeits are of rare dates, meant to sell at high prices. Some were meant to circulate.

23. 1966 5-cent piece: Two Proof Jefferson 5-cent pieces were struck to mark the addition of designer Felix Schlag's initials, F.S., to the obverse design. At least one coin was presented to Schlag; the other may have been retained by the Mint.

24. 1971 5 cents: Some Proof sets contain 5-cent coins which were struck from a Proof die without a Mint mark. This was an engraver's oversight and is not a filled die. Official estimate of 1,655 sets released.

25. P Mint mark: The P Mint mark, placed on the 1979 Anthony dollar, was added to all 1980 denominations from the Philadelphia Mint except for the cent.

26. 1838-O half dime and dime: Both are of Seated Liberty, Without Stars design (type of 1837). 1838 Philadelphia coins have stars, as do all others through 1859.

27. 1856-O half dime: One Proof known, reason for issue unknown.

28. 1860-(P), O, S half dime and dime: Beginning in 1860 (with the exception of the 1860-S dime), the half dime and dime were redesigned by eliminating the stars, moving the legend UNITED STATES OF AMERICA to the obverse, and using a larger, more elaborate wreath on the reverse. A number of fabrications with the obverse of 1859 and the reverse of 1860 (thereby omitting the legend UNITED STATES OF AMERICA), were struck by order of the Director of the Mint. These consist of half dimes dated 1859 or 1860, and dimes dated 1859. Although they are considered by some to be patterns, that designation is doubtful as the intentions of the Director were highly questionable.
29. 1860-O half dime: Three Proofs known, reason for issue unknown.
30. 1873-CC dime: One known, all others presumably were melted.
31. 1894-S dime: Twenty-four Proof or specimen strikings were made for private distribution by the Superintendent of the San Francisco Mint. Twelve can be traced today, including two circulated pieces.
32. 1906-D dime: Proofs struck in honor of the opening of the Denver Mint.
33. 1968 dime: Some Proof sets contain dimes which were struck from a Proof die without a Mint mark. This was an engraver's oversight and is not a filled die. It has been unofficially estimated that only 20 specimens from this die are known. Beware of sets opened and reclosed with "processed" P-Mint coins inserted. Check the edge of the case for signs of tampering.
34. 1970 dime: Some Proof sets contain dimes which were struck from a Proof die without a Mint mark. This was an engraver's oversight and is not a filled die. Official estimate is that 2,200 sets were released with this error.
35. 1982 No-P dimes: Some 1982 dimes were released without a Mint mark, although dimes have been Mint marked since 1980. Distribution of the coins, many found in the Sandusky, Ohio, area, indicates they were from the Philadelphia Mint.
36. 1875-S 20 cents: Six to seven Proofs known, probably struck to celebrate the first (or last) year of this denomination at this Mint.
37. 1876-CC 20 cents: Virtually all remelted at the Mint. A few escaped, possibly as souvenirs given to visitors. Fewer than 20 are known today.
38. 1827 quarter dollar: Although the Mint Report lists a mintage of 4,000 pieces for this year, it is likely that all of these coins were dated 1825 except for a few Proofs. Later this date was unofficially (but intentionally) restruck at the Mint using an obverse die dated 1827 and a reverse die which had been used in 1819, and which had a Square Base 2 in quarter dollar, rather than the Curled Base 2 of the original 1827.
39. 1855-S quarter dollar: One Proof known, presumably struck to celebrate the beginning of silver coinage at the San Francisco Mint.
40. 1866 coinage: It was decided to add the motto IN GOD WE TRUST to the reverse of all double eagles, eagles, half eagles, silver dollars, half dollars and quarter dollars beginning in 1866. Early in the year, before the new reverse dies had arrived, the San Francisco Mint produced $20, $10, $5, and half dollar coins without the motto. These are regular issue coins and are not patterns or errors. They are not to be confused with a peculiar set of Philadelphia Mint silver coins without motto, consisting of two dollars, one half dollar and one quarter dollar, which was clandestinely struck inside (but not by) the Mint for sale to a collector. A three-piece set containing the unique quarter dollar and half dollar and one of the two known silver dollars was stolen from the Willis H. DuPont collection in 1967 and never recovered. Beware of regular coins with motto or Mint mark removed.
41. 1879 quarter dollar: The Proof figure is official, but may be wrong. The true number might be near or equal to 1,100.
42. 1891-O quarter dollar: Two Proofs known, probably struck to celebrate the resumption of fractional silver coinage at this Mint.
43. 1974-1976 quarter dollars, half dollars and dollars: The circulating commemorative coinage dated 1776-1976 in celebration of the nation's Bicentennial wreaked havoc on mintage bookkeeping. In anticipation of the program, 1974-dated coins of these denominations were struck in calendar years 1974 and 1975. No 1975-dated quarter dollars, half dollars or dollars were struck; 1975 Proof and Mint sets contain Bicentennial dates. 1776-1976-dated dollars, half dollars and quarter dollars were struck in calendar years 1975 and 1976. The 1976-S mintages for these denominations includes copper-nickel clad Proofs sold in 1975 and 1976 in six-piece Proof sets, and 40 percent silver clad Proofs and Uncirculateds, of which 15 million pieces of each denomination were struck.
44. 1817 half dollar: Only one Proof known, with overdate 1817/3.
45. 1836 Reeded Edge half dollar: Actually a pattern of the design adopted the following year, but much of the mintage was placed into circulation.
46. 1838-O half dollar: It is thought that 20 Proof specimens were struck as souvenirs in honor of the opening of the New Orleans Mint. No regular issue coins of this date and Mint were struck, and it is possible that these were struck in 1839.
47. 1839-O half dollar: Three or four Proofs known.
48. 1839-(P) half dollar: Although Christian Gobrecht's half dollar design was slightly modified during 1839 by the addition of a small drapery fold beneath the elbow, the design was never as fully modified as the other Seated Liberty denominations

were in 1840. In subsequent years individual dies would occasionally be over-polished, thus removing this small drapery fold. Coins struck from these inferior dies are sometimes referred to as having a "No-Drapery design," when in fact no design change was intended or made.

49. 1853-(P), O half dollar: All 1853-(P) and virtually all 1853-O half dollar are of the new weight. Two or three 1853-O are known without the arrows and rays. Beware of alterations from 1858-O.

50. 1855-S half dollar: Three Proofs known, presumably struck to celebrate the beginning of silver coinage at the San Francisco Mint.

51. 1861-O half dollar: Mintage includes 330,000 struck by the USA; 1,240,000 by the State of Louisiana; and 962,633 by the Confederate States of America. It is impossible to tell them apart. One obverse die is identifiable as having been used with the CSA reverse to strike four pattern coins, but there is no way of telling when that die was used with a regular reverse die or who issued the coins struck from it. Three to six Proofs known, probably struck under the authority of either the state of Louisiana or the CSA .

52. 1873-S half dollar: The 1873-S Seated Liberty, Without Arrows half dollar is unknown in any condition in any collection. Presumably they were all melted with the 1873-S silver dollars. Beware of any regular 1873-S with the arrows removed. The difference in weight between the two issues is insignificant, and useless in checking a suspected altered coin.

53. 1895-O half dollar: Proofs issued to mark reopening of New Orleans Mint.

54. Proof set sales suspended 1965-67.

55. 1970-D and 1987 half dollar: Struck only for inclusion in Mint sets. Not a regular issue coin. 1987 coins were struck for Uncirculated sets, Proof sets and Souvenir Mint sets only, forcing a change in the Mint's accounting procedures. Previously, business strikes intended for Uncirculated Mint sets and Souvenir sets had been reported with coins intended for circulation. However, upon seeing "circulation" mintages where none should be, the Mint began separating the mintages of coins intended for sale to collectors from those intended for commerce.

56. 1798 silver dollar: Mintage includes both reverse designs.

57. 1801, 1802, and 1803 silver dollar: All three dates were restruck in Proof in 1858 with a plain edge, using obverse dies made in 1834-5 and the reverse die from the Class I 1804 dollar, which was also made in 1834. Due to the scandal caused by the private issue of 1804 dollars in 1858, these coins were not offered for sale to collectors until 1875, by which time their edges had been lettered.

58. 1804 silver dollar: Although the Mint Report lists 19,570 dollars for this year it is assumed that they were all dated 1803. The 1804 dollars were first struck in 1834-35 for inclusion in diplomatic presentation sets. A few pieces, possibly flawed Proofs or production overruns, reached collectors via trades with the Mint or in circulation and the coin was popularized as a rarity. In 1858 the son of a Mint employee used the obverse die prepared in 1834 and a newly prepared reverse die plus a plain collar to secretly strike 1804 dollars, a few of which were sold to collectors. While the Mint had intended to do exactly the same thing with dollars dated 1801-04, Mint officials were forced to cancel the project due to the public scandal over the privately-issued 1804s. The privately struck coins were recalled, and all but one (which went to the Mint Cabinet collection) were allegedly melted. Instead, they and the plain edged 1801-03s were put in storage and offered for sale in 1875, by which time their edges had been mechanically lettered.

59. 1805 silver dollar: The 321 dollars listed in the Mint Report for 1805 were older dollars which were found in deposits of Spanish-American silver and which were re-issued through the Treasury. On the basis of this misinformation a few coins have been altered to this date in the past.

60. 1836, 1838, and 1839 silver dollar: Gobrecht dollars, some patterns and some intended for circulation, were struck in these years. Also, some varieties were restruck in later years, making mintage figures questionable. Varieties exist with or without stars and/or the designer's name, some of them exceedingly scarce. The 1,600 mintage figure for 1836 represents 1,000 struck for circulation on the 1836 standard of 416 grains, and 600 pieces struck in 1837 (dated 1836) on the new standard of 412.5 grains.

61. 1853 silver dollar: All Proofs are restrikes, made 1864-5.

62. 1858 silver dollar: It is estimated that 80 Proofs were struck, some of them possibly at a later date.

63. 1870-CC silver dollar: Proofs mintage unknown, possibly struck to mark first Carson City dollar coinage.

64. 1870-S silver dollar: Not listed in the Mint Report, but a few pieces may have been struck as souvenirs of the opening of the new Mint.

65. 1873-S silver dollar: Presumably all or most were melted at the Mint after production of standard silver dollars was suspended.

66. 1878-(P) silver dollar: Three slightly different designs were used for both the obverse and reverse of this date, including some dies with the second designs impressed over the first. All 1878-CC and 1878-S are from the second designs. Most 1879-1904 dollars are of the third design, except for some second design reverses on 1879-S and 1880-CC coins. New, slightly different master hubs were pre-

pared for 1921. Proof mintage includes 700 of the 8 Tail Feathers variety and 300 of the 7 Tail Feathers, flat eagle breast variety. Beware of any early strike, prooflike surface Morgan dollar being sold as a Proof.

67. 1879-O silver dollar: Two Proofs now known of 12 struck to celebrate the re-opening of the New Orleans Mint.

68. 1882-CC silver dollar: Proof mintage unknown, reason for issue unknown.

69. 1883-CC silver dollar: Proof mintage unknown, reason for issue unknown.

70. 1883-O silver dollar: One Proof now known of 12 struck for presentation to various local dignitaries. Occasion uncertain.

71. 1884-CC silver dollar: One Proof reported, reason for issue unknown.

72. 1893-CC silver dollar: 12 Proofs struck for presentation to Mint officials to mark the closing of the Carson City Mint.

73. 1895 silver dollar: Apparently virtually all business strike coins were never issued and were probably melted in the great silver melt of 1918. One circulated business strike coin has reportedly been authenticated. Beware of altered dates and removed Mint marks.

74. 1921-(P) Peace silver dollar: The 1921 Peace dollars, (and a very few Proof 1922s), are of a higher relief than the 1922-35s.

75. 1873 Trade silver dollar: All Proofs are of the Open 3 variety.

76. 1884-85 Trade dollar: Struck in Proof in the Mint for private distribution by person or persons unknown. Not listed in the Mint Report.

77. S-Mint clad dollars: Struck only for sale to collectors. In 1971-72 struck in 40 percent clad silver in Proof and Uncirculated for individual sale. Beginning in 1973 a copper-nickel clad dollar was added to the Proof sets.

78. 1973-(P), D copper-nickel dollar: Struck only for inclusion in Mint sets. Not a regular issue coin. 1,769,258 Mint sets were sold. 439,899 excess dollars melted, presumably of near-equal distribution. 21,641 coins were kept for possible replacement of defective sets and may have been melted.

79. Anthony dollars: Anthony dollars were sold in three-coin sets only in 1981. None were released into circulation.

80. 1861-D gold dollar: A small number were struck by the CSA.

81. 1870-S gold dollar: 2,000 coins were struck without a Mint mark. It is unknown if they were melted and recoined or released as is and included in the Mint Report figure of 3,000 coins.

82. 1834 $2.50: Most or all were melted. It may be that all survivors are Proofs and circulated Proofs.

83. 1841-(P) $2.50: Struck in Proof only, possibly at a later date. Unlisted in Mint Report. Nine known, several of them circulated or otherwise impaired.

84. 1848-(P) $2.50: Approximately 1,389 coins were counterstamped CAL. above the eagle to show that they were made from California gold. This was done while the coins were resting on an inverted obverse die on a worktable. This virtually eliminated distortion of the obverse, which will probably show on a genuine coin with a fake counterstamp.

85. 1860-S $3: Out of 7,000 coins struck, 2,592 pieces were not released because of short weight. They were melted in 1869 for use in other denominations.

86. 1870-S $3: Not included in the Mint Report, supposedly one piece was struck for inclusion in the cornerstone of the new San Francisco Mint. One piece is known in a private collection, and the present whereabouts of the cornerstone piece is unknown. It is possible there is only one piece.

87. 1873 $3: All original Proofs are of the more Open 3 variety. There were two restrikes with the Closed 3 and one with the Open 3.

88. 1798 $5: Mint Report of 24,867 coins includes Small Eagle reverse coins dated 1798, as well as Heraldic Eagle coins dated 1795, 1797 and 1798. This mixture of mulings is the result of an emergency coinage late in 1798 after the Mint had been closed for a while due to yellow fever. Quantities struck of each are unknown and can only be a guess.

89. 1822 $5: Although the Mint Report says 17,796 coins were struck, only three pieces are known and it is likely that most of this mintage was from dies dated 1821.

90. 1825 $5: Struck from the regular overdated dies. 1825/4, one known, and 1825/1, two known.

91. 1828 $5: Includes at least one overdate, 1828/7.

92. 1844-O half eagle: One Proof known, reason for issue unknown.

93. 1861-C $5: Mintage includes 5,992 pieces coined by USA and 887 by CSA. It is impossible to prove the issuer.

94. 1899-S half eagle: One or two Proofs known, reason for issue unknown.

95. 1906-D and 1907-D $5: These were, of course, struck at the Denver Mint. This is the only design which was struck at both Dahlonega and Denver.

96. 1797 $10: Mintage includes both reverse types.

97. 1839 $10: Includes first design head (type of 1838) and modified head (type of 1840-1907). Proofs are of the type of 1838, with large letters and different hair style.

98. 1844-O eagle: One Proof known, reason for issue unknown.

99. 1852-O eagle: Three Proofs known, reason for issue unknown.

100. 1853-O eagle: Proof mintage unknown, reason

for issue unknown.

101. 1906-D eagle: Proofs struck in honor of the opening of the Denver Mint.

102. 1907 $10: An unknown number of Indian Head patterns were also struck in Proof.

103. 1933 $10: Very few of these were issued, perhaps several dozens known. Beware of counterfeits.

104. 1849 $20: One specimen in gold survives of a small number of trial strikes produced in December 1849. The dies were rejected, allegedly because of improper high relief, but in actuality to discredit Longacre in an attempt to force his removal. The attempt failed and Longacre eventually produced a second set of dies, but they were not completed until the following month and so they were dated 1850. The one known Proof gold specimen is in the National Numismatic Collection at the Smithsonian Institution and all others were melted.

105. 1850 $20: One Proof was once owned by the engraver, James B. Longacre. Whereabouts presently unknown.

106. 1854-S double eagle: One Proof known, in the Smithsonian Institution. Struck in honor of the opening of the San Francisco Mint.

107. 1861-(P) $20: A few trial pieces are known with a reverse as engraved by Paquet, with taller, thinner letters and a narrow rim. The design was judged unacceptable because the narrow reverse rim would not stack easily.

108. 1861-O $20: Mintage includes 5,000 coins struck by the USA; 9,750 by the State of Louisiana; and 2,991 by the Confederate States of America. It is impossible to prove the issuer of any given coin.

109. 1861-S $20: Mintage includes 19,250 pieces struck with the Paquet reverse and released into circulation. Most of these were recalled and melted during the next few years, but specie hoarding during the Civil War probably preserved a number of them until later years when the problem was forgotten.

110. 1866-(P), S $20: When the reverse of the double eagle was altered to include the motto there were also a few minor changes made in the scrollwork, the most prominent being the change in the shield from flat-sided to curved. Check any alleged 1866-S No Motto $20 for this feature.

111. 1877 $20: In this year the master hubs were redesigned slightly, raising the head and changing TWENTY D. to TWENTY DOLLARS.

112. 1906-D double eagle: Two Proofs now known of 12 struck in honor of the opening of the Denver Mint.

113. 1907-D double eagle: One Proof known, possibly struck as a specimen of the last year of this design.

114. 1907 $20: An unknown number of Saint-Gaudens type coins of pattern or near-pattern status were also struck in extremely high relief Proof.

115. 1933 $20: This issue was officially never released, so the coins are considered illegal to own. A few are reported to exist, including one in the National Numismatic Collection at the Smithsonian Institution. Most late-date gold never filtered down through the banks and so it was returned to the Mint for melting.

116. 1994-P 5 cent: The Mint double-struck 167,703 "Uncirculated" pieces from specially prepared, sandblast dies, essentially creating a Matte Proof, for inclusion in a special packaging set with the 1993 Jefferson commemorative silver dollar.

117. American Eagle gold bullion: Roman numerals used in date.

118. 1996-W Roosevelt dime: Produced with a West Point Mint mark for inclusion in 1996 Uncirculated Mint sets on the occasion of the 50th anniversary of the Roosevelt dime.

119. 1995-W American Eagle silver bullion dollar: Produced for sale only in special "10th Anniversary" sets.

6 Proof & Uncirculated Sets

The United States Mint has had a longstanding relationship with American coin collectors. Although the primary business of the Mint is to produce sufficient coinage for use in commerce, it has produced special collectors' products for much of its existence. The Mint's most popular collectors' products, no doubt, have been Proof coins and sets and Uncirculated Mint sets, including since 1994 some low-mintage coins with a special Matte Finish.

The first Uncirculated Mint sets, dated 1947, were offered in 1948. After the 1947 sets sold out, 1948-dated sets were offered to the public. Sets were again offered in 1949, but none were offered in 1950 due to a Treasury decision to conserve appropriations and manpower during the Korean War, and because Uncirculated coins were available from banks. From 1951 through 1964, sets were offered every year. The numbers of coins offered fluctuated from year to year, depending upon what denominations were being struck for circulation.

Before 1959, Uncirculated Mint sets were individually packaged in cardboard folders; each set containing two specimens of each coin struck that year. Beginning in 1959, sets were packaged in polyethylene packets, and contained just one example of each coin struck that year.

No Uncirculated Mint sets or Proof sets were offered from 1965-67 because of a major coin shortage sweeping the country. However, Mint officials did offer Special Mint sets, featuring coins not the quality of Proofs but better than those found in the pre-1964 Uncirculated Mint sets.

Production and sales of Uncirculated Mint sets resumed in 1968. From 1973-78, Philadelphia and Denver Mint specimens of the Eisenhower dollar were contained in the set. In 1979, the Eisenhower dollar was replaced by the Anthony dollar, and a San Francisco Assay Office specimen added. No Uncirculated Mint sets were offered in 1982-83, with Mint officials blaming budgetary cutbacks. Congress passed a law in 1983 requiring annual sales of both Uncirculated Mint sets and Proof sets.

As noted earlier, some Uncirculated Mint sets contain coins not struck for circulation. This generally increases the value of the sets because collectors saving an example of each coin struck each year will be unable to find the needed coins in circulation. In 1970, no half dollars were struck for circulation; thus, the 1970-D Kennedy half dollar could only be found in the set. In 1973, no Eisenhower dollars were struck for circulation, but were included in the set. The only way to obtain the three 1981 Anthony dollars was to buy the Uncirculated Mint set of that year, and in 1987, no Kennedy half dollars were struck for circulation but were included in the set. The 1996 Uncirculated sets include a 1996-W Roosevelt dime — available nowhere else — added to commemorate the 50th anniversary of the coin's introduction.

Proof coins and sets

While coins in Uncirculated Mint sets are no different from those struck for circulation, Proof coins are a special breed. A Proof coin is struck on a specially prepared planchet, using special minting techniques, generally on a specialized coining press.

"Proof" in numismatics refers to a special manufacturing process designed to result in coins of the highest quality produced especially for collectors. "Proof" is not a grade, as many beginning collectors think.

Proof coins result from the same basic processes used in producing the dies and planchets used in producing business strikes for circulation. Business strike refers to the everyday coin, struck for use in circulation. However, Mint employees use special techniques in preparing the surfaces of the dies and planchets intended for Proof coins. Special presses and striking techniques are used to produce Proof coins.

The Proof coins sold by the United States Mint today are Frosted Proofs. The flat fields are mirror-like, reflective and shiny. The frosting refers to the white, textured, nonreflective finish found on the raised devices, lettering and other points in relief. Both finishes are the results of the special techniques used in preparing the dies.

Proof coins are struck on special hand-fed presses that operate at slower speeds than the high-speed presses used for striking business-strike coinage. Each Proof coin is struck two or more times, depending on the size of the coin, the design and the composition of the metal. The multiple striking ensures that the detail is brought up fully on each coin. Proof coins are then sealed into plastic capsules or plastic holders to protect their surfaces from damaging environmental factors.

The Philadelphia Mint struck its first true Proof coins in 1817, not for collectors but as presentation pieces. From 1817 to 1859, Proof coins were made in small batches whenever a number of orders were assembled.

Proof coins were first offered to the public at large in 1858, the result of a decision by Mint Director John Ross Snowden. It was not until 1860, however, that mintages jumped as collector interest caught hold and the Mint began anticipating demand rather than striking the Proof coins to order.

Coins were sold individually and in complete sets, the latter in limited quantities. Sets were sometimes sold as sets of minor coins and gold coins in addition to the complete sets.

From 1907-16, the Mint began experimenting with various Proof finishes, including Matte Proof, Sandblast Proof and Roman Finish Proof finishes.

The Mint stopped offering Proof coins in 1916. Walter Breen in his *Encyclopedia of United States and Colonial Proof Coins: 1722-1977* notes: "At first ostensibly because of the war, later more likely because of administration changes (there being no coin collectors in high office until William H. Woodin became Secretary of the Treasury), no Proofs were publicly sold. The few made went to VIPs and most are controversial."

Proof coinage resumed in 1936 with the production of Brilliant Proofs. Coins were sold by the piece with five denominations making a complete set. Mintages of the Proof sets from 1936 through 1942 are based on the coin with the largest mintage. Abandoned were the experiments with Matte Proofs and other experimental finishes. Proof production halted again at the end of 1942 because of World War II, and did not resume until 1950.

Beginning in 1950, customers could no longer purchase single Proof coins. The five-coin sets were housed in individual cellophane envelopes, stapled together and placed into a cardboard box. The Mint changed to new packaging in mid-1955 (the 1955 set is available each way): a plastic soft-pack inserted into an envelope. This packaging remained in use through 1964.

No Proof sets were struck in 1965-67 because of the massive coin shortage haunting the nation.

Proof set production resumed in 1968, but at San Francisco instead of the Philadelphia Mint.

Special Proof and Uncirculated sets were offered in recognition of the 1976 Bicentennial of American Independence. The Bicentennial

U.S. Mint Proof set

event was numismatically celebrated with changes in the reverse designs of the Washington quarter dollar, Kennedy half dollar and Eisenhower dollar. Copper-nickel versions of all three were issued for circulation and for the regular Proof set.

Collectors were offered two three-coin sets of the same coins composed of 40 percent silver, in Proof and Uncirculated versions.

From 1976-81, standard Proof sets were issued with either the Eisenhower dollar or Anthony dollar. With the resumption of commemorative coinage production in 1982, and the introduction of American Eagle bullion coins in 1986, Proof production was spread to all four coining facilities, in Philadelphia, Denver, San Francisco and West Point. The San Francisco Mint continues to strike the regular five-coin Proof set in addition to Proof commemorative and bullion coins. Prestige Proof sets were offered since 1983 in years when the Mint issued commemoratives. Prestige Proof sets contain the regular set and one or more Proof commemorative coins. The last Prestige Proof sets were produced in 1998.

Congress mandated annual sales of a Silver Proof set in 1990; it authorized a Proof set with 90 percent silver versions of the dime, quarter dollar and half dollar. The Mint did not issue the first Silver Proof sets until 1992, citing 1991 production difficulties. The Mint offered two packaging versions of the new Proof set: a set in the same kind of holder as the standard Proof set marked with the word "silver," and a Premier Silver Proof set containing the same coins in a higher quality package.

The latest wrinkles in Proof coin production occurred in 1999 because of changes in coinage designs and the need to strike new denominations.

The State quarter dollars program, introduced in 1999, is reflected in the 1999 Proof sets. The traditional Proof set contains all five quarters for nine coins total. A second Proof set containing only the five State quarters is also being offered. The Mint is offering two versions of the nine-coin set — one with the dime through half dollar struck on copper-nickel clad planchets and the second with the same coins struck on 90 percent silver planchets.

The siphoning of 1979 and 1980 Anthony dollars from Treasury vaults throughout the end of the 1990s and the delay in production of the new Sacagawea dollar (set for 2000) resulted in the need to strike 1999-dated Anthony dollars for circulation. Mint officials announced that they would offer Proof and Uncirculated versions of the Anthony dollar later in the year in single-coin packaging. The decision to strike the coins came after Proof set production had begun, making it difficult to include with the other Proof coins.

Matte Finish coins

As the United States Mint began offering more collector coin products in the 1980s and 1990s, officials began experimenting with special finishes to enhance some of the Uncirculated commemorative coins. By the early 1990s, for example, commemorative silver dollars were given a matte surface similar in appearance to the Matte Proof coins of the early 20th century mentioned earlier. Collectors took little note of this special finish, however, because the Mint referred to it as their Uncirculated finish (although it differed considerably from the Uncirculated finish given to coins in the standard Uncirculated Mint sets). Then, in 1994, the special Uncirculated finish was applied to a noncommemorative denomination placed in a limited-edition set.

Congress authorized a commemorative silver dollar celebrating the 250th anniversary of Thomas Jefferson's birth for release in 1994. The Mint offered the 1994 Jefferson silver dollar in Proof and Uncirculated versions, the latter bearing the special matte surfaces developed over the years. Mint officials also offered the dollar in a variety of purchasing options. Among the special options was a Jefferson Coin and Currency set, which contained a 1994-P Jefferson silver dollar, a $2 Federal Reserve note (with Jefferson's portrait) and a 1994-P Jefferson 5-cent coin. While Mint officials intended to limit this set to 50,000 pieces, they forgot to mention that fact on any sales literature. Thus the Mint produced the set to order, selling 167,703 sets.

Mint officials also forgot to tell collectors that the Jefferson 5-cent coin in the set was given the same matte surfaces that had been given to the Jefferson silver dollar in the set, to give the two coins uniform finishes. A collector, however, noted the special finish and informed *Coin World* of that fact. That suddenly made the Jefferson Coin and Currency set a hot property. Many collectors collect Jefferson 5-cent coins, and many seek to acquire Proof and traditional Uncirculated specimens of each date and Mint mark. As collectors and dealers began referring to the coin as having a Matte Finish, many sought specimens of the special 5-cent coin to complete their collections of the denomination. Many Matte Finish 5-cent coins probably were removed from their holders for placement in whatever holders the collectors were storing their Jefferson 5-cent sets. Prices for this special 5-cent coin remain high, as much as $200 in nearly perfect condition.

Three years later, Mint officials offered a second Matte Finish Jefferson 5-cent coin (although Mint officials were still not using this terminology), this one dated 1997-P and housed in the Botanic Garden Coin and Currency set (also containing a Botanic Garden silver dollar and $1 Federal Reserve note). Production of the set was limited to 25,000 sets, meaning just 25,000 Matte Finish 1997-P Jefferson 5-cent coins would be offered, making this set an even hotter property than the Jefferson sets of three years earlier. In what became one of the most criticized offerings by the U.S. Mint in recent years, the Botanic Garden Coin and Currency set sold out in about a week, before many collectors even received their order forms in the mail. Dozens of irate collectors called *Coin World* to complain about being shut out of the offering because other collectors living closer to where the order form was placed into the mail had an advantage over those living farther away. Few if any of the callers wanted the sets for the Botanic Garden dollar. Most wanted the extremely limited, 25,000 mintage Matte Finish 1997-P Jefferson 5-cent coin for their collections.

Mint officials learned from this experience, so in 1998, when it offered a Kennedy Collectors set bearing a 1998-P Robert F. Kennedy silver dollar and 1998-P John F. Kennedy half dollar, it limited sales to a specific ordering period, not to a specific number of sets. Sales totaled more than 63,000 sets. By this time, Mint officials had also accepted the terminology that had caught on in hobby circles, and noted that the half dollar in the set had been given the special Matte Finish.

Will the popularity of the two Matte Finish 5-cent coins and half dollar prompt Mint officials to make similar offerings in the future? Stay tuned.

Proof Sets

Year Minted	Sets Sold	Prestige Commemorative	Selling Price	Face Value
1950	51,386		2.10	0.91
1951	57,500		2.10	0.91
1952	81,980		2.10	0.91
1953	128,800		2.10	0.91
1954	233,300		2.10	0.91
1955	378,200		2.10	0.91
1956	669,384		2.10	0.91
1957	1,247,952		2.10	0.91
1958	875,652		2.10	0.91
1959	1,149,291		2.10	0.91
1960 ‹1›	1,691,602		2.10	0.91
1961	3,028,244		2.10	0.91
1962	3,218,019		2.10	0.91
1963	3,075,645		2.10	0.91
1964	3,950,762		2.10	0.91
Production suspended during 1965, 1966, 1967				
1968 ‹2›	3,041,506		5.00	0.91
1969	2,934,631		5.00	0.91
1970 ‹3›	2,632,810		5.00	0.91
1971 ‹4›	3,220,733		5.00	0.91
1972	3,260,996		5.00	0.91
1973	2,760,339		7.00	1.91
1974	2,612,568		7.00	1.91
1975 ‹5›	2,845,450		7.00	1.91
1976 ‹6›	4,123,056		7.00	1.91
1977	3,236,798		9.00	1.91
1978	3,120,285		9.00	1.91
1979 ‹6›	3,677,175		9.00	1.91
1980	3,554,806		10.00	1.91
1981	4,063,083		11.00	1.91
1982 ‹7›	3,857,479		11.00	0.91
1983 ‹8›	3,138,765		11.00	0.91
1983 Prestige	140,361	1983-S Olympic silver dollar	59.00	1.91
1984	2,748,430		11.00	0.91
1984 Prestige	316,680	1984-S Olympic silver dollar	59.00	1.91
1985	3,362,821		11.00	0.91
1986	2,411,180		11.00	0.91
1986 Prestige	599,317	1986-S Immigrant half dollar, 1986-S Ellis Island silver dollar	48.50	2.41
1987	3,356,738		11.00	0.91
1987 Prestige	435,495	1987-S Constitution silver dollar	45.00	1.91
1988	3,031,287		11.00	0.91
1988 Prestige	231,661	1988-S Olympic silver dollar	45.00	1.91
1989	3,009,107		11.00	0.91
1989 Prestige	211,807	1989-S Congress half dollar 1989-S Congress silver dollar	52.00	2.41
1990 ‹9›	2,793,433		11.00	0.91
1990 Prestige	506,126	1990-P Eisenhower silver dollar	46.00	1.91

Year Minted	Sets Sold	Prestige Commemorative	Selling Price	Face Value
1991	2,610,833		11.00	0.91
1991 Prestige	256,954	1991-S Mount Rushmore half dollar 1991-S Mount Rushmore silver dollar	55.00	2.41
1992 ‹10›	2,675,618		11.00/12.50	0.91
1992 Prestige ‹11›	183,285	1992-S Olympic half dollar 1992-S Olympic silver dollar	49.00/56.00	2.41
1992 Silver ‹11, 12›	1,009,586		18.00/21.00	0.91
1992 Premiere ‹11,12›	308,055		29.50/37.00	0.91
1993	2,337,819		12.50	0.91
1993 Prestige ‹11›	232,063	1993-S James Madison half dollar 1993-S James Madison silver dollar	51.00/57.00	2.41
1993 Silver ‹11, 12›	589,712		18.00/21.00	0.91
1993 Premiere ‹11,12›	201,282		29.00/37.00	0.91
1994	2,308,701		12.50	0.91
1994 Prestige ‹11›	175,893	1994-P World Cup half dollar 1994-S World Cup silver dollar	49.00/56.00	2.41
1994 Silver ‹11, 12›	636,009		18.00/21.00	0.91
1994 Premiere ‹11,12›	149,320		29.00/37.00	0.91
1995	2,018,945		12.50	0.91
1995 Prestige ‹11›	105,845	1995-S Civil War Battlefields half dollar 1995-S Civil War Battlefields dollar	55.00/61.00	2.41
1995 Silver ‹11, 12›	537,374		18.00/21.00	0.91
1995 Premiere ‹11,12›	128,903		29.00/37.00	0.91
1996	2,085,191		12.50	0.91
1996 Prestige ‹11›	59,886	1996-S Olympic Soccer half dollar 1996-P Olympic Rowing dollar	55.00/61.00	2.41
1996 Silver ‹11, 12›	623,264		18.00/21.00	0.91
1996 Premier ‹11,12›	151,817		29.00/37.00	0.91
1997	1,975,000		12.50	0.91
1997 Prestige	80,000	1997-S Botanic Garden dollar	44.00	1.91
1997 Silver <11,12>	605,289		18.00/21.00	0.91
1997 Premier <11,12>	135,905		29.00/37.00	0.91
1998	Pending		12.50	0.91
1998 Silver <11,12>	Pending		18.00/21.00	0.91
1998 Premier <11,12>	Pending		29.00/37.00	0.91
1999 <19>	Pending		19.95	1.91
1999 State <20>	Pending		13.95	1.25
1999 Silver <12,19>	Pending		Not announced	1.91

40% silver clad dollars
Struck in San Francisco

Year Minted	Uncirculated	Proof
1971	6,868,530	4,265,234
1972	2,193,056	1,811,631
1973	1,883,140	1,013,646
1974	1,900,156	1,306,579

Special Mint Sets

Year Minted	Sets Sold	Prestige Commemorative	Selling Price	Face Value
1965	2,360,000		4.00	0.91
1966	2,261,583		4.00	0.91
1967	1,863,344		4.00	0.91

Uncirculated sets

Year Minted	Sets Sold	Prestige Commemorative	Selling Price	Face Value
1947	12,600		4.87	4.46
1948	17,000		4.92	4.46
1949	20,739		5.45	4.96
1951	8,654		6.75	5.46
1952	11,499		6.14	5.46
1953	15,538		6.14	5.46
1954	25,599		6.19	5.46
1955	49,656		3.57	2.86
1956	45,475		3.34	2.64
1957	34,324		4.40	3.64
1958	50,314		4.43	3.64
1959	187,000		2.40	1.82
1960	260,485		2.40	1.82
1961	223,704		2.40	1.82
1962	385,285		2.40	1.82
1963	606,612		2.40	1.82
1964	1,008,108		2.40	1.82
1965	2,360,000		4.00	0.91
1966	2,261,583		4.00	0.91
1967	1,863,344		4.00	0.91
1968	2,105,128		2.50	1.33
1969	1,817,392		2.50	1.33
1970	2,038,134		2.50	1.33
1971	2,193,396		3.50	1.83
1972	2,750,000		3.50	1.83
1973	1,767,691		6.00	3.83
1974	1,975,981		6.00	3.83
1975	1,921,488		6.00	3.82
1976	1,892,513		6.00	3.82
1977	2,006,869		7.00	3.82
1978	2,162,609		7.00	3.82
1979	2,526,000		8.00	3.82[13]
1980	2,815,066		9.00	4.82[13]
1981	2,908,145		11.00	4.82[13]
1984	1,832,857		7.00	1.82
1985	1,710,571		7.00	1.82
1986	1,153,536		7.00	1.82
1987	2,890,758		7.00	1.82
1988	1,447,100		7.00	1.82
1989	1,987,915		7.00	1.82
1990	1,809,184		7.00	1.82
1991	1,352,101		7.00	1.82

UNCIRCULATED SETS (CONTINUED)

Year Minted	Sets Sold	Prestige Commemorative	Selling Price	Face Value
1992	1,500,098		7.00/8.00	1.82
1993	1,297,094		8.00	1.82
1994	1,234,813		8.00	1.82
1995	1,013,559		8.00	1.82
1995 Deluxe	24,166		12.00	1.82
1996	1,450,440		8.00	1.92[14]
1997	940,047		8.00	1.82
1998	Pending		8.00	1.82
1999 <21>	Pending		14.95	3.82

Proof American Eagle issue prices[15]

Year	Metal	1/10 oz	1/4 oz	1/2 oz	1 oz	Set
1986	Gold	—	—	—	550.	—
	Silver	—	—	—	21.00	—
1987	Gold	—	—	295.	585.	870.
	Silver	—	—	—	23.00	—
1988	Gold	65.00	150.	295.	585.	1065.
	Silver	—	—	—	23.00	—
1989	Gold	65.00	150.	295.	585.	1065.
	Silver	—	—	—	23.00	—
1990	Gold	70.00	150.	285.	570.	999.
	Silver	—	—	—	23.00	—
1991	Gold	70.00	150.	285.	570.	999.
	Silver	—	—	—	23.00	—
1992	Gold	70.00	150.	285.	570.	999.
	Silver	—	—	—	23.00	—
1993	Gold	70.00	150.	285.	570.	999.
	Silver	—	—	—	23.00	—
1993 Philadelphia set[16]					499.	
1994	Gold	70.00	150.	285.	570.	999.
	Silver	—	—	—	23.00	—
1995	Gold	70.00	150.	285.	570.	999.
	Silver	—	—	—	23.00	—
1995 10th Anniversary set[17]					999.	
1996	Gold	70.00/75.00	150./159.	285./299.	570./589.	999./1025.
	Silver	—	—	—	23.00	—
1997	Gold	75.00	159.	299.	589.	1,025.
	Silver	—	—	—	23.00	—
	Platinum	99.00	199.	395.	695.	1,350.
1997 Impressions of Liberty set[18]					1,499.	
1998	Gold	70.00	150.	285.	570.	999.
	Silver	—	—	—	24.00	—
	Platinum	99.00	199.	395.	695.	1,350.
1999	Gold	70.00	150.	285.	570.	999.
	Silver	—	—	—	24.00	—
	Platinum	NA	NA	NA	NA	NA

Bicentennial sets

Final mintages are 3,998,621 for the Proof set, and 4,908,319 for the Uncirculated set.

Notes

1. Includes Large Date and Small Date cents. The Small Date is rarer.
2. Some Proof sets contain dimes struck from Proof die missing the Mint mark, an engraver's oversight, not a filled die. Unofficially estimated that 20 specimens are known. Beware of sets opened and reclosed with "processed" P-Mint coins inserted. Check edge of case for signs of tampering.
3. An estimated 2,200 Proof sets contain dimes struck from Proof die missing the Mint mark, an engraver's oversight, not a filled die.
4. An estimated 1,655 Proof sets contain 5-cent coins struck from Proof die missing the Mint mark, an engraver's oversight, not a filled die.
5. Contains 1776-1976 dated Bicentennial quarter dollar, half dollar and dollar.
6. 1979 Proof set: The Anthony dollar replaced the Eisenhower dollar. During latter 1979, a new, clearer Mint mark punch was used on the dies. Sets with all six coins bearing the new Mint mark command a premium.
7. 1982 Proof set: A new Mint mark punch with serifs was introduced.
8. 1983 10-cent piece: Some 1983 sets were issued with dimes missing the S Mint mark, similar to errors on 1968, 1970, 1971 and 1975 Proof coins.
9. The Mint released an estimated 3,555 1990 Proof sets with a cent missing the S Mint mark. The die was for business strikes at Philadelphia, but was inadvertentely sent to San Francisco, prepared as a Proof and placed into Proof production.
10. Price increased from $11 to $12.50 July 1, 1992.
11. Prices are pre-issue discount/regular price.
12. Beginning in 1992 a new type of Proof set was issued, consisting of a regular Proof cent and 5 cents, but with the dime, quarter dollar and half dollar struck on 90 percent silver planchets, rather than the copper-nickel clad planchets of the circulating and regular Proof coinage. A "Premiere" edition — essentially fancy packaging — was sold at an additional premium.
13. 1979-81 Uncirculated sets: It has been erroneously reported in previous editions of this book and elsewhere that the 1979 Unicirculated set has a face value of $4.82. In fact, it was a 12-coin set with a face value of $3.82. While Anthony dollars were struck for circulation at the San Francisco Assay Office, the Unc. S dollar was not included in sets until the 1980 and 1981 sets, which are 13-coin sets with a face value of $4.82.
14. 1996 Uncirculated set set: A 1996-W Roosevelt dime, availableonly in these sets, was added at no additional cost to mark the 50th anniversary of the coin.
15. Prices are for single-coin or -set purchase only; bulk discounts may apply; in 1996, a pre-issue discount was offered on gold coins.
16. Includes tenth-, quarter-, half-ounce gold, 1-ounce silver coin and 1-ounce silver medal.
17. Includes four gold coins and one silver, all with West Point Mint mark.
18. Includes one each Proof 1-ounce platinum, gold and silver bullion coin.
19. Includes one each Delaware, Pennsylvania, New Jersey, Georgia and Connecticut quarter dollars, plus cent, 5-cent coin, dime and half dollar.
20. Includes one each Delaware, Pennsylvania, New Jersey, Georgia and Connecticut quarter dollars only.
21. Includes Philadelphia Mint and Delaware Mint example of Delaware, Pennsylvania, New Jersey, Georgia and Connecticut quarter dollars.

7 Commemoratives

America's commemorative coins are graphic reminders of the United States' past, honoring its history, its heroes and its accomplishments.

They are special coinage issues, authorized by acts of Congress to recognize the people and events that have shaped the United States. They occasionally honor an individual, like Ulysses S. Grant. They may honor a historical event such as the Battle of Gettysburg or a more recent event such as the 1996 Olympic Games in Atlanta.

They are rarely issued for circulation, although that changed in 1999. The United States Mint began a 10-year program that when completed, will have resulted in 50 different circulating quarter dollars, one each commemorating one of the 50 states in the Union.

The first series of U.S. commemorative coins dates from 1892 until 1954, when Department of Treasury support for commemorative coins ended. The abuses were many, with many coins issued for events of purely local interest or even to commemorate nonevents. Administrations since the Eisenhower presidency opposed all commemorative coinage. There was so much opposition that when the 1976 Bicentennial of the Declaration of Independence quarter dollars, half dollars and dollars were issued in 1975-76, Treasury officials carefully avoided any and all use of the word "commemorative," although clearly the coins are commemorative in nature.

It came as a surprise, then, when in 1981 United States Treasurer Angela M. Buchanan announced Treasury Department support for a commemorative half dollar honoring George Washington's 250th birthday in 1982. Buchanan said that Treasury "has not objected to special coinage authorized by Congress for the government's own account," referring specifically to the 40 percent silver versions of the Bicentennial coinage. Buchanan said that Treasury had always objected to "the issuance of commemorative coins for the benefit of private sponsors and organizations." Congress passed the Washington half dollar bill and President Reagan signed it into law. Thus, the commemorative coin program in the United States was reborn.

Since 1982, commemorative coins have been issued in every year but 1985, often with more than one program in each year. In fact, many of the abuses of the past have resurfaced. Some recent years have witnessed multiple programs, making the acquisition of one of every coin an expensive proposition. Congress has also authorized programs of extremely limited interest (as shown by shrinking sales figures). Special-interest groups have come to consider coin collectors a "cash cow," since surcharges added to the cost of modern commemorative coins are given to various special-interest groups to fund a variety of memorials and projects. In one case, $1 million in surcharges originally intended for funding scholarships for disadvantaged youth (from the sales of the Jackie Robinson commemoratives) was diverted to the Botanic Garden, even though the Botanic Garden had already received money from the sales of its own commemorative coin program. The diversion of funds occurred because the wife of the member of Congress sponsoring the diversion of funds was closely connected to the Botanic Garden.

In this section, commemorative issues are presented by year of their first issuance. For early commemoratives, those produced from 1892-1954, original mintage, number melted and final mintage are listed. For commemorative coins produced since 1982, the final, net mintage only (reflecting sales figures) is listed. The U.S. Mint no longer makes public the original mintage, number of coins melted, or whether coins have been held in inventory or stored in Treasury vaults. Each coin listing includes the designer's name, and original issue prices are also given, so that the collector may determine the coin's performance against its original cost.

For a detailed history of the commemorative coin story, complete with politics and intrigue, consult *Commemorative Coins of the United States* by Anthony Swiatek, published by *Coin World.*

Commemoratives 1892-1954

Commemorative / Date	Original Mintage	Melted	Final Mintage	Designer / Original Price
Columbian Exposition half dollar				**Charles E. Barber/George Morgan**
1892	950,000	None	950,000	$1.00
1893	4,052,105	2,501,700	1,550,405	$1.00
Isabella quarter dollar				**Charles E. Barber**
1893	40,023	15,809	24,124	$1.00
Lafayette-Washington silver dollar				**Charles E. Barber**
1900	50,026	14,000	36,026	$2.00
Louisiana Purchase Exposition gold dollar				**Charles E. Barber**
1903	250,258	215,250	each type 17,375	$3.00
Lewis and Clark Exposition gold dollar				**Charles E. Barber**
1904	25,028	15,003	10,025	$2.00
1905	35,041	25,000	10,041	$2.00
Panama-Pacific Exposition half dollar				**Charles E. Barber**
1915-S	60,030	32,896	27,134	$1.00
Panama-Pacific Exposition gold dollar				**Charles Keck**
1915-S	25,034	10,034	15,000	$2.00
Panama-Pacific Exposition quarter eagle				**Charles E. Barber**
1915-S	10,017	3,278	6,749	$4.00
Panama-Pacific Exposition $50				**Robert Aiken**
1915-S Round	1,510	1,027	483	$100
1915-S Octag.	1,509	864	645	$100
McKinley Memorial gold dollar				**Charles E. Barber/George T. Morgan**
1916	20,026	10,049	9,977	$3.00
1917	10,014	14	10,000	$3.00
Illinois Centennial half dollar				**George T. Morgan/John R. Sinnock**
1918	100,058	None	100,058	$1.00
Maine Centennial half dollar				**Anthony de Francisci**
1920	50,028	None	50,028	$1.00
Pilgrim Tercentenary half dollar				**Cyrus E. Dallin**
1920	200,112	48,000	152,112	$1.00
1921	100,053	80,000	20,053	$1.00
Missouri Centennial half dollar				**Robert Aitken**
1921 2*4	5,000	None	5,000	$1.00
1921 No 2*4	45,028	29,600	15,428	$1.00
Alabama Centennial half dollar				**Laura Gardin Fraser**
1921 2X2	6,006	None	6,006	$1.00
1921 No 2X2	64,038	5,000	59,038	$1.00
Grant Memorial half dollar				**Laura Gardin Fraser**
1922 Star	5,006	750	4,256	$1.00
1922 No Star	95,055	27,650	67,405	$1.00
Grant Memorial gold dollar				**Laura Gardin Fraser**
1922 Star	5,016	None	5,016	$3.50
1922 No Star	5,000	None	5,000	$3.00
Monroe Doctrine Centennial half dollar				**Chester Beach**
1923-S	274,077	None	274,077	$1.00

Commemorative Date	Original Mintage	Melted	Final Mintage	Designer Original Price
Huguenot-Walloon Tercentenary half dollar				**George T. Morgan**
1924	142,080	None	142,080	$1.00
Lexington-Concord Sesquicentennial half dollar				**Chester Beach**
1925	162,099	86	162,013	$1.00
Stone Mountain half dollar				**Gutzon Borglum**
1925	2,314,709	1,000,000	1,314,709	$1.00
California Diamond Jubilee half dollar				**Jo Mora**
1925-S	150,200	63,606	86,594	$1.00
Fort Vancouver Centennial half dollar				**Laura Gardin Fraser**
1925	50,028	35,034	14,994	$1.00
American Independence Sesquicentennial half dollar				**John R. Sinnock**
1926	1,000,528	859,408	141,120	$1.00
American Independence Sesquicentennial quarter eagle				**John R. Sinnock**
1926	200,226	154,207	46,019	$4.00
Oregon Trail Memorial half dollar				**James E. and Laura G. Fraser**
1926	48,030	75	47,955	$1.00
1926-S	100,055	17,000	83,055	$1.00
1928	50,028	44,000	6,028	$2.00
1933-D	5,250	242	5,008	$2.00
1934-D	7,006	None	7,006	$2.00
1936	10,006	None	10,006	$1.60
1936-S	5,006	None	5,006	$1.60
1937-D	12,008	None	12,008	$1.60
1938	6,006	None	6,006	$6.25
1938-D	6,005	None	6,005	for
1938-S	6,006	None	6,006	three
1939	3,004	None	3,004	$7.50
1939-D	3,004	None	3,004	for
1939-S	3,005	None	3,005	three
Vermont Sesquicentennial half dollar				**Charles Keck**
1927	40,034	11,872	28,162	$1.00
Hawaiian Sesquicentennial half dollar				**Juliette Mae Fraser/Chester Beach**
1928	10,000	None	10,000	$2.00
Maryland Tercentenary half dollar				**Hans Schuler**
1934	25,015	None	25,015	$1.00
Texas Independence Centennial				**Pompeo Coppini**
1934	205,113	143,650	61,463	$1.00
1935	10,0078	12	9,996	$1.50
1935-D	10,007	None	10,007	$1.50
1935-S	10,008	None	10,008	$1.50
1936	10,008	1,097	8,911	$1.50
1936-D	10,007	968	9,039	$1.50
1936-S	10,008	943	9,055	$1.50
1937	8,005	1,434	6,571	$1.50
1937-D	8,006	1,401	6,605	$1.50
1937-S	8,007	1,370	6,637	$1.50
1938	5,005	1,225	3,780	$2.00
1938-D	5,005	1,230	3,775	$2.00
1938-S	5,006	1,192	3,814	$2.00
Daniel Boone Bicentennial half dollar				**Augustus Lukeman**
1934	10,007	None	10,007	$1.60

Commemorative Date	Original Mintage	Melted	Final Mintage	Designer Original Price
1935	10,010	None	10,010	$1.10
1935-D	5,005	None	5,005	$1.60
1935-S	5,005	None	5,005	$1.60
1935 W/1934	10,008	None	10,008	$1.10
1935-D W/1934	2,003	None	2,003	$3.70
1935-S W/1934	2,004	None	2,004	for two
1936	12,012	None	12,012	$1.10
1936-D	5,005	None	5,005	$1.60
1936-S	5,006	None	5,006	$1.60
1937	15,010	5,200	9,810	$1.60, $7.25 set
1937-D	7,506	5,000	2,506	$7.25 in set
1937-S	5,006	2,500	2,506	$5.15
1938	5,005	2,905	2,100	$6.50
1938-D	5,005	2,905	2,100	for
1938-S	5,006	2,906	2,100	three
Connecticut Tercentenary half dollar				**Henry G. Kreiss**
1935	25,018	None	25,018	$1.00
Arkansas Centennial half dollar				**Edward E. Burr**
1935	13,012	None	13,012	$1.00
1935-D	5,005	None	5,005	$1.00
1935-S	5,506	None	5,006	$1.00
1936	10,010	350	9,660	$1.50
1936-D	10,010	350	9,660	$1.50
1936-S	10,012	350	9,662	$1.50
1937	5,505	None	5,505	$8.75
1937-D	5,505	None	5,505	for
1937-S	5,506	None	5,506	three
1938	6,006	2,850	3,156	$8.75
1938-D	6,005	2,850	3,155	for
1938-S	6,006	2,850	3,156	three
1939	2,104	None	2,104	$10
1939-D	2,104	None	2,104	for
1939-S	2,105	None	2,105	three
Arkansas-Robinson half dollar				**E.E. Burr/Henry Kreiss**
1936	25,265	None	25,265	$1.85
Hudson, N.Y., Sesquicentennial half dollar				**Chester Beach**
1935	10,008	None	10,008	$1.00
California-Pacific International Expo				**Robert Aitken**
1935-S	250,132	180,000	70,132	$1.00
1936-D	180,092	150,000	30,092	$1.50
Old Spanish Trail half dollar				**L.W. Hoffecker**
1935	10,008	None	10,008	$2.00
Providence, R.I., Tercentenary				**John H. Benson/Abraham G. Carey**
1936	20,013	None	20,013	$1.00
1936-D	15,010	None	15,010	$1.00
1936-S	15,011	None	15,011	$1.00
Cleveland, Great Lakes Exposition half dollar				**Brenda Putnam**
1936	50,030	None	50,030	$1.50
Wisconsin Territorial Centennial half dollar				**David Parsons/Benjamin Hawkins**
1936	25,015	None	25,015	$1.50
Cincinnati Music Center half dollar				**Constance Ortmayer**
1936	5,005	None	5,005	$7.75

Commemorative				Designer
Date	Original Mintage	Melted	Final Mintage	Original Price
1936-D	5,005	None	5,005	for
1936-S	5,006	None	5,006	three
Long Island Tercentenary half dollar				**Howard K. Weinmann**
1936	100,053	18,227	81,826	$1.00
York County, Maine, Tercentanary half dollar				**Walter H. Rich**
1936	25,015	None	25,015	$1.50
Bridgeport, Conn., Centennial half dollar				**Henry G. Kreiss**
1936	25,015	None	25,015	$2.00
Lynchburg, Va., Sesquicentennial half dollar				**Charles Keck**
1936	20,013	None	20,013	$1.00
Elgin, Ill., Centennial half dollar				**Trygve Rovelstad**
1936	25,015	5,000	20,015	$1.50
Albany, N.Y., half dollar				**Gertrude K. Lathrop**
1936	25,013	7,342	17,671	$2.00
San Francisco-Oakland Bay Bridge half dollar				**Jacques Schnier**
1936-S	100,055	28,631	71,424	$1.50
Columbia, S.C., Sesquicentennial half dollar				**A. Wolfe Davidson**
1936	9,007	None	9,007	$6.45
1936-D	8,009	None	8,009	for
1936-S	8,007	None	8,007	three
Delaware Tercentenary half dollar				**Carl L. Schmitz**
1936	25,015	4,022	20,993	$1.75
Battle of Gettysburg half dollar				**Frank Vittor**
1936	50,028	23,100	26,928	$1.65
Norfolk, Va., Bicentennial half dollar				**William M. Simpson/Marjorie E. Simpson**
1936	25,013	8,077	16,936	$1.50
Roanoke Island, N.C., half dollar				**William M. Simpson**
1937	50,030	21,000	29,030	$1.65
Battle of Antietam half dollar				**William M. Simpson**
1937	50,028	32,000	18,028	$1.65
New Rochelle, N.Y., half dollar				**Gertrude K. Lathrop**
1938	25,015	9,749	15,266	$2.00
Iowa Statehood Centennial half dollar				**Adam Pietz**
1946	100,057	None	100,057	$2.50/$3.00
Booker T. Washington half dollar				**Isaac S. Hathaway**
1946	1,000,546	?	?	$1.00
1946-D	200,113	?	?	$1.50
1946-S	500,279	?	?	$1.00
1947	100,017	?	?	$6.00
1947-D	100,017	?	?	for
1947-S	100,017	?	?	three
1948	20,005	12,000	8,005	$7.50
1948-D	20,005	12,000	8,005	for
1948-S	20,005	12,000	8,005	three
1949	12,004	6,000	6,004	$8.50
1949-D	12,004	6,000	6,004	for
1949-S	12,004	6,000	6,004	three
1950	12,004	6,000	6,004	$8.50
1950-D	12,004	6,000	6,004	for
1950-S	512,091	?	?	three

Commemorative Date	Original Mintage	Melted	Final Mintage	Designer Original Price
1951	510,082	?	?	$3 or $10
1951-D	12,004	5,000	7,004	for
1951-S	12,004	5,000	7,004	three
Booker T. Washington/George Washington Carver				**Isaac S. Hathaway**
1951	?	?	110,018	$10
1951-D	?	?	10,004	for
1951-S	?	?	10,004	three
1952	?	?	2,006,292	$10
1952-D	?	?	8,006	for
1952-S	?	?	8.006	three
1953	?	?	8,003	$10
1953-D	?	?	8,003	for
1953-S	?	?	108,020	three
1954	?	?	12,006	$10
1954-D	?	?	12,006	for
1954-S	?	?	122,024	three

Commemoratives 1982-1996

George Washington half dollar		**Elizabeth Jones**
1982-D Unc.	2,210,458	$8.50/$10[1]
1982-S Proof	4,894,044	$10/$12[1]
Los Angeles Olympic Games silver dollar		**Elizabeth Jones**
1983-P Unc.	294,543	$28 or $89[2]
1983-D Unc.	174,014	for
1983-S Unc.	174,014	three
1983-S Proof	1,577,025	$24.95[2]
Los Angeles Olympic Games silver dollar		**Robert Graham**
1984-P Unc.	217,954	$28 or $89[2]
1984-D Unc.	116,675	for
1984-S Unc.	116,675	three
1984-S Proof	1,801,210	$32[2]
Los Angeles Olympic Games gold eagle		**James Peed/John Mercanti**
1984-P Proof	33,309	$352[2]
1984-D Proof	34,533	$352[2]
1984-S Proof	48,551	$352[2]
1984-W Proof	381,085	$352[2]
1984-W Unc.	75,886	$339[2]
Statue of Liberty, Immigrant half dollar		**Edgar Steever/Sherl Winter**
1986-D Unc.	928,008	$5/$6[3]
1986-S Proof	6,925,627	$6.50/$7.50[3]
Statue of Liberty, Ellis Island dollar		**John Mercanti/Matthew Peleso**
1986-P Unc.	723,635	$20.50/$22[3]
1986-S Proof	6,414,638	$22.50/$24[3]
Statue of Liberty half eagle		**Elizabeth Jones**
1986-W Unc.	95,248	$160/$165[3]
1986-W Proof	404,013	$170/$175[3]
Constitution Bicentennial silver dollar		**Patricia L. Verani**
1987-P Unc.	451,629	$22.50/$26[3]
1987-S Proof	2,747,116	$24/$28[3]
Constitution Bicentennial half eagle		**Marcel Jovine**
1987-W Unc.	214,225	$195/$215[3]

Commemorative Date	Original Mintage	Melted	Final Mintage	Designer Original Price
1987-W Proof			651,659	$200/$225[3]
1988 Olympic Games silver dollar				**Patricia L. Verani/Sherl J. Winter**
1988-D Unc.			191,368	$22/$27[3]
1988-S Proof			1,359,366	$23/$29[3]
1988 Olympic Games gold half eagle				**Elizabeth Jones/Marcel Jovine**
1988-W Unc.			62,913	$200/$225[3]
1988-W Proof			281,465	$205/$235[3]
Congress Bicentennial half dollar				**Patricia L. Verani/William Woodward**
1989-D Unc.			163,753	$5/$6[3]
1989-S Proof			767,897	$7/$8[3]
Congress Bicentennial silver dollar				**William Woodward**
1989-D Unc.			135,203	$23/$26[3]
1989-S Proof			762,198	$25/$29[3]
Congress Bicentennial half eagle				**John Mercanti**
1989-W Unc.			46,899	$185/$200[3]
1989-W Proof			164,690	$195/$215[3]
Eisenhower Birth Centennial silver dollar				**John Mercanti/Marcel Jovine**
1990-W Unc.			241,669	$23/$26[3]
1990-P Proof			1,144,461	$25/$29[3]
Mount Rushmore 50th Anniversary half dollar				**Marcel Jovine/James Ferrell**
1991-D Unc.			172,754	$6/$7[3]
1991-S Proof			753,257	$8.50/$9.50[3]
Mount Rushmore 50th Anniversary silver dollar				**Marika Somogyi/Frank Gasparro**
1991-P Unc.			133,139	$23/$26[3]
1991-S Proof			738,419	$28/$31[3]
Mount Rushmore 50th Anniversary half eagle				**John Mercanti/Robert Lamb**
1991-W Unc.			31,959	$185/$210[3]
1991-W Proof			111,991	$195/$225[3]
Korean War Memorial silver dollar				**John Mercanti/James Ferrell**
1991-D Unc.			213,049	$23/$26[3]
1991-P Proof			618,488	$28/$31[3]
USO 50th Anniversary silver dollar				**Robert Lamb/John Mercanti**
1991-D Unc.			124,958	$23/$26[3]
1991-S Proof			321,275	$28/$31[3]
1992 Olympics clad half dollar				**William Cousins/Steven Bieda**
1992-P Unc.			161,607	$6/$7.50[3]
1992-S Proof			519,645	$8.50/$9.50[3]
1992 Olympics silver dollar				**John R. Deecken/Marcel Jovine**
1992-D Unc.			187,552	$24/$29[3]
1992-S Proof			504,505	$28/$32[3]
1992 Olympic gold half eagle				**Jim Sharpe/Jim Peed**
1992-W Unc.			27,732	$185/$215[3]
1992-W Proof			77,313	$195/$230[3]
White House Bicentennial silver dollar				**Edgar Z. Steever/Chester Y. Martin**
1992-D Unc.			123,803	$23/$28[3]
1992-W Proof			375,851	$28/$32[3]
Columbus Quincentenary clad half dollar				**T. James Ferrell**
1992-D Unc.			135,702	$6.50/$7.50[3]
1992-S Proof			390,154	$8.50/$9.50[3]

Commemorative				Designer
Date	Original Mintage	Melted	Final Mintage	Original Price
Columbus Quincentenary silver dollar				**John M. Mercanti/Thomas D. Rogers Sr.**
1992-D Unc.			106,949	$23/$28[3]
1992-P Proof			385,241	$27/$31[3]
Columbus Quincentenary half eagle				**T. James Ferrell/Thomas D. Rogers Sr.**
1992-W Unc.			24,329	$180/$210[3]
1992-W Proof			79,730	$190/$225[3]
Bill of Rights/Madison silver half dollar				**T. James Ferrell/Dean E. McMullen**
1993-W Unc.			193,346	$9.75/$11.50[3]
1993-S Proof			586,315	$12.50/$13.50[3]
Bill of Rights/Madison silver dollar				**William J. Krawczewicz/Dean E. McMullen**
1993-D Unc.			98,383	$22/$27[3]
1993-S Proof			534,001	$25/$29[3]
Bill of Rights/Madison gold $5 half eagle				**Scott R. Blazek/Joseph D. Pena**
1993-W Unc.			23,266	$175/$205[3]
1993-W Proof			78,651	$185/$220[3]
World War II 50th Anniversary clad half dollar				**George Klauba/Bill J. Leftwich**
1991-1995-P Unc. (1993[4])			197,072	$8/$9[3]
1991-1995-S Proof (1993[4])			317,396	$9/$10[3]
World War II 50th Anniversary silver dollar				**Thomas D. Rogers Sr.**
1991-1995-D Unc. (1993[4])			107,240	$23/$28[3]
1991-1995-W Proof (1993[4])			342,041	$27/$31[3]
World War II 50th Anniversary half eagle				**Charles J. Madsen/Edward Southworth Fisher**
1991-1995-W Unc. (1993[4])			23,672	$170/$200[3]
1991-1995-W Proof (1993[4])			67,026	$185/$220[3]
Thomas Jefferson 250th Anniversary silver dollar				**James Ferrell**
1743-1993-P Unc. (1994[5])			266,927	$27/$32[3]
1743-1993-S Proof (1994[5])			332,891	$31/$35[3]
World Cup Soccer clad half dollar				**Richard T. LaRoche/Dean E. McMullen**
1994-D Unc.			168,208	$8.75/$9.50[3]
1994-P Proof			609,354	$9.75/$10.50[3]
World Cup Soccer silver dollar				**Dean E. McMullen**
1994-D Unc.			81,524	$23/$28[3]
1994-S Proof			577,090	$27/$31[3]
World Cup Soccer gold $5 half eagle				**William J. Krawczewicz/Dean E. McMullen**
1994-W Unc.			22,447	$170/$200[3]
1994-W Proof			89,614	$185/$220[3]
Prisoner of War silver dollar				**Tom Nielsen and Alfred Maletsky/Edgar Z. Steever IV**
1994-W Unc.			54,790	$27/$32[3]
1994-P Proof			220,100	$31/$35[3]
Vietnam Veterans Memorial silver dollar				**John Mercanti/Thomas D. Rogers Sr.**
1994-W Unc.			57,317	$27/$32[3]
1994-P Proof			226,262	$31/$35[3]
Women in Military Service silver dollar				**T. James Ferrell/Thomas D. Rogers Sr.**
1994-W Unc.			53,054	$27/$32[3]
1994-P Proof			213,201	$31/$35[3]
U.S. Capitol Bicentennial silver dollar				**William C. Cousins/John Mercanti**
1994-D Unc.			68,332	$32/$37[3]
1994-S Proof			279,579	$36/$40[3]

Commemorative				Designer
Date	Original Mintage	Melted	Final Mintage	Original Price
Civil War Battlefields clad half dollar				**Don Troiani/T. James Ferrell**
1995-D Unc			113,045	$9.50/$10.25[3]
1995-S Proof			326,801	$10.75/$11.75[3]
Civil War Battlefields silver dollar				**Don Troiani/John Mercanti**
1995-P Unc			51,612	$27/$29[3]
1995-S Proof			327,686	$30/$34[3]
Civil War Battlefields gold half eagle				**Don Troiani/Alfred Maletsky**
1995-W Unc.			12,623	$180/$190[3]
1995-W Proof			54,915	$195/$225[3]
Special Olympics World Games dollar				**Jamie Wyeth & T. J. Ferrell/Thomas D. Rogers Sr.**
1995-W Unc.			89,298	$29/$31[3][6]
1995-P Proof			352,449	$31/$35[3][6]
Games of the XXVI Olympiad, Atlanta clad half dollar				**Clint Hansen/T. James Ferrell**
1995-S Basketball Unc.			169,527[8]	$10.50/$11.50[7]
1995-S Basketball Proof			170,733[8]	$11.50/$12.50[7]
Games of the XXVI Olympiad, Atlanta clad half dollar				**Edgar Steever/T. James Ferrell**
1995-S Baseball Unc.			164,759[8]	$10.50/$11.50[7]
1995-S Baseball Proof			119,396[8]	$11.50/$12.50[7]
Games of the XXVI Olympiad, Atlanta silver dollar				**Jim Sharpe/William Krawczewicz**
1995-D Gymnastics Unc.			43,003[8]	$27.95/$31.95[7]
1995-S Gymnastics Proof			185,158[8]	$30.95/$34.95[7]
Games of the XXVI Olympiad, Atlanta silver dollar				**John Mercanti/William Krawczewicz**
1995-D Cycling Unc.			20,122[8]	$27.95/$31.95[7]
1995-S Cycling Proof			127,465[8]	$30.95/$34.95[7]
Games of the XXVI Olympiad, Atlanta dollar				**John Mercanti/William Krawczewicz**
1995-D Track & Field Unc.			25,425[8]	$27.95/$31.95[7]
1995-S Track & Field Proof			143,304[8]	$30.95/$34.95[7]
Games of the XXVI Olympiad, Atlanta silver dollar				**Jim Sharpe/William Krawczewicz**
1995-D Paralympic, blind runner Unc.			29,015[8]	$27.95/$31.95[7]
1995-S Paralympic, blind runner Proof			139,831[8]	$30.95/$34.95[7]
Games of the XXVI Olympiad, Atlanta gold half eagle				**Frank Gasparro/Frank Gasparro**
1995-W Torch Runner gold Unc.			14,817[8]	$229/$249[7]
1995-W Torch Runner gold Proof			57,870[8]	$239/$259[7]
Games of the XXVI Olympiad, Atlanta gold half eagle				**Marcel Jovine/Frank Gasparro**
1995-W Atlanta Stadium gold Unc.			10,710[8]	$229/$249[7]
1995-W Atlanta Stadium gold Proof			43,399[8]	$239/$259[7]
Games of the XXVI Olympiad, Atlanta half dollar				**William Krawczewicz/Malcolm Farley**
1996-S Swimming clad Unc.			50,077[8]	$10.50/$11.50[7]
1996-S Swimming clad Proof			114,890[8]	$11.50/$12.50[7]
Games of the XXVI Olympiad, Atlanta clad half dollar				**Clint Hansen/Malcolm Farley**
1996-S Soccer clad Unc.			53,176[8]	$10.50/$11.50[7]
1996-S Soccer clad Proof			123,860[8]	$11.50/$12.50[7]
Games of the XXVI Olympiad, Atlanta silver dollar				**Jim Sharpe/Thomas D. Rogers Sr.**
1996-D Tennis Unc.			16,693[8]	$27.95/$31.95[7]
1996-S Tennis Proof			93,880[8]	$30.95/$34.95[7]
Games of the XXVI Olympiad, Atlanta silver dollar				**Bart Forbes/Thomas D. Rogers Sr.**
1996-D Rowing Unc.			16,921[8]	$27.95/$31.95[7]
1996-S Rowing Proof			155,543[8]	$30.95/$34.95[7]

Commemorative Date	Original Mintage	Melted	Final Mintage	Designer Original Price
Games of the XXVI Olympiad, Atlanta silver dollar				**Calvin Massey/Thomas D. Rogers Sr.**
1996-D High Jump Unc.			16,485[8]	$27.95/$31.95[7]
1996-S High Jump Proof			127,173[8]	$30.95/$34.95[7]
Games of the XXVI Olympiad, Atlanta silver dollar				**Jim Sharpe/Thomas D. Rogers Sr.**
1996-D Paralympic, wheelchair athlete Unc.			15,325[8]	$27.95/$31.95[7]
1996-S Paralympic, wheelchair athlete Proof			86,352[8]	$30.95/$34.95[7]
Games of the XXVI Olympiad, Atlanta $5				**Frank Gasparro/William Krawczewicz**
1996-W Olympic Flame brazier Unc.			9,453[8]	$229/$249[7]
1996-W Olympic Flame brazier Proof			38,871[8]	$239/$259[7]
Games of the XXVI Olympiad, Atlanta $5				**Patricia L. Verani/William Krawczewicz**
1996-W Flag Bearer Unc.			9,397[9]	$229/$249[7]
1996-W Flag Bearer Proof			33,214[9]	$239/$259[7]
National Community Service silver dollar				**Thomas D. Rogers Sr./William C. Cousins**
1996-P Unc.			23,463	$30/$32[3]
1996-S Proof			100,749	$33/$37[3]
Smithsonian 150th Anniversary silver dollar				**Thomas D. Rogers/John Mercanti**
1996-P Unc.			31,320	$30/$32[3]
1996-S Proof			129,152	$33/$37[3]
Smithsonian 150th Anniversary gold half eagle				**Alfred Maletsky/T. James Ferrell**
1996-W Unc.			9,068	$180/$205[3]
1996-W Proof			21,772	$195/$225[3]
Botanic Garden silver dollar				**Edgar Z. Steever IV/William C. Cousins**
1997-P Unc.			83,505	$30/32[3]
1997-P Proof			269,843	$33/37[3]
Franklin Delano Roosevelt gold half eagle				**T. James Ferrell/Jim Peed**
1996-W Unc.			29,417	$180/$205[3]
1996-W Proof			11,887	$195/$225[3]
National Law Enforcement Officers Memorial silver dollar				**Alfred Maletsky / Maletsky**
1997-P Unc.			28,575	$30/32[3]
1997-P Proof			110,428	$32/37[3]
Jackie Robinson silver dollar				**Al Maletsky/T. James Ferrell**
1997-S Unc.			30,180	$30/32[3]
1997-S Proof			110,002	$33/37[3]
Jackie Robinson gold half eagle				**William C. Cousins/Jim Peed**
1997-W Unc.			5,174	$180/205[3]
1997-W Proof			24,072	$195/225[3]
Robert F. Kennedy silver dollar				**Thomas D. Rogers/Jim Peed**
1998-S Unc.			106,422	$30/32[3]
1998-S Proof			99,020	$33/37[3]
Black Revolutionary War Patriots silver dollar				**John Mercanti/Ed Dwight**
1998-S Unc.			37,210	$30/32[3]
1998-S Proof			75,070	$33/37[3]
Dolley Madison silver dollar				**Tiffany & Co./Tiffany & Co.**
1999-P Unc.			Pending	$30/32[3]
1999-P Proof			Pending	$33/37[3]
George Washington gold half eagle				**Laura Gardin Fraser/L.G. Fraser[9]**
1999-W Unc.			Pending	$180/205[3]
1999-W Proof			Pending	$195/225[3]

Commemorative Date	Original Mintage	Melted	Final Mintage	Designer Original Price
Yellowstone National Park silver dollar				**Edgar Z. Steever IV/William C. Cousins**
1999-P Uncirculated			Pending	$30/32[3]
1999-P Proof			Pending	$33/37[3]

Notes

1. Prices for 1982 George Washington half dollar are for 1982 and 1983-85.
2. Prices for 1983-84 Olympic coins in some cases are first prices charged and do not reflect higher prices charged later.
3. Prices since 1986 are pre-issue/regular issue of single coins only. Most modern commem programs have offered various packaging options and combinations.
4. Although produced and sold in 1993, none of these coins actually carries the year of issue in its legends, in apparent violation of law. The anniversary dates 1991-1995 refer to the 50th anniversaries of the beginning and ending of United States involvement in World War II. More clearly, it would have been stated "1941-1991/1945-1995."
5. Although produced and sold in 1994, the coin does not carry the year of issue in its legends, in apparent violation of law. 1743 is the year of Jefferson's birth; 1993 is the 250th anniversary of that date.
6. The Special Olympics World Games silver dollar was offered "encapsulated only" without the usual presentation case. The case option was also available, at a slightly higher price.
7. Price options for individual coins. The coins were offered on a subscription basis from Dec. 2, 1994, through Feb. 3, 1995. The coins were then to be released four at a time — one gold, two silver, one clad — in February 1995, July 1995, January 1996 and sometime in the spring of 1996. Pre-issue prices and options were to be offered during the first few weeks of each release.
8. Figures represent sales totals that may not be final. As of August 1999, Mint officials have been unable to provide final sales figures for this program.
9. The designs are based on Fraser's submissions in the design contest for the 1932 Washington quarter dollar. The Commission of Fine Art recommended Fraser's designs but was overruled by the secretary of the treasury, who selected the designs used from 1932-98. A popular movement supporting Fraser's 1932 quarter dollar designs led to them being used on the 1999 half eagle.

8 Grading

Probably no other subject has been more hotly debated in American numismatics by collectors, dealers and investors than grading. Since a dealer first charged more for one specimen of a coin than for another of the same type, date and Mint mark simply because the second had less wear than the other, there has been controversy.

The grade of a coin (note, medal or token) represents what professional numismatist and researcher Dr. Richard Bagg aptly called its "level of preservation." The grading controversy arises both from disagreements over the grade of a coin and often the enormous differences in price between two specimens of the same type and date of a U.S. coin, even when the only difference lies in the placement of one or two marks or surface abrasions from contact with other coins, commonly referred to as "contact marks" or "bag marks."

The grade measures the amount of wear, natural mishaps and other surface degradation a coin has received after leaving the coining press. The more wear and surface marks a coin has received, the less it is worth compared to other specimens of the same coin with less surface degradation.

However, not all coins have received circulation wear since they were struck. These coins are called Uncirculated or Mint State. Rather than being easier to grade because there are no points of wear to determine, Uncirculated coins become much harder to grade.

A noncollector unexposed to the intricacies of grading might be expected to show surprise at this last statement. After all, he might think, it seems logical that a coin that has received less wear is worth more than one that has received more wear. However, if a coin hasn't received any wear, how can it be different from other unworn specimens of the same coin? Suffice to say, there are graduated levels of Mint State, at least 11 (from Mint State 60 to Mint State 70), determined by such factors as contact marks, luster and — depending on the grading standard being used — the strength of the strike and toning. Therein lies the heart of the controversy.

For decades, the controversy lay mainly in the differences between the dealer's grade for a specific coin and that of the collector. As grading became more complicated and values increased in greater increments between coins of different grades, third-party grading services began operation.

The first third-party grading service, the International Numismatic Society Authentication Bureau, began grading coins in December 1976, several months after it began authenticating coins. It laid the groundwork for third-party grading services, all of which provide an opinion about a coin's grade for a fee. INSAB was followed March 1, 1979, when the American Numismatic Association Certification Service began grading coins for a fee.

Another major step in third-party grading services was taken by the Professional Coin Grading Service, a private business founded in February 1986. PCGS is responsible for two firsts. It was the first grading service to encapsulate the coins it graded into hard plastic holders, nicknamed "slabs," and it was the first grading service to use 11 levels of Mint State, from Mint State 60 to MS-70. It rapidly overtook ANACS, until then the most active of grading services in terms of numbers of coins graded. PCGS also published a grading guide, in 1998, the first of the private grading services to do so.

PCGS was followed by the Numismatic Guaranty Corporation of America. As encapsulated coins became more popular with dealers and collectors, existing services expanded their services. INSAB offered a "slab" service beginning in 1989, as did the ANA with its ANACS Cache.

In 1990, the American Numismatic Association sold ANACS — its grading and certification service — to Amos Press Inc. ANA retained the right to authenticate — but not grade — coins, and now operates under the acronym ANAAB, the American Numismatic Association Authentication Bureau. Amos Press Inc. retained the ANACS name, but it no longer refers to the American Numismatic Association Certification Service. Amos Press moved ANACS from ANA headquarters in Colorado Springs, Colo., to Columbus, Ohio.

Over the years, other grading services have surfaced, some specializing in paper money and world coins. One of the newest opened in 1998 — the Independent Coin Grading Company. Not all of the companies have succeeded; several have closed over the years.

Grading: What's involved?

Dr. Richard Bagg, in *Grading Coins: A Collection of Readings* that he co-edited in 1977 with James J. Jelinski, described the grade of a coin as its "level of preservation." It is not entirely accurate to call grading the charting of wear on a coin. The very definition of an Uncirculated coin (also called Mint State) is "a coin which has seen no circulation" (in *Official American Numismatic Association Grading Standards for United States Coins*) and a coin with "no wear" (in *New Photograde: A Photographic Grading Guide for United States Coins*). However, Uncirculated coins are subject to forms of surface degradation other than circulation wear.

A coin becomes subject to external factors affecting its surface from the second it leaves the press. The moment a coin is struck, it is pushed from the surface of the anvil die. The coin then falls into a bin of other coins. When the coin hits the previously struck coins lying in the bin, the portion of its surface coming into contact with the other coins will probably be marred. Then, as the coins are bundled into bags for shipment to banks, the coins will scrape, scratch and bump each other.

Contact marks

The collisions between coins create a variety of surface marks called "contact marks" or "bag marks." A contact mark may range in severity from a light, minor disruption of the coin's surface to a large, heavy scrape. Generally, the bigger and heavier the coin, the larger and more unsightly the contact marks, due to the heavier weight of the coins.

The location of contact marks plays a major role in determining at what level of Mint State a coin may be categorized. For example, marks that are clearly visible in the field of a coin, or on the cheeks, chin or forehead of a Liberty Head device are more distracting than marks of equal severity hidden in curls of Liberty's hair or the wing feathers of the eagle found on the reverse of many U.S. coins.

The size of contact marks also plays a role in determining the proper Mint State level. Larger marks, of course, are more distracting than smaller marks. Remember, however, that a contact mark 1 millimeter long is less distracting on a large coin such as a silver dollar (diameter of 38.1 mm) than it is on a smaller coin such as a silver half dime (diameter of 15.5 mm).

The number of contact marks also plays a significant role in determining the proper level of a Mint State coin. A coin with numerous contact marks is less appealing to the eye than a coin with one or two distracting marks. The diameter of the coin plays a role here too. A silver dollar with five contact marks scattered across its surfaces may be judged appealing; a much smaller half dime with five contact marks may be judged less appealing, since the half dime has a smaller surface area in which the marks appear.

Luster

Another factor involved in determining the level of Mint State and high-level circulated grades is luster. "Luster is simply the way light reflects from the microscopic flow lines of a coin," according to ANACS grader-authenticator Michael Fahey in "Basic Grading," a reprint from his series of articles in the American Numismatic Association's *The Numismatist.* James L. Halperin, author of the Numismatic Certification Institute's *The NCI Grading Guide*, defines luster as, "The brightness of a coin which results from the way in which it reflects light."

Luster is imparted to the surfaces of a coin at the moment of striking. The immense pressures used in the coining process create flow lines, the microscopic lines that trace the paths the metal took while filling the crevices of the die that compose the designs.

A coin with full luster is generally one that has a bright, shiny surface (although toning, to be discussed later, may obscure full luster), caused by the light reflecting off the surface of the coin. If the luster has been disturbed, the light reflects from the surface of the coin differently; the coin may appear dull.

Circulation wear erases the microscopic flow lines that cause the luster. Heavy cleaning or cleaning with a substance that removes a microscopic layer of the surface metal will also damage the flow lines and disrupt or eliminate the luster of a coin.

A Mint State coin cannot be lackluster. At best, an Uncirculated coin without full luster can be no higher than Mint State 63 under the American Numismatic Association grading standards. High-level circulated coins may show small patches of luster in protected areas.

Wear vs. friction

Once a coin enters the channels of commerce, it begins to receive wear. An individual reaches into his pocket to pull out some change and his fingers rub across the surfaces of the coin, creating wear. A coin is thrown into a cash register drawer where it bumps against other coins, creating more wear. A dime is used as an impromptu screwdriver, damaging the edge and creating more wear.

The amount of wear a coin receives determines its grade among the circulated grade levels. The high points of a design are usually the first to depict wear, since they are the most exposed. Then the raised inscriptions and date depict wear, and finally, the flat fields.

Circulation wear erases design details, ultimately to the point where the design features are only slightly visible to the naked eye. The separate curls of hair tend to merge, the eagle's feathers are rubbed away and the inscriptions begin to disappear into the fields.

Coins with only the slightest hint of wear are called About Uncirculated, a term that, if studied closely, defies logic. A coin is either Uncirculated or it is not. Then, in descending order, are Extremely Fine, Very Fine, Fine, Very Good, Good, About Good, Fair (and many years ago, Poor). Graders use several levels for some of the higher circulated grades to denote, for example, an Extremely Fine coin of higher quality than another legitimate Extremely Fine coin.

Many hobbyists differentiate between circulation wear and another form of wear labeled "friction." According to Halperin, friction is "a disturbance which appears either on the high points of a coin or in the fields, as a result of that coin rubbing against other projections." It is often referred to as cabinet friction, a term applied to the minute wear a coin received when sliding back and forth in the drawer of a cabinet used for storage by earlier numismatists.

According to some grading services, friction does disturb the luster of the coin, but it should not disturb the metal underneath. If it does, the disturbance falls into the category of wear, they believe. However, Numismatic Guaranty Corporation of America graders make no distinction between circulation wear and friction. Professional Coin Grading Service graders do not consider cabinet friction to be wear unless it is heavy.

Some grading standards permit coins with friction to be Mint State. For example, ANACS distinguishes between a coin with circulation wear and one with friction wear, permitting Mint State coins to possess small amounts of friction wear. NGC, however, would consider a coin with just the slightest amount of friction to be no better than About Uncirculated.

Strike

Strike is "The sharpness of detail which the coin had when it was Mint State," according to Halperin; Fahey defines it as "the evenness and fullness of metal-flow into all the crevices of a die."

The amount of pressure used to strike a coin controls the sharpness of a strike. Design elements may also affect the strike; if two large design features are centered on both sides of the same coin, there may not be enough metal to flow into every little crevice of the design, thus leaving some details weak and ill-defined.

A coin with a sharp strike has sharp design details. For example, the curls of hair on Liberty's head are strong and distinct. The feathers on the eagle's wings and breast are clearly visible. All of the other design details, legends and other elements are sharp and well defined.

A coin with a weak strike has weak and ill-defined design details. It may look worn, since design details are missing from the high points of a coin. However, luster is unimpaired. Lower striking pressures may not force the metal into the deepest crevices on the die (the highest point on the coin), thus the weaker design details.

Grading services, dealers and collectors consider strike an important part of a coin's grade. An Uncirculated coin relatively free of marks and with full luster may still be placed at the lower end of the Mint State scale if it has a weak strike.

Strike affects the value of a coin. A coin with a sharp strike will generally have a higher value than a coin with a weak strike, all other factors being equal.

Toning and color

As a coin ages, the original color changes in reaction to the environment. The original red of copper coins becomes brown (or green). Silver coins may tone into any color of the rainbow, depending on environmental factors. Gold is a more stable metal and even when immersed in seawater for centuries, generally shows little change in tone and color.

Many years ago, toned coins, particularly silver coins, were judged unattractive. Silver coins were "dipped," placed into a chemical solution that removed the toning and restored the shiny surface by stripping away the outer surface of the silver or the dirt.

However, in the last decade or so in the United States, attractively toned coins have become more appreciated from an aesthetic viewpoint. A silver dollar with rainbow toning may bring a considerable premium because of its coloration. Still, coins that exhibit bright white, original surfaces are prized. Coins that exhibit unattractive toning (referred to as tarnish) are considered to be of lesser quality.

Because attractively toned coins often bring higher prices, some unscrupulous individuals have devised ways of artificially toning coins. Some use the bluing materials used by gunsmiths. Others bake their coins in ovens using various substances to impart different colors. Some chemically treat coins.

Novices will find it difficult to judge between natural toning and artificial toning. Experience is important here. An individual who has looked at a large number of coins will find that he can determine at a glance whether the toning is natural or whether it has been artificially generated. Collectors should not pay a premium for an artificially toned coin.

Other factors

Other factors under some grading standards do not affect the grade but may affect the value. Under other standards, those same factors affect both the grade and the value of the coin.

Among these factors are die scratches, not to be confused with "hairline" scratches. Die scratches are thin raised lines on a coin, resulting from minute scratches in the surface of the die. A hairline is a thin scratch scraped into the surface of a coin inflicted after the coin is struck.

A close examination of a coin's surface through a magnifying glass should indicate whether a line on a coin is raised, and thus a die scratch, or incused, making it a hairline scratch.

Hairlines tend to affect the value more than die scratches. Most grading services, however, will lower the grade of a coin for more extensive, distracting die scratches. For example, NGC considers die scratches when determining a coin's grade.

Adjustment marks are often found on older U.S. silver and gold coins. Planchets (unstruck coins) were individually weighed before striking. If found to be a little overweight, the excess gold or silver was filed away. The striking pressures often did not obliterate the adjustment marks, which may resemble a series of parallel grooves. According to NGC practices, adjustment marks may affect both the grade and the value.

Eye appeal

All of the factors mentioned earlier are ultimately considered when graders, dealers and collectors decide on the "eye appeal" of a coin. Eye appeal relates to the overall attractiveness of a coin and ultimately determines its value. A potential buyer, whether he is a dealer, collector or investor, decides just how attractive he believes the coin to be.

Judging eye appeal is a purely subjective action. For example, a coin could have a strong strike and full details, possess full luster and have few large, distracting contact marks and still not have eye appeal if it has toned to an unattractive color.

When examining a coin, a buyer must decide for himself just how "pretty" the coin is and whether its attractiveness warrants the price being asked. Only the buyer can decide the eye appeal. Aesthetic judgments differ from person to person.

"Raw" coins vs. "slabbed" coins

When the Professional Coin Grading Service began grading coins in early 1986, it introduced a new product onto the market: the "slabbed" coin. A "slab" is the hard plastic holder into which a coin graded by a third-party grading service is sealed. The grading information is sealed into the slab as well. The slab permits both obverse and reverse of the coin to be viewed.

An encapsulated , or slabbed, coin

Proponents of the "slab" cite several benefits: 1. A coin encased within a slab is protected somewhat from environmental factors that could cause a deterioration in the coin's surfaces, and a lowering of its grade. 2. By sealing a coin into the same holder that contains the grading certificate, a buyer is "assured" that a coin meets the grading requirements of a specific grading service, if graded accurately. 3. It permits the "sight unseen" trading of a coin (in other words, various dealers have agreed to purchase coins graded by a particular grading service at the grade indicated in the slab, even without seeing the coin first).

However, in recent years, testing has shown that coins sealed in grading services' slabs can continue to tone. That's because the plastic is permeable; the chemicals that cause a coin to tone can permeate through the plastic or along the slab's seals. Collectors who own slabbed coins should inspect them routinely to ensure that the environment in which they are stored is not causing the coins to tone unattractively. (Unslabbed coins should also be examined regularly as well.)

Individuals who do not like slabbed coins cite detracting factors: 1. A collector cannot handle the coin directly. 2. Slabs do not permit the edge of the coin to be viewed. 3. It may be difficult to form one's own opinion about a coin's grade if it has already been encapsulated, since many like to grade a coin without having to examine it through a holder.

Related to the "slabbed" coin is the "raw" coin. A "raw" coin is the nickname used by some hobbyists for a coin that has not been graded and encapsulated by a third-party grading service.

Grading guidelines

The following guidelines are not presented as grading standards, but as introductions to the terminology of grading and its usage.

A few words regarding grading usage. When two grades are linked together by a virgule — as in Mint State 64/65 — it may mean that the coin has two grades (the first grade represents the obverse and the second, the reverse) or that the coin falls into a range between the two grades. When two grades are linked by a hyphen — as in Mint State 64-65 — it means that the grade for both sides lies somewhere between the two grades given. Collectors might want to exercise caution about buying a coin graded AU-BU. Most collectors believe a coin is either circulated or Uncirculated — it cannot fall somewhere in between.

Plus signs are used by many to indicate a coin slightly better than the numerical grade indicated, but not as good as the next numerical grade. A coin graded MS-60+ is better than an average MS-60 coin, but not as good as an MS-61 coin. The term "premium quality" means the same thing as a plus sign: that a coin is in the upper range for that grade and is very close to the next grade level.

Many dealers and collectors use adjectives instead of numerals, or combine adjectives and numerals when speaking about Mint State coins. A superb or superb gem coin is generally MS-67. A gem coin is usually MS-65. Some dealers use choice to describe an MS-63 coin, and others use choice for an MS-65 coin. Mint State 60 coins are generally referred to as Uncirculated or Brilliant Uncirculated; sometimes an MS-60 coin is called typical Uncirculated. Collectors should determine what adjectival "system" the dealer uses when no numerals are present because of the disagreement over what the adjectives represent.

Buyers should remember that different dealers, different collectors and investors use different grading systems. Although various grading services use an 11-point Mint State system, this does not necessarily mean they use the same criteria for assigning grades. In fact, there is no universally accepted standard for determining grades for U.S. coins.

Collectors should also know that grading standards can change over time. Standards sometimes tighten up, with a coin once considered Mint State 65 now considered MS-64. Standards can also loosen, with an MS-64 coin grading MS-65 under the looser standards. This can be troublesome, especially if a novice collector buys a slabbed coin graded during a period of loose standards; even if the slab is marked as MS-65, current standards might consider the coin no higher than MS-64. That's why it is vital that collectors learn how to grade coins, in order to protect themselves when buying coins.

Proof: Traditionally, Proof describes a method of manufacture, not a grade. However, since numerals are often assigned to Proof coins, there are different qualities of Proof coins; in effect, different grades. A circulated Proof is often called an "impaired Proof." Proof is rarely abbreviated.

Brilliant Proof: These coins are struck on highly polished planchets. Slower, high-pressure presses are used; coins are struck two or more times to bring up greater detail in the design.

Mint State and Uncirculated: The two terms are interchangeable and describe a coin that has no wear. To qualify as Mint State, a coin must not have any level of wear. Even the slightest amount of wear will drop the coin into the About Uncirculated level. (Coins described by some dealers as "Borderline Uncirculated" have wear and are actually About Uncirculated.) Mint State is most often used with numerals.

The numerical Mint State system so widely used in the current rare coin market is based on a system created by Dr. William H. Sheldon for the U.S. large cents of 1793-1814. When the numerical system began to spread to other series, three levels of Mint State were used: Mint State 60, for an Uncirculated coin of average luster, strike and marks; MS-65, an Uncirculated coin of above average quality; and MS-70, a perfect coin as regards luster, strike and marks. All 11 numbers are now used from MS-60 to MS-70.

Uncirculated is usually abbreviated as Unc. It often appears as Brilliant Uncirculated, abbreviated as BU. Sometimes used with numerals, generally as Unc. 60, and so on. Some dealers use a plus sign to indicate a coin better than one level of Mint State, but not as good as the next level.

About Uncirculated: This is a coin with only the barest traces of wear on the highest points of the design. It is abbreviated AU and often appears with numerals as AU-50, AU-55 and AU-58. The term has gained acceptance despite seeming inconsistency. Some people in the hobby still say that no coin can be About Uncirculated — it is either Uncirculated or it is not. Some use Almost Uncirculated, although all major U.S. grading guides use "About." The AU-58 grade has been described as an MS-63 coin with just the slightest hint of wear. It should have fewer contact marks than lower level Mint State coins: MS-60, MS-61 and MS-62. It may be more attractive and more valuable than these lower Mint State coins.

Extremely Fine: Light overall wear on highest points, but with all design elements sharp and clear, distinguishes this grade. Most hobbyists abbreviate it as EF, although a few use XF. It appears as EF-40 and EF-45.

Very Fine: The coin has light to moderate even wear on surface and high points of design. Abbreviated VF, it appears with numerals as VF-20 and VF-30. The abbreviations VF-25 and VF-35 are infrequently used.

Fine: The wear is considerable although the entire design is still strong and visible. It is abbreviated as F-12.

Very Good: The design and surface are well worn, and main features are clear but flat. Abbreviated as VG, it is used with numeral as VG-8 and VG-10.

Good: Design and surface are heavily worn, with some details weak and many details flat. It is abbreviated only when used with numeral, G-4; G-6 is infrequently used. Ironically, a coin in Good condition is not a "good" coin to collect; a Good coin is generally the lowest collectible grade.

About Good: The design is heavily worn with surface fading into rim and many details are weak or missing. Abbreviated as AG, it is used with a numeral as AG-3. Few coins are collectible in About Good condition. Dealers also use the terms Fair and Fair 3 to describe a coin in this state of preservation.

9 U.S. Coinage History

United States coinage history is a fascinating subject involving economics, politics, artistic expression, personal rivalry, technological breakthroughs, gold and silver discoveries and more. In short, the history of the country's coinage is the history of the United States.

Prior to the Revolution and the ratification of the U.S. Constitution, coinage in the British Colonies was a mixed bag of foreign coins, privately minted tokens and a few pieces authorized by the crown, and later, individual states.

Leading thinkers of the United States — Benjamin Franklin, Robert Morris and Thomas Jefferson, among them — suggested coinage systems. Franklin is even credited with the design concepts for the first true United States coin, the 1787 Fugio cent, struck under the provisions of the Articles of Confederation.

However, it was Alexander Hamilton, the country's first secretary of the treasury (later killed in a duel with Vice President Aaron Burr), who suggested a decimal coinage plan similar to what would be adopted in 1792. Hamilton's proposal, submitted to Congress in January 1791, recommended six denominations: gold $10 and $1 coins, silver $1 and 10-cent coins, and copper cents and half cents. Congress considered Hamilton's proposal, wrestled over the desires of many in Congress to place George Washington's portrait on U.S. coins (Washington vehemently opposed it), tinkered with weights and finenesses and finally arrived at the famous act that, to this day, still exerts controls over U.S. coinage.

The American coinage system was authorized under the Mint Act of April 2, 1792. The act also authorized the construction of a minting facility, provided for the positions that would be required, and outlined the responsibilities of the officers and set their salaries.

The 1792 act authorized 10 coinage denominations, eight of them legal tender. The two smallest denominations, the copper cent and half cent, had no legal tender status, unlike the silver and gold coins. Five silver denominations were authorized: the 5-cent half disme (later spelled as half dime), 10-cent disme, 25-cent quarter dollar, 50-cent half dollar and dollar. Three gold denominations were authorized: quarter eagle, or $2.50 coin; half eagle, or $5 coin; and eagle, a $10 coin. The act even outlined what design elements should appear on the coins (Liberty, and an eagle on the silver and gold coins).

Denominations

Since coinage began at the Philadelphia Mint in 1793, more than 20 denominations have appeared on the circulating, commemorative and bullion coins of the United States. In platinum, the denominations have been $100, $50, $25 and $10. In gold, the denominations have been $50 (commemorative and bullion coins only), $25 (the American Eagle bullion coin), $20, $10, $5, $3, $2.50 and $1. Among silver coins (many later changed to copper-nickel by the Mint Act of 1965), there have been the silver dollar, the Trade dollar, the half dollar, the quarter dollar, 20-cent coin, dime, half dime and 3-cent coin. The other denominations are copper-nickel 5-cent, 3-cent and 1-cent coins; a bronze 2-cent coin; cents in six different alloys; and a copper half cent.

Production of U.S. coinage began in earnest in 1793 with the production of copper half cents and cents. However, the striking of the two copper denominations came several months after the 1792 half disme was struck in small quantities for circulation, according to a report by George Washington. Silver coinage began on a more regular basis one year after copper coinage production began. The Mint began striking silver half dimes, half dollars and dollars in 1794; and silver dimes and quarter dollars in 1796. Gold coinage began in 1795 with the $5 half eagle and the $10 eagle, followed by the $2.50 quarter eagle in 1796.

During the earlier years of the U.S. Mint, not all denominations were struck in all years. In 1804, coinage of the silver dollar ceased with the striking of 1803-dated coins; dollar coinage was not resumed until 1836. A few gold eagles were struck in 1804, but coinage of the $10 coin then ceased until 1838. No quarter eagles were struck from 1809 through 1820. Production of the other denominations was sporadic except for the cent; planchet shortages prevented any 1815-dated cents from being produced. Otherwise, the cent series has been issued without interruption since 1793.

Meanwhile, as the country's borders and population grew, the monetary system grew with them. The denominations authorized in 1792 were no longer sufficient to meet the country's monetary needs at the midpoint of the 19th century. New denominations were authorized at the century's halfway mark. Congress authorized a gold dollar and gold $20 double eagle, both under the Act of March 3, 1849. Two years later, a silver 3-cent coin was authorized to facilitate the purchase of 3-cent postage stamps (Act of March 3, 1851). A gold $3 coin was introduced in 1854 (Act of Feb. 21, 1853), again to help in the purchase of 3-cent stamps (in sheets of 100). A smaller, copper-nickel cent was approved in 1857, replacing the pure copper large cent. The half cent was eliminated, also in 1857.

The American Civil War erupted in 1861, causing massive hoarding and exporting of coinage and the necessity of coinage substitutes like encased postage stamps, privately produced cent-like tokens and finally, the first federal paper money. More changes to U.S. coins began in 1864, when the composition of the cent was changed to 95 percent copper and 5 percent tin and zinc (bronze), and a bronze 2-cent coin was introduced (both under the Act of April 22, 1864).

A copper-nickel 3-cent coin was issued beginning in 1865 (Act of March 3, 1865) to circulate alongside the silver 3-cent coin (which was struck in decreasing numbers until the last coins were produced in 1873). A copper-nickel 5-cent coin was introduced in 1866 (Act of May 16, 1866); the silver half dime was eliminated after 1873.

In a bit of numismatic trivia that might be surprising to most non-collectors, the first coin to be called a "nickel" was the copper-nickel cent issued from 1857-64. The copper-nickel 3-cent coin was also called a "nickel" by 19th century users of the coin, with the copper-nickel 5-cent coin introduced in 1866 finally appropriating the nickname. The nickname persists to this day although the term "nickel" appears in none of the legislation authorizing the 5-cent coin. The nickname is based on the copper-nickel alloy that composes the coin, although ironically, the alloy used in the 5-cent coin since its inception has been 75 percent copper and just 25 percent nickel.

The year 1873 brought significant, unprecedented changes to the U.S. coinage system, under a law called by some the "Crime of '73." The Act of Feb. 12, 1873, is called by numismatic historian Don Taxay "the most exhaustive [coinage act] in our history." Four denominations were abolished by the act: the 2-cent coin, the silver 3-cent coin, the half dime and the standard silver dollar. A Trade silver dollar was authorized to circulate among merchants in Asia; Congress revoked the coin's legal tender status in the United States in 1876. The weights of the silver dime, quarter dollar and half dollar were increased. In addition, the act, in effect, demonetized silver and placed the United States on a gold standard, triggering a national debate that would last for the next quarter century.

Another new denomination was authorized under the Act of March 3, 1875 — the silver 20-cent coin. The coin was struck for circulation in 1875-76, setting the record for the shortest-lived silver denomination in U.S. coinage history. Coinage of Proof 20-cent coins continued for collectors only in 1877-78.

Meanwhile, the powerful silver interests in the United States, faced with the demonetization of silver left by the Crime of '73, fought in Congress. The Act of Feb. 28, 1878, reinstituted the standard silver dollar abolished by the Act of Feb. 12, 1873. The specifications were unchanged from the silver dollar of 1837-73: an alloy of 90 percent silver and 10 percent copper, weighing 26.73 grams. Obverse and reverse designs created by Mint Engraver George T. Morgan were selected for the dollar, today generally called the Morgan dollar (it was also called the Bland-Allison dollar, after the names of the congressmen responsible for the bill). Coinage of the Morgan dollar continued through 1904. Coinage denominations in use continued unchanged through 1889, when the gold dollar and gold $3 denominations were struck for the last time.

The circulating silver dollar was resurrected twice for circulation: in 1921, to continue through 1935; and in 1964, although the 1964-D Peace silver dollars were all destroyed before entering circulation. After the government withdrew support for the 1964-D Peace dollars, the coins were destroyed, in part to ensure that none entered circulation or collector circles inadvertently. Rumors persist, never confirmed, that the Denver Mint allowed employees to purchase some of the 1964-D dollars before the order came to destroy them; according to speculation, not all of the employees returned the coins they had purchased.

The copper-nickel clad dollar was introduced in 1971, and a smaller dollar (the Anthony dollar) was issued briefly from 1979-81. The standard silver dollar lives on in commemorative coinage, with approximately 40 different commemorative dollars struck between 1983 and 1999. In addition, there is a 1-ounce silver bullion coin that bears a $1 denomination, introduced in 1986 as part of the American Eagle bullion coin program.

Since the Mint Act of 1875, only three new denominations have been authorized, none for circulation. A gold $50 coin was approved to commemorate the 1915 Panama-Pacific Exposition being held in San

Francisco. More than 70 years later, in 1986, the $50 denomination was revived for the American Eagle bullion program. That same legislation (Act of Dec. 17, 1986, Public Law 99-185) also approved the United States' first $25 coin, the American Eagle half-ounce gold bullion coin. A $100 denomination was given the 1-ounce platinum American Eagle bullion coin, which was introduced in 1997.

The last gold denominations were struck for circulation in 1933, when coinage of the eagle and double eagle ceased under President Franklin Roosevelt's anti-gold executive orders. The gold quarter eagles and half eagles were last struck in 1929. All gold coins struck since 1984 have been commemorative or bullion coins.

A new dollar coin will go into circulation in 2000. The authorizing legislation requires it to have a distinctive golden color and edge, to help distinguish the coin from the similarly sized quarter dollar.

Designs

The story behind the designs of U.S. coinage is one of artistic experimentation and drone-like uniformity; of political necessity and political favoritism; of beauty tempered by the realities of the coining process.

The congressmen who approved the U.S. monetary system created design parameters that affect new U.S. coin designs even today, more than 200 years after that initial legislation. The Mint Act of April 2, 1792, specified that certain design features and legends appear on the coins that were authorized. On one side of all coins was to be an impression symbolic of Liberty, plus the word liberty and the year of coinage. For the silver and gold coins, an eagle and UNITED STATES OF AMERICA were to appear on the reverse. The denomination was to appear on the reverses of the half cents and cents.

For more than 115 years in the history of U.S. coinage, Liberty was portrayed by allegorical female figures, appearing either as a bust or a full-length portrait. Liberty's changing face through the years says a lot about the artistic abilities of the craftsmen employed on the Mint staff and the artists hired from outside to design certain coins. Some of the most attractive U.S. coins were designed by non-Mint employees, often in the face of opposition from a jealous Mint engraving staff that seemed more concerned about whether a coin would stack than its physical beauty. Beautiful designs created by Mint staff engravers never went beyond the pattern stage in favor of the uniformity that characterized

U.S. designs from the mid-1830s into the early 20th century.

The changing portrait of Liberty also reveals the embodiment of the "ideal woman" by the physical standards set by the American men of the time, and men had always dominated U.S. coinage design until the 1980s. (The Mint engraving staff was exclusively male until the Reagan administration appointed Elizabeth Jones chief sculptor-engraver.) The first coinage portraits of Liberty are "Rubenesque" by modern standards. Among the most recent allegorical figures to appear on U.S. coins is on American Eagle gold bullion coins — depicting a reproduction of an 80-year-old design, "slimmed down" to resemble the trimmer woman championed by American advertising and dietary standards in the 1980s and 1990s.

The 1793 half cents and cents introduced the allegorical themes used on U.S. coins: The half cent depicts a bust of Liberty with her hair flowing free. A Liberty Cap on a pole, a familiar symbol of Liberty in the American and French revolutions of the latter 18th century, rests on her right shoulder, giving the design its name: the Liberty Cap. On the first cents of 1793, another Flowing Hair Liberty appears. Contemporary reports claimed Liberty looks frightened on the cent. The designs are somewhat crude by modern standards. However, the Liberty busts were cut directly into steel by hand. Mint technicians had no access to the modern equipment and techniques available today.

Since the Mint Act of 1792 required only the denomination to appear on the reverses of the copper coins, the Mint engravers had a free rein. The first half cents have a wreath on the reverse, a device used as late as 1958 on the reverse of the Lincoln cent in the form of two "ears" of wheat. The reverse device on the first cents lasted only months. A 15-link chain meant to represent the unity of the 15 states appears on the first 1793 cents. The public believed the chain was a symbol of enslavement perceived to represent "a bad omen for Liberty." Changes in the design of both sides of the cent came rapidly. The Chain reverse was replaced by a wreath, then the obverse design of the "frightened Liberty" was replaced with a Liberty Cap design similar to that on the half cent. Thus, three distinct cents were struck with the 1793 date: the Flowing Hair Liberty, Chain cent; the Flowing Hair Liberty, Wreath cent; and the Liberty Cap, Wreath

LIberty Cap With Pole

cent.

Additional design changes were instituted for the cent in 1796, when a Draped Bust design was introduced and used through 1807. Liberty appears without a cap, her hair falling over bare shoulders. Loose drapery covers Liberty's bust. Another Liberty Head design called the Classic Head design was used on the cent from 1808-14. It differs considerably from the earlier allegorical motifs, with Liberty wearing a ribbon inscribed with LIBERTY around her hair.

Flowing Hair Liberty

The Coronet design was introduced in 1816 on the large cent. This design would prove one of the most versatile of the 19th century. A variation of the Coronet design would appear on both copper coins until 1857 and on most of the gold denominations from the 1830s to the first decade of the 20th century. The design is similar on all of the coins, depicting Liberty wearing a coronet inscribed with LIBERTY.

Chain reverse

Designs for the half cent were generally similar to the cent's designs, although the timetable for introduction was often different. The half cent used a Liberty Cap design until 1797 and from 1800-08 a Draped Bust design was used. The Classic Head design was used on the half cent from 1809-36 and the Coronet design was introduced in 1840.

The silver coins of the 18th century feature designs similar to those on the copper coins. The silver coins used a Flowing Hair design in 1794-95, and in 1795-96, a Draped Bust design was introduced on all silver coins. The Capped Bust design was used first for the half dollar in 1807, with the dime following in 1809, the quarter dollar in 1815 and the half dime in 1829. The eagles appearing on the reverse of the silver coins appeared in several forms. The first was in a Small Eagle design that some critics likened to a pigeon; a Heraldic Eagle was used on the dollar beginning in 1798, the half dollar in 1801 and the quarter dollar in 1804.

Allegorical Liberty figures with similar themes but somewhat different details were used on the early gold coins. A Capped Bust, Heraldic Eagle design was used from 1796-1807 for the quarter eagle, then replaced in 1808 with the one-year-only Capped Draped Bust type. The Capped Head quarter eagle was struck between 1821-34. On the half eagle, the Capped Bust design was used from 1796-1807; the Small Eagle reverse was used from 1796-98, and a Heraldic Eagle design was used from 1795-1807, concurrently with the Small Eagle at first. The Capped Draped Bust was used on the half eagle from 1807-12, and the Capped Head, from 1813-29. The Classic Head design was used briefly, from 1834-38. For the $10 eagle, the Capped Bust design was used from 1795 to 1804, when production of the denomination ceased. On the reverse of the $10 coin, the Small Eagle was used from 1795-97, and the Heraldic Eagle design was used from 1797 to 1804.

Draped Bust

Several events took place in the mid-1830s that were to affect coinage designs for decades. Among them was the Act of Jan. 18, 1837, which eliminated the need for an eagle on the reverses of the half dime and dime. The other event was the resumption of coinage of the silver dollar in 1836, and the adoption of a new design that eventually would appear on six different denominations, on some of them for more than half a century.

Production of the silver dollar resumed in 1836 with the Gobrecht dollar. The obverse depicts a Seated Liberty figure on a rock, her body wrapped in robes. The reverse depicts a Flying Eagle design. The Seated Liberty dollar was the first of four coins that would use a similar Flying Eagle theme.

Coronet cent

With the creation of the Seated Liberty design, a new age of uniformity ensued on U.S. coins. The Seated Liberty obverse design was introduced on the half dime and dime in 1837, the quarter dollar in 1838 and the half dollar in 1839. Wreaths were placed on the half dime and dime in 1837; eagles appeared on the new quarter dollar and half dollar; and the dollar received a new eagle design in 1840, with the Flying Eagle replaced by an eagle similar to those on the quarter dollar and half dollar.

Gold coins, too, entered the uniform age of coin design when the Coronet (sometimes called Liberty Head on gold coins) design was introduced in 1838 for the $10 eagle, 1839 for the $5 half eagle and 1840 for the $2.50 quarter eagle. When the gold dollar and $20 double eagle were introduced in 1849 and 1850, the Coronet design was used for both. Like the silver coins, the gold coins would not break out of uniformity until the early 20th century, except for the dollar.

A new theme was introduced in 1854 on the gold dollar, replacing the Coronet figure. An Indian Head portrait by James B. Longacre was introduced. It was the first in a series of medallic tributes to Native Americans that would last until shortly before the beginning of World War II. Ironically, this first use of an Indian as a symbol of Liberty occurred even as the American movement to push the Indians into decreasingly smaller portions of the West accelerated. However, the gold dollar portrait was not a true Indian; Longacre simply placed an Indian headdress on the same Liberty figure he would use in many different versions of the design. A slightly larger Indian Head was used beginning in 1856 on the gold dollar. The gold $3 coin depicts an Indian Head portrait, and the reverse depicts not an eagle but a wreath.

Heraldic Eagle

When the large cent was abandoned in 1857 for a smaller cent (see section titled "specifications"), a Flying Eagle design was placed on the obverse (the 1856 Flying Eagle cents are patterns, struck before Congress authorized a change in composition). This was the first nonhuman portrayal of Liberty and the only time an eagle would appear on the cent. The obverse design was changed to an Indian Head design in 1859. Wreaths of various types appear on the reverses of both.

Several nonallegorical designs began to appear on U.S. coins in the 1850s. On the silver 3-cent coin, a six-point star appears as the central obverse design; the reverse depicts the Roman numeral III inside what resembles a large letter "C." Shields appear on the obverses of the 2-cent coin and the first copper-nickel 5-cent coin.

A Liberty Head design replaced the Shield design on the 5-cent coin in 1883. The silver dollar, abandoned in 1873 and reinstated in

Seated Liberty 50¢

Coronet gold $20

1878, depicts a Liberty Head and an eagle (the coin is called the Morgan dollar).

The Seated Liberty coinage design was dusted off and placed on the short-lived 20-cent coin of 1875-78. The Seated Liberty design, used on most of the silver coins since 1836, was finally abandoned at the end of 1891. Chief Mint Sculptor-Engraver Charles Barber replaced it in 1892 with his Liberty Head design. Barber also created a Heraldic Eagle for use on the reverse of the quarter dollar and half dollar; the reverse wreath appearing on the Seated Liberty dime was maintained on the reverse of the "Barber" dime. The Barber designs were used through mid-1916 for the dime and quarter dollar, and through 1915 for the half dollar.

Silver 3-cent coin (enlarged)

The first two decades of the 20th century resulted in two major design trends for U.S. coins. One, beginning in 1907, resulted in what is often called the "Golden Age of U.S. Coin Designs." The other, beginning in 1909, was the first step away from the allegorical depictions that had characterized U.S. coins since 1793 in favor of medallic tributes to prominent political figures from American history.

The "golden age" began with the election of Theodore Roosevelt as president of the United States. Roosevelt, best known among non-numismatists as a vibrant president who built the Panama Canal and advocated the carrying of a "big stick," did more to improve the aesthetics of U.S. coins than any politician since Washington. He invited Augustus Saint-Gaudens, the premier U.S. sculptor of the day, to create

Saint-Gaudens double eagle, ultra-high relief

coin designs Roosevelt hoped would relive the beauty of ancient Greece. Saint-Gaudens submitted designs for the cent, $10 eagle and $20 double eagle. Roosevelt choose from the submissions the designs for the two gold coins. The $10 coin depicts an allegorical Liberty Head wearing an Indian headdress on the obverse and a standing eagle on the reverse; the double eagle depicts a Standing Liberty facing the viewer on the obverse and a Flying Eagle design for the reverse.

The Mint engraving staff, led by Charles Barber, was not happy with the hiring of outside talent, although Saint-Gaudens' double eagle design is considered by many collectors to be the finest ever portrayed on a U.S. coin. The first $20 coins struck in 1907 have high relief features, an artistic creation that caused problems in production. The coins required too many strikings for efficient production, so the relief was lowered later in 1907. Saint-Gaudens, who had been in ill health for some time, was dead by this time and unable to protest the changes.

The "golden age" continued in 1908, with new designs for the $2.50 quarter eagle and $5 half eagle by Bela Lyon Pratt: an American Indian on the obverse and a Standing Eagle on the reverse. These were the first true Indians to appear on U.S. coins. What made the designs so unusual, however, was their placement on the coin. The designs were created in the oxymoronic "incused relief." Often incorrectly referred to as incused, the designs are raised, but sunken into the fields so the highest points are level with the flat fields. This design feature was criticized, with some suggesting that the "incused" portions would permit enough germs to accumulate to prove a health hazard.

In 1913, the designs for the 5-cent coin were changed. An American Indian was placed on the obverse and an American bison was placed on the reverse. The coin, known variously as the Indian Head,

Bison or Buffalo 5-cent coin (also nicknamed the Buffalo nickel), is considered the most American of U.S. coin designs because of the two themes portrayed. The Indian design appearing on the obverse is probably the finest to be placed on a U.S. coin. Three Indians — Iron Tail, Two Moons and Chief John Tree — posed for designer-sculptor James Earle Fraser, who created a composite portrait. The model for the bison was Black Diamond, a resident of the New York Zoological Gardens.

More design changes were made in 1916, when the Barber designs for the dime and quarter dollar were replaced in mid-year. The dime features a Winged Liberty Head on the obverse. The design is often called the "Mercury" dime. However, Mercury was a Roman male god with wings on his ankles who wore a winged hat, while the figure on the dime is female and wears a winged cap. The artist never intended the figure to represent Mercury. The reverse depicts a fasces.

The quarter dollar design introduced in 1916 proved controversial. The Standing Liberty figure had an exposed right breast. The offending breast was covered with a coat of mail in 1917 (both varieties of the 1917 coin exist). Although many numismatic books claim there was an outcry over Liberty's bare breast, no contemporary evidence exists that backs the theory that the cover-up was a form of censorship. In fact, the coat of chain may indicate the nation's preparation to enter the war in Europe, a common allegorical theme. The reverse depicts a Flying Eagle; its position was modified slightly in 1917 when Liberty was given additional clothing. Amusingly, correspondence between Mint officials and designer A.A. Weinman refer to changes in the placement of the eagle but apparently do not mention the unclad Liberty. The coat of mail was added very quietly. The change may have been illegal, since Congress did not authorize it as required by law.

The Walking Liberty half dollar was also introduced in 1916. The obverse depicts a Walking Liberty figure. The reverse depicts one of the most attractive eagles on a regular issue of U.S. coins.

The Peace dollar replaced the Morgan dollar in 1921, which had been briefly resurrected in 1921 (coinage had ceased after 1904). The Peace dollar commemorates the peace that followed the end of World War I. Coinage of the dollar ceased at the end of 1935 when the denomination was temporarily abandoned.

The second coinage trend to begin in the early 20th century occurred in 1909 when a portrait of Abraham Lincoln replaced the Indian Head on the cent. For the first time, a historical, nonallegorical figure was used on a circulating coin of the United States. Lincoln's 100th birthday was celebrated in 1909. His 150th birthday in 1959 resulted in the Lincoln Memorial replacing the wheat found on the Lincoln cents of 1909-58.

The trend continued in 1932, when the Standing Liberty quarter dollar was replaced with the Washington portrait on the bicentennial of Washington's birth. A portrait of Thomas Jefferson replaced the American Indian in 1938 on the 5-cent coin (the Treasury Department held a design contest) and Franklin Roosevelt's portrait was placed on the dime in 1946, a year after his death. A portrait of Benjamin Franklin was placed on the half dollar in 1948, replacing the Walking Liberty designs. Franklin was replaced in turn in 1964 by a portrait of John F. Kennedy in a numismatic tribute to the assassinated president.

Lincoln's portrait ended allegory

In 1971, a copper-nickel dollar coin was introduced bearing President Dwight D. Eisenhower's portrait on the obverse and an allegorical figure of an eagle landing on Earth's moon, commemorating the Apollo 11 moon landing.

The Bicentennial of the Declaration of Independence in 1976 brought changes to the reverses of the quarter dollar, half dollar and dollar. The reverse of the 1976 quarter dollar depicts a Revolutionary War drummer, the half dollar depicts Independence Hall in Philadelphia and the dollar depicts the Liberty Bell superimposed over the moon. The designs reverted to their original versions in 1977.

In 1979, a new copper-nickel dollar sized between the quarter dollar and half dollar was introduced, replacing the Eisenhower dollar. The coin depicts feminist Susan B. Anthony and a reduced version of the moon-landing design. Anthony was the first nonallegorical U.S. woman

Dual date and commemorative reverse design were in celebration of the nation's Bicentennial.

to appear on a circulating coin. The choice was not a popular one, since many collectors had hoped a reincarnation of the Flowing Hair Liberty, designed by Chief Sculptor-Engraver Frank Gasparro especially for the smaller dollar, would appear. Many letters from collectors focused on the supposed unattractiveness of Anthony, who was shown in her later years on the coin. Ironically, a descendant of Anthony was critical of an early version of Gasparro's Anthony portrait as too "pretty" and not at all indicative of the woman's strong character; Gasparro modified the design before it was placed on the coin. However, the coin did not circulate well, mainly because of its similarity in size to the quarter dollar (many found the two coins too close to each other in diameter) and because the dollar bill remained in circulation. Poor public usage of the smaller dollar resulted in none being struck after 1981 (the 1979-80 coins were struck for circulation, and the 1981 coins were struck for collectors only). During the 1990s, however, the increasing use of Anthony dollars began to deplete the government's stocks of the coin, once expected to remain in the vaults forever. By June 1999, the Treasury Department's vaults had been emptied of Anthony dollars and the Mint had placed orders for dollar coinage strip in preparation to begin striking 1999 Anthony dollars. Production began during the summer of 1999.

Anthony dollar

The reintroduction of commemorative coins and the American Eagle bullion coins has brought renewed interest in coinage designs, and renewed controversy. Collectors and others have been critical of some of the designs on the commemorative coins (the two torchbearers on the 1984 Olympic $10 eagle were lampooned as "Dick and Jane running" by members of Congress). Others, most notably the obverse of the 1986-W Statue of Liberty half eagle, designed by Chief Sculptor-Engraver Elizabeth Jones, have been praised.

Reusing older designs on the American Eagle coins has proven controversial.

The obverse of the silver dollar depicts the Walking Liberty half dollar obverse, enlarged for placement on the larger coin. A new Heraldic Eagle appears on the reverse.

The designs chosen for the gold bullion coins were even more controversial. Saint-Gaudens' obverse Liberty for the double eagle was chosen, but not until Treasury Secretary James A. Baker III ordered Liberty on a diet in 1986. The Mint engraver assigned to the project was ordered to reduce Liberty's apparent weight by giving her slimmer arms and legs. Members of the Commission of Fine Arts decried the changes to what is considered a classic design. Members were also critical of the reverse, a Family of Eagles design by Dallas sculptor Miley Busiek. The legislation authorizing the gold coins mandated the Busiek design. Busiek had been an untiring champion of her design, which shows two adult eagles and two younger birds. She lobbied Congress and the Treasury Department for months in a politically successful attempt to have her design placed on the bullion coins. She says the design reflects the values of the American family.

American Eagle
silver bullion dollar

The newest members of the bullion coin family, the platinum American Eagles, stay near the tried-and-true designs of the past. On the obverse, John Mercanti rendered a medium close-up view of the Statue of Liberty, but deliberately thinned Liberty's lips and made other cosmetic changes. The reverse depicts a rendering of an eagle in flight with the sun in the background. In an interesting decision, Mint officials decided that beginning in 1998, the Proof versions of the platinum coin would depict a new reverse design every year for five years. The Proof 1998 American Eagle platinum coins depict an eagle in flight over a seashore scene (complete with lighthouse), with the moon in the sky. The 1999 Proof coins show an eagle in a swamp scene. The original reverse design remains in use on the Uncirculated versions of the coins.

Family of Eagles

For years, hobbyists and others have called for new designs on circulating coins, which the Treasury secretary may change without

Platinum
bullion coin

congressional approval after they have been in use 25 years. The 25-year limitation was placed on the coinage system in the Act of Sept. 26, 1890. Until then, there were no limitations concerning the life of a coin design. This act is now a part of Title 31 of the U.S. Code.

For decades, Mint officials had publicly opposed changes to U.S. coinage designs, stating that to change coinage designs would cause hoarding of the old designs, thus generating a coinage shortage. However, that policy briefly changed in April 1988 when Mint Director Donna Pope, appearing before the Senate Banking Committee, reported that the Treasury had no major objections to a bill calling for the redesign of all circulating U.S. coins.

Congress had split over the redesign issue. The Senate had supported the measure for years, having passed redesign legislation more than a half dozen times. The House of Representatives, however, long opposed coinage redesign as unnecessary and unwanted by a majority of the American public. Repeatedly the House voted down redesign legislation. At one point in early 1992, it appeared as though the Senate and House had reached agreement on coinage redesign. The measure was added to an omnibus coin bill seeking a variety of commemorative coins for 1992 and beyond. However, on the day the vote was scheduled, someone began spreading the false rumor that the legislation would eliminate "In God We Trust" from U.S. coinage. The House defeated the bill because of the false rumors.

Finally, Congress changed its mind and in 1996 authorized limited coinage redesign through the 50 States circulating commemorative quarter dollar program. Fifty new reverse designs will be introduced over a 10-year period beginning in 1999. Collectors are eagerly waiting to see what designs will be selected from 2000 to 2008.

New designs will also be used on the new dollar coin, to be introduced in 2000 with a portrait of Sacagawea and her infant son. This design concept was selected after unprecedented public discourse on the subject on June 8-9, 1998, in Philadelphia. Members of the public were invited to speak before a panel empowered to recommend coinage designs for the dollar coin. Artists, coin collectors and others recommended such subjects as Eleanor Roosevelt, allegorical portraits of Liberty and other themes, with the Sacagawea theme selected by the panel. The decision was controversial, since no portrait of Sacagawea exists. (The reverse depicts an eagle.)

However, the other circulating denominations remain unchanged in design, and even Washington remains on the obverse of the State quarter dollars. However, these first steps provide hope to collectors that more changes may be in the wings.

Specifications

The physical specifications of U.S. coins — metallic content, weights and diameters — have been ever changing. Changes were in response to increases and decreases in metal prices, public rejection of large-diameter coins and other factors.

Even before the first copper coins were struck in 1793, their weights were reduced under the Act of May 8, 1792. The modified weights are 6.74 grams for the half cent and 13.48 grams for the cent (weights are given in grams for modern convenience; the early coinage laws specified the weights in grains). Weights for both copper coins were reduced in 1795, to 5.44 grams for the half cent and to 10.89 grams for the cent.

Arrows signify change

The 1794-95 silver coinage was struck in a composition of 90 percent silver and 10 percent copper, according to some sources. When additional silver denominations were added in 1796, the composition for all five coins was changed to 89.2427 percent silver and 10.7572 percent copper, until additional change came in 1836-37.

Composition of the first gold coins is 91.6667 percent gold and 8.3333 percent copper and silver.

The only changes made to U.S. coins from the first decade of the 19th century and 1834 were to the designs. Then, on June 28, 1834, the weight of gold coins was reduced and the alloy changed for two years to 89.9225 percent gold and 10.0775 percent copper and silver. In 1836, the gold alloy was changed again, to 90 percent gold and 10 percent copper and silver, an alloy unchanged until 1873. Changes were made to silver coins in 1836 as well, when the silver content was changed to 90 percent silver and 10 percent copper, an alloy used until the mid-1960s.

The rising price of silver resulted in a reduction in weights for the silver coins during 1853 (except for the silver dollar). Arrows were added to both sides of the dates on the reduced weight half dimes, dimes, quarter dollars and dollars, a design feature used for 1853-54. The arrows were removed in 1855 although the weights of the silver coins remained the same.

Major changes were made to the country's copper coinage in 1857. The half cent was eliminated and the large copper cent was replaced with a smaller cent composed of 88 percent copper and 12 percent nickel (Act of Feb. 21, 1857). Diameter of the old cent is approximately 29 millimeters; the new cent has a diameter of 19 mm.

The weights of the Seated Liberty silver coinage increased in 1873, and again arrows were placed at either side of the date to signify the increased weight. Silver was dropped from the gold coin alloy, which changed to 90 percent gold and 10 percent copper.

The next major changes in U.S. coins were made during World War II. At the beginning of the United States' entry into World War II, several metals used in coinage became critical for wartime use. The first to be affected was the 5-cent coin, which had nickel removed in mid-1942 after some copper-nickel specimens were struck. The new composition was 56 percent copper, 35 percent silver and 9 percent manganese. The old alloy was resumed in 1946.

Also during the war, the composition of the cent changed. First, tin was removed late in 1942. Then, in 1943, a zinc-coated steel cent was introduced to conserve copper. The brass alloy of 95 percent copper and 5 percent zinc was resumed in 1944 through 1946. The 95 percent copper, 5 percent tin and zinc composition resumed in 1947 and continued until late 1962. Again, tin was removed from the bronze alloy, turning the alloy into the same composition used in 1944-46.

The 175-year-old history of United States coinage was changed with the stroke of a pen on July 23, 1965. On that day President Lyndon B. Johnson signed into law the Coinage Act of 1965, the most sweeping changes to the U.S. coinage system since the Mint Act of 1873. The 1965 act eliminated silver in dimes and quarters and reduced the silver content of the halves to 40 percent.

Silver-alloy war nickel

Special congressional hearings relative to the nationwide coin shortage were first held in 1964. Coin shortages had continually worsened in the decade prior to 1965 as a result of the population growth, expanding vending machine businesses, popularity of Kennedy half dollars and the worldwide silver shortage.

In the face of the worldwide silver shortage, it was essential that dependence on silver for coinage be reduced. Otherwise, the country would be faced with a chronic coin shortage.

Because of studies conducted by both the Treasury and the Battelle Memorial Institute, a clad metal composed of three bonded layers of metal was selected for the new composition. Battelle tested various alloys to determine their suitability for coinage. (Battelle is a Columbus, Ohio-based company that specializes in high-tech experimentation and research.)

The dimes and quarter dollars are composed of two layers of 75 percent copper and 25 percent nickel bonded to a core of pure copper. The half dollars of 1965-70 are composed of two layers of 80 percent silver and 20 percent copper bonded to a core of approximately 20 percent silver and 80 percent copper, such that the entire coin is composed of 40 percent silver. Half dollars struck for circulation since 1971 are composed of the same copper-nickel clad alloy.

The combination of copper-nickel and copper gave the new coins the required electrical conductivity, a necessary property for vending machines. The copper-nickel surfaces also continued the traditional silvery color of the coins and would be much harder to counterfeit.

At first, all of the strip (coinage metal rolled out into the proper thickness) was produced at the Olin Brass Division of Olin Mathison Chemical Corp. in East Alton, Ill. From there it was shipped to the U.S. Mints at Philadelphia and Denver and to the San Francisco Assay Office. As time had passed and the Mints built new facilities, more and more of the cladding was produced at the Mints. However, the Mint currently buys all strip from outside manufacturers. Mint officials claim it is more efficient and less expensive to do so. In addition, the Mint buys some of its planchets from private contractors, including all of the copper-plated zinc cent planchets and all of the precious metal planchets for special programs.

In an effort to maximize coin production, 1964-dated silver coins were struck into 1965. The Coinage Act of 1965 also made it mandatory that clad coins be dated not earlier than 1965. All clad coins actually made in 1965 bear that date. The first clad dimes were struck in late December 1965 and were released March 8, 1966. The first clad quarter dollars were struck Aug. 23, 1965, and released Nov. 1, 1965. The first silver-clad half dollars were released March 8, 1966, but were struck starting Dec. 30, 1965. The 1965 date was retained until July 31, 1966, when the date was changed to 1966. Normal dating resumed Jan. 1, 1967.

The last great compositional change to U.S. circulating coinage came in mid-1982, when the brass cent was replaced with a cent of nearly pure zinc, plated with a thin layer of pure copper to retain its copper appearance. Rising copper prices were the cause. The switch was made with few noting the difference.

When the American Eagle bullion coins were introduced in 1986, some numismatists were critical of the .9167 gold content, a composition they deemed "nontraditional"; there was some preference for a .900 gold content. However, the chosen composition is virtually identical to the alloy first used for U.S. gold coins, from 1795 to 1834. A new silver composition was introduced with the production of the .999 fine silver American Eagle dollar. The platinum American Eagle bullion coins, introduced in 1997, are .9995 fine.

Mint officials experimented with ring bimetallic experimental pieces in early 1993. The coins — consisting of an outer ring of one metal bonded to an inner ring of another, different-colored metal — are being used in circulation by many countries.

As this book is going to press, Mint officials have been studying what composition to select for the new dollar coin, which by law must be gold in color to help users distinguish it from the quarter dollar. As of July 1999, officials had already struck .9167 fine gold versions of the new dollar (under debatable legal authority), 12 of which were launched into orbit during a July 1999 space shuttle mission. Mint officials said gold versions would be offered to collectors in 2000.

10 Mints and Mint Marks

The United States Mint built in Philadelphia in 1792 has the distinction of being the first building constructed by the federal government. The importance of a federal coinage was widely recognized by national leaders following the ratification of the Constitution. The newly elected president, George Washington, had spoken about coinage issues and the need for a national Mint in his first three addresses to Congress, in 1789, 1790 and 1791. Congress passed a resolution March 3, 1791, stating, "That a Mint shall be established under such regulations as shall be directed by law." That law came a little more than a year later, with passage of the Mint Act of April 2, 1792, the same legislation that set denominations, specifications and legal tender status for the first U.S. coins. The Mint Act specified, "That a Mint for the purpose of a national coinage be, and the same is established; to be situate[d] and carried on at the seat of the Government of the United States, for the time being. ..."

The 1792 Mint Act also specified which officials would be required to conduct operations at the Mint, including the chief position, that of director. David Rittenhouse, widely considered America's top scientist at the time, was selected as the nation's first Mint director in April 1792 and wasted little time in beginning construction of a new Mint. Rittenhouse laid the foundation stone of the new Mint at 10 a.m. July 31, 1792. Construction moved promptly, with the building completed Sept. 7. However, much of the minting equipment was beyond the capabilities of America to manufacture and had to be ordered from abroad.

The first U.S. coins struck under the provisions of the Constitution were the 1792 half dismes. (The act called for half dismes and dismes, and those spellings appear on the 1792 pieces. This spelling remained in use in Mint documents until well into the 19th century, although never on any coins after the 1792 coins.) Research by numismatist Walter Breen indicates the 1792 half dismes were struck outside of the Mint facility on presses newly arrived from Europe. The striking of coins within the walls of the Philadelphia Mint for circulation began in 1793, with copper half cents and cents. Silver and gold coins followed.

First Philadelphia Mint

The first Philadelphia Mint was primitive by modern standards. The presses were hand-operated, with the other equipment powered by human or horse. The typical coining press in use at the Mint was the screw press, powered by human muscle. A planchet was placed on the bottom die by an early feed system and two men grasped ropes tied to the two arms of the press and pulled quickly, causing the upper die to descend and strike the coin. The first steam-powered equipment was installed June 24, 1816. Steam powered the machines that rolled the coinage metal to the proper thickness and the punch press used to produce planchets. Further mechanization came in 1833, when the second Philadelphia Mint was opened. The man-powered screw presses were replaced with steam-powered coining presses. Other equipment was also mechanized.

The growth of the United States Mint was linked to the westward expansion of the nation. Despite the improved output of the second Philadelphia Mint, by the mid-1830s additional coining facilities were needed. Gold discoveries in the Appalachian Mountains triggered America's first gold rush.

To meet the growing coinage needs of an ever-expanding country and population, Congress authorized the first Branch Mints in 1835: Dahlonega, Ga.; Charlotte, N.C.; and New Orleans. All of the Southern Branch Mints opened for coining in 1838. The Dahlonega and

Charlotte Mints were never prolific; they struck gold coins only, generally in smaller numbers than struck at Philadelphia. The New Orleans Mint was a better match for the Philadelphia Mint, striking both silver and gold coins.

Meanwhile, William Marshall gold discovered in California on the American River in 1848. The find triggered the biggest gold rush in U.S. history. Ever larger numbers of men with visions of unlimited wealth undertook the hazardous journey. California became a state in 1850; the population grew, as did the need for coinage. However, the closest Mint was in New Orleans. A number of private mints sprang up in California, striking native gold and fulfilling a need for coinage the U.S. Mint was unable to fill until Congress authorized the San Francisco Mint in 1852. It began operations in 1854, striking both silver and gold coins.

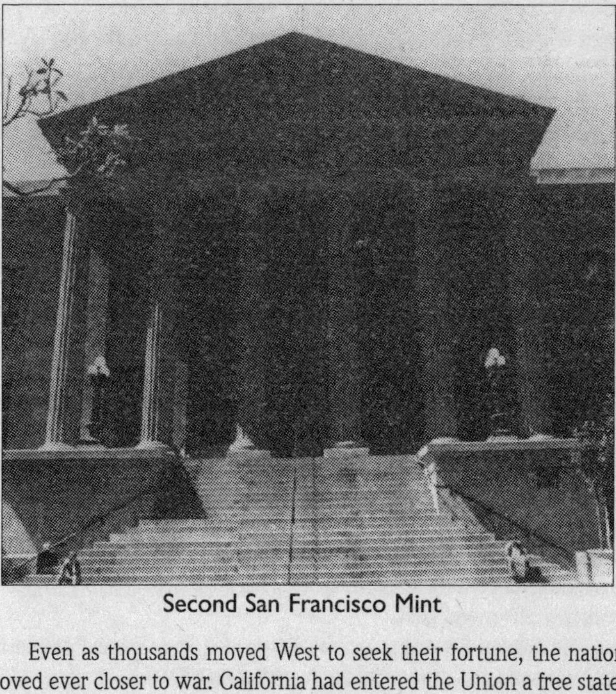

Second San Francisco Mint

Even as thousands moved West to seek their fortune, the nation moved ever closer to war. California had entered the Union a free state, without slavery, the result of the Compromise of 1850. However, the

Denver Mint in 1962

Compromise only postponed the inevitable. The sectional troubles that had been tearing the country apart for decades burst into full, horrible bloom with the election of Abraham Lincoln as president in 1860. One by one, the Southern states seceded from the Union. As Louisiana, Georgia and North Carolina left the Union, the federal Mints in those states changed hands. There was no need for Southern troops to use force to capture the facilities; the majority of Mint officials and employees at the three facilities were sympathetic to the Confederate cause. All three facilities struck small quantities of coins in early 1861, the New Orleans facility even striking four half dollars with a special Confederate design on one side. However, coinage at all three Mints ended in 1861 due to dwindling resources. The Dahlonega and Charlotte Mints never reopened following the war; however, New Orleans resumed coining activities from 1879 to 1909.

Other gold and silver discoveries in the West, particularly in Nevada and Colorado, triggered the need for additional Mints.

The federal government in 1863 purchased the private Clark, Gruber & Co. mint in Denver and extensively remodeled the building. Although officially designated a Branch Mint, it served instead as an Assay Office. A new Mint was built in Denver at the turn of the century, opening for coining in 1906. Denver has struck coins of copper, copper-nickel, silver and gold.

The Carson City Mint in Nevada opened in 1870 and closed in 1893. Carson City struck silver and gold coins only.

The San Francisco Mint closed after striking 1955 coinage, its presses no longer needed to keep up with the national demand for coinage. Congress revised its status in 1962, naming it the San Francisco Assay Office. However, a coin shortage struck the country and in 1965 the Assay Office resumed striking coins. The facility regained Mint status in 1988.

Currently, there are four federal Mints in operation in the United States. The Philadelphia Mint strikes all denominations of coins for circulation and some collectors' coins; the engraving staff works there; and the Philadelphia Mint produces coining dies. The Denver Mint is in its original 1906 building, although there have been recent additions; it, too, strikes a combination of circulation issues and collectors' coins, and has had a die production shop since 1996. The San Francisco Mint is in its third building, opened in 1937; today, it strikes coins for collectors only, although it struck coins for circulation as recently as 1980. The West Point Mint is the newest facility, having gained Mint status in early 1988; previously, it had been the West Point Bullion Depository (opening in 1938) although its coining facilities have been used since 1974. West Point is currently used only for collectors' programs and bullion coins although it has struck coins for circulation in the recent past. All platinum and gold bullion and commemorative coins are struck at West Point. A special 1996-W Roosevelt dime was struck at West Point to commemorate the 50th anniversary of the coin's introduction. It was included at no extra charge in 1996 Uncirculated sets.

History of Mint marks

A Mint mark on a United States coin is a small letter (or letters) placed on the field (the flat, featureless areas surrounding the designs and lettering) of the coin to show which Mint manufactured it. Mint marks on U.S. coins were authorized by the act of March 3, 1835.

Mint marks:

C for Charlotte, N.C., (gold coins only), 1838-1861
CC for Carson City, Nev., 1870-1893
D for Dahlonega, Ga. (gold coins only), 1838-1861
D for Denver, Colo., 1906-present
O for New Orleans, La., 1838-1861; 1879-1909
P for Philadelphia, Pa., 1793-present
S for San Francisco, Calif., 1854-1955; 1968-present
W for West Point, N.Y., 1984-present

With one four-year exception, U.S. coins struck at the Philadelphia Mint bore no Mint marks until 1979. The initial use of the "P" on a

U.S. coin appears on the Jefferson, Wartime 5-cent coins, struck from 1942 to 1945 in a silver alloy. The "P" Mint mark on these issues was designed to distinguish the silver alloy issues from regular copper-nickel 5-cent coins.

With the passage of the Coinage Act of 1965, which gave the United States copper-nickel clad coinage, Mint marks were not used on coins dated 1965 through 1968. The move was designed to help alleviate a coin shortage by removing the distinction between coins struck at Branch Mints and those struck in Philadelphia so collectors could not determine which were the more limited strikes.

With the announcement Jan. 4, 1968, that Mint marks would return to coins, Mint Director Eva Adams made several changes in Mint mark application. First, to achieve uniformity, she directed that all Mint marks be placed on the obverse. Second, she announced Proof coins would be manufactured at the San Francisco Assay Office with an "S" Mint mark. Previously, all Proof sets were produced at Philadelphia and had no Mint mark, except for some 1942 5-cent coins.

Mint marks were again omitted from certain U.S. coins when cents were struck at the West Point Bullion Depository in 1974 and later, and when dimes were struck in San Francisco in 1975.

Major changes were made in Mint mark policy beginning in 1978. Mint officials in 1978 announced that the 1979 Anthony dollar would bear the "P" Mint mark for Philadelphia business strikes. The list of coins to bear the "P" Mint mark grew in 1980, when all other denominations but the 1-cent coin received the new Mint mark.

A new Mint mark, "W," was established in September 1983, when the West Point Bullion Depository (now the West Point Mint) began striking 1984-dated $10 gold eagles commemorating the Los Angeles Olympic Games.

Additional changes were placed into effect beginning in 1985 to forestall Mint mark errors, when the Mint mark was placed on the master die instead of the working dies for all Proof coinage. In 1986, Mint officials decided to add the Mint mark on all commemorative and Proof coins at the initial model stage. Thus, on these special collectors' coins, the Mint mark appears on all stages of models, hubs and dies.

In 1990, Mint officials decided to add the Mint mark at the master die stage for coins intended for circulation. The cent and 5-cent coins underwent the change in procedure in 1990, with the remaining denominations following in 1991.

11 How Coins are Made

The various coining facilities of the United States Mint are factories, whose products happen to be coinage of the realm. Like any other metal-working factory, the U.S. Mint has a variety of presses, engraving and reducing machines and metal-working equipment.

Like any metal product, coins don't "just happen." A number of intricate steps must be taken, from the preparation of the raw metal used in the coins to the striking of the coins. And before the coins can be struck, dies must be produced.

The dies used for striking coins start out as an approved sketch in the Engraving Department at the Philadelphia Mint. The sculptor-engraver makes a model in bas-relief (with the design portions raised above the surface of the coin) from the sketch. The model will be anywhere from three to 12 times as large as the finished coin. Next, a plaster-of-paris negative is cast from the model. The negative is touched up and details are added, including legends (think of the skill necessary to engrave the letters of the legends backwards). Then a plaster-of-paris positive is made. The positive is used as the model to be approved by the Mint director and the secretary of the treasury if a new design is being created.

When final approval is received, another negative is made from which a hard epoxy positive model is prepared.

The completed epoxy model is then mounted on a Janvier transfer-engraving machine. This machine cuts the design into soft tool steel — tracing the exact details of the epoxy model — and produces a positive replica of the model called a "hub." The hub, which is the exact size of the coin, is then heat treated to harden it and is placed in a hydraulic press. The hub is slowly pressed into a blank piece of soft die steel until a negative replica is made, called a master die. The original hub is stored in a safe place to ensure against loss of the original reduction.

Working hubs are made from the master die in the hydraulic press in the same way as the original, master hub. Working dies are made from the working hubs in the same way. A blank piece of soft die steel is impressed with the working hub, an act that hardens the metal.

Janvier reducing machine transfers image from large epoxy model at right to coin-sized steel hub at left

The number of impressions of hub into die or die into hub to fully form a usable image depends on the equipment in use. Since 1997, most dies produced at the Philadelphia and Denver Mints have been produced on newer equipment that permits single-impression hubbing, with the complete image formed during one impression of die into hub. That technology was introduced when a new die shop went into operation at the Denver Mint (the first there) on May 13, 1996. Half dollar and other larger denomination dies continued to be produced on older equipment requiring multiple impressions of die into hub to fully form the image throughout 1998. However, the two Mints began producing half dollars dies in a single hubbing operation in 1999.

Mint marks — found on all U.S. coins since 1980 but the Lincoln cent struck at the Philadelphia Mint — are added at various stages of the die-production process. Traditionally, Mint engravers had placed the Mint mark by hand on each of the thousands of working dies. That is no longer the case. Beginning in 1990, the Mint began placing the Mint mark on the master die for the cent and 5-cent coin. The other denominations — dime, quarter dollar and half dollar — followed in 1991. Mint marks on commemorative coins and Proof coins are placed at the initial modeling stage and have been since the mid- to late 1980s. Later in the 1990s, the D Mint mark was added to the models for the Denver

Mint cents, but not for other circulating coinage. All of these changes decrease the possibility of producing Mint mark errors and varieties.

Modern United States coins have their beginnings in the private sector, where a number of companies produce some coinage blanks and planchets and all coils of strip metal the Mint purchases. Blanks and planchets represent the same product at different stages of production: the unstruck, circular pieces of metal that become coins when struck between the dies. The Mint produced its own strip metal as late as Fiscal Year 1982 at the Philadelphia Mint, but the operations were closed officially in Fiscal 1983. The Mint still produces some of its coin blanks and planchets.

In preparing the raw metals used in coining, the coinage metals are assayed, melted and formed into slabs that are then rolled to the proper thickness. For clad coinage, bonding operations are required to bond the two layers of copper-nickel to the core of pure copper. The strip is then coiled and shipped to the Mint for blanking.

Blanks are unfinished planchets that haven't been through all of the processing steps necessary before they can be struck into coins. Once a blank has been through all of the processing steps, it becomes a planchet and is ready to be struck in a coining press to become a coin.

Blanks are produced on blanking presses, which are simply punch presses similar to those found in any machine shop. They have a bank of punches (or rams) that travel downward through the strip of coinage metal and into a steel bedplate that has holes corresponding to the punches. The presses punch out blanks each time the punches make their downward cycle. The blanks made at this stage are slightly larger than the finished coins. Because of the shearing action of the punches, the blanks have rough edges. Most of the rough edges (or burrs) are removed during succeeding operations.

The blanks are next passed over sorting screens that are supposed to eliminate all of the defective pieces. Thin and incomplete blanks will fall through the screens. Rejected blanks are remelted.

During the finish rolling and blanking press operations the blanks have again been hardened and must now be softened by being heated to controlled temperatures, approximately 1400 degrees Fahrenheit, changing their crystal structure to a softer state. Planchets are "frozen" into that state by a water quench bath. The annealing process prolongs the life of the coining dies by ensuring well-struck coins with lower striking pressures.

Despite a protective atmosphere, annealing causes some discoloration on the surfaces of the blanks that must be removed. The blanks are tumbled against each other and passed through a chemical bath. Then they are dried by forced hot air. Many of the blanks' next stop is an upsetting mill. (The Mint no longer finds it necessary to upset the rims of 5-cent blanks at the Denver Mint.)

The upsetting mill consists of a rotating wheel with a groove on its edge. The grooved edge of the wheel fits into a curved section (or shoe) that has a corresponding groove. The distance between the wheel and the shoe gets progressively narrower so that, as the blank is rolled along the groove, a raised rim is formed on both sides of the blank. This raised rim serves several purposes. It sizes and shapes the blank for better feed at the press and it work-hardens the edge to prevent escape of metal between the obverse die and the collar.

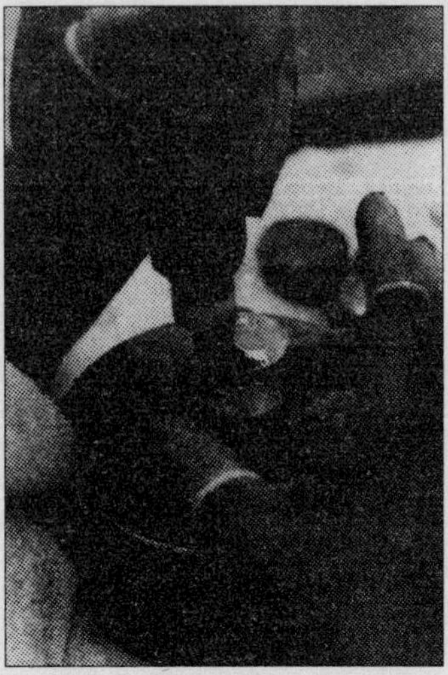

Die being polished for a Proof coin

The blanks are now planchets and are ready to be struck into coins on the Mint's coining presses.

Coining presses are designed for any denomination of coin. Dies and are interchangeable and striking pressures are adjustable for the various denominations and metals. A circular piece of hardened steel forms the collar, which acts as the wall of the coining chamber, and one die forms the bottom. The dies impress the various designs and devices on the obverse and reverse for the coin while the collar forms the edge of the coin, flat and smooth on cents, 5-cent coins and Sacagawea dollar and reeded on the dime, quarter dollar and half dollar. The collar, which is five-thousandths of an inch larger in diameter than the dies, is mounted on springs that allow slight vertical movement.

Generally, the reverse die is the lower (or anvil) die while the obverse die is the upper (or hammer) die; however, there are exceptions. The dies are mounted horizontally so that they move parallel to the floor on some presses. Still, the terms anvil die and hammer die are appropriate on these latter presses.

Planchets are fed by gravity from a basin attached to the press through a cylindrical tube. This tube stacks 20 or so planchets. From this stack, the bottom planchet is fed into the press by one of several feed devices.

One device is called the feed fingers: two parallel pieces of metal joined in such a way that they can open and close; on one end of the two pieces is a covered recessed slot and in the center is a hole. A second device is a dial feeder: a circular piece slotted with holes that transport the planchets to the coining chamber and then transport the newly struck coin from the dies.

No matter which feed device is used, the coining process is the same. The anvil die at this point is stationary. The hammer die moves toward the anvil die, the dies impress the designs of both sides into the planchet and then the hammer die completes its cycle by moving back to its original position. On presses using the dial feeder, the dial remains stationary so that the hole transporting the planchet remains centered over the anvil die, with the hammer die passing through the hole to strike the coin. Then, the anvil die moves above the collar, actuated by an eccentric cam, raising the struck coin out of the coining chamber. Depending on the feeder system used, one of two things happens.

As the anvil die moves, about the same time the feeder fingers, in a closed position, start to move forward with a planchet lying in the center hole. At this time the anvil die reaches the top of its cycle, the recessed slot (ejection slot) slides over the struck coin and pushes the coin away from the coining chamber. The feed fingers have completed their forward movement and now the center hole is moving toward the coining chamber. Having imparted movement to the struck coin, that coin continues onward until it hits a shield that deflects it into the struck coin hopper. The feed fingers open, allowing the planchet to fall into the coining chamber. Then the feed fingers reverse direction to return to their original position.

On presses using a dial feeder, the struck coin is pushed back up into the hole that had carried the planchet; the dial rotates, moving the coin away from the coining chamber while the next hole drops a new planchet onto the lower die. The cam action now causes the lower die to move to its stationary position. This process repeats for each coin that is struck.

Presses fed by dial feeders have sensors that automatically stop the press if a planchet is mispositioned, of the wrong size or incomplete, or is completely missing. The Mints have made good use of this feature to decrease production of many of the error coins that entice collectors.

Frequently, while a press is in operation, the press attendant will pick up a finished coin for inspection to catch some of the remaining varieties and errors that are still produced. The inspector examines the coin under a magnifier to search for any defects made in the die during operation. Another attempt is made to prevent improperly shaped coins from reaching circulation by passing them through a second device to remove improperly sized or shaped coins.

Throughout the minting process, computers track such statistics as the productivity of each press operator, any repairs to a coining press, quantities of coins struck per press, plus installation, movement and destruction of the dies.

After the coins have been struck, they are ready for a final inspection. After passing the inspection, they are counted automatically by machines, weighed and bagged or boxed. The bags are sewn shut and the boxes shut. The coins now are ready for shipment from the Mint to the Federal Reserve Banks or private money-handling firms like Brinks for distribution.

12 Errors

What is an error coin? An error coin deviates from the norm as a result of a mishap in the minting processes; in effect, an error represents a "substandard" product of the Mint. However, some collectors prefer these items over normal coins.

Values for error coins depend on the same factors affecting normal numismatic merchandise: supply, demand and condition. Errors are in very short supply when compared to total mintages. However, error collectors represent a fraction of the total number of collectors, so demand is less for most items. Some error coins, such as the 1955 Lincoln, Doubled Die cent, because of publicity and dealer promotion, "cross over" and become popular with general collectors; thus, demand is higher for a fixed supply, and values are correspondingly higher. Condition is important, although error collectors seem less concerned with "perfection" than other collectors.

Rare does not necessarily mean great value. Many error coins struck in small quantities are available for a few dollars. Even errors that are considered unique are often available for several dollars. Sometimes, many persons not familiar with errors, including some dealers, place uncharacteristically high values on error coins.

Another factor affecting value is the type of coin involved. For example, in June 1999, State quarters bearing errors considered relatively common were selling for prices many times more than 1998 quarters bearing the same errors. For example, a 50 percent off-center 1998 quarter dollar was selling for about $30 while the same error on a 1999 State quarter was selling for $500! The individual State quarters are being struck in much smaller quantities than the traditional quarters, meaning fewer errors are likely to exist per State coin. Error dealers contacted by *Coin World* were somewhat astonished by the prices they were paying and offering for the State quarter errors.

At the same time, error dealers were cautioning collectors against paying high premiums for State quarters with minor errors, such as those missing a letter in a legend due to a filled die or having die cracks. At that time, there was no indication that a secondary market was being established for such pieces, which are considered very common. *Coin*

World received many reports from readers who were finding State quarters bearing these and other minor errors.

Any discussion of error coins must include a discussion of varieties. A numismatic variety is defined as the difference between individual dies (for example, the difference in the placement of the four digits of the date may differ from die to die for 18th and 19th century coins, making each die a different variety). Among the coins considered varieties are such coins as the 1955, 1972 and 1995 Lincoln, Doubled Die cents, and the 1937-D Indian Head, Three-Legged Bison 5-cent coin.

Error and variety coins can be found in circulation, unlike many other collectors' items. Some collectors go to banks and obtain large quantities of coins to search through; coins not bearing errors are returned to the bank. Many errors, particularly of the minor classification, can be discovered simply by going through pocket change and wallets. Major errors, particularly those that leave the coin misshapen, are generally acquired from individuals who work at private companies that receive large quantities of unsearched coins directly from the Mint (the employees find the coins while rolling them for banks and other customers; they purchase the coins at face value and sell them to dealers with whom they have regular contact). All it takes are sharp eyes and knowledge of what to look for.

Many error collectors are adept at what they call "cherry picking." They use their superior knowledge of errors and varieties when going through a dealer's stock to obtain scarcer pieces at prices less than what a specialist might charge.

Some of that knowledge comes from a clear understanding of the minting process. The minting of a coin is a manufacturing process and should be fully understood by anyone interested in collecting and studying error coins (see **Chapter 11, "How coins are made"**). Many forms of alteration and damage received outside the Mint resemble certain types of errors, but none precisely duplicate genuine Mint errors. Collectors who understand the minting process should be better able to distinguish between errors, damage and alteration.

The following section presents error coins in three parts: **die errors, planchet errors** and **striking errors.** Our categorization of error types may differ from other specialists. Die errors are those produced due to a mishap involving the die or hub. Planchet errors are the result of defective or improperly selected planchets. Striking errors are created during the actual coining process; each is unique.

Die errors

BIE: The term commonly used for minor errors affecting the letters of the word LIBERTY on Lincoln cents. A small break in the die between the letters, especially BE, often resembles the letter I, hence the BIE designation. Such errors are much more common on the coins of the 1950s and early 1960s than more recent issues. Collectors tend to be less interested in such errors in the late 1990s than they were 20 years ago. However, interest picked up in 1995 when the discovery of the 1995 Lincoln, Doubled Die cents prompted collectors to closely examine their cents, resulting in the discovery of many BIE cents and other minor varieties and errors.

Clashed dies: When during the striking process two dies come together without a planchet between them, the dies clash (come into direct contact). Depending on the force with which the dies come together and the nature of the designs, a portion of the obverse design is transferred to the reverse, and a portion of the reverse is transferred to the obverse. Coins struck from the clashed dies will show signs of the transferred designs. Although the cause of this type of error occurs during the striking process, the die is affected; thus, it is considered a die error.

Clashed Dies

Die breaks, chips, cracks, gouges, scratches: Dies, like any other piece of steel, are subject to all sorts of damage. Any incused mark on the die leaves raised areas on coins. Breaks and cracks are similar, appearing on coins as raised lines. A die break affects a larger area than the die crack, and breaks often result in pieces of the die falling out. A die chip occurs when a small portion of the die breaks away, while gouges and scratches generally occur when a foreign object scores the surface of the die.

A major die break is often though misleadingly referred to as a "cud." It occurs when the die breaks at the rim and a piece of the die falls out of the press. The metal of coins struck from that die flows up into the missing area, resulting in a raised blob of metal bearing no image; these are nicknamed "cud" errors. The side of the coin

Die crack

opposite the raised blob is often weak and indistinct; this is because metal flows along the path of least resistance, flowing into the broken area and not the recesses of the other die. A retained major die break occurs when the die breaks at the rim, but the piece does not fall out. Coins struck from these dies show the break, but also depict the image inside the break.

Major die break

Doubled dies: If during the hubbing and die making process, a misalignment between hub and partially completed die occurs, overlapping, multiple images may appear on the die. Coins struck from the die will show the overlapping images, like the doubled date, IN GOD WE TRUST and LIBERTY on the 1955 Lincoln, Doubled Die cent. Die doubling on coins with raised designs feature a rounded second image; on coins with incused designs, the second image is flat and shelf-like. At the corners of the overlapping images are distinct "notches" on coins with raised designs. A tripled or quadrupled die is caused by the same misalignment, but bears a tripled or quadrupled image. Doubled dies may become impossible due to technological improvements at the Mint. Doubled dies can only occur when more than one impression of hub into die is required, and the alignment between hub and die shifts between hubbing operations. The new single-hubbing equipment eliminates the possibility that doubled dies can be created.

Doubled die

Engraving varieties and errors: While more common on the dies of the 18th and 19th centuries, engraving errors and varieties have been made on modern dies. On the earlier dies, numerals and letters were often repunched to strengthen the design, punched in upside down or otherwise out of alignment, and sometimes, wrong letters or numbers were punched into the die. On more modern dies, engraving errors include the use of the wrong size Mint mark by mistake and Mint marks placed too close to design elements or too far from their intended locations. Other "engraving" errors, discussed in separate sections, include doubled dies, overdates and multiple Mint marks.

Misaligned dies: Although one side of the coin appears to have been struck off-center, it is not a striking error. A misaligned die occurs when one die is horizontally displaced to the side, causing only a partial image to appear on that side of the coin. However, unlike the off-center coin that it resembles, only one side is affected. The other side is normal. Some specialists classify misaligned dies as striking errors.

Misplaced dates: A misplaced date is a relatively recently studied variety. Researchers have discovered numerous coins with numbers from the date punched well away from the region of the die where the date was punched. For example, coins have been found with a number or numbers punched into the dentils along the rim or into a major design element. While theories abound, no one is sure whether this punching was accidental or deliberate, or why it was done.

Overdate

Overdates: When one or more numerals in the date are engraved, punched or hubbed over a different numeral or numerals, both the original date and the second date can be seen. Modern hubbed examples include the 1943/2-P Jefferson 5-cent coin and the 1942/1 Winged Liberty Head dime (both are also doubled dies). The traditional, pre-20th century overdate occurred when one date was punched over another date, as on the 1818/5 Capped Bust quarter dollar.

Over Mint mark

Over Mint marks: A form of repunched Mint mark, but when punches of two different Mints are used. Examples include the 1944-D/S Lincoln cent and the 1938-D/S Indian Head 5-cent coin. These can occur accidentally or deliberately. Mint officials as late as 1955 salvaged dies intended for one Mint by repunching a different Mint mark over the original Mint mark and using them at the second Mint. The 1955-D/S Jefferson 5-cent coins fall into this category.

Polished dies: Mint employees polish dies to extend their working life and to remove such things as clash marks, die scratches, dirt and grease. If the die is polished too much, details may be erased or small raised lines may appear on the coins. Most over-polished errors have little value, but there are exceptions, including the 1937-D Indian Head, Three-Legged 5-cent coin.

Repunched Mint marks: Mint marks were punched into each

individual working die (for coins issued for circulation) by hand with mallet and punch until changes were made to the process in 1990-91 (see **Chapter 11, "How Coins Are Made,"** and **Chapter 10, "Mints and Mint marks,"** for details). Under the old system, several blows to the punch were needed to properly sink the Mint mark into the working die. If the punch was not properly placed after the first blow, a multiple image could result. A coin identified as a 1960-D/D Lincoln cent has a repunched D Mint mark, for example.

Rotated dies: Most U.S. coins have the obverse and reverse sides oriented so each side is upright when rotated vertically. The alignment between the two is 180 degrees. However, if the dies are aligned at anything other than 180 degrees, the dies are considered rotated. The Mint considers coins rotated 5 degrees or less within tolerance. Some specialists consider rotated dies to be striking errors since the die's face is unchanged.

Worn dies: Dies have a limited life, based on the hardness of the coinage metal being struck and the striking pressures involved. When a die wears beyond a certain point, details around the rim tend to flow into the rim, while other details weaken. The surface of the die becomes scarred, as if heavily polished. Coins struck from worn dies rarely have collector value as die errors.

Planchet errors

Alloy errors: All U.S. coins are produced from alloyed metals that are mixed when molten to strict specifications. If mixed incorrectly, the metals may cool in nonhomogeneous form, with streaks of different metals appearing on the surface of the coin.

Damaged planchet

Brass-plated cent: A post-1982 error is the brass-plated cent. Zinc planchets are plated with copper to form a copper-plated zinc planchet. Zinc planchets sometimes remain within the molten copper and dissolve, adding their zinc content to the copper, thus forming brass. Subsequent planchets are plated with brass instead of pure copper. A number of brass-plated 1998 cents were produced.

Damaged planchets: Planchets are subject to various sorts of damage, including cracks (not to be confused with die cracks), holes and major breaks.

Fragments, scrap struck: Small pieces of coinage metal — fragments and scrap left over from the blanking process — sometimes fall between the dies and are struck. Fragments must be struck on both sides and weigh less than 25 percent of a normal coin's weight to qualify as a struck fragment. Planchet scrap is generally larger than a fragment, and usually has straight or curved edges as a result of the blanking process.

Struck fragment

Incomplete planchets: Often, though erroneously, called a "clip," an incomplete planchet results from a mishap in the blanking process. If the planchet strip does not advance far enough after a bank of punches rams through the metal, producing planchets, the punches come down and overlap the holes where the planchets were already punched out. Where the overlapping takes place, there is a curved area that appears to be "missing" from the planchet. The word "clip," commonly used, suggests a piece of the planchet was cut off, which is not the cause of the incomplete planchet. "Clip," when properly used, refers to the ancient process of cutting small pieces of metal from the edges of precious metal coins for the bullion; that is why U.S. gold and silver coins have lettered or reeded edges, to make it more difficult to clip a coin. Other incomplete planchets occur when the strip shifts to the side, causing the punches to overlap the strip's edge, or when the punches overlap the end of the strip. The missing area is represented by a straight edge, not curved. An "incomplete planchet planchet" occurs when the punch does not completely punch out a planchet, but leaves a circular groove. If the strip advances improperly, planchets overlapping the incomplete punch will bear a curved groove; the groove remains visible after the coin is struck. It is sometimes called an incomplete clip. Most but not all incomplete planchet errors have a "signature" known as the Blakesley effect. The area of the rim 180 degrees opposite the "clip" is weak or nonexistent since the "clip" negates the rim-making process in the upset mill. The

Incomplete planchet

lack of pressure in the upset mill at the clip results in improper formation of the rim on the opposite side.

Lamination

Laminations: During the preparation of the planchet strip, foreign materials — grease, dirt, oil, slag or gas — may become trapped just below the surface of the metal. Coins struck from this strip later may begin to flake and peel since adhesion is poor in the location of the trapped material. The Jefferson, Wartime 5-cent coins are particularly susceptible to lamination, due to the poor mixing qualities of the metals used during the war metal emergency.

Split planchet

Split planchets: Planchets can split due to deep internal laminations or in the case of clad coinage, because of poor adhesion of the copper-nickel outer layers to the copper core. Planchets may split before or after striking. Those splitting before generally exhibit weak details due to lack of metal to fill the dies, while those split afterwards usually depict full detailing. On nonclad coins, the inner portion of the split shows parallel striations typical of the interior structure of coinage metal.

Thick and thin planchets: Planchets of the wrong thickness are produced from strip that was not rolled properly. Too little pressure can result in planchet stock that is too thick; too much pressure can result in a thin planchet. If the rollers are out of alignment on one side, a tapered planchet — thicker on one side than the other — is created.

Unplated planchets: New in U.S. coinage, unplated planchets became possible in 1982 with the introduction of the copper-plated zinc cent (and briefly in 1943 with the zinc-coated steel cents). The zinc-copper alloy planchets are plated after they are punched from the strip but some planchets miss the plating process. Coins struck on the unplated planchets are grayish-white in color. Beware of cents that have had their plating removed after leaving the Mint. Although beyond the ability of a neophyte to detect, any authentication service should be able to distinguish between a genuine piece and an altered version.

Wrong metal, planchet, stock: A wrong metal error is struck on a planchet intended for a denomination of a different composition. This includes 5-cent coins struck on cent planchets, cents on dime planchets, and higher denominations struck on cent and 5-cent planchets. A second type is the wrong planchet error, defined as a coin struck on a planchet of the correct composition, but the wrong denomination. These include quarter dollars struck on dime planchets, half dollars struck on quarter dollar and dime planchets, and dollars struck on other clad planchets. Some specialists claim that wrong metal and wrong planchet errors are striking errors, not planchet errors. Their argument? The planchet is OK. It was just fed into the wrong coining press. A third type is the wrong planchet stock error. It occurs when clad coinage strip rolled to the thickness of one denomination is fed into the blanking press of another denomination; the diameter is correct, but the thickness is thicker or thinner than normal. The most common appears to be 1970-D quarter dollars struck on planchet stock intended for dimes. A fourth, rarer form is the double denomination. It occurs when a coin is struck on a previously struck coin, such as a cent struck over a dime. Since the U.S. Mint has struck coins for foreign governments in the past, it has been possible to find in circulation U.S. coins struck on planchets intended for foreign coins, as well as U.S. coins struck on previously struck foreign coins. Another rare type of wrong metal error is called the transitional error. It occurs as a coin's composition changes. Some 1965 coins are known struck on silver planchets of 1964 composition, while some 1964 coins were struck on clad planchets (1964 coins were struck through 1965, with planchets for both types of coins available side by side). One fact for all errors of this broad category is that the planchets must be of an equal size or smaller than the intended planchet. A 5-cent planchet, for example, would not fit between the dies of the smaller cent.

Wrong planchet

Wrong stock

Double denomination

Striking errors

Broadstrike

Broadstrikes: If the surrounding collar is pushed below the surface of the lower die during the moment of striking, the metal of the coin being struck is free to expand beyond the confines of the dies. The design of the coin is normal at center, but as it nears the periphery, becomes distorted due to the uncontrolled spread of the metal of the coin being struck.

Brockage and capped die strikes: If a newly struck coin sticks to the surface of one of the dies, it acts as a die itself — called a die cap — and produces images on succeeding coins. The image produced by any die is the direct opposite on a coin, and brockages are no different. Since the image is raised on the coin adhering to the die, the image on the brockage is incused and reversed — a true mirror image. The first brockage strikes, perfect mirror images and undistorted, are most prized. As additional coins are struck from the capped die, the die cap begins to spread and is made thinner under the pressures of striking, distorting its image. Although the image is recognizable, the design expands, producing an image that can be several times the normal size. At some point, as the die cap becomes thinner and the brockage image disappears, the coins struck cease to be brockages and are known as capped die strikes. While a brockage bears a recognizable though mirror and often distorted image, capped die strikes are simply a form of struck-through coin (see later explanation). At first, few of the original design elements from the obscured die are visible, though as the cap becomes thinner, more and more of the original design elements are transferred from the obscured die through the die cap. Finally, the die cap breaks off or is pounded so thin it ceases to affect succeeding strikes. Sometimes, the die caps fall off early and in a relatively undistorted state. Die caps resemble bottle caps, with the metal wrapping around the surface of the die. Die caps are very rare and collectible, much more so than capped die strikes.

Brockage

Double and multiple strikes: Double strikes are coins struck more than once. If the coin rotates slightly between strikes, but remains centered within the coining chamber, two images will appear on both sides of the coin. The first strike will be almost totally obliterated by the second strike, and the first strike will be flattened and have almost no relief. Sometimes, a struck coin will flip — somewhat like a pancake on a hot griddle — and fall upside down onto the surface of the die; thus, the second strike has an obverse image obliterating the original reverse, and a reverse image flattening the first obverse image. If the coin falls partially outside the dies after the first strike, the second image is only partial. The partial second strike obliterates the original image beneath it, but the rest of the first strike is undistorted, except in the immediate vicinity of the second strike. A saddle strike is generally not a true double strike, but usually the result of having a planchet fall partially between two pairs of dies on a multi-die press. Saddle strikes have two partial images and an expanse of unstruck planchet between the struck areas, resembling Mickey Mouse's head with the partial coin images representing his ears. Examples of coins struck three, four or more times are known.

Filled die

Filled dies: The Mint factory has its share of dirt, grease and other lubricants, and metal filings. The recessed areas of the dies sometimes fill with a combination of this foreign material, preventing the metal of the coins from flowing into the incused areas. This results in weak designs or missing design details, and is probably the most common type of error. Filled-die coins are a form of struck-through error (see later explanation). Filled-die coins rarely carry significant premiums.

Indented error

Indented errors: An indented error is a coin struck with another coin or planchet lying partially on its surface. The area covered by the planchet does not come into contact with the die and thus is blank if indented by a planchet, or shows a partial brockage if indented by a struck coin. The most desirable of the indented errors are larger coins with the indentation of a smaller planchet centered on one side. Indented error coins are a form of struck-through error (see later explanation).

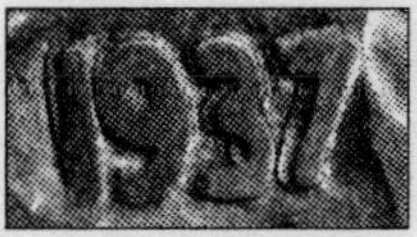

Strike doubling

Machine, mechanical or strike doubling: A form of doubling, this is probably the most common type of Mint error. Some do not consider it an error, but believe it to be a form of Mint-caused damage. Most, however, believe it a true form of error coin. The cause is a looseness of the die or other

Off-center strike

parts in the press that causes the die to twist or bounce across the surface of the newly struck coin. In twisting or bouncing, the die shoves the metal of the raised designs to one side, creating the doubled image. The doubling is flat, like a shelf. Machine-doubling coins are often mistaken for doubled die coins. However, the two forms of doubling have different causes and are distinct in appearance. Machine-doubled coins rarely carry significant premiums.

Off-center coins: If a planchet lies partially outside of the dies during the striking, it receives an off-center strike. Each coin struck off center is unique, but due to the large numbers available, are very inexpensive in the lower denominations. Off-center coins with dates are more valuable than coins without dates. Generally, on dated coins, the greater the off-center strike, the more it is worth.

Partial collar

Partial collar: Often known as "railroad rim" errors, the edge, not the rim, is the portion of the coin affected. It occurs when the collar is pushed somewhat below the surface of the lower die, so that the upper portion of the coin is free to expand beyond the confines of the collar, while the lower portion is restrained. On coins struck from a reeded collar, partial reeding exists on the area restrained by the collar. The error gets the nickname "railroad rim" from its appearance — the coin, viewed edge-on, resembles the wheel from a railroad car.

Struck through

Struck-through errors: Struck-through errors occur when foreign objects fall between die and planchet during striking. Pieces of cloth, metal fragments, wire, slivers of reeding, grease, oil, dirt, wire bristles (from wire brushes used to clean dies, resembling staples), die covers, a thin die cap, other coins, planchets and other objects may fall between the dies and the coin. The most collectible struck-through errors are those with the foreign object still embedded in the surface of the coin.

Weak strikes: Weak strikes often resemble coins struck from grease-filled dies, but can be identified. They occur either when the press has been turned off — it tends to cycle through several strikings,

13 Mysterious Rarities

Through the years, some "coins" have achieved a certain notoriety in the numismatic field because of their rarity, their mysterious background and dealer promotion. These are coins that when sold may bring prices in the five- and six-figure range and that when displayed at a show, bring a gleam to the eyes of even the most experienced numismatists.

Ironically, many of these "coins" are in reality fantasies, produced under cloudy circumstances, usually at the United States Mint but without official sanction, practices that sometimes brought official investigations and condemnation. For example, during the mid-19th century, a number of Mint employees profited from the sale of fantasy pieces produced for collectors.

Then there are the legitimate coins, produced under official sanction but consigned to the melting pot before they ever entered circulation. Examples include the 1964-D Peace dollar and the 1974 Lincoln cents struck in aluminum or bronze-clad steel. Other rarities discussed include patterns — proposed coin designs, compositions or denominations not adopted for circulation in the year in which they are struck, possibly never.

Some of these fantasies, patterns and others are of questionable legal status — pieces that would prompt a visit by Treasury Department agents were a collector or dealer to publicly admit owning them.

Whatever their status, official or unofficial, legal or illegal, their stories are fascinating and deserve to be told. A listing of some of these mysterious pieces follows, with details about their origin noted, when known. The listing is by denomination.

Half cents

1831-36, 1840-49, 1852 Coronet half cents: None were struck for circulation; all were struck for sale to collectors. They are characterized as Original strikes and Restrikes, with the latter struck in the period of 1858-59. (A restrike is a coin struck from the original dies by the original minting authority, but in a later year than appears on the coin; restrikes are generally produced specifically for collectors and not for use in circulation.)

Cents

1795 Liberty Cap, Jefferson Head cent: Opinions differ concerning this piece. Many believe it was struck outside of the U.S. Mint by John Harper, who hoped to obtain a contract to strike U.S. coinage at a time when some congressional leaders tried to eliminate the Mint. If true, the piece is a contemporary counterfeit.

1804 Draped Bust, Restrike cent: A counterfeit produced about 1860 outside of the Mint, using genuine though mismatched dies. The reverse design is of the type used in 1820 and the obverse die was altered from an 1803 die.

1823 Coronet, Restrike cent: A counterfeit struck at the same time as the 1804 counterfeit, using mismatched dies. The reverse die was originally used for 1813 cents.

1856 Flying Eagle cent: A pattern, struck before the Act of Feb. 21, 1857, authorized the replacement of the copper large cent with a smaller copper-nickel cent. The 1856 patterns were produced to show congressmen what the proposed smaller cent would look like. Restrikes also exist.

1942 Experimental cents: A number of private companies struck cent-sized experimental pieces under Mint contract using special dies. In addition to various metallic alloys, pieces were struck in uranium-bearing glass and an early plastic. Collectors appear to be free to collect them despite their experimental nature.

1974 and 1975 Lincoln, Aluminum cent and 1974 Bronze-Clad Steel cent: The 1974 aluminum cent and bronze-clad steel cent were struck by Mint officials in 1973 as copper prices rose to a point where the copper content became worth more than its face value. A total of 1,579,324 1974 aluminum cents were struck. Like the 1856 Flying Eagle cent, a number of the aluminum patterns were given to members of Congress and their staff members to illustrate what an aluminum cent would look like. However, when the copper crisis passed and Mint officials asked for the aluminum cents back, approximately a dozen were missing. Not all of the cents have been returned and presumably are "hidden or lost" somewhere, although one was turned over by a congressional aide to the Smithsonian Institution for the National Numismatic Collection, where it remains. All Mint specimens were destroyed. The 1974 bronze-clad steel cent was unknown to collectors until 1994, when a collector sent one to *Coin World*, staff members became convinced it was genuine after examining the coin. The collector had been an employee at a Pennsylvania steel mill in 1974 when Mint officials brought bags of the bronze-clad steel cents to be destroyed in the mill's furnaces. A bag of the experimental cents broke open and Mint officials failed to scoop up all of the pieces. Five to eight pieces survived, although several are somewhat damaged by the heat of the furnaces. Interestingly, the Treasury Department's official report on the 1973 and 1974 testing denied that the Mint used Lincoln cent dies to strike anything other than aluminum cents. The report claimed "nonsense dies" were used to strike the other compositions; nonsense dies replicate coin-like legends and designs without duplicating existing coins. The discovery of the bronze-clad steel cent and Mint officials' later admission that they did strike them, proved that original statement false. An unknown number of bronze-clad steel cents were struck. *Coin World* was also to the first publication to reveal that the Mint struck 66 1975 aluminum cents, a fact unknown until 1996. The Mint never made this information public until an attorney and coin collector used the Freedom of Information Act to get some information about the 1933 Saint-Gaudens double eagle (see below for information on this coin). The 1975 aluminum cents were struck as part of the continuing experimentation in alternative compositions for the cent. Two of those cents — sent to top Treasury officials for examination — may be missing. The 1974 and 1975 aluminum cents and 1974 bronze-clad steel cents have questionable legal status, and are probably subject to confiscation. The owner of the 1974 bronze-clad steel cents remains anonymous for obvious reasons. The only known 1974 aluminum cent is held in the Smithsonian Collection, although some others may survive. *Coin World* News Editor William T. Gibbs is probably the only collector to have examined specimens of both the 1974 aluminum cent and 1974 bronze-clad steel cent.

Two-cent coins

1873 Open 3 2-cent coin: A restrike and companion piece to the 1873 Closed 3 2-cent coin. Both varieties were struck in Proof only.

Five-cent coins

1913 Liberty Head 5-cent coin: A fantasy. The Liberty Head design was replaced with the Indian Head design (more commonly known as the "Buffalo nickel") in 1913. Four or five pieces turned up in 1919 in the hands of a former U.S. Mint employee, who left the Mint in November 1913. Dies were apparently prepared in 1913 for the Liberty Head coinage but were never officially used. Somehow, someone at the Mint managed to strike four or five of the coins. One piece may be missing and hasn't been seen in decades.

Half dimes

1859 and 1860 Seated Liberty, Transitional half dime: The so-called "transitional" coins, struck without the legend UNITED STATES OF AMERICA. The legend was moved from the reverse to the obverse in 1860, but a small number of pieces were struck from pairs of dies not bearing the legend. Numismatic researcher and author Walter Breen labeled them fantasies.

Dimes

1859 Seated Liberty, Transitional dime: A fantasy. See explanation for similar half dime.

1894-S Barber dime: No one is sure of the origin of these pieces. One version of their origin, according to former *Coin World* Collectors' Clearinghouse Editor James G. Johnson, is that San Francisco Mint Superintendent J. Daggett was approached by a banking friend and asked to strike a small number of dimes in 1894. Although production of dimes was not scheduled in San Francisco that year, Daggett apparently complied with the request, and 24 coins were struck and distributed among eight individuals. Daggett reportedly received three coins, as did his daughter. About a dozen are known today.

Quarter dollars

1866 Seated Liberty, No Motto quarter dollar: The motto IN GOD WE TRUST was added to the reverse of the quarter dollar, half dollar and dollar in 1866. However, at least four coins were struck with the 1866 date and no motto. The quarter dollar and half dollar are unique, and there are two of the silver dollars. There are no Mint records of the coins having been struck.

Half dollars

1866 Seated Liberty, No Motto half dollar: See quarter dollars above.

Silver dollars

1804 Draped Bust dollar: A fantasy. The Mint Report for 1804 records 19,570 silver dollars being struck. However, the 1804 dollar is one of the greatest of U.S. rarities, with just 15 pieces known. So what happened to all those dollars struck in 1804? Rumors about the coins abounded in the 19th century. One story is linked to 19th century terrorism in the Middle East. That story claims that all of the 1804 dollars were sent to the Barbary pirates as ransom for the release of American hostages captured in 1804 when the *USS Philadelphia* ran aground in Tripoli Harbor. Another rumor said all of the dollars were relegated to the melting pot. None of the rumors, however, had any basis in fact. In fact, none of the dollars struck in 1804 bore that date. In the early days of the U.S. Mint, it was common practice to continue to use dated dies in later years — even though the year marked on the die had ended. This saved materials and expense and cut down on the number of new dies that had to be made. Mintages for the silver dollar dropped annually from 1798 to 1804. The Spanish Pillar dollar was considered legal tender in the United States at that time, even though it contained less silver than the U.S. dollar. Also, the silver dollar was the basic unit in payment for commercial goods shipped from overseas. Thus, dollars were shipped abroad almost as quickly as they could be struck and few were returned to the United States. Dollar production was halted between 1805 (although a few 1803-dated dollars were struck in 1805) and 1835. Meanwhile, in 1832, the U.S. government was seeking to establish diplomatic and commercial relationships with several countries in the Far East. At that time, rulers of many countries expected foreign diplomats to bring gifts to them. Gifts of coins were one of the more popular gifts, so diplomat Edmund Roberts requested that complete sets of coins be struck and placed in presentation cases. Dollar production still had not resumed at this time. Mint officials, desiring to place a dollar coin in the set, examined Mint records and found that silver dollars were last struck in 1804. What they failed to account for was that those coins were dated 1803, not 1804. Nevertheless, silver dollar dies dated 1804 were prepared in 1834 and several coins struck. Several of the presentation sets were given to foreign rulers, notably the King of Siam and the Sultan of Muscat. The remaining 1804 dollar fantasies were held in Mint vaults. The remaining specimens were gradually distributed, beginning in the early 1840s. One was sold to collector Matthew A. Stickney in 1843. A total of eight of the pieces struck about 1834, referred to as the Class I specimens, are known. Demand, however, quickly outstripped the supply and in 1858, additional pieces were struck for sale and trade to prominent collectors (referred to as Class II and Class III coins). The sole Class II coin known today was struck over an 1857 shooting taler from Switzerland, thus confirming its illegitimate birthday; it resides today in the National Numismatic Collection at the Smithsonian Institution. The six Class III pieces were all sold to collectors. Eventually, the scandal of striking and restriking rare coins for wealthy collectors became public and their production slowed but did not stop until about the turn of the century. The Class II and III coins were struck from a different reverse than the Class I coins. (The Proof 1801, 1802 and 1803 Draped Bust dollars date from the time of the Class I 1804 dollars, and are generally labeled restrikes.)

1836, 1838, 1839 Gobrecht, Restrike dollars: The Gobrecht dollar is one of the most confusing series in U.S. coinage history. Of the nine different varieties, three were struck for circulation, two are legitimate patterns and four are restrikes.**1866 Seated Liberty, No Motto dollar:** See listing for quarter dollars. Two pieces; one has been missing since a 1967 robbery.

1884, 1885 Trade dollars: Proof only. For years, many numismatists considered these two coins to be fantasies, struck years later. However, recent research indicates that the 1884 Trade dollars were struck that year, and it is likely the 1885 Trade dollars were coined in 1885 as well. Specimens did not appear until 1908 in the hands of dealer John W. Haseltine. They were apparently struck specifically for collectors, as are all Proof coins.

1964-D Peace dollar: Even as Treasury officials considered proposals to eliminate silver from U.S. coinage in 1964, special-interest groups persuaded Congress to authorize the striking of Peace dollars, last struck in 1935. Forty-five million coins were authorized by the Act of Aug. 3, 1964, and 316,076 pieces were struck at the Denver Mint. However, those who recognized the reality of the silver shortage won out over the special-interest groups and none of the dollars were released into circulation. All were eventually melted although rumors persist that some escaped the Mint. At least one person who was an employee of the Denver Mint at the time insists that the coins were never offered to employees, directly contradicting the rumors. Treasury officials would likely consider it illegal to own a 1964-D Peace dollar, if any survive.

$4 Stellas

1879 and 1880 $4 Stellas: The $4 Stellas are patterns. However, these pieces are often listed with other gold coins, although only the gold patterns are cited. The off-metal pieces (aluminum, copper, white metal) are not listed in other price guides.

Eagles

1907 Indian Head, Wire Rim, Periods eagle: A pattern. Often referred to incorrectly as a Wire Edge variety.

1907 Indian Head, Rounded Rim, Periods eagle: A pattern. Often incorrectly referred to as a Rounded Edge variety. The circulation issues do not have periods separating the words E PLURIBUS UNUM.

Double eagles

1849 Coronet double eagle: A pattern piece, and unique. In the Smithsonian collection.

1907 Saint-Gaudens, Extremely High Relief double eagle: The 1907 double eagles bearing the Saint-Gaudens designs were struck in varying reliefs. The High Relief variety with Roman Numerals and the Low Relief variety with Arabic Numerals were struck for circulation. All of the Extremely High Relief pieces, however, are considered patterns. (The differences between the High Relief and Low Relief varieties are obvious when compared side-by-side. The design areas on the Low Relief variety are raised the same height above the flat fields as on modern coins; on the High Relief variety, the relief rises much higher above the field.)

1933 Saint-Gaudens: The Mint struck 445,500 1933 double eagles but before they were released, President Franklin D. Roosevelt signed several executive orders making it illegal for American citizens to own most forms of gold. Thus, the coins were never released. However, specimens of the 1933 double eagle appeared at auction in the 1940s and several private sales occurred. Treasury officials confiscated several specimens, although it is believed by some in numismatic circles that specimens remain in hiding. The specimen in Egypt's King Farouk auction was removed from the offering at the request of U.S. Treasury officials, but the coin was not turned over by Egyptian officials. In early 1996, a specimen surfaced in dealer hands. The United States government promptly confiscated it and as this book is being edited, legal action is pending. In addition, the Smithsonian Institution has two specimens in the National Numismatic Collection.

14 Glossary

Numismatics (pronounced nu-mis-mat-iks), like any science, has a language of its own spoken by its practitioners and students. New collectors unfamiliar with terms like obverse, reverse, Mint mark and double eagle may feel confused by a bewildering lexicon. But the language need not be confusing.

The terms defined here are those that may be commonly encountered during the normal course of coin collecting.

Alloy: Mixture of more than one metal.

Altered: A coin that has been deliberately changed to make it resemble a rare or more valuable piece.

American Eagle: A legal tender bullion coin struck and issued by the United States Mint. The Mint strikes four .9995 fine platinum coins, four .9167 fine gold coins and a .999 fine silver coin. Refer to "Values" section for other specifications.

Bag marks: See Contact marks.

Bicentennial coins: Quarter dollar, half dollar and dollar struck in 1975-76 with special reverse designs commemorating the 200th anniversary of the signing of the Declaration of Independence.

Buffalo nickel: Nickname given the Indian Head 5-cent coin. Nickname is commonly though incorrectly used; most U.S. coins are named after their obverse design; the creature on the reverse is a bison, not a buffalo; and no U.S. coin denomination is legally called a "nickel."

Clad: Composite coinage metal strip composed of a core, usually of a base metal such as copper, and surface layers of more valuable metal like copper-nickel. The U.S. dimes, quarter dollars and half dollars struck since 1965 are a clad coinage.

Coin: Usually a piece of metal, marked with a device, issued by a governing authority and intended to be used as money. Coins may or may not be legal tender.

Colonial coins: Coins struck by one of the 13 British Colonies prior to the American Revolution. Few of the Colonial coins were struck with the authority of the British throne, which legally had all coinage rights in Great Britain and the Colonies.

Contact marks: Surface abrasions found on U.S. coins, as a result of coins striking the surfaces of other coins during bagging and shipping procedures. See Chapter 8, "Grading," for details.

Coronet: A style of Liberty Head used on U.S. copper and gold coins for much of the 19th century. Liberty wears a coronet (usually marked with the word LIBERTY).

Denomination: The face value of a coin; the amount of money it is worth as legal tender.

Device: The principal design element, such as a portrait, shield or heraldic emblem, on the obverse or reverse of a coin.

Die: A hardened metal punch, the face of which carries an intaglio or incused mirror-image to be impressed on one side of a planchet.

Disme: Original spelling of "dime." May have been pronounced "deem."

Double eagle: A $20 gold coin of the United States.

Eagle: A $10 gold coin of the United States.

Edge: Often termed the third side of a coin, it is the surface perpendicular to the obverse and reverse. Not to be confused with the rim. Edges can be plain, reeded, lettered or carry other designs.

Fantasy: An object having the physical characteristics of a coin, issued by an agency other than a governing authority (or without official sanction) yet purporting to be issued by a real or imagined governing authority as a coin.

Field: The flat part of a surface of a coin surrounding and between the head, legend or other designs.

Flow lines: Microscopic striations in a coin's surface caused by the movement of metal under striking pressures.

Frost: Effect caused by striking a coin with sandblasted dies, often used in reference to Proof coins.

Half dimes, half dismes: A silver 5-cent coin of the United States. The Mint Act of April 2, 1792, authorized "half dismes." See disme.

Half eagle: A $5 gold coin of the United States.

Hub: A right-reading, positive punch used to impress incused, mirror-image dies.

Large cent: Refers to the U.S. cents of 1793-1857, with diameters between 26-29 millimeters, depending on the year it was struck.

Legal tender: Currency (coins or paper money) explicitly determined by a government to be acceptable in the discharge of debts.

Lettered edge: An incused or raised inscription on the edge of a coin.

Minor coin: A silver coin of less than crown weight or any coin struck in base metal.

Mint mark: A letter or other symbol indicating the Mint of origin. Also spelled Mintmark.

Money: A medium of exchange.

Nickel: A silver-white metal widely used for coinage. It is factually incorrect to use "nickel" for the copper-nickel 5-cent coin. In the mid-19th century, copper-nickel cents and 3-cent coins were also nicknamed "nickel," like the modern 5-cent coin. The U.S. Mint has never struck a coin officially called a "nickel."

Numismatics: The science, study or collecting of coins, medals, paper money, tokens, orders and decorations and similar objects.

Numismatist: A person knowledgeable in numismatics, with greater knowledge than a collector.

Obverse: The side of a coin that bears the principal design or device, often as prescribed by the issuing authority. In informal English, the "heads."

Pattern: Coin-like pieces designed to test coin designs, mottoes or denominations proposed for adoption as a regular issue and struck in the metal to be issued for circulation, but which were not adopted, at least in year of pattern issue. The 1856 Flying Eagle cent is a pattern; the coin was not struck for circulation or authorized until 1857.

Penny: The nickname given the 1-cent coin. The United States Mint has never struck a penny for use in the United States. The nickname derives from the country's English origins; England still uses a denomination called a penny.

Pioneer gold: Gold coins, often privately produced, struck in areas of the United States to meet the demands of a shortage of coins, generally in traditional U.S. coin denominations. Often called "private gold," which is correct for many but not all of the issues, and "territorial gold," which is incorrect since none of the coins were struck by a territorial government authority.

Planchet: The disc of metal that when placed between the dies and struck becomes a coin. Also called flan or blank.

Restrike: A numismatic item produced from original dies at a later date. In the case of a coin, the restrike usually occurs to fulfill a collector demand and not a monetary requirement.

Reverse: The side opposite the obverse, usually but not always the side with the denomination (the denomination appears on the obverse of the State quarters, for example). The side opposite the side containing the principal design. Informally, the "tails."

Slab: A rigid plastic, permanently sealed holder, usually rectangular, especially those used by third-party grading services.

Series: Related coinage of the same denomination, design and type, including modifications and varieties.

Type: A basic coin design, regardless of minor modifications. The Indian Head and Jefferson 5-cent coins are different types.

Variety: The difference between individual dies of the same basic design or type.

INDEX